FUR
A Sensitive History

FUR
A Sensitive History

JONATHAN FAIERS

YALE UNIVERSITY PRESS
NEW HAVEN AND LONDON

Countless thanks to my darlings Dell, Inez, Kurt and Lottie for their love, guidance, inspiration and fur.

First published by
Yale University Press 2020
302 Temple Street,
P.O. Box 209040,
New Haven CT 06520-9040
47 Bedford Square,
London WC1B 3DP
yalebooks.com |
yalebooks.co.uk

Copyright
© 2020 Jonathan Faiers

All rights reserved. This book may not be reproduced or transmitted in any form or by any means, electronic or mechanical, including photocopy, recording or any other information storage and retrieval system (beyond that copying permitted by Sections 107 and 108 of the US Copyright Law and except by reviewers for the public press), without prior permission in writing from the publisher.

ISBN 978-0-300-227208-0 HB
Library of Congress Control Number: 2020931948

10 9 8 7 6 5 4 3 2 1
2024 2023 2022 2021 2020

Designed by Kathrin Jacobsen
Copy edited by Denny Hemming

Printed in China

Cover: Dyed white mink (detail). Courtesy of Kopenhagen Fur and Mikkel Østergaard Schou

Frontispiece: Mink 'petals'. Dyed and embellished fur. Courtesy of Kopenhagen Fur and Mikkel Østergaard Schou

CONTENTS

INTRODUCTION: FUR THINKING   7

1   **HAIR**   13

2   **PELT**   41

3   **COAT**   79

4   **SKIN**   161

5   **FLEECE**   191

CONCLUSION: FUTUREFUR   225

NOTES   228
BIBLIOGRAPHY   233
ACKNOWLEDGEMENTS   235
INDEX   236

CLOTHES

FUR

Long, long ago, when people lived in caves, they used animal skins for clothing. Boys and girls snuggled warmly in the fur of the wild beasts that their fathers killed. This was all that they had to wear.

This happened many thousand years ago, before anybody knew about the clothes we wear today. There was no cotton or wool or silk. But fur skins were fine for people who did not have warm houses to live in.

INTRODUCTION

FUR THINKING

Fur, once the ultimate vestimentary signifier of social and economic status, has now become an unspeakable subject and is either absent from, or given only cursory and fleeting attention in, nearly all available studies of fashion and luxury consumption. Fur as clothing has a long, complex and rich history, yet a brief, largely forgotten presence within the literature of dress history and theory. When it is present, it is within discussions concerning the ethics of wearing fur and the rights of animals, or debates focusing on its sustainability, two distinct issues which, however, are often incorrectly conflated. As fashion historian Elizabeth Ewing, in one of the few attempts to chart the history of fashionable fur, suggests, 'Fur has been an element of dress for longer than any other, but despite this it probably has the shortest history and literature of any'.[1] Although written nearly 40 years ago, this situation remains unaltered. However, as a material it is unparalleled in its combination of economic value, rarity, thermal properties, traditional artisanal skills essential to its transformation into garments and other products, and the specialised knowledge and connoisseurship required on the part of both producer and consumer.

Philosophically fur promises transformation, offers a supremely tactile experience in an increasingly immaterial world, and is imbued with an emotional, immersive intensity absent from our contemporary navigation through the universe of things. Fur's power has meant that historically it has been the subject of concentrated regulation, both official and unofficial, and although the days of sumptuary legislation have passed, fur remains uniquely proscribed and quarantined.

The concept of the journey is central to this study of fur. Sensate and emotional journeys, journeys of exploration and exploitation, journeys vast and almost imperceptible, map the spaces within this book. Running parallel to its narratives of exploration, technological innovation and desire are voyages of colonialism, decimation and subterfuge. As a result of these often uncomfortable itineraries, contemporary attitudes to fur mean that its economic, political, psychological and, indeed, fashionable significance is largely forgotten. While the subject of fur today is

0-1 'Fur' from *The Story Book of Clothes*, 1937. Maud and Miska Petersham. Published by J.M. Dent and Sons Ltd. Courtesy of the author almost unmentionable, when it is uttered the topic polarises, confounds and excites, a testament to its fundamental significance. Fur has built nations, decimated species, subjugated communities and driven fashion. It has inspired great works of art, created fortunes, demarcated society and has been the catalyst for desire and disgust in equal measure.

While this book is in no way intended to be understood as promoting the use of fur, it is undertaken in a spirit of genuine enquiry that seeks to excavate the influential and excessively rich history of fur and fur production from its carapace of contemporary condemnation. To explore and discuss a subject is not an endorsement of that same subject, but rather an acknowledgement of its power and influence. Problematic and sensitive subjects deserve as much attention, if not more, as those with which we can establish a comfortable critical distance. The notion of distance and its companion, proximity, will be crucial to this book. For it is our innate sensory connection to fur that makes it such a commanding subject, one that needs to be acknowledged and indeed re-discovered.

This introduction has been subtitled 'Fur Thinking' in acknowledgement of the burgeoning discipline of fashion thinking, a critical perspective that seeks an alternative to the popularly understood definition of fashion theory, which typically utilises established models (say feminism, Marxism, psychoanalysis etc.) to understand fashion. What has led me and others to call our work fashion thinking is a refusal to be bound by limited, sequential, chronological histories, the histories of manufacturing, design, production and consumption that much dress history is informed and inspired by. Nor do we submit to being confined by one strict methodology, which we feel is too limiting for the globally experienced and historically central phenomenon that is fashion. Fashion thinking recognises, values and is animated by the essentially social, ludic, democratic and rapidly shifting and transformative qualities of fashion. Put simply, fashion as a sensual, erotic, self-affirming practice is in danger of being atomised by the weight of a critical apparatus that is ill-fit to fully explore its persistent and pervasive influence.

What fashion thinking hopes to achieve is an understanding of fashion as both subject and verb, so to 'fashion' as in to 'make' thinking is crucial here, and that thinking can, as in the process of making fashion, take a variety of forms. Just as the way in which a piece of cloth, or in this case an animal skin, can be cut, shaped, sewn and made up into a garment, but then just as easily unpicked, recut and re-assembled to make an entirely new item of clothing, so too can the material we choose to study be used to explore any number of fashion products, be they garments, texts, films, artworks or environments. This belief led to the decision to commence each of the five principal chapters of this work with an image of a contemporary artwork relevant to the way fur is being thought about in that section.

My formulation of fur thinking is indebted to the notion of 'indiscipline', as suggested by the art historian W.J.T. Mitchell, when he stated that within his field he was more interested in 'forms of "indiscipline", turbulence or incoherence at the inner and outer boundaries of discipline'.[2] This discontinuity, moments of breakage or rupture that open up spaces between and outside disciplines, encourages a diversity of thought to match the richness of our many encounters with fur be they historical, metaphorical or real. Fur's complexity demands a study that is fluid, necessarily critical but also ultimately sensate. Therefore this book will try to avoid becoming enmeshed in specific debates that prohibit the opportunity to embark on the necessary journeys offered by fur's dazzling polysemy. Similarly it will call upon critical and philosophical voices that, while often not addressing fur directly, can offer perspectives on 'Furland', a space created and territorialised by fur, the space of the body and the screen, the spaces of production and consumption, spaces vanished and terrifying, insistently present, tactile and seductive. Michel Serres, for example, whose journey through the senses has been fundamental to this work, calls on the figure of Hermes, the messenger god, to travel back and forth between the disciplines he interrogates in his work.[3] Hermes, the god of boundaries and also their transgressor, the trickster god at the crossroads, adept at trade and commerce, proves a useful navigator for the successive journeys back and forth, near and far, which chronicle our relationship with fur.

Understanding that fur's journeys are never direct, always digressive and in many respects unfinished, this book adopts a structure that allows for the necessary departures, arrivals and, indeed, becomings that 'fur thinking' discovers. Therefore the book is divided into five chapters: **HAIR**, **PELT**, **COAT**, **SKIN** and **FLEECE**. These titles, and their associated subtitles, have been chosen not only for their obvious relationship to our understanding of fur, whether physiological, mercantile, fashionable, sensory or mythical, but also for the possibilities those same terms promise. Indeed fur's extraordinarily rich linguistic formation and its influence on cultural discourses has been one of the pleasures and surprising discoveries of this work.

HAIR, the book's first chapter, commences with the subsection 'Manimal', an exploration of the physiological structure of human and animal hair, our emotional and political responses to both human hair and animal fur, and some of the possible causes of what I suggest is a prevailing climate of trichophobia, or fear of hair. 'I'd Rather Go Hairless' picks up the theme of trichophobia as a means by which to discuss developments within recent anti-fur campaigns, which are also situated in this chapter within the broader context of the history of human and animal right movements. This first chapter also introduces and establishes many of the characteristic methods of fur thinking. For example, mainstream film is employed throughout this work as evidence of fur's dissemination in popular culture and the prominent position it occupied in twentieth-century western consciousness as a visual signifier of aspiration, sensuality and fashion. Fur in film acts as a form of haptic visuality, to borrow theorist Laura Marks's formulation of the term, where a sense of physical touching or being touched is triggered by, in these instances, fur's integration into mainstream cinematic narratives of glamour and desire.[4] In turn, these visual representations of fur trigger memories in the viewer of their own experience of the touch, smell and wearing of fur. While the central chapter of this work, Coat is devoted to developments within fur clothing and its relationship to fashion, examples of garments made from or incorporating fur are deployed in this and subsequent chapters of the book as demonstrations of fur thinking, in order to understand its use in garments as indicative and expressive of a range of theoretical and political positions.

PELT, the term most commonly associated with the trade in fur and its commodification, is the title for the book's second chapter that navigates the reader through some of the routes and spaces established by the fur trade. 'Soft Gold', the epithet for fur used by early traders at the height of its commercial desirability, presents an abbreviated history of the fur trade, necessarily condensed due to the scope of the current work and also acknowledging that the history of the fur trade, in particular the Hudson's Bay Company, is the one aspect of fur that has been widely and expertly researched and published. This section then takes a different direction, exploring fur in relationship to the concept of territorialisation, as principally formulated by philosophers Gilles Deleuze and Félix Guattari, a furry territorialisation that has demarcated landscapes, animal populations, indigenous peoples and the commercial and retail spaces of fur.[5] While briefly addressing the western fur trade's impact on indigenous populations, a full discussion of this aspect is beyond the range of this work. Similarly, indigenous design and production of fur clothing is limited to a consideration of it as a form of inspiration for, and appropriation by, western fur fashion. As with the Hudson's Bay Company, there are a number of excellent studies of indigenous people's relationship to fur-bearing animals, to which this work makes reference and is indebted. 'Wearer's Rights' offers a revisioning of the sumptuary legislation against fur and argues that legislation against the wearing of fur remains a prominent form of vestimentary proscription, the only difference between Renaissance and modern-day regulation being its intended subject and on what grounds.

COAT, the central and largest chapter, is devoted to an exploration of fashionable fur, the principal focus of this book. However, rather than attempting a chronological history, the development of western fur clothing is understood as a series of journeys – temporal, spatial and psychological. Comprising seven subsections, Coat opens with 'Modern Primitives', a consideration of fur's enduring reading as primal, functional and economical, no matter how fashionably translated. 'Now You See Me, Now You Don't' is an account of fur's use throughout the majority of western fashion history as a lining, simultaneously prized both for its thermal properties as well as status affirmation. 'Heads or Tails' follows fur's migration from the interior of the garment to its edges and away from the body in the form of accessories, such as hats, tippets and muffs. Following this, 'Furland' explores the association of specific types of fur with certain locales, be they real or imagined, and how fur has been instrumental in fashion's conceptualisation of the 'foreign' and the exotic. 'In Black and White and Colour' addresses fur's relationship to cinema, its mediated image in the twentieth century and new advances in the dyeing and dressing of fur, while 'The Force of Fur' continues the discussion of technological developments in fur fashion, and how it is obtained, processed and developed stylistically. It also considers the impact technology has had on the way we wear fur, especially the advent of modern forms of transport, including the automobile, which led to the development of what today we recognise as the modern fur coat. The chapter ends with 'The F Word', which reveals that faking fur, its methods and intentions, has been a parallel journey to that of real fur and commences long before our current preoccupation with synthetic fur might suggest. In this section, as elsewhere in the book, specific case studies of significant varieties of fur are presented, not to provide an exhaustive catalogue but in order to consider how fur has been subject to socio-cultural and psychological imperatives as well as the vagaries of fashion itself.

SKIN, the penultimate chapter, calls upon a range of philosophical, literary and visual material in order to consider our fundamental tactile affinity with fur. 'Under my Skin' explores the sensate response to fur, its negotiation and demarcation of the borders between the interior and the exterior, and the erotic force of fur. 'Furnishing' extends the concept of fur as covering in order to consider its use in interior and object design, and the displacement of fur as a catalyst for fine art.

The final chapter of the book, **FLEECE**, as its title suggests, journeys through fur's mythical, ritual and symbolic uses and representation. 'Shape Shifters' discusses fur's transformative potential and how this has been celebrated and imagined throughout global culture from the earliest times. 'Translation' considers how fur has been represented, both historically and today, via specific visual systems such as heraldic symbolism or media, which range from precious metals to digital image-making.

0-2 'Fur' from *The Story Book of Clothes*, 1937. Maud and Miska Petersham. Published by J.M. Dent and Sons Ltd. Courtesy of the author

To embark on the various expeditions this study takes to Furland, certain equipment has been essential. As mentioned previously, fur's cinematic presence has been an essential navigational aid, as has its various constructions in literature. Fur's occupation of the space of commerce in the form of fashion journalism, advertising and retailing has indicated unexpected routes and passages. Critical guides have also proved indispensable companions: Michel Serres's poetic understanding of touch has shared the journey with Elspeth Veale's meticulous study of the early English fur trade and Elizabeth Ewing's pioneering account of fashionable fur, while Gilles Deleuze and Félix Guattari ensure that fur is experienced both territorially and as 'becoming'.[6]

No apology is made for assembling such a diverse expeditionary party as the journey to Furland needs equipment for all eventualities and all encounters. Similarly, in the desire to fully understand fur's centrality not only to the development of western fashion but also its cultural landscape, the book has focused on fashion from the nineteenth century onwards as this is where we can still find evidence of fashionable fur's most inventive development in the form of extant garments, many of which are illustrated here for the first time.

Contemporary fashion has often been utilised to illustrate historical discussions about particular aspects of fur garments in order to demonstrate that many of our attitudes concerning fashionable fur have remained unchanged since their formulation and continue to inspire. Similarly, when discussing fur's centrality to the history of western art, *Fur: A Sensitive History* has preferred to explore some of fur's lesser known artistic territories and, while historical examples including portraiture are included, it is hoped that many of the contemporary artworks and design objects discussed here will confirm fur's enduring aesthetic and conceptual value.

PART ONE

HAIR

1 HAIR

MANIMAL

'But the very haires of your head are all numbred' [1]

Our attraction to, and possibly fear of, fur can be explained by the fact that in many respects human hair and animal fur share remarkable similarities. Both serve thermoregulatory and waterproofing functions, can act as camouflage, elicit sexual attraction, and register fear, anxiety or excitement by becoming raised, a reflex known as pilo-erection. However, all these properties are greatly reduced in human hair as compared to fur. As with fur, human hair grows everywhere (except on mucous membranes and glabrous skin, which includes the palms of the hands, soles of the feet and lips), can be pigmented, straight or curly, and can moult, but again not as plentifully, or with as much variety, as fur.

Belying human hair and animal fur's superficial visual and tactile similarities, however, is the structure, distribution and composition of each, which is markedly different. Human hair is composed of a protein filament that grows from follicles in the dermal layer of the skin and is divided into two basic types: terminal and vellus. Vellus hair, from the Latin for fleece, is the very fine, short, often imperceptible hair that covers the majority of the human body from childhood, while terminal hair is thicker, coarser and often darker as found on the head. Terminal hair is further subdivided into androgenic hair, that is hair growth stimulated during puberty by the male androgen hormones resulting in pubic and armpit (also known as axillary) hair, and (typically in males) beard and darker body hair.

The visible, external hair that emerges from the surface of the skin, otherwise known as the shaft, can be roughly divided into three distinct layers; the cuticle, cortex and the medulla. The outer layer, or cuticle, is composed of flat overlapping cells, which contribute to hair's water-repellent properties, and keratin, the structural proteins that also form the outer layer of human skin, nails, horns, claws and hooves. The middle layer, or cortex, contains melanin, which gives hair its pigmentation: eumelanin is responsible for brown or black hair, pheomelanin for red, while blond hair is the result of a lack of pigmentation and grey hair is due to the decrease or cessation of melanin production. The medulla is an open, unstructured area at the centre of the hair. Hair growth occurs in the cuticle, beneath the skin's surface, so the hair that emerges above the surface is technically 'dead' as no biochemical activity takes place in the hair shaft.

In contrast to human hair, an animal's pelage, a collective term for the fur, hair or wool of a quadruped, is typically but not exclusively composed from three different hair types: guard hair, awn hair and underfur. Underfur (or down hair) is closest to the skin and is commonly made up of numerous fine, short, wavy hairs, its principal function being that of thermoregulation by providing an insulating layer that traps air against the skin. The guard hairs that form the outer layer

PREVIOUS PAGE Royal Canadian Mounted Police overcoat (detail), 1965–70. Quebec; buffalo fur, leather and satin lining. With permission of the Royal Ontario Museum. © ROM

1-1 OPPOSITE Nick Cave (b. 1957), *Soundsuit*, 2011. Mixed media including human hair, 307 x 107 x 84 cm. Courtesy of the artist and Jack Shainman Gallery, New York of the pelage are generally longer, coarser, often oily and straighter, and give the fur its sheen, colour pigmentation and markings. They also provide protection from harmful ultraviolet rays, repel water and with the aid of the pilo-motor reflex become raised when the animal is threatened or excited. In between these two can be found the awn hair, a hybrid of both being mid-length, and curly at the base before becoming straighter towards the end, which aids thermoregulation and water resistance. In addition to these three principal types of hair some species also possess vibrissae, or sensory hairs, most commonly seen in the form of whiskers or spines, such as those borne by the porcupine, which are modified guard hairs covered in a dense layer of keratin and used for defence.

If we accept the physical sensation produced by touching fur as essential to understanding its practical, economic, fashionable and cultural importance, then it is worth considering how this sensation is produced. Hair grows in tufts, and in humans on average one to three hairs develop from each follicle, with the greatest concentration of follicles, on average 290 per square centimetre, found on the head. If we compare this to that of the chinchilla, which is widely accepted

1-2 Leopard skin showing characteristic ring-like markings termed rosettes. Courtesy of the author

as having the densest and softest of all furs, we find that each chinchilla follicle may bear from 50 to 100 hairs and can reach a density of 20,000 per square centimetre. While the chinchilla may have the softest of furs, with other furs less dense or indeed fine, the overall greater quantity and concentration of hair forming an animal's pelage is what gives it its unique tactile quality and differentiates it from human hair.

In addition to the thermal, protective and water-repellent functions of fur, it can of course act as camouflage. The tiger's stripes, the leopard and jaguar's rosettes and the cheetah's spots are the most recognisable amongst a dazzling array of furry markings, all of which have developed to disguise the animal in its individual environment, whether

1-3 Martin Parr (b. 1952), *Italy. Reggio Emilia*, 2006.
© Martin Parr/Magnum Photos

that be a forest with its dappled light or amongst tall grasses, with their interplay of sunshine and shadow (fig. 1-2). Animals can also be polymorphic, that is, different forms occur within the same species, so, for example, what are termed panthers are in fact black-coated or melanistic variants of either the jaguar or leopard. Erythrism, a genetic mutation, can produce an unusual amount of red pigmentation in fur, as seen in polecats, or, as with humans, can also result in albino forms lacking all pigmentation. Seasonal polyphenism describes the reaction when an animal changes the pigmentation of its fur according to the changing seasons, as is the case with the Arctic fox, which morphs from summer brown to winter white or blue-grey if living in coastal areas, and whose fur provides the best insulation of any mammal, or the stoat, whose winter coat we know as ermine. Some animals have markings that warn potential predators of their toxic, foul-smelling or aggressive behaviour, known as aposematism, hence the distinctive black-and-white fur of the skunk and the similarly contrasted coat of the ferocious honey badger.

Having briefly considered the material similarities and differences between human and animal hair, can we utilise these facts further to explore some of the broader philosophical, cultural and emotional responses both to our own hair and that of animals?

1-4 Joris Hoefnagel (1542–c.1600), Petrus Gonsalvus and his wife from *Animalia Rationalia et Insecta*, Plate I, c.1575–80. Watercolour and gouache on vellum, 14.3 x 18.4 cm. Courtesy National Gallery of Art, Washington D.C. Gift of Mrs Lessing J. Rosenwald

As noted earlier, the human body is covered with fine vellus hair, often almost imperceptible but immediately noticeable when excited, fearful or cold. Its response to what is an involuntary reflex is to become raised in the characteristic form of 'goose bumps'. This vestigial reminder of our former, much furrier, selves collapses the distance between us and other fur-bearing animals as we too become urgently and sensorially awake to our surroundings, impending danger, or mounting excitement, a primal response akin to the tactile pleasure we receive on touching fur. This awareness of our hairier, sensate selves is both disquieting and pleasurable, and explains our multivalent and fluctuating reaction to hair and fur. Michel Serres expresses this simultaneous awareness of our own skin, its hair and its exteriority, and the deeper responses that begin to be felt once our original tactile self is triggered, when he suggests, 'The senses haunt the skin, pass beneath it and are visible on its surface'.[2] The hairy primeval body haunts fact and fiction, history and the present, offering uneasy pictorial and literary visions as a counterpoint to contemporary neuroses centred on the maintenance of the hirsute body.

The remarkable *Soundsuit* created by Nick Cave, which opens this chapter, is made from human hair and when worn provides both an unmistakeable reminder of our hairy essential selves, and also the possibility of transformation (see fig. 1-1). As Cave explains, 'The Soundsuits are about a kind of search for an understanding of identity, whatever it is that can make someone the same as or different from others, and this is a topic each one of us explores everyday. Wouldn't you like a new identity every once in a while – just to see what it feels like?'[3]

Tangible evidence of our former hairier selves can be found in the phenomenon of lanugo hair (from *lana*, the Latin for wool), which is produced in the womb by foetal hair follicles, covering the foetus with very fine, normally un-pigmented hair at about five months into the gestation period. This is usually shed at about seven or eight months but in some instances is retained, resulting in markedly hirsute babies, one of the most celebrated examples being actress Elizabeth Taylor,

1-5 OPPOSITE Joris Hoefnagel (1542–c.1600), Tognina and Arrigo Gonsalvus from *Animalia Rationalia et Insecta*, Plate II, c.1575–80. Watercolour and gouache on vellum, 14.3 x 18.4 cm. National Gallery of Art, Washington D.C. Gift of Mrs Lessing J. Rosenwald

1-6 ABOVE Postcard of 'Lionel the Lion-Faced Boy' (detail), c.1910–32. Sufferers from hypertrichosis (or excessive hairiness), such as Stephan Bibrowski, achieved celebrity status in travelling exhibitions. Wellcome Collection, London

who not only retained her lanugo hair for a period but was also born with a double set of eyelashes. Some animals, too, develop and retain lanugo hair at birth, most relevant to this study being the seal. The function of lanugo hair remains mysterious, with the consensus suggesting it fulfils a hormonal regulatory function. But its other explanation as an early attempt to insulate the body is possibly reaffirmed by the development of lanugo hair by people suffering from anorexia nervosa.

The lanugo phenomenon is not to be confused with the rare condition hypertrichosis, which describes abnormal hair growth either all over the body, or restricted to certain areas. Hypertrichosis can be either congenital or may occur later in life, with the most severe form of the condition – known as congenital terminal hypertrichosis – resulting in fully pigmented hair covering the entire body, often accompanied by gingival hyperplasia, an abnormal enlargement of the gums. Although extremely rare, due to the remarkable appearance of people with the condition it has been comparatively well documented throughout history. Petrus Gonsalvus is perhaps the most celebrated early case due to the remarkable portraits of himself and his son and daughter, who also had the condition. These are preserved at Ambras Castle, the Renaissance palace located on the hill above Innsbruck that houses Archduke Ferdinand II's great cabinet of curiosities, hence the condition is also known as Ambras syndrome. Gonsalvus was born in Tenerife in about 1500 and was sent as a child to the court of Henry II of France, where he was educated, raised as a nobleman and later 'gifted' to the governor of the Netherlands, Alessandro Farnese. Now married with a family, including a son and daughter – Arrigo and Tognina – who had both inherited their father's hypertrichosis, Gonsalvus was next despatched to the Farnese court at Parma. As medical curiosities and 'living marvels', Gonsalvus and his family achieved considerable fame and were chronicled extensively in written accounts and visually, including exquisite illuminations made of them by Joris Hoefnagel, which are included in a bestiary produced for Rudolf II (figs 1-4, 1-5).

By the nineteenth century the private Wunderkammer of the Renaissance had become the public spectacle of the sideshow. Celebrated 'hairy' people who achieved global fame in travelling exhibitions included the somewhat obviously named 'Jo-Jo the Dog-Faced Man' (Fedor Jeftichew), a Russian performer discovered and exhibited by B.T. Barnum, and 'Lionel the Lion-Faced Boy' (Stephan Bibrowski) (fig. 1-6). Most celebrated of all the nineteenth-century hypertrichosic cases was Julia Pastrana, the performer and singer who toured America and Europe attracting the attention of artists and writers, and who was billed variously as a 'hybrid' between human and ape, a 'bear woman' and most poignantly as a 'nondescript' (fig. 1-7). The fascination and fear that these hairy luminaries generated speaks loudly of the all too proximate condition of being human and becoming animal, with hair turning to fur as the tactile proof of such a transformation, which is discussed further in 'Shape Shifters' (p. 193).

Hair, human and animal, goes through four distinct phases: the anagen or growing phase, which in humans lasts between two and seven years but decreases over time; the catagen or regressive phase, which marks the end of active growth of the hair; the telogen or resting phase, which sees the hair become fully keratinised and dormant; and the final exogen phase, during which the hair is shed and new growth starts to develop. Humans lose on average between 50 and 100 hairs daily, but with age the hair follicles also start to diminish leading to balding. Understanding that at any given time hair is both active and dormant, or 'living' and 'dead', can account for the contradictory responses we find throughout global culture and history to human and animal hair. We not only nurture and 'dress' our hair to maintain its vitality but also understand hair as 'dead matter', especially when it grows too abundantly, in the

1-8 Lucas Cranach the Elder (1472–1533), *Samson and Delilah* (detail), c.1528–30. Oil on beech, 57.2 × 37.8 cm. The Metropolitan Museum of Art, New York. Bequest of Joan Whitney Payson, 1975

wrong place or, most disconcertingly of all, is detached from the body and finds its way into drains or food, becoming, as anthropologist Mary Douglas famously explained, 'matter out of place'.[4]

Hair is a sign of our strength, especially masculine strength, and so Samson's confession that 'There hath not come a razor upon mine head' has been the tonsorial regimen for a host of lion-locked strongmen ever since (fig. 1-8).[5] Long, uncut hair is cherished in many global cultures, including that of Native Americans for whom it is regarded as an extension of the nervous system, acting as a conduit able to transmit information to the brain. Hence many Navajo or Diné People cut their children's hair for the only time on their first birthday, while Sikhs encourage head and beard hair to grow naturally out of respect for God's creation, a practice known as *kesh*. Hair's central position in many ceremonial and transitional rites connected with mourning, puberty and marriage, in which hair is often, but not exclusively, cut, recognises the essential libidinous symbolism of hair. It also accounts for its removal by those seeking to follow a spiritual way of life, bestowing on hair a supernatural significance interrogated by social anthropologist Edmund Leach in his essay 'Magical Hair'. Here he observed that typically in ritual situations, 'long hair = unrestrained sexuality; short hair or partially shaved head or tightly bound hair = restricted sexuality; close shaven head = celibacy'.[6]

1-7 Exhibition advertisement for Miss Julia Pastrana, 'The Nondescript', 1855–60. Coloured woodcut. Wellcome Collection, London

1-9 Alexander McQueen, hair coat, *Eclect Dissect,* Givenchy Haute Couture, Autumn/Winter 1997. Hair. Fairchild Archive/Penske Media/Shutterstock

Magical hair is also what Alexander McQueen invoked so often in his use of longer haired furs, and even real human hair (fig. 1-9). 'Hair, whether human or animal, is crucial to an understanding of McQueen's ability to weave together the primitive, the mythical, the mortal and the tactile, rendering the body into a site of ceaseless experimentation'.[7]

Hair's apparent disregard for the boundaries between growth and stasis, a product of the body that is both living and dead, has nourished many of our deepest anxieties concerning decay, mortality and even immortality; trichological nightmares populated by the hairy undead. The frisson of unease experienced when looking at mummies that still retain hair, for example, is the same shock felt when the obvious decay of the body is coupled with an unnatural villosity (fig. 1-10). Death after all is typically personified as bald and skull-like. Hair as evidence of the transcendence of death is a belief both chilling and comforting, as German novelist Erich Maria Remarque observed of his fallen First World War comrade, imagining his fingernails and hair continuing to grow after death, 'twisting like corkscrews and growing and growing, and with them the hair on his caved-in skull, like grass on good earth, just like grass – how can all that be?'[8] Remarque's analogy between hair and earth or dirt has a precedent. In the early Modern period the condition of a man's beard was understood to be an indicator of his general health, as beard hair was believed to be a form of waste matter akin to sweat, which issued through the pores in the face and then congealed when coming into contact with the air as a sort of hairy excrement.

This emotional, literary response to hair has a logic that is absent from some of the more clinically acute reactions to hair, such as chaetophobia, sufferers from which avoid touching hair, human or animal, or indeed their own in the belief that it is 'dirty' or harmful; loose, fallen or cut hair, as might be found on the floor of a barber's shop, causes alarm. Similarly, trichopathobia is the fear of losing one's hair or developing scalp and hair disorders, while trichotillomania, which may be the result of a hormonal imbalance or brought on by stress, manifests itself in the excessive pulling out of one's own hair, resulting in bald patches.

Whether, ritually, artistically or cosmetically induced, we have arrived at a juncture where our attitude to hair has never been more ambivalent and which, it could be argued, also saturates the prevailing

1-10 Mummified male, *c.*1200–1400. Possibly from Chimu people, northern Peru. Wellcome Collection, London

1-11 Workshop of Rogier van der Weyden, *Portrait of a Lady*, c.1460. Oil with egg tempera on oak, 37 x 27.1 cm. National Gallery of Art, Washington D.C. Andrew W. Mellon Collection, 1937.1.44. Eileen Tweedy/Shutterstock

1-12 Advertisement for mink and sable eyelash extensions, Toronto, 2017. Courtesy of the author

contemporary attitude to fur. Paradoxically, as bodies, both female and male, become increasingly depilated, the care and attention given to head hair in the form of cosmetic preparations and professional hairdressing is magnified. Historically, female axillary hair (that is, underarm and pubic hair), together with noticeable body hair, has since the ancient world been under constant threat of extinction from a depilatory onslaught, trimmed, plucked, shaved, waxed and electrolysed into invisibility. In ancient Egypt women customarily removed all body and pubic hair, while both men and women were often shaven-headed and wore wigs. Patrician Greeks and Romans, who regarded excess body and pubic hair as undesirable, removed it with the aid of volsella, a prototype of our modern tweezers. Fashion historian Patricia Lurati notes that 'The twelfth-century medical compendium on female health known as *The Trotula* included hair-removal formulas using quicklime "in order that a woman might become very soft and smooth and without hairs from her head down"'.[9] Coming closer to the Modern period, aristocratic and fashionable women of the Middle Ages turned their attention to facial hair, plucking eyebrows, eyelashes and shaving the forehead hairline to accentuate and elongate the brow. The haunting *Portrait of a Lady* from the workshop of Rogier van der Weyden (c.1460) is perhaps one of the most celebrated examples of 'bald' beauty (fig. 1-11). This fashionable Burgundian woman wears a truncated hennin, or cone-shaped headdress, popular in Northern Europe in the late Middle Ages, which meets her shaved hairline as the edge of her veil brushes her plucked brows and lashless eyes, creating a startlingly bare sculptural effect, the only 'hair' in the work being that of the dark fur trimming her dress. She may well recognise her twenty-first century sister in today's plucked and shaved ideal, and possibly covet a pair of real mink false eyelashes available in a range of qualities and thicknesses for between $40 and $300 a pair (fig. 1-12), but not perhaps the contemporary perversity whereby shaved eyebrows are now permanently restored by tattooing.

Understandably less is known about the grooming fashions for pubic or ancillary hair in the early Modern period, although merkins, or pubic wigs, were thought to have been adopted especially by prostitutes, who, having had to remove their pubic hair to avoid lice, resorted to a merkin to disguise the depilated signs of carnality and possibly to obscure further signs of sexual infection. Pubic hair was also collected and kept as an amorous keepsake in the late eighteenth and early nineteenth centuries, and was even worn in the hats of libertines as a form of hairy cockade.

The pubic souvenir is a lesser-known counterpart to the customary locks of hair from the heads of loved ones included in sentimental jewellery, which could also be arranged into scenes or woven to produce the typical net forms of Victorian mourning jewellery (fig. 1-13). George IV, perhaps unsurprisingly, indulged in pubic accessorising evidenced by the snuffbox packed with ginger hair that he bequeathed in 1822 to the Beggar's Benison, a gentlemen's club founded in Fife, Scotland, in 1732 and dedicated to the 'convivial celebration of male sexuality'. The snuffbox and contents survives in the special collections of the University of St Andrews accompanied by a handwritten card, which reads: 'Hair from the Mons Veneris of a Royal Courtesan of George IV'.[10] The king made his gift while on a tour of Scotland, a political exercise intended to unify Britain under Hanoverian rule. His bequest was meant to act as a replacement for a famed wig, made from the pubic hair of Charles II's conquests, which had been the Beggar's Benison's prized possession until it was removed to the rival Wig Club in 1775.[11]

Although far removed from the libertine sensibilities of Georgian Scotland, three remarkable and highly individual examples of contemporary fashion that conflate merkins, pubic and displaced hair, using real fur, synthetic fur and human hair respectively, can provide suitable attire for our journey towards human hairlessness and its relationship to fur. In 1963 the furrier Georges Kaplan, together with his son Jacques, commissioned leading American artists to create a series of coats, which they would then showcase along with other fur designs from that year's collection. Art-loving Jacques had by this time begun to amass a collection of contemporary works of art, acquired mostly by trading fur coats, and so using artists to create furs was a logical progression (see 'Furnishing' and 'Soft Gold', pp. 182, 43). The coats, made of cow hide, were used primarily as canvases on which the artists, including Frank Stella, painted abstract designs using a plastic paint especially developed by the famous New York pigments manufacturer Bocour. The coat by pop artist Marisol, however, departed from this pattern and is painted front and back with an animated pink, naked female body with the startling addition of black mink 'pubic hair' (fig. 1-14). The coat (now in the collection of the Metropolitan Museum of Art, New York) – a transgressive garment that clothes the wearer in human nakedness constructed from the external covering of animals – poses a number of dermic questions concerning the relationship between the real and represented body, human and animal skin, and fur and hair.[12]

1-13 Brooch containing human hair, 18th century. Europe. Science Museum, London

1-14 Jacques Kaplan, coat, 1963. Cowhide and mink, painted by Marisol. Photograph by Marina Hays, The Metropolitan Museum of Art, New York

1-15 Vivienne Westwood, coat, *On Liberty*, Autumn/Winter 1994. Fake chinchilla. Ken Towner/Associated Newspapers/Shutterstock

Vivienne Westwood's 1994 Autumn/Winter collection, *On Liberty*, included, amongst the designer's hallmark historicist revisioning of the contemporary female form, a series of looks utilising synthetic fur, Westwood would renounce real fur in 2007. Then-supermodel Carla Bruni's appearance in a voluminous, wrapped, brown chinchilla-inspired coat, which she then opened to reveal a matching fake fur G-string or more accurately merkin, effectively mimicking the shape of human pubic hair, ensured the collection received global media attention and a prominent position in the Westwood canon (fig. 1-15). The substitution of fake fur for real, the heightening of attention paid to the pubic area by its 'disguise' and the direct historical reference to the archaic merkin is characteristic of Westwood's abiding interest in society's shifting attitudes to sexuality. In this case its fascination with, and denial of, intimate body hair is cloaked by yet another artifice – fake fur.

British designer Andrew Groves's 1997 Autumn/Winter debut collection, entitled *Ordinary Madness*, featured garments inspired by Central African nail fetish figures, or *nkondi*, and the history of Bedlam. However, it is surrealist concepts of displacement that are most apparent in the elegant sheath of pale fleshy-pink satin, which was simultaneously eminently wearable and also shocking due to the addition of a meticulously grafted fuzz of red pubic hair. Paying homage to René Magritte's disquieting vision *Philosophy in the Boudoir* (1947), which shows a dress metamorphosed into a face, with breasts for eyes and a hairy genital region for the mouth, Groves's dress plays with the idea of being both dressed and undressed in public. Similarly, as the hair was real (albeit head hair rather than pubic), the sheath is suggestive of the readymade, with a prosthetic embellishment that is at once mundane and rare, especially as Groves had each individual hair knotted into the front panel of the dress by a professional wigmaker (fig. 1-16). As with the Marisol coat, the interchangeability of surfaces is interrogated as hair is displaced from its usual position, separated only by the sensuous membrane of satin from which it now sprouts rather than the skin veiled beneath it.

Having paused to consider three examples of fashion that seek to question the relationship between the body and its hair, it is fashion in an alliance with depilatory technology that completes the passage from hirsute to shorn. From its introduction in 1680 in Sheffield, the steel-edged straight or cut-throat razor remained the dominant mode of shaving for some 200 years until 1901, when King Camp Gillette applied for the patent for an easy-to-use safety razor, with disposable, double-edged blades that obviated the need for sharpening, which went into production in 1904 (fig. 1-17). The newly found ease with which men could shave themselves safely at home without having to go to a barber ensured the success of the safety razor and women were swiftly targeted as additional lucrative

1-16 Andrew Groves, dress, *Ordinary Madness*, Autumn/Winter 1997. Satin with human hair addition. Courtesy Andrew Groves

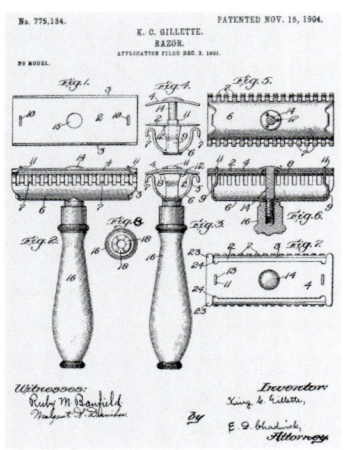

1-17 Drawing from the patent application for the Gillette safety razor. Filed in 1901 by King C. Gillette and approved in 1904. Granger/Shutterstock

consumers with an onslaught of depilatory powders, creams and other preparations, the advertising for which defined underarm hair as undesirable and unclean. Gillette's launch of the Milady Decolleté razor in 1915 coincided with the exact moment when women's fashion became more revealing, as indicated in an advertisement of the same year: 'The vogue of the sleeveless evening gown, the popularity of the dance, the filmy dress fabrics, have made an insistent demand for an *underarm* as smooth as the face.'[13] Fashion continued to play a vital role in the stripping of the body from its hair, with hem lines rising steadily throughout the 1920s, encouraged in the 1930s by a focus on the newly athletic, sporting body revealed by figure-hugging fashions that naturally required grooming as part of the overall shift towards the public exhibition of the body. Just as the First World War had played a vital role in advancing the clean-shaven man, when it was necessary to be clean-shaven to ensure the close fitting of the seals on gas masks, so too, in the United Kingdom at least, the Second World War encouraged women to shave their legs, newly exposed by the absence of silk and nylon stockings due to rationing.

Whether war and the shortage of fabric was responsible for the development of the bikini is questionable, but nevertheless in 1946 both established designer Jacques Heim and engineer-turned-lingerie designer Louis Réard unveiled their revolutionary two-piece bathing suits, although precursors to the bikini have been identified in Roman mosaics and in the Modern era have been worn since the 1930s. Echoing the nuclear tests of the time, Heim's 'atome' bathing suit was relatively modest compared to Réard's shocking 'bikini', the first two-piece to reveal the navel. Nevertheless its fame and popularity presaged a renewed focus on the pubic region and the control of its hair. Almost immediately the bikini, a quintessentially displacing garment that both preserves modesty and satisfies our desire for exhibitionism (thus underlining the essential ambivalence J.C. Flügel proposed in his *The Psychology of Clothes*), was also used to emphasise the tension between hairless modernism and hairy primitivism.[14] Nowhere is this seen more forcefully than in the concept of the fur bikini, an impossible

1-18 *One Million Years B.C.*, dir. Don Chaffey, 1966. Film still. Moviestore Collection/Shutterstock

1-19 Jacket, c.1965. Embroidered suede trimmed with crimped sheep's hair, lined in shorter pale fur. Label reads 'Made in Turkey'. Texas Fashion Collection, University of North Texas Libraries

garment that is dysfunctional as swimwear and makes vestimentary mockery of our animalistic inheritance. Diana Dors, who appeared at the 1955 Venice Film Festival in a mink bikini, increased her celebrity status overnight due to this furry publicity stunt. The erotic potential of the 'primitive' striptease was soon exploited in cabarets and strip clubs, such as the Casino de Paris in London, which in 1963 exhibited three dancers wearing real and printed versions of bikini briefs topped off by fur nipple pasties. The most celebrated and possibly ironic fur bikini is without doubt that worn by Raquel Welch as the Neanderthal 'Leona the Fair One' in the 1966 film *One Million Years B.C.*, a furry two-piece that reaches a high point of cinematically cultivated 'primitivism' (fig. 1-18).[15]

On reaching the 1960s and fashion that celebrated the nubile, smooth physique influenced by science fiction, in which bodies are resolutely hairless (body hair has no function in a temperature-controlled future), the denuded ideal of today dawned. Periodic reversions to hairy bohemianism, typified by the hippie movement and the Afghan coat, attempted to ruffle the absent pelage of the newly fit future body (fig. 1-19). This was assisted by the advent of the women's liberation movement, which fought hairlessness and supported the retention of underarm hair as an anti-patriarchal protest, but to little lasting effect against an increasingly hairless standard. The explosion of the pornography industry in the late twentieth century propagated the image of completely hair-free genitals, both male and female, with what is reputed to be the first widely circulated image of depilated female genitalia, appearing in *Hustler* magazine in September 1974. Bodybuilding, fitness regimes and the growth of 'gym culture' during the same period also encouraged the hairless male body, which demanded muscular definition free from distracting body hair.

Despite a growing contemporary reaction to the 'norm' of hairlessness, the resurgence of the beard being an example, the ascendancy of hair removal (fig. 1-20) and the rise of waxing parlours specialising in extreme forms of depilation, such as Brazilians for women and the much derided 'back, crack and sack' for men, is a testament to contemporary trichophobic culture. Male hair removal is a major growth (no pun intended) industry, explained not only by the dominance of the hairless body in both heterosexual and homosexual erotic imagery, but also by other factors varying from the increase in cycling (demanding the removal of lower body hair) to the preponderance of body tattooing (which requires a 'blank' canvas to be seen to full advantage). As mentioned previously, backlashes against the drift towards hairlessness have occurred throughout the late twentieth and twenty-first centuries with varying degrees of success. The most fervent advocates of hairiness, however, remain marginalised, and are

1-20 *Representation of the New Shaving Machine* critiquing mechanisation, 18th century. Coloured etching. Wellcome Collection, London

often dismissed as eccentric and reactionary, or regarded as somehow aberrant. Caricatured as 'hairy feminists' or homosexual 'bears' (hairy, heavy-set or muscular gay or bisexual men), the latter have appositely adopted a suitably furry classificatory system, where 'otters' denote thinner but hairy bodies, 'cubs' indicate younger hairy bodies and 'pups' are hairless (fig.1-21). Finally, a hirsute body is simply understood as an attribute of ageing and a sign of mortality, which bolsters contemporary western attitudes to body hair as unwanted, abject and 'dirty', and has contributed significantly to the contemporary attitude to fur.

If cultural shifts in the acceptance or indeed rejection of hair have been presaged and consolidated by comparative fluctuations in fashionable dress, then until the current 'fear of fur', or doraphobia as it is medically termed, fashion has been able to deploy fur visibly to reflect, augment or question prevailing attitudes to hair, often acting as a vestimentary reminder of our primordial, hairier selves. The selection of fur according to colouring, length and texture, or its positioning and quantity on a garment, have been dependant since the late nineteenth century on a variety of factors: developments in hunting, trapping and latterly the farming of fur; technological advances in transportation, starting with the development of the automobile; the influence of cinema; the escalation of the anti-fur movement; and not least the rise of fashion media itself.

Fashionable fur's serial devotion to longer, shaggier, hairier furs, manifested in the fraternity raccoon coat popular with male college students in the 1920s, chic simians clad in 1930s monkey fur (see 'The Force of Fur' and 'Shape Shifters', pp. 141, 193) or counter-cultural activists dropping out in Afghan coats, is a result of many of the previously listed stimuli, but must also express a desire to put on, if momentarily, a primal guise where hair and

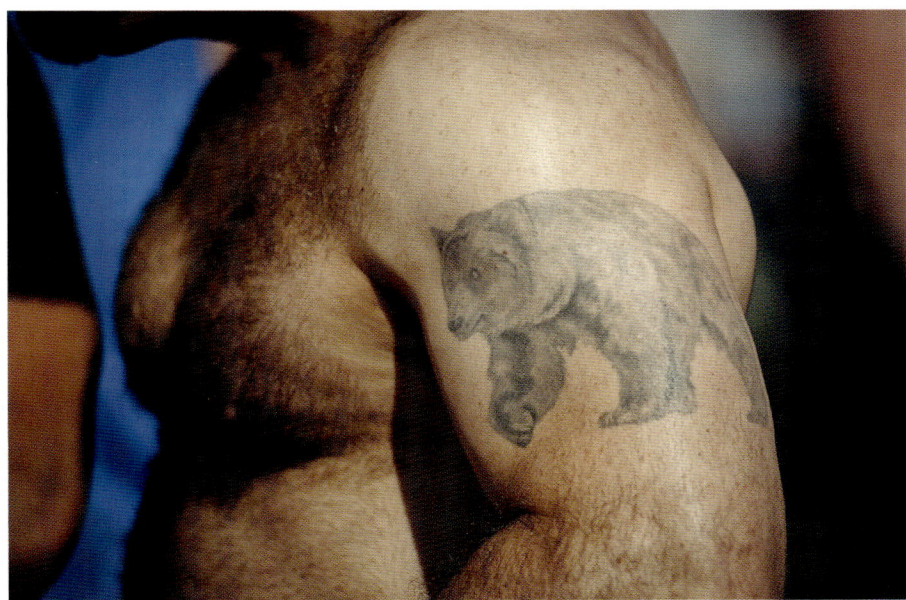

1-21 Bear tattoo on a 'Bear', Pride in the Park, Shoreditch, London, 2013. Dosfotos/Shutterstock

1-22 Albert Alfus, coat for Nieman Marcus, New York, 1969/70. Curly lamb or possibly goat hair, stand-up collar, placket and pockets of brown leather. Texas Fashion Collection, University of North Texas Libraries

fur's separation is fused once again and the wearer is rendered newly sensate (fig. 1-22). The border between human and animal is always permeable and fashionable fur has been instrumental in sartorially weakening or defending this border. The projection of our primal self, where a period of inadequate grooming or the donning of fur is all that is needed to render us 'primitive' or 'animal' once more, is so deeply embedded in the collective psyche that it can be used as a salutary warning against judging by appearances, as Frank Tashlin, that quintessential post-war commentator on social mores, demonstrated in his 1946 parable *The Bear That Wasn't*. This relates the story of a bear waking from hibernation to find that no matter how strongly he protests the opposite, every human and bear he meets declares 'You're not a bear! You're just a silly man who needs a shave and wears a fur coat!'[16]

I'D RATHER GO HAIRLESS

'Nobody needs a mink coat but the mink'[17]

This line of dialogue from the seasonal 1945 comedy film *Christmas in Connecticut*, prompted by the delivery of a mink coat to the film's leading character Elizabeth Lane (Barbara Stanwyck), is the first of many similar references to the mink coat. In the film it represents inessential and profligate desire and is also the root cause of Lane's increasingly comedic pretence at being the perfect mid-twentieth-century American homemaker.

While this comment suggests a concern for the animal's wellbeing unusual for the period, the emphasis on need and the film's subsequent use of the mink coat to trigger discussions centred around financial security, status, sexuality and worth, construct the mink as an ideal object of the libidinal economy, as the philosopher Jean-François Lyotard termed it; an excessive garment in terms of its practicality, its expense and the strong emotions it induces.[18] The mink coat, as with many similar cinematic fur garments, functions as a nexus of libidinal intensity, affecting protagonists and events with a force that transcends their theatrical fiction. As a consequence, it leaves a troubling residue redolent of opposing arguments arising from the commercial production of fur and the rights of the animal that continue to divide opinion.[19]

The polarisation that today characterises the arguments put forward by the fur industry itself and those opposed to it – broadly speaking animal rights groups and more specifically the anti-fur lobby – suggests a simplistic opposition between those who regard the wearing of fur as wrong and those who don't (fig. 1-23). This basic perspective belies the complexity of the arguments on both sides and indeed the often surprising, and largely overlooked, history of the animal rights movement. Therefore, this section of the book will attempt to briefly trace both the development of the animal rights movement in general and specifically its opposition to wearing fur, concluding

1-23 Dan Mathews, Senior Vice-President of Campaigns for PETA, and member Julia Sloane launch the 'We'd Rather Go Naked Than Wear Fur!' campaign, Tokyo, 1992. Itsuo Inouye/Shutterstock

with that same movement's transformation under the aegis of today's headline grabbing organisations.

The early history of the animal rights movement, certainly in terms of published writing on the subject, is inexorably bound up with the abolitionists and their opposition to slavery. In simple terms, the argument put forward by abolitionists – that slavery denied those in bondage basic rights – was extended by some to include animals, which as living entities also deserved to be afforded similar rights. Searching for a suitable starting point for the wider promotion, if not acceptance, of animal rights, one of the earliest and most significant figures was the philosopher and founder of utilitarianism, Jeremy Bentham. In a footnote to the chapter entitled 'On the Limits of the Penal Branch of Jurisprudence' in his *Introduction to the Principles of Morals and Legislation*, published in 1789, Bentham includes this now famous passage, widely regarded as one of the earliest and most impassioned pleas for animal rights:

> *The day has been, I grieve to say in many places it is not yet past, in which the greater part of the species under the denomination of slaves, have been treated by the law exactly upon the same footing as, in England, for example, the inferior races of animals are still. The day may come when*

the rest of the animal creation may acquire the rights which never could have been witholden from them but by the hand of tyranny. The French have already discovered that the blackness of the skin is no reason why a human being should be abandoned, without redress, to the caprice of a tormentor. It may come one day to be recognised that the number of the legs, the villosity of the skin, or the termination of the os sacrum, are reasons equally insufficient for abandoning a sensitive being to the same fate. What else is it should trace the insuperable line? Is it the faculty of reason, or, perhaps, the faculty of discourse? But a full-grown horse or dog is, beyond comparison, a more rational, as well as more conversable animal than an infant of a day, a week, or even a month old. But suppose the case were otherwise, what would it avail? The question is not, Can they reason? Nor, Can they talk? But, Can they suffer?[20]

Although Bentham was not against animals being killed for food, used in medical experiments or killed in defence of human life, he did make plain his objection to causing unnecessary suffering to animals, and while he makes no mention of animals used for fur, his equation between the rights of humans and animals to live their lives free from torment has informed and inspired many subsequent champions of animal rights (fig. 1-24).

Following Bentham's publication, various milestones in the progress of the animal rights movement were reached including, in 1822, the passing of the Ill-Treatment of Cattle Act, commonly known as 'Martin's Act' after the humanitarian and animal rights campaigner Richard Martin who formulated it. Although only pertaining to cattle and 'beasts of burden', it marked an important legislative precedent. The passing of the bill galvanised a growing group of animal rights sympathisers, no doubt

1-24 *Animal Cruelty*, 1865. American newspaper engraving. This image inspired Henry Bergh to found the American Society for the Prevention of Cruelty to Animals the following year. Granger/Shutterstock

encouraged by the increasing condemnation by many English reformers of the cruelties of bull- and bear-baiting and cock-fighting. They included the Reverend Arthur Broome, who organised a meeting in 1824 of like-minded sympathisers, such as the leading abolitionist William Wilberforce, who oversaw the passing of the Abolition of the Slave Trade Act in 1807, and Lewis Gompertz, animal rights campaigner and early vegan. It was at this meeting that the Society for the Prevention of Cruelty to Animals (later the RSPCA) was created.

The presence of both Wilberforce and Gompertz at this seminal meeting in the history of animal rights signals the increasingly complex, worldwide imbrication of a number of emancipatory and reforming ideologies. These included those of abolitionists, supporters of women's rights and the growing suffrage movement, vegetarians and vegans, dress reformers, those opposed to blood sports, anti-vivisectionists and, by the end of the nineteenth century, those specifically campaigning against the use of animals in the fashion and clothing industries, including, of course, the use of fur and feathers.

1-25 *The Woman Behind the Gun*, *Puck* magazine, May 1911. Illustration by Gordon Ross; photomechanical print. This anti-plumage image shows a woman wearing a large hat with feathers, shooting at birds with a rifle. Two cartoon gun dogs, labelled 'French Milliners', retrieve the dead birds in their mouths. Public Domain/WikiCommons

While many of the earliest advocates for animal rights were men, from the mid-nineteenth century onwards, both within Europe and North America, it would be fair to say that the development of animal rights, including opposition to the use of animals in fashion, was primarily due to female advocacy. Battersea Dogs Home (established in 1860), the National Anti-Vivisection Society (1875) and the British Animal Defence and Anti-Vivisection Society (1903) are just a few of the institutions founded by women, many of whom, alongside their support for animal rights, were committed to the women's suffrage movement and were promoters of temperance and vegetarianism amongst other social reforms. While the use of fur in the fashion industry was a major target for these pioneering and reforming women, it is the use of feathers that gained more widespread support and indeed popular attention (fig. 1-25). A key figure in the anti-plumage movement, who typified the strong-minded, articulate, upper- and middle-class women who made such an important contribution to animal rights in this period, was Eliza Phillips. She was an ardent opponent of the use of birds' feathers in ladies fashion, holding afternoon meetings of the 'Fur, Fin and Feather Folk' at her house in Croydon. Another was Emily Williamson, who headed an anti-plumage group based in Manchester, which generated attention concerning the plight of birds used in the millinery trade. These groups were representative of a groundswell of public opinion that gathered momentum and, together with the Plumage League and the Selborne Society for the Protection of Birds, Plants and Pleasant Places, led to the creation of the Society for the Protection of Birds (SPB) in 1891 (the 'Royal' prefix was added in 1904).[21] Similar anti-plumage sympathisers worked industriously in North America, most notably two Boston socialites, Harriet Hemenway and Minna B. Hall, whose bird preservation tea parties led to the foundation of the Massachusetts Audubon Society in 1896. Their campaign resulted in the Weeks-McLean Migratory Bird Act of 1913, which effectively ended 'millinery murder' in North America.

Opposition to the use of fur in fashion at this period was centred on the trade in sealskin (fig. 1-26). Much like the egret, seals were killed with no attention paid to breeding patterns or seasons, and owing to the enormous popularity of sealskin fashions from the mid-nineteenth to the early twentieth century, fur seal populations were severely depleted and put at risk of extinction. The plight of the fur seal galvanised the burgeoning anti-fur lobby and its inclusion in an address given by Margaretta Lemon, a founding member of the SPB, entitled 'Dress in Relation to Animal Rights' at the International Congress of Women held in London in 1899, is typical:

Undoubtedly, terrible abuses exist; many beautiful and useful animals are becoming extinct because they are hunted and killed without due regard to the breeding season, and we know that indescribable cruelties have been practised in the killing and skinning of the fur-bearing seals, and in the procuring of certain kinds of astrakhan, which is the skin of the unborn lamb.[22]

Seven years prior to Lemon's address, animal rights benefitted from the publication of what is still possibly the most comprehensive, reasoned and well argued condemnation of human-inflicted animal suffering in all of its forms: Henry Salt's *Animals' Rights Considered in Relation to Social Progress*. Salt was an ardent prison and school system reformer, vegetarian, pacifist and campaigner for the humane treatment of animals, who counted amongst his circle a dazzling array of radicals and thinkers including George Bernard Shaw, William Morris, Beatrice Webb and Havelock Ellis; while Gandhi, whom Salt befriended upon his arrival in England, declared that he owed his ideas on civil disobedience to Salt's writings. In the preface to the 1980 edition of *Animals' Rights*, Peter Singer,

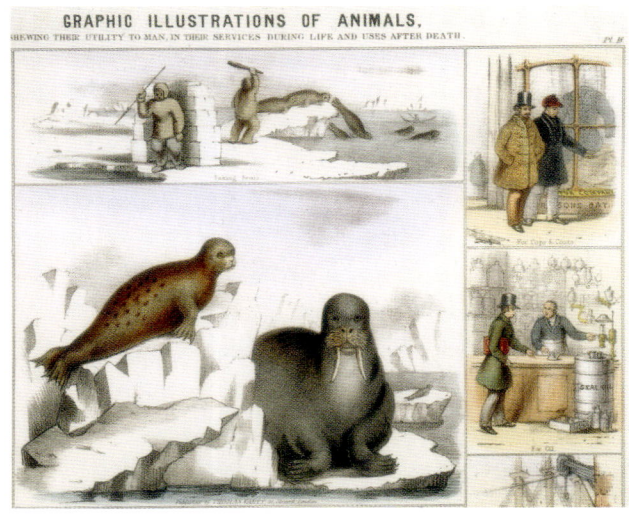

1-26 *Graphic Illustrations of Animals* (detail), plate XVIII, c.1850. Benjamin Waterhouse Hawkins; coloured lithograph, published by Roake and Varty, London, including scenes of capture and the use of seal fur for 'Caps and Coats' as depicted by the men outside a Hudson's Bay Company shop. Universal History Archive/UIG/Shutterstock

1-27 Reverse side of a fur coat. Courtesy of the author

whose own highly influential *Animal Liberation* (1975) promoted vegetarianism, coined the term 'speciesism' and had a formative influence on the modern animal liberation movement, writes: 'He anticipates almost every point discussed in the contemporary debate over animal rights' and adds that campaigners 'have been able to add relatively little to the essential case Salt outlined in 1892'.[23] Indeed Salt tackles what we would now understand as factory farming, animal experimentation, the abolition of blood sports and the use of animals in the fashion industry. Again, it is an indication of where popular support lay at the time Salt was writing that the section in the book that deals explicitly with the fur trade is to be found in the chapter entitled 'Murderous Millinery', prioritising an awareness of the evils of the plumage industry.

Interestingly, much of Salt's condemnation of the wearing of fur arises from the concept that a fur coat is made from many small individual pieces sewn together and not a continuous skin, which it purports to be, seeing it as an essentially duplicitous garment that bears a direct relationship to the concept of deception and disguise (fig. 1-27):

It makes patch-work, one may say, not only of the hides of its victims, but of the conscience and intellect of its supporters. A fur garment or trimming, we are told, appearing to the eye as if it were one uniform piece, is generally made up of many curiously shaped fragments. It is significant that a society which is enamoured of so many shams and fictions, and which detests nothing so strongly as the need of looking facts in the face, should pre-eminently esteem those articles of apparel which are constructed on the most deceptive and illusory principle.[24]

Salt's circle of supporters and like-minded public figures is typical of the formative period of the animal rights movement, which from its outset attracted what might today be termed celebrities. Many renowned writers of the period used their popularity as a platform to advance the course of animal rights. Wilkie Collins, for example, produced what is probably the first anti-vivisection novel – *Heart and Science: A Story of the Present Time* – in 1883, which he himself ranked alongside his masterpiece, *The Woman in White*. Similarly, the Animals' Friend Society, founded by Lewis Gompertz, included both John Galsworthy and Jerome K. Jerome amongst its supporters. Galsworthy's *Treatment of Animals* and *For Love of Beasts* were both available as titles in the Animals' Friend Pamphlet Series (priced at 2d each, postage paid), which was billed as 'The best and most comprehensive Series dealing with the Treatment of Animals', while Jerome's *The Cruel Steel Trap* was published as a 'Pass On' leaflet (supplied free).[25]

After the initial explosion of interest in the welfare of animals in the late nineteenth and early twentieth centuries, the animal rights movement progressed slowly. The First World War highlighted the inhumane treatment of animals, such as the plight of horses, which then receded from public attention during the Second World War, although a disturbing anomaly to this was Hitler's advocacy of vegetarianism and the passing of various animal protection laws by the Nazi Party, commencing with the first German Animal Welfare Act (Reichstierschutzgesetz) in 1933. However, the Act's reforms with regard to the slaughter of animals were targeted at Jewish kosher practices, and in a chilling reversal of the early supporters of animal rights, their edicts with hindsight would suggest that some humans had the same, or even fewer rights than animals.[26]

It was not until the 1960s and 1970s that a crystallisation of reforming ideologies, similar to that at the end of the nineteenth century and including the rights of animals, occurred. It is during this later period that we see the movement's cause furthered by the formulation of concepts such as Singer's 'speciesism' (that is, treating one species more favourably than another with the same interests, which, as argued by animal rights supporters, displays the same prejudicial foundation as racism or sexism) and 'animal liberation' with its advocacy of direct action. The growth of anti-blood sports campaigners in England during the 1960s and the actions of fox hunt saboteurs can be seen as the first instances of a new militant advancement of animal rights, galvanised by Singer's *Animal Liberation* and the formation of the Animal Liberation Front in 1976. The newsworthy activities of animal liberationists included attacks on animal experimentation laboratories, the release of mink from mink farms and the slashing of fur coats. Documentaries such as the opinion-changing *The Animals Film*, narrated by Julie Christie, and the continued endorsement of animal rights by world-famous figures such as Brigitte Bardot alongside the burgeoning ecology movement, meant that by the 1980s the protection of animals had reached an unprecedented level of global awareness and concern (fig. 1-28).[27]

Exploding into British, and later worldwide, public consciousness in 1985, the same year that Live Aid mobilised popular awareness of the famine in Ethiopia through the deployment of pop music, came Lynx, the highly successful and controversial anti-fur campaigning organisation. It was formed by Lynne Kentish, hailing from a background of music industry PR, and Mark Glover, environmentalist and activist, who met whilst both were members of Greenpeace, the environmental movement (fig. 1-29). Glover and Kentish, both passionate anti-fur campaigners, left Greenpeace to form Lynx following Glover's disappointment with Greenpeace's level of anti-fur activism, primarily due to its involvement with Inuit communities. Kentish and Glover's winning formula of activism, PR experience and music industry contacts proved immediately effective. Lynx's first venture, the now famous 'It takes up to 40 dumb animals to make a fur coat ... But only one to wear it' campaign,

1-28 Julie Christie with members of the Animal Liberation Front, 1982. Photograph by Richard Young. Richard Young/Shutterstock

1-29 *Rainbow Warrior*. The vessel owned by Greenpeace used in anti-whaling, anti-seal hunting and anti-nuclear testing campaigns during the late 1970s and early 1980s. Pierre Gleizes/AP/Shutterstock

1-30 'Rich bitch/Poor bitch' campaign poster, issued by animal rights group Lynx, 1989. Photograph by Linda McCartney. The Advertising Archives Ltd

was photographed by David Bailey (who took no fee for his services). It featured a black-and-white image of a leather-skirted, high-heel-wearing woman, shot from the waist downwards. She is dragging a fur coat along the ground, which leaves a graphic trail of bright red blood behind it. The campaign immediately proved controversial, not least because of the reaction of certain feminist groups who objected to the sexist language and imagery used. This was shortly followed by a promotional film, shown in cinemas, depicting a fur fashion show watched by an adoring front row of stereotypes: effeminate male designer; decrepit, sneering wealthy woman; and salivating young fashionista. As the models parade, they take off and swing their coats in typical fashion show choreography, splattering the increasingly shocked onlookers with trails of blood that issued from the coats. More controversial campaigns followed, including that shot by Linda McCartney, the animal rights campaigner, successful vegetarian-packaged-meal entrepreneur and photographer. It showed a supine fur-coated woman on the left and a dead and bloody fox, caught in a trap, on the right, with the text 'Rich bitch' and 'Poor bitch' under each image respectively (fig. 1-30). These campaigns, which used sexist language to vilify as moronic and cruel all fur-wearing women, as opposed to more obvious targets such as fur trappers, producers and retailers, proved highly successful. Obscuring the traditional glamorous imagery of fashionable fur with a bloody screen of outrage and disgust had an immediate impact on the British fur industry, which saw the sales of fur drop by 75 per cent between 1985 and 1990, and the closure of mink farms across the country, while many stores closed their fur departments, as did Harrods in 1990.[28] (see fig. 1-31). Lynx's remarkably successful activities came to an ironic end in 1992, when it was decided in the High Court that Lynx had disseminated literature to MPs, which wrongly accused a West Yorkshire mink farmer of running a 'hell hole'. Faced with crippling damages and court costs, the organisation was made bankrupt and ceased its activities.

The re-situating of the modern fur-clad woman as hopelessly unfashionable, in contrast to her contemporary counterpart the conscientious consumer, is an approach that was resurrected in 2015 by the fashion designer Stella McCartney.[29] This can be understood as the reversal of an earlier attack on the fur-wearing woman of the late nineteenth century as depicted by Ouida (the pen name of Maria Louise

Ramé), the popular dog-loving, anti-vivisectionist and reactionary novelist, in her essay 'The New Woman'. The essay, a riposte to an article promoting women's suffrage and equal rights for women, attacks the 'New Woman' for behaving like a man, behaviour that included, crucially for Ouida, hunting, shooting and fishing. She 'wears dead birds as millinery and dead seals as coats' and 'is very sorry, but she has so many claims on her already' that she has no time for attending to the welfare of animals.[30]

Whether the wearing of fur is seen as symptomatic of modernity, as was the case in the late nineteenth century, or as hopelessly old fashioned and irrelevant, as organisations such as Lynx in the United Kingdom and PETA (People for the Ethical Treatment of Animals) in the United States were so successful in promulgating, what remains constant is that it is the consumer, rather than the producer, who is the subject of condemnation, and that consumer is resolutely female. Julia Emberley, in her authoritative work on the sexualisation, and indeed marginalisation, of women by the anti-fur movement and its advertising campaigns, sees the anti-fur movement's expansion in the 1980s as arising from a series of complex social and ideological concerns that characterised the end of the twentieth century.[31] The anti-fur debate took a central position in an ideological battleground that mobilised widely conflicting viewpoints, or 'antagonisms' as Emberley terms them. These were realised in such actions as the throwing of red paint at women wearing fur. British feminist graffiti artists defaced Lynx campaigns for being sexist and the product of a patriarchal system. The Inuit communities of Alaska, Greenland and Canada were radicalised to counter misinformation disseminated by groups such as Greenpeace and Lynx, and what could be considered their neo-imperialist attitude towards the hunter-gatherer communities of the far north (fig. 1-32).[32]

PETA, founded in Norfolk, Virginia, in 1980 by Ingrid Newkirk and Alex Pacheco, had from its inception a larger remit than Lynx, declaring that 'Animals are not ours to experiment on, eat, wear, use for entertainment, or abuse in any other way.' Even PETA's fiercest critics admit that it has been remarkably effective in changing global public opinion, making it today the world's largest animal rights organisation with, it is claimed, some 6.5 million members and supporters.[33] In 1981 the organisation achieved international fame as a result of the Silver Springs Monkey case, which resulted from Pacheco going undercover and exposing the treatment of 17 monkeys at a behavioural research unit in Maryland,

1-31 Closing-down sale at Birger Christensen fur store, New Bond Street, London, 1991.
Mike Floyd/Associated Newspapers/Shutterstock

1-32 Seal hunting protest and Inuit opposition, Ottawa, 2005.
Canadian Press/Shutterstock

leading to a 10-year legal battle and the first American raid on an animal laboratory.

Much like Lynx, PETA's anti-fur lobbying has unashamedly continued to use sexualised female imagery and references to get their message across. The organisation's riposte to continued accusations of sexism is that all their models willingly offer their services and therefore are not being objectified. Fully realising the old adage that sex, and indeed sexism, sells (Newkirk regularly confirms this with the widely reported retort that 'PETA has a duty to be press sluts'), the group is still probably most widely known for its campaign 'I'd Rather Go Naked than Wear Fur'. Ongoing, it features an ever-expanding number of predominantly female, naked celebrities and models, although it is perhaps a testament to the economic weight of the fashion industry, and indeed the changing status of fashionable fur, that of the original quintet of supermodels who launched the campaign in 1994, only Christy Turlington has remained resolutely fur-free.[34] In addition to the press campaigns, PETA's various media-ready public demonstrations and protests typically consist of naked, or near naked, often bloodied women, simulating scenarios of torture and captivity (fig. 1-33).

How effective PETA's anti-fur campaigns are is difficult to assess, its increasing extremism and scattergun approach potentially losing as many supporters as its newsworthy actions gain new ones. A notorious example of this featured Dan Mathews, PETA's Senior Vice-President of Campaigns and responsible, amongst many others, for the 'I'd Rather Go Naked' campaign (see fig. 1-23). When asked by a journalist who he would nominate as a notable homosexual, he replied 'Andrew Cunanan, because he got Gianni Versace to stop using fur'.[35]

Alienation of the LGBTQ community is just one of PETA's achievements, which also include offending the black community, in particular the NAACP (National Association for the Advancement of Colored People), the civil rights organisation founded in 1909, which, in 2005, objected to PETA's 'Are Animals the New

1-33 'Bloody Burberry' protest by PETA, Burberry store, Regent Street, London, 2006. Tony Kyriacou/Shutterstock

Slaves?' exhibition. This consisted of images of Afro-American slaves, Native Americans, child labourers and women alongside pictures of chained elephants and slaughtered cows. Another notorious campaign that caused outrage amongst the Jewish community was its 2003 touring exhibition, *Holocaust on Your Plate,* which juxtaposed images of Holocaust victims with animal carcasses being transported for slaughter, and which, in 2010, the German courts banned from being shown there as it was deemed an offence against human dignity.

The successive changes in the public perception of fur and its use in the fashion industry, while no doubt affected by groups such as PETA, are also part of a larger and accelerating fluctuation of public opinion. Since the 1980s, characterised by Emberley as the 'anti fur season', fur's fashionable fortunes have risen

1-34 TOP Supporters of New York City's proposed fur ban, City Hall, New York, May 2019. Gabriele Holtermann Gorden/Pacific Press via ZUMA Wire/Shutterstock

1-35 ABOVE Opposers of New York City's proposed fur ban, City Hall, New York, May 2019. Gabriele Holtermann Gorden/Pacific Press via ZUMA Wire/Shutterstock

and fallen with increasing rapidity. The rise of new markets, principally Asian, for fashionable fur has boosted sales, while recent developments, such as the growing ranks of designers renouncing the use of fur in their collections, have seen fur sales plummeting again. This fall has been accelerated by a ban on the manufacture and sale of fur within city limits, voted for by the citizens of Los Angeles. Other cities have followed suit: San Francisco and West Hollywood with, at the time of writing, a similar ban being proposed by New York City Council (figs 1-34, 1-35; and see p. 76).[36] The level of anti-fur feeling, it would appear,

as with many other causes, is increasingly the result of a generation reared on social media, constantly searching for the next cause to 'like', and while PETA is resolute in its anti-fur mission, the organisation's current concentration on promoting veganism is representative of this social oscillation.

However much PETA (and before it Lynx) upholds the maxim that no publicity is bad publicity, it is surely ironic that today's most influential advocate for animal rights, a movement that from its infancy owed its effective organisation and expansion to a succession of pioneering women and was often inextricably linked to the suffrage movement, should resort so tirelessly to misogyny and sexism to promote its cause. Recent controversies surrounding PETA's vegan campaign, which compares larger women with whales, have obscured a new and, for this study at least, disturbing variant of its anti-fur agenda: that of opposing hair of all varieties, animal or human. The 'Fur trim: Unattractive' campaign of 2012 features model and TV reality star Joanna Krupa, naked except for a pair of sheer pink briefs, sprouting from each side of which are long, shaggy brown tufts suggestive of impossibly abundant pubic hair. Accompanied by the byline 'Don't Ruin Your Look With Fur Trim', the campaign is, according to PETA's website, all about bringing to our attention the use of fur as trimming, referred to on the website as Krupa's 'little extra something'.[37] While signalling the use of unregulated farmed fur as trimming, the advertisement can simultaneously be construed as both sexist and an endorsement of the current fashion for depilation, encouraging women to spend time and money trimming and waxing in the belief that pubic hair is somehow undesirable.[38] This apparent collusion between the anti-fur lobby and the anti-hair lobby, represented by the cosmetic industry, is borne out by a more direct campaign launched a year earlier. The 'Wear "Bare Skin" Not Fur!' advertisement, which ran in *Glamour* magazine, featured an open, fur-covered, zippered purse, accompanied by the exhortation: 'Get waxed and charitable all at once thanks to Ministry of Waxing's collaboration with

animal protection charity PETA. From now until December, MoW will be donating £2 from every Brazilian and XXXX Wax in-store to the charity.'[39] This simultaneous denigration and commodification of female genitalia seems far removed from animal rights and is more indicative of an escalating trichophobia.

As discussed previously, men are also increasingly identified as victims of undesirable hair and PETA's 'Ink Not Mink' campaign taps into the fear of male body hair (fig. 1-36). Featuring a roster of American professional sportsmen (with the addition of a few rock stars and tattoo artists), the campaign shows the celebrities stripped to reveal their extensively tattooed and hairless bodies. The parade of smooth, athletic men, over half of them black, which includes football stars Chad Johnson and Willis McGahee and basketball legend Dennis Rodman, who pose completely naked, offers up an unsettling post-colonial vision of the objectified male black body that seems more concerned with titillation than activism.

Jeremy Bentham's eighteenth-century plea that animals should be accorded the same consideration

1-36 Dennis Rodman launches PETA's 'Ink not Mink' campaign during New York Fashion Week, February 2005. Sipa/Shutterstock

as the recently emancipated slave seems almost inaudible amidst the clamour of PETA's commodified sensationalism. It is perhaps indicative of not just the anti-fur lobby's position today but the depth of feeling generated by the subject of fur itself, that in order for the subject to be considered at all Salt's words remain both prophetic and indispensible:

> *While not hesitating to speak strongly when occasion demanded, I have tried to avoid the tone of irrelevant recrimination so common in these controversies, and thus to give unmistakeable emphasis to the vital points at issue.*[40]

PART TWO

PELT

2 PELT

SOFT GOLD

Richard Davey in his classic, if idiosyncratic, history of the fur trade of 1895, in which he seeks possible origins for the trade, suggests that the myth of Jason and the Golden Fleece could be a metaphor for the wealth that could be accumulated from trading furs and skins: 'Thus, possibly, Jason was merely a fur trader, round whose very doubtful commercial and domestic morality poetry has woven one of her most glorious legends' (fig. 2-2).[1] If we could chart Jason's mythical trading expedition we would discover Jason and his crew sailing with skins originating from Russia, Siberia, Persia and Bokhara, the most important suppliers of furs to Western Europe and parts of Asia until the development of the North American fur trade in the seventeenth century. Jason would most likely have loaded his furs at the principal early fur-trading centre of Armenia (the origin of the word ermine), before sailing back across the Black Sea, through the Bosporus and the Dardanelles, on into the Aegean and home.

Davey rightly locates the origins of the fur trade in myth, as any attempt to establish its beginnings becomes ever more elusive. Garments made from the skins of animals have, of course, been worn since pre-history, but as to when furs first started to be traded or exchanged is impossible to determine. However, many ancient civilisations have left evidence of the wearing of furs that must have been acquired through trade with other countries. The ancient Greeks learned about fur from campaigns waged in Asia by Alexander the Great, while the Romans conducted a significant trade in furs with the Northern European tribes they encountered. With the fall of Rome and the relocation of the centre of government to Byzantium

2-2 Attributed to the Orchard Painter, column-krater depicting Jason about to seize the Golden Fleece (detail), c.470–460 BCE, Terracotta, H: 29.2 cm. The Metropolitan Museum of Art, New York. Harris Brisbane Dick Fund, 1934

PREVIOUS PAGE Dolman (detail), Hudson's Bay Furriers, c.1885. England; mink lined with satin. © Victoria and Albert Museum, London. Given by Mrs A. C. Bryant

2-1 OPPOSITE Rebecca Belmore (b. 1960), *Rising to the Occasion*, 1987–91. Mixed media. Art Gallery of Ontario. Gift from the Junior Volunteer Committee, 1995

(modern-day Istanbul), and because of its strategic location spanning the known eastern and western worlds, Byzantium (later Constantinople) became and remained the principal location through which most of the world's fur trade passed until it fell under Ottoman rule in 1453. During this period Kastoria, in northern Greece (its name is said to be derived from the Greek name for the European beaver, *kastóri*), developed as an important fur manufacturing and trading centre, supplying furs for the robes of the Byzantine court, and Kastoria remains to this day one of the world's pre-eminent fur manufacturing locations.

In the fifteenth century Venice and Genoa grew in importance due to their strategic geographical locations, their status as important commercial centres of trade, including fur, between Europe and the East, and their investment in mercantile exploration (figs 2-3, 2-4). London also emerged as a significant fur trading and manufacturing city, principally as a result of becoming a foreign trading post of the Hanseatic League, the powerful mercantile federation that dominated Northern Europe's coastal trade with Russian and Siberian furs a significant part of that business. As the League declined in importance and Britain, Holland and Scandinavia became independently powerful trading nations, fur continued to be a central component of their financial success.

This history of the early fur trade is necessarily abbreviated here due to the limitation of space and aims of this book; however, there are many authoritative works on the subject, including the seminal study of the early English trade by Elspeth Veale, to which this current work is indebted.[2] What this chapter will attempt to discuss, however, is the creation of a specific economic and mercantile space of fur, similar to the topographical imaginings of place encountered in 'Furland' (see p. 118) but here concerned more with the production and marketing of fur, rather than its fashioning and wearing, with the North American fur trade as a model. Again, it is not within the remit of this book to present a comprehensive history of the trade in North America, on which there are many authoritative works, especially that of the Hudson's Bay Company.[3] Indeed this aspect of the history of fur is

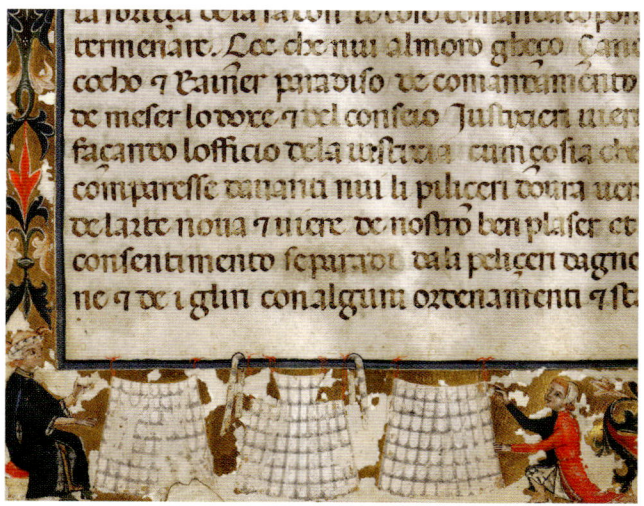

2-3 *La Mariegola* or statutory regulations for furriers, showing *vair* or squirrel skins being displayed (detail), 14th century. Venice, Italy. Alfredo Dagli Orti/Shutterstock

2-4 Exterior of the Church of Orsanmichele, Florence (detail). The chapel was used by the city's powerful trade and craft guilds. The emblem is that of the Guild of Furriers and Skinners, situated in the niche housing a statue of St James, the patron saint of furriers, c.1415. Courtesy of the author one of the few that have been extensively researched and published, and so what follows uses that history to understand the production and the territorialisation of the space of fur that has emerged since the seventeenth century. A space of fur that can be considered, in the words of Davey, to be marked by a 'very doubtful commercial and domestic morality'.

Indigenous North American peoples had been trading furs and other products amongst themselves throughout the pre-Columbian era. The commercial fur trade in North America and present-day Canada, as we understand it today, grew out of the initial contact in the sixteenth century between First Nations People and European, principally Basque, fishermen, catching cod off the coast of Newfoundland. In return for knives and other iron-based products and textiles, indigenous peoples would trade essential supplies including beaver pelts, locally tanned and made up into garments, which Europeans wore on the long cold, transatlantic journeys home (fig. 2-5). These processed pelts, or *castor gras* as they became known (see 'Heads or Tails', p. 102), were a highly prized material used in the felting process by the European hat-making industry. By the latter half of the sixteenth century the growing demand for fur as a result of the increasing popularity of beaver hats, and the resulting decimation of European beaver populations, led to the trade in fur becoming more organised. What had originated as a random exchange became, by the seventeenth century, a highly lucrative and systematised industry based in the French- and English-governed territories of the region. The best quality beaver pelts were obtained where winters were harshest and so the trade was concentrated in present-day Canada, but also extended along the Mississippi River and into the Rocky Mountains. The French were the first to exploit the vast quantities of indigenous fur-bearing animals, followed in the seventeenth century by Dutch and English traders who gradually moved inland from the coast, following the beaver along the St Lawrence and Ottawa Rivers and into the Great Lakes area.

The French traders Médard Chouart des Groseilliers and Pierre-Esprit Radisson were the first to propose

2-5 James Isham, *Indians Hunting Beaver* (detail), 1743. Isham was a trader and chief factor for the Hudson's Bay Company at York Factory and Fort Prince of Wales. He recorded in notes and drawings the landscape, customs and people he encountered there, compiled as *James Isham's Observations on Hudson's Bay, 1743*. Harper Collins Publishers/Shutterstock

a trading company that would reach into the interior and its fur resources via Hudson's Bay. Failing to get the full support they needed from the French government, they travelled to England and enlisted the help of Prince Rupert, cousin of Charles II, to present their scheme to the king who, with a number of other prominent parties, backed the enterprise and dispatched the first ships to the territory in 1668. This initial foray was followed in 1670 by the proclamation of a Royal charter forming the Hudson's Bay Company, or to give it its full title The Governor and Company of Adventurers of England Trading into Hudson's Bay (fig. 2-6). The company was granted wide powers including exclusive trading rights in the area, which became known as Rupert's Land. There was a fundamental difference between French and English trading patterns. English trade was organised along hierarchical lines with salaried managers, whereas the French monopoly issued licences or *conges*, allowing independent traders to use their posts. The English structure was centralised and controlled from London, and required systems that could monitor the managers of their trading posts. The leasing and licensing arrangements of the French, conversely, made monitoring unnecessary, but led to centralised government having far weaker control over how the trade was conducted, while being more flexible and conducive to expansion. How the English and French interacted with indigenous peoples also differed greatly, with representatives of the Hudson's Bay Company establishing posts throughout the area to which First Nations traders, often the middlemen between indigenous trappers further inland and Company representatives, would bring pelts to trade. The French, by contrast, moved into the interior themselves and frequently traded directly with First Nations trappers, often forming relationships with, including marriages to, women of prominent indigenous families.

The next 100 years would see fierce rivalry, principally between the French and the English, for control of the fur trade in the area. This was a period that would establish, as political economist Harold Adams Innis suggested in his seminal work of 1930, *The Fur Trade in Canada*, the 'infrastructure of colonization'.[4] European models of extraction, transportation and exchange replaced First Nations organisations that had existed for centuries, and so roads replaced paths and tracks, sailing and subsequently steamships took over from canoes, towns grew up where previously there had been camps and trading posts, and maps became standardised. As well as developing and imposing a foreign infrastructure, the fur trade also conformed to the patterns of many similar colonising ventures, entailing the systematic stripping away and translation of indigenous knowledge concerning land, shelter, food, etc., an overture to the destruction of cultural practices and habits.

The principal rival to the Hudson's Bay Company, the North West Company, emerged in the eighteenth century, formed in 1779 by a confederation of Montreal-based traders, many of them Scottish. Unlike the stationary 'Baymen', the traders of this newly formed company penetrated far into the interior, encountering as yet unexploited populations of fur-bearing animals. They had the advantage of mobility and the specialised knowledge that came from living in the area and being familiar with the indigenous population, unlike the Hudson's Bay representatives who were often new to the territory and controlled from afar by London-based financiers. Crucially, however, the Hudson's Bay Company presided over the sea route from England to the Bay, where goods could be unloaded and fur picked up in a fraction of the time it took the North West Company to gather their goods, transport them over land and by canoe, load them into ships and set sail. After a series of confrontations and disputes the two companies merged in 1821, making the newly augmented Hudson's Bay Company the most powerful fur-trading organisation in the world at that period.

The other organisation to reap the benefits of the North American fur trade was the American Fur Company, founded in 1808 by a German immigrant, John Jacob Astor (fig. 2-7). On his arrival in America around 1784 Astor began working for a Quaker fur dealer and soon started to buy and trade furs with the money he made from a variety of business ventures. By 1800 he was reputedly worth $250,000, mostly made from fur trading, which included lucrative trading ventures with China and the exchange of furs for cargoes of silk, tea and porcelain. Capitalising on anti-British sentiment, and arguing that American fur should be controlled and sold by Americans, he

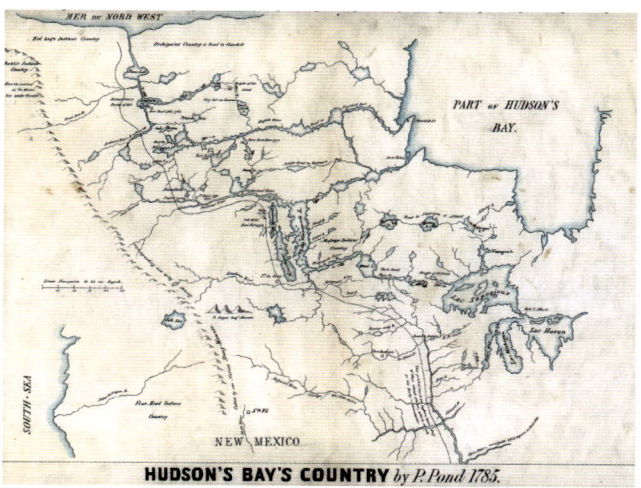

2-6 Map of the Hudson's Bay area (detail), 1785. Produced for the Hudson's Bay Company by explorer, trader and mapmaker Peter Pond. Granger/Shutterstock

2-7 Edward Dalton Marchant (1806–1887), *John Jacob Astor*, 1836. Oil on canvas. Granger/Shutterstock

gained the support of Thomas Jefferson, and so Astor's company swiftly grew to monopolise the fur trade in the newly established United States. By 1830 Astor, foreseeing the decline in the demand for fur, had withdrawn from the company and shifted his attentions to real estate, the fortune he had accrued from fur making him one of the wealthiest people in the world and America's first multi-millionaire.

As the nineteenth century progressed, the North American fur industry's fortunes changed, partly due to the decline in demand for beaver fur as a result of the development of alternatives such as silk plush (see 'Heads or Tails', p. 102), partly due to the decimation of the beaver population and its habitats, and partly due to changing fashions in fur. Like Astor, the Hudson's Bay Company had also diversified its interests to accommodate the diminishing demand for fur and in 1870 agreed to transfer back to the Crown the lands it had once occupied, which were then reincorporated into the new Dominion of Canada following its federation in 1867.

Innis rightly understood the study of the beaver as central to an understanding of the subsequent economic, social and geographical changes brought about as a consequence of the colonial imposition of the industrialised fur trade. The territorialisation of the beaver and its habitat, initially that which it imposed on its own natural environment including the building of lodges and the damming of waterways, was extended to the indigenous population that hunted it and developed complex ritual and societal codes that facilitated the territorial exchange between hunter and hunted (fig. 2-8). This process then penetrated and diversified even further with the arrival of European colonising forces, which ecologically, economically and culturally territorialised both beaver and First Nations inhabitants. As Deleuze and Guattari proposed, 'A territory borrows from all the milieus; it bites into them, seizes them bodily (although it remains vulnerable to intrusions). It is built from aspects or portions of milieus. It itself has an exterior milieu, an interior milieu, an intermediary milieu, and an annexed milieu.'[5]

Beavers have long been celebrated for their ability to construct their own environment, diverting waterways and building dwellings from material shaped by gnawing. Early travellers marvelled both at their numbers, soon to be decimated, and their remarkable ability to engineer their watery habitats. The Jesuit historian Pierre François de Charlevoix wrote in his *Journal of a Voyage to North America* of 1761: 'There are sometimes three or four hundred together in one place, forming a town which might properly enough be called a little Venice'. He continued in similar anthropomorphic fashion when describing the accuracy with which beavers felled and cut wood: 'For these architects foresee everything'.[6] This representation of the beaver as an architect was merely a European rationalisation of the same admiration for the animal's ingenuity that pervaded many indigenous peoples' creation myths. Traditionally, for many, the beaver represents industry, creativity and persistence. Its ability to shape the environment, to territorialise it, for example, is celebrated in the Haida myth of the Beaver, the Salmon and the Raven. In the legend the raven steals salmon from the beaver people (beavers are often portrayed as once being human) by rolling up the lakes and rivers like a carpet and then flying off with them. The raven's burden is heavy and so it has to rest frequently in the trees. This prompts the beaver people to transform themselves back into beavers and gnaw down the trees in which the raven perches. Each time they do so, elements of water and salmon fall down to earth forming the great lakes and rivers of the West Coast.

The ancient processes of animal topographical structuring, both mythical and real, are continued with the advent of the fur trade, which not only physically altered the terrain, but also often renamed it as a fundamental part of the processes of colonisation. It is estimated that there are some 79 beaver lakes in Canada and 155 in America, and that every Canadian province and every American state (except Hawaii) has places named after the animal, which in turn often supplanted original indigenous place names honouring the beaver.[7] Finally, the original space of the colonising force itself becomes territorialised and the fur trade symbolised by the beaver still imprints the built environments of London and New York, as well as modern-day Canada.

Astor Place subway station in New York, completed in 1904, is one of the original 28 stations in the transport system. It is decorated with terracotta plaques depicting beavers, produced by the Grueby Faience Company, thus acknowledging the fortune Astor made from the fur trade (fig. 2-9). While the famous Astor House hotel, now demolished, did not include beavers in its interior decoration, one of its most illustrious guests, Davy Crockett, is supposed to have declared on seeing the hotel's opulence, 'Lord help the poor beavers and bears!' Beaver Street in the financial district of New York is one of Manhattan's oldest thoroughfares, named in the 1660s to commemorate the trade in furs between Dutch settlers and the newly established British inhabitants of New Amsterdam, as New York was then known. Even the seal of New York City is emblazoned with two beavers, within a shield at its centre and flanked by a sailor and a Native American.

If New York's principal evidence of the fur trade's territorialisation is subterranean, in London a similar process is most evident when one looks skywards. All that remains of Hudson's Bay House in Bishopsgate is a weather vane in the shape of a golden beaver, which surmounts the modern development that replaced the original building, while at 105–109 Oxford Street, the site of the former Henry Heath Hat Factory, carved beavers decorate the pediment that crowns this red brick building. Beaver House, the headquarters and fur auction rooms of the Hudson's Bay Company in London, exists in name only now

2-8 'Beaver', from the Quadrupeds series of cigarette cards produced to promote Allen & Ginter cigarettes, 1890. United States. The Metropolitan Museum of Art, New York. The Jefferson R. Burdick Collection, Gift of Jefferson R. Burdick

2-9 Wall plaque of a beaver at Astor Place subway station, New York. Produced by Heins & LaFarge; faience, 1904. Courtesy of the author

2-10 'The Threepenny Beaver' stamp. The first Canadian postage stamp designed by Sir Sandford Fleming and issued in April 1851. Granger/Shutterstock

but is close to the original Skinners' Hall and the Church of St James Garlickhythe in the City of London, respectively the guild headquarters and spiritual home to the Worshipful Company of Skinners since the seventeenth century.

Modern Canada, of course, is thoroughly territorialised by the beaver (fig. 2-10). Perhaps the most widely disseminated evidence of this is the Canadian five cent piece, which bears on the reverse an image of a beaver on a rock, while the Threepenny Beaver is generally considered to be the first Canadian postage stamp. Designed by Sir Sandford Fleming, Scottish Canadian engineer and inventor of standard worldwide time, it was the first stamp to picture an animal rather than a monarch.

Territorialisation also informs the construction of the space of fur encountered in Jules Verne's 1873 novel *Le Pays des fourrures*, or *The Fur Country* (fig. 2-11). The novel follows the exploits of a group of Hudson's Bay employees, astronomers and lady adventurers as they seek to establish a trading fort some 70 degrees north of the Arctic Circle, but in typical Vernian fashion the expedition party ends up detached from the mainland, floating on an iceberg to unknown lands and encountering avalanches, hostile and friendly natives, earthquakes, ferocious animals and solar eclipses. Permeating the book is a remarkable geographical animism, constantly reminding the reader of the relationship between the fur trade and its, quite literal, territorialisation of the environment. The shape of Great Bear Lake, for example, is described by Verne not as a living animal but as a commodity: 'Two long promontories almost bisect it, giving it a very irregular shape. The northern half is like a flattened triangle, and the whole lake resembles a large animal's hide stretched out'.[8]

To regard animals as commodities was, of course, completely antithetical to indigenous peoples' relationship to the animals they subsisted with. Traditional methods of trapping were gradually replaced by technologically advanced and more effective means, resulting in the rapid decimation of many fur-bearing animal populations. The indiscriminate pelagic seal hunting at the end of the nineteenth century that replaced traditional Inuit

2-11 Jules Verne, *The Fur Country*, 1874. Published by Samson Low, Marston, Low and Searle, London (4th edn). Heritage Auctions, HA.com

methods was just one example of the fur trade's accelerating demands, which brought about the near extinction of a species (see 'The Force of Fur', p. 141). The beaver did not escape this process, and the introduction of the steel trap, which was less time-consuming and more productive in terms of the number of animals caught, replaced traditional hunting methods (fig. 2-12). Instead of the ancient method of catching beavers using nets made from knotted caribou cords, or wooden traps sunk into the river bed, foreign trappers discovered as early as 1728 that the combination of a steel trap baited with *castoreum*, the pungent liquid produced by the beaver from its castor glands to mark its territory, increased the yield dramatically. These modern industrial methods of capture violated the traditional codes of behaviour between hunters and their prey, which had been observed for centuries and which regulated the numbers of animals that could be killed.

The uncomfortable relationship between survival and commerce is re-presented for a contemporary audience by Anishinaabekwe artist Rebecca Belmore, whose video performance, *Twelve Angry Crinolines*, marked the Duke and Duchess of York's official visit to Thunder Bay in 1987 (fig. 2-13; see also fig. 2-1). The royal couple toured a reconstructed fur-trading fort and rode in a birch-bark canoe, 'replaying colonial history' as Belmore has suggested. Belmore's performance included a remarkable construction, a dress that she wore to greet officials, which was part pastiche nineteenth-century crinoline, part beaver dam. Entitled *Rising to the Occasion*, it included a headdress of erect 'Pocahontas' braids, a bodice of fringed and beaded buckskin, and breastplates fashioned from English porcelain plates. The beaver dam/bustle was fashioned from twigs in which were trapped clichéd cultural objects, such as royal souvenir mugs and cutlery. Belmore's work follows Deleuze and Guatarri's advice: 'How very important it is, when chaos threatens, to draw an inflatable, portable territory. If need be, I'll put my territory on my own body, I'll territorialize my body' because 'a territory has two notable effects: *a reorganization of functions and a regrouping of forces.*'[9]

Belmore's work is also suggestive of the notion of exchange, not only the exchanging of identities and subject positions but also the unfair literal exchange represented by the legal tender introduced for the fur trade. In order to standardise trade and make it more economically advantageous, the Hudson's Bay Company introduced the Made Beaver. This was the equivalent of one adult, full-size beaver pelt, which had been worn for at least a year and from which most of the long guard hairs had been shed, rendering it the most useful form for hat-making. Other skins were priced relative to the value of a Made Beaver; so, for example, two otter skins might be the equivalent of one beaver. The beaver pelts could be exchanged for a variety of European trade goods. In 1733, at Fort Albany, amongst the items one beaver pelt could buy were three-quarters of a pound (some 340 grams) of coloured glass beads, four spoons, a gallon (4.5 litres) of brandy, one handkerchief and two looking-glasses, while a gun cost between ten and twelve pelts.[10] Some 100 years later, in about 1860, trading tokens also known as Made Beavers were introduced in the form of a small coin, roughly the same size as today's American quarter. Bearing the arms of the Hudson's

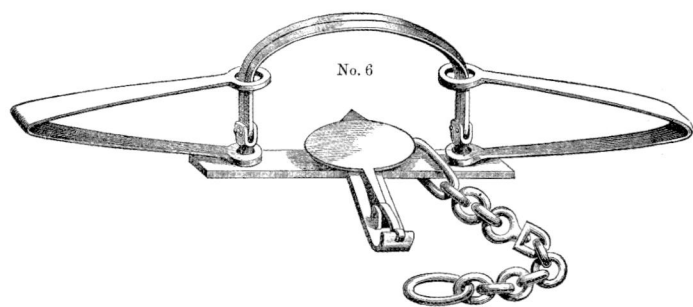

2-12 ABOVE Animal trap used by fur traders, 19th century. United States; engraving. Granger/Shutterstock

2-13 OPPOSITE Rebecca Belmore (b. 1960), *Rising to the Occasion* (detail), 1987–91. Mixed media. This detail shows British royal family commemorative souvenirs caught in the 'beaver dam bustle'. Art Gallery of Ontario. Gift from the Junior Volunteer Committee, 1995

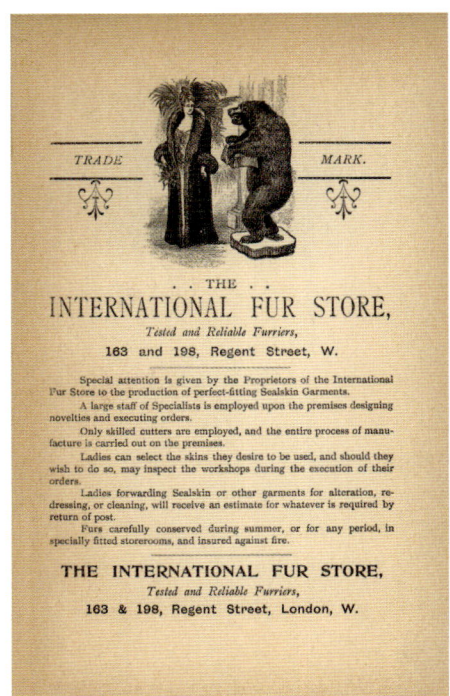

2-14 a&b Advertisements for the International Fur Store, Regent Street, London, 1895. Courtesy of the author

Bay Company, it became the unit of currency for everything bought and sold at trading posts, the last of these tokens being produced for the St Lawrence-Labrador region in the 1920s.

From the very first page of Jules Verne's *The Fur Country*, the reader is made aware of the value of fur as a unit of currency, or 'soft gold' as fur was described by early traders, so lucrative was this commodity. It led Gustave Flaubert, in the same decade as Verne was writing his novel, to define fur in his *Dictionary of Received Ideas* as the 'sign of wealth.'[11] Verne's novel opens with a party at Fort Reliance, a Hudson's Bay trading post, the opening page describing the space where the party takes place:

> *The interior wall, with its narrow single door leading to the adjoining room, was ornately decorated with as magnificent a display of furs as could be seen in the exclusive shops of Regent Street or Nevsky Prospect. It was as if every species of wild animal known to the Arctic – wolf, grizzly bear, polar bear, otter, wolverine, mink, beaver, muskrat, silver fox, ermine – had contributed its finest pelts. Above, in letters artistically cut from a piece of coloured cardboard, hung the motto of the famous Hudson's bay company: PRO PELLE CUTEM*[12]

The immediate collapsing of geographic space between Fort Reliance 'within five degrees of the Arctic Circle' and the shops of London and St Petersburg, in tandem with manufacture and the space between raw material and finished garment, is indicative of the nineteenth century's specific marketing of fur (figs 2-14 a&b).[13] This took place in a series of idealised 'milieus', to use Deleuze and Guattari's term, reimagined as the space in which fashionable and technical mastery overcomes the seductive yet terrifying forces of the natural world, with its inherent ferocity, primitivism and carnality. This tension is present in the retailing of fur, whether seen within the context of nineteenth-century commerce, twentieth-century advertising or contemporary cinema.

Verne's reference to the exclusive shops of Regent Street and Nevsky Prospect would have been inspired by the famous European furriers and fur showrooms, which were at the peak of their success at the time he was writing *The Fur Country*. Revillon Frères, the Parisian furriers founded in 1723 and associated with the advertising maxim 'Elegance needs the most precious fabrics and furs', had branches in London, Montreal and New York by the time of Verne's novel (figs 2-15, 2-16). Direct access to Russian furs was enabled by an agency in Moscow and trading posts in Siberia, Mongolia and Turkestan. The company also operated a network of trading posts in northern Canada in direct competition with the Hudson's Bay Company, and in 1922, in a remarkably contemporary awareness of media promotion, it financed the film *Nanook of the North*.

The interiors of fur showrooms, such as those of Revillon, were designed to impress. A photograph of Laliberte's Fur Parlor in Quebec, advertised as the 'Finest in the World', presents a claustrophobic chaos of fur garments, taxidermied animals in various contorted poses supporting mirrors and carrying baskets, pelts suspended from bars, tiger skin rugs and indigenous craft artefacts (fig. 2-17).

Lost amongst this furry terrain, two assistants or possibly customers merge into the environment in their fur-trimmed outfits. Although Laliberte is perhaps an extreme example of nineteenth- and early twentieth-century fur retail spaces, it was customary for stuffed animals to form part of the decorative schemes of these interiors. This remarkably direct reminder to prospective customers of the origin of the garments for sale reflects the contemporary attitude to fur: the presence of taxidermied specimens stood as a testament not only to the skill required to render animals into fashion items but also the authenticity and quality of the skins used (fig. 2-18). The proximity to 'lifelike' animals was also reflective of the period's fascination with fur as part of a larger process of transformative consumerism, in which garments and accessories made from animals allowed the wearer to assume some of the characteristics of the animal, a concept prevalent in art and literature of the period. It is a concept that remains an effective marketing device for fur, witness the success of the promotional film *A Therapy*, directed by Roman Polanski for Prada in 2012. In the film, widely regarded as one of the

2-15 Advertising card for Revillon Frères, Rue de Rivoli, Paris, 1912. Kharbine–Tapabor/Shutterstock

2-16 Advertisement for Revillon, 1940. Designed by Paul Colin. Kharbine–Tapabor/Shutterstock

2-17 *Laliberte's Fur Parlor – Finest in the World, Quebec, Canada* Keystone View Co., c. 1900. United States; gelatin silver print. Digital image courtesy of the Getty's Open Content Program. Gift of Weston J. and Mary M. Naef

first important narrative 'fashionfilms', Ben Kingsley plays an analyst distracted by the fur coat of his client (Helena Bonham Carter). While she continues 'her talking cure', Kingsley rises from his chair, caresses her coat lovingly and eventually puts it on, admiring himself in the mirror while adopting a number of cat-like poses and indulging in an auto-erotic touching and rubbing of the fur.[14] Space is a fluid, constantly changing construct and its ability to transform itself – not just in geographical and physical terms, as we have seen with respect to the territorialising effects of the North American fur trade, but also socially, culturally and economically – is central to an understanding of these new retail spaces of the raw and the cooked, the wild and the tamed, the space of fashionable fur.

The display of fur also constructed complex narratives of colonialism, where the slaughter of animals, the commercial quest for profitable skins and their subsequent processing into garments is comparable to the invasion, subjugation and making 'intelligible' of the foreign, the 'other' and the 'primitive'. In the nineteenth century this

2-18 *A London Furrier*, 19th century. France; watercolour. The Metropolitan Museum of Art, New York. The Elisha Whittelsey Collection, The Elisha Whittelsey Fund, 1955

54 FUR: A SENSITIVE HISTORY

2-19 Fur display, Great Exhibition, London, 1851. From *Dickinsons Comprehensive Pictures of the Great Exhibition of 1851*. Published by Dickinson Brothers; lithograph, 1854. © Victoria and Albert Museum, London

political production of knowledge was made possible by the new exhibitionary spaces of the museum, department store and what would become known as the World Fair (fig. 2-19). In these spaces art, artefacts and indeed people from other cultures were brought under a western rationalising gaze and placed in hierarchical narratives of colonial dominance (fig. 2-21). In the north-west transept of the Crystal Palace, erected for the Great Exhibition of 1851, J.A. Nicholay & Sons, the Court Furriers with establishments in London's Oxford Street, mounted a display of their products (fig. 2-20). It establishes an economic and imperialist taxonomy, with the most valued and prized furs at the apex of a pyramidal edifice. Ermine, in the form of what looks like the robes of a peer of the realm, resides at the pinnacle, followed by sable and sealskin capes and jackets. Next come fur-trimmed garments, concluding with tippets and accessories at the base, a decreasing scale of economic and aesthetic value. Similarly, the stuffed animals 'guarding' the display represent the extent of imperial dominion, with lions and gazelles representing Africa, and a tiger skin denoting India, surmounted by a European deer's head and smaller North American fur-bearing animals scattered about the floor. Encounters of a decidedly proto-surrealist nature punctuate the display, such as the fox apparently curled up asleep on a chair and a

2-20 J.A. Nicholay & Sons display, Great Exhibition, London, 1851. Salted paper print. Digital image courtesy of the Getty's Open Content Program

2-21 A group portrait from the Russian Booth at the Albany Army Relief Bazaar, 1864. Churchill & Denison. Albumen silver print. The bazaar was held to raise money for sick and wounded Union soldiers. Digital image courtesy of the Getty's Open Content Program

squirrel contemplating the skull of what looks like a ram. To the Great Exhibition's British visitors the visual semiotics of the display would have been clear: not only was it presented by Nicholay & Sons, the pre-eminent and royally endorsed furrier, but also it represented the might of the British Empire and the maintenance of that Empire's social and economic hierarchy, affirmed by the use of fur.

Looking at displays such as this we are reminded of the highly influential ideas of philosopher and sociologist Henri Lefebvre concerning different models of space, or 'spatialisation' as it has been termed. The hallucinatory spaces of fur are contradictory, conflicted and ultimately political, the product of a society that is structured around notions of power. Such power expresses itself firstly through the subjugation of the animal kingdom, and secondly through the internal economic divisions between those who manufacture garments made of fur and those who wear them and receive their attendant historic symbolic potency, both of which necessitate a direct encounter with the physical spaces of fur. These forms of directly experienced or perceived space are then incorporated into a third space, that of the imaginary, an animate and transformative space whose promise we can trace via the mediated imagery of fur.[15]

During the late 1930s and early 1940s the surrealist artist Dorothea Tanning worked as a freelance illustrator for a number of clients including Macy's, the prominent New York department store. Macy's and many similar stores, such as Bergdorf Goodman, Saks and the now defunct Henri Bendel, all had dedicated fur departments or salons, often run by specialist fur companies, such as Revillon at Saks (a store today owned by the Hudson's Bay Company). For Macy's newly opened Fur Muff and Hat Bar on the third floor ('where you will find every fur you can think of, and some you haven't yet learned the names of!') Tanning produced a remarkable advertisement that appeared in the *New York Times* in September 1940.[16] Under the title of *Tales of the American Woods*, Tanning's drawing depicts a forest glade in which a variety of fur hats and muffs are suspended from the branches of trees, from within which emerges the head of a dryad wearing an ocelot toque priced at $5.98. Accompanied by a suitably patriotic verse that suggests there are 'No woods so deep, so wild, so mysteriously beautiful as our own American forests', the advertisement sends a clear message to consumers that in wartime it is their duty to purchase American furs rather than imported ones. A bewildering variety of styles is on offer in this forest, with its 'primitive fascination for American women', including a 'silver fox shako', 'a sable-dyed muskrat baby bonnet' and 'a blended mink halo', which is perched anthropomorphically on a branch, the 'neck' of which is tied with a net fichu. The advertisement succeeds in creating a surreal space of fur, at once economic, chauvinistic, transformative and carnal, in which 'Every hat, except one, is under $10.00!'

If Tanning's imagining of the space of fur is typical of mid-twentieth-century America's effective merging of the worlds of art, fashion and commerce, then the famous 'Blackglama' campaign, launched in 1968, reflects the fur industry's search for new ways in which to promote their product in a climate of opposition, and represents an astute understanding of what today is termed celebrity culture and its pivotal role in the promotion of consumer goods, especially luxury fashion (fig. 2-22). In 1968 the Great Lakes Mink Association (GLMA), a group of some 400 farmers producing exclusively black mink, was seeking a way to 'remodel public opinion' at a time of counter-cultural opposition to fur, which was seen by a younger generation as economically and ecologically offensive.[17] The GLMA approached the advertising agency of Jane Trahey, who conceived the campaign together with Peter Rogers. As dark furs are especially hard to photograph, it was decided to showcase the 'lustre' of the famous people who wore mink. 'Legends' rather than mere 'stars' or 'celebrities', as Rogers describes them, who needed no introduction, were selected, hence their names are absent. In fact the only copy that appears is the tag line 'What becomes a Legend most?', the response being 'Blackglama'.[18] The insertion of the extra 'a' into the acronym GLMA provided the necessary 'Glama'. While celebrity endorsement was certainly not new and had functioned symbiotically since the dawn of Hollywood, what distinguished the Blackglama campaign was the simple visual synthesis of fur and fame, an association that echoes the historic period of sumptuary legislation and the consolidation of fur with status. So successful was the campaign that the GLMA's fortunes were reversed and Blackglama became a name asked for by customers, rather than a branded designer product, a significant achievement for the producers of a raw material. The personalities, who were photographed by Richard Avedon and Bill King, were given a mink coat as a fee, and in 1970 included soon-to-be animal rights activist and staunch anti-fur campaigner Brigitte Bardot. The campaign continues today but rather than using 'legends', it is promoting younger 'faces', models wearing not one but a variety of mink garments, and is largely indistinguishable from the majority of mainstream fashion editorials.

A mere three years separates the launch of the aspirational Blackglama campaign and the revolutionary fashion editorials featured in *Nova*

2-22 Diana Ross in mink for Blackglama, 1973. Designed by Bill King (1939–1987). Poster, 70.3 x 55.2 cm. The Advertising Archives Ltd

magazine, a decidedly more problematic representation of fashionable fur created by Caroline Baker, 'the original stylist' as Iain R. Webb has described her.[19] *Nova*, published between 1965 and 1975, was billed as 'a new kind of magazine for the new kind of woman'. A radical, intellectually stimulating and visually startling magazine, it tackled social issues such as contraception, race and homosexuality alongside cutting-edge fashion featuring the work of photographers such as Helmut Newton and Terence Donovan in advertisement-free editorials. Baker's fashion features offered a groundbreaking alternative to the relatively staid, designer-led fashion journalism of the time and showed models in unconventional environments and poses, dressed in a radical combination of high street and high fashion, secondhand clothes and do-it-yourself accessorising. The feature 'Every Hobo Should Have One' appeared in the November 1971 issue and immediately angered the fur trade. Saul Leiter photographed the model wearing the shaggy, long-haired furs fashionable at the time, firstly sleeping rough on a park bench, then slumped in a rubbish-strewn street and finally pushing an old pram filled with her possessions, accompanied by her dog tied to the handle by a piece of string. As fashion writer Alice Beard points out, 'Baker removed fur coats from their context of glamour, wealth and couture and used them as props to dress her model as a tramp ... The fur coat in each shot performs the essential task of keeping the woman warm; whether it is wrapped around her loosely or spread out over her body like a blanket as she sleeps on the grass'.[20] The copy accompanying the photographs informs the reader that 'above all furs must be worn as casually as clothes are nowadays – looking as if no thought had gone into that nonchalant, put-together style that takes such agonising hours to work out.'[21] With acute awareness of the period's burgeoning anti-fur feeling, a proviso assured readers that the featured coats were 'made from animals not threatened by extinction and certified by the British Fur Trade Association'.[22] Baker incurred the displeasure of the fur industry again in the feature 'We're Just Good Fur-Reinds' of January 1974, this time photographed by Hans Feurer at the Grosvenor Hotel, London. A mixture of real and fake fur coats were used to dress the models, who were posing as prostitutes, caught by the paparazzi *in flagrante* with a variety of visiting foreign dignitaries, all of whom ended up in police custody. Fur in these magazine pages is portrayed as ignominious, associated with corruption, and at best of use only thermally when down and out, a far cry from the aspirational glamour promoted by the fur industry at the time.

The awareness of the growing antipathy to the fur trade that Baker anticipated, and which found its logical, yet still fashionable, position within the alternative pages of *Nova*, was also understood, and indeed capitalised upon, by possibly the most innovative and radical furrier of the latter half of the twentieth century – Jacques Kaplan. A reluctant furrier, Kaplan came from a fur dynasty, the business having been founded in 1889 in Paris by his grandfather, a Russian émigré. Fleeing the Nazi occupation, Jacques's father Georges moved the business to New York in 1942. Jacques meanwhile had joined the French Resistance and was awarded the Croix de Guerre. He then studied at the Sorbonne with the intention of teaching philosophy, but family responsibilities saw him move to New York in the 1950s to help his father run the company.

Finding the fur business staid but lucrative, Kaplan started to experiment, working with more unusual skins and discovering new ways to treat fur, as reported in a *Life* magazine article of 13 December 1968. 'For him, skins are just the beginning – blank canvases to be painted, printed, cut up and reassembled on the principle that anything cloth can do fur can do wittier.'[23] The reference to painting is intentional as Kaplan had developed a passion for contemporary art, after walking into a gallery in the late 1950s, seeing a work of art he admired and acquiring it in exchange for a fur coat. This unconventional approach proved so popular with artists and dealers that he swiftly gained an entrée into the New York art world and amassed a sizeable collection, even commissioning new works, which often incorporated, or were inspired by, furs. Perhaps the most famous of these were the cowhide coats, painted by leading artists such as Frank Stella, Richard Anuszkiewicz and Marisol (see 'Manimal', p. 15). He even created his own artworks, 'exploded' pieces consisting of wall-mounted, stretched and embellished skins and kinetic assemblages, one of which incorporated rotating discs of monkey fur.

While his career as an artist, collector and dealer progressed, so too did the Kaplan fur business, its shop now located on 5th Avenue, close to Bergdorf Goodman. Kaplan introduced a number of innovative lines that injected new life into traditional furriering,

including less expensive garments in cheaper furs such as weasel, rabbit and squirrel but dyed and stencilled in vibrant colours that appealed to a younger, less conservative clientele (figs 2-23, 2-24). This led to him being credited as the inventor of 'fun fur', not to be confused with the fake version (see 'The F Word', p. 151). As he declared, 'We have taken the trauma out of buying fur. The wilder they are, the faster they sell.'[24] He also introduced unusual furs, such as wildebeest, zorino (skunk) and gayal (Indian ox), manufactured fur furniture (see 'Furnishing', p. 182) and interior decorations, and staged fur fashion shows in art galleries. Perhaps his most far-sighted business decision came in the late 1960s when, becoming aware of the plight of endangered species, he announced he would no longer use furs such as cheetah and leopard, much to the consternation of rival furriers, which earned him the praise of the World Wildlife Fund.

2-23 'Jacques Kaplan's Tour de Furs', *Life* magazine, 13 December 1968. Courtesy of the author

The story that he made a skirt out of domestic cat skins as an alternative to rarer species was commented on by Tom Wolfe in his 1970 article 'Radical Chic': 'Freddy Plimpton had Jacques Kaplan, the number one Society furrier, make her a skirt of alley cat pelts … He must have seen Radical Chic coming a mile away. Early in the game he himself, a furrier, started pitching in for the embattled ocelots, margays, fitch and company like there was no tomorrow.'[25] This turned out to be a publicity stunt. Facing protests from domestic cat lovers the skirt was revealed to have been made from the skins of the genet, a spotted cat-like animal found in North Africa and parts of Europe and much used in the medieval fur trade (see 'Wearer's Rights', p. 63).

On sofa of nutria and giraffe is a stenciled calfskin pantsuit ($850). Large painting is one of Larry Rivers' major works, "The Dutch Masters." At left are two de Koonings.

Model wearing a sheared-lamb coat-dress ($1,250), trimmed with unsheared lamb, sprawls on a calf rug designed and painted by Kaplan's friend Richard Anuszkiewicz.

Kaplan made this long jumper dress with a deep slit ($550) out of zorino, a South American skunk which he likes because it resembles sable but is much cheaper. The paintings are by Larry Rivers (left) and French artist Martial Raysse, while the bedspread of Mongolian lamb is again Kaplan's work.

His collections include calf, skunk and Rivers

Entering the family business as a youth some 20 years ago, Jacques Kaplan was a reluctant furrier. When he discovered that he could combine pelts with his passion for modern art, however, he opened up a new direction not only for himself but for fur design in general. Often prompted by his artist friends' experiments, his design audacities sold—and so helped launch an era in which exuberance counted more than awe. Since that time Jacques Kaplan has acquired plenty of art, mostly by swapping furs, and a reputation for the unexpected in design. For him, skins are just the beginning—blank canvases to be painted, printed, cut up and reassembled on the principle that anything cloth can do fur can do wittier. These selections from his current collection, priced from $450 to $2,200, include everything from pantsuits to jumpers and testify to his belief in *lèse majesté* and more merriment.

CONTINUED

Kaplan sold his fur business in 1969 and the showroom closed in 1972, allowing him to pursue his love of art and open his own gallery in Connecticut in 1984.

Kaplan's many innovations, however, did not include the earlier twentieth century's commercial extension of fur into the olfactory space; a unique example of furry synaesthesia that incorporated the sense of smell along with touch and sight into the marketing of fur. In 1928 the Parisian furriers Weil, established in 1892, launched what they termed *parfum des fourrures*, a series of perfumes specifically designed to harmonise with fur and cover up its sometimes musty smell. Advertised as 'strictly an odour for furs', the four perfumes – *Zibeline* (Sable), *Ermine, Chinchilla Royal* and *Une Fleur de Fourrure* (A Flower for Furs) – were sold in bottles made by Baccarat and became immediately successful, so successful in fact that when Weil closed their fur business during the Second World War and relocated to New York, perfumery eventually replaced furriering. Drawing on their knowledge of furs, *Ermine*, for example, was supposed to evoke tenderness and virginity (see 'Now You See Me, Now You Don't', p. 89), while *Zibeline* recalled in its 'woody' notes the steppes and oak forests of Russia, the habitat of the sable.[26]

Weil was not the only furrier to produce perfume. The illustrious Revillon Frères also introduced a line of perfumes in 1934. The relationship between animal parts and fragrance is, of course, well known with the glandular secretions of the musk deer and civet cat, and the previously mentioned *castoreum* obtained from the beaver, all highly prized and used to provide base notes. Traditionally castoreum would add a

2-24 'Jacques Kaplan's Tour de Furs', *Life* magazine, 13 December 1968. Courtesy of the author 'leather' note. While considerably more downmarket than either Weil or Revillon, Fabergé Cosmetics, remembered now primarily for the still popular mass-market men's fragrance *Brut*, launched *Tigress* in 1938. Originally promoted as 'The perfect perfume for furs', when repackaged in the 1970s in a bottle with a fake tiger skin top, its marketing shifted to the perfume's transformative power, turning women who wore it, according to its marketing campaign, into 'Wild, willful, uninhibited' tigresses.

The hunting, capture and killing of animals for their fur, fundamental to the history of the fur trade, has created its own cinematic space. Such representational spaces, Lefebvre suggests, 'tend towards more or less coherent systems of non-verbal symbols and signs'.[27] Typically characterised by limitless terrains of wealth, power and sensuality, fur's cinematic landscape is sublime, composed of horizonless snowy vistas, vast mountain ranges and surging, tumultuous waterways, waiting to be explored and traversed; it is peopled not only with trappers but also guides, frontiersmen and expedition leaders, all in search of elsewhere. The fur trade itself is transitional, comprised of camps and trading posts or, more accurately, entrepôts where goods are exchanged at the crossroads between origin and destination. These transitional spaces use fur as a stimulus, its seductive surface demarcating a world of possibility and desire similar to that Lucy experienced when pushing through the fur coats on her way to Narnia in C.S. Lewis's cherished novel, *The Lion, the Witch, and the Wardrobe* (1950). Whilst any lengthy discussion of individual cinematic productions is not possible in this volume, in general what is apparent is that the cinematic characterisation of fur is infinitely adaptable and emblematic of wider social and political concerns and interests.

Robert F. Flaherty's silent 1922 docu-drama, *Nanook of the North*, was financed by Revillon Frères, and met with immediate box office and critical success (fig. 2-25).[28] Following the story of an Inuit man, his wife and family, and their means of survival in the Canadian Arctic by hunting walrus, visiting a trading post and building an igloo, *Nanook*, as with all films, documentary or otherwise, is a construct. It is a construct similar to that found in the exhibitionary spaces of the nineteenth century mentioned previously, where the customs, and indeed peoples, of other cultures were displayed in living tableaux as part of a process of western 'preservation' (see fig. 2-21). This necessitated the safeguarding of the 'other' as exotic, 'primitive', untouched by technological progress and in danger of extinction. In reality, by the time the film was made Nanook (real name Allakariallak) would have hunted with guns rather than the harpoons Flaherty insisted on for the film, and far from being technologically ignorant, Inuit people formed Flaherty's film crew, some acting as camera operators. As writer and director Fatimah Tobing Rony notes, 'Because fur prices were at their height in the 1920s, the Inuit in Quebec were introduced to a cash economy, and the Inuit portrayed in Nanook thus were using guns, knew about gramophones, wore Western clothing'.[29]

Hudson's Bay, filmed in 1941, while not directly financed by a fur company received historical advice and considerable support from the Hudson's Bay Company, which promoted the film through its Canadian retail outlets. These were increasing in number with the aim of taking back control of the fur trade from the threat of Revillon, which, at the time of the film's release, was growing.[30] A routine Hollywood biopic, starring Paul Muni as Radisson and Laird Cregar as Groseilliers (nicknamed 'Gooseberry' in the film), while presenting an idealised account of the formation of the Hudson's Bay Company, it is also a thinly disguised wartime call to arms for a unified Canada. As expressed by Chantal Nadeau, in her authoritative study of this and other 'snow flicks', as she terms Canadian-set Hollywood productions, 'As much as *Nanook* was all about the exotic Other, *Hudson's Bay* was about the contrasting points of the internal other: the French and the British becoming one unified couple, fighting for progress, and the preservation and triumph of the British/colonial presence in the "peace" of the new country.'³¹ With thick accents and fur costumes to match, designed by Travis Banton, we see the French trappers and British adventurers bond in an isolated male space composed of pelts, canoes and snowy peaks. Here, 'the obviously male homosocial quality of the trade is sealed in the corporate skin/fabric', a corporation whose initials 'HBC', Nadeau records, was known by its employees to also stand for 'horny boys club'.³²

The homosocial landscape of fur trapping is submerged in the waterlogged and snowbound 1966 Canadian/British co-production *The Trap*. Filmed in British Columbia, it starred Oliver Reed as Jean la Bête (or John the Beast), adopting another thick French accent (a unifying trope across many of these 'snow flicks'), and the silent Rita Tushingham as Eve, the mute wife he purchases to relieve his solitary wilderness existence (fig. 2-26).³³ Here nation building and homoerotic potential gives way to feminism and ecology, reflecting the growth of these concerns in the 1960s. From the opening scenes we see the treatment of women equated to animals, with the disembarkation of the 'jailbirds' – prior to meeting their prospective trader husbands, who have bought their freedom from captivity in England – contrasted with piles of skins being unloaded on the dock. The story of Jean la Bête's conquest of the silent Eve (initially tethered to him as an indigenous trapper to his prey) is played out against her objections to the cruelty of trapping. Jean in turn becomes the prey, caught in his own trap, and in a role reversal Eve amputates his leg, symbolically emasculating him, and learns to trap and fend for herself while Jean is left crippled and domesticated.

This brief expedition across the frontiers of cinematic 'Furland' concludes with the Oscar-winning *The Revenant* (fig. 2-27) and the Netflix period drama *Frontier*, which so far has run to three series.³⁴ Although set in different locales and periods, *The Revenant* in the Upper Missouri River area in the 1820s and *Frontier* around Hudson's Bay in the late 1700s, their success suggests that in a pervasive climate of protest with dwindling numbers wearing fur, the history of its trade is sufficiently remote and indeed unknown, making it ripe for mainstream reinvention. In *The Revenant* the trade is seen as the catalyst for prolonged bloody violence, the violence that comes with the promise of wealth. At the beginning of the film we see trappers encamped, preparing skins in gory detail in readiness to be transported down river, when they are attacked by the Arikara People.

2-25 *Nanook of the North*, dir. Robert J. Flaherty, 1922. Poster. Granger/Shutterstock

2-26 *The Trap*, dir. Sidney Hayers, 1966. Film still. ITV/Shutterstock

2-27 *The Revenant*, dir. Alexander González Iñárritu, 2015. Film still. 20th Century Fox/Regency Enterprises/Kobal/Shutterstock

During this graphic encounter, wise frontiersman Hugh Glass (Leonardo DiCaprio) orders them to leave the furs and escape, whilst the treacherous and avaricious trapper Fitzgerald (Tom Hardy) counters this instruction with 'Grab some pelts! C'mon, grab some pelts!'[35] The fur trade is understood as a force that transforms its participants morally, physically and emotionally, setting the scene for the traditional revenger's tragedy that unfolds throughout the film. In *Frontier* justice is also sought, but by indigenous people personified by the half-Irish, half-Cree hero, Declan Harp (Jason Momoa). The story pivots around Harp's attempts to halt colonial exploitation by forming the Black Wolf Company, an indigenous rival to the Hudson's Bay Company. It is possible that the success of both productions is partly due to the *Game of Thrones* effect, where warring fur-clad tribes, clashing against dramatic scenery in this American fantasy TV series, have made audiences 'fur trade-ready', especially as *Frontier* lead Momoa previously starred as the prominent *Game of Thrones* character Khal Drogo.

The space of the fur trade has been marked by the past, by its translation into art and myth, its topographies a response to major social and political shifts. It has colonised and subjugated, deconstructed and fabricated, consumed and ejected, but as Lefebvre affirms, 'Nothing disappears completely, however; nor can what subsists be defined solely in terms of traces, memories or relics. In space, what came earlier continues to underpin what follows.'[36]

WEARER'S RIGHTS

The right to wear fur, by whom and of what sort, has been a significant consideration throughout the early history of western fashionable dress (fig. 2-28). The various proscriptions against fur, whether legally instituted or popularly received, provide an explanation of fur as an effective signifier of status and, more equivocally, can be a testament to the morality of its wearers. Owing to its beauty, practicality and expense, fur has always been highly prized and much sought after, and understandably has been the object of sumptuary legislation since the advent of this form of judicial sartorial intervention. Sumptuary laws, that is, legislation designed to restrict personal expenditure and excessive consumption, can be traced back to the ancient world. Greek and Roman edicts were primarily alimentary, and were concerned with limiting the amounts and sorts of food and wine consumed at feasts

as well as expenditure on ceremonial events, such as weddings and funerals. It is not until the Middle Ages that dress, and fur especially, becomes the primary object of sumptuary legislation, which was widespread throughout Europe from the twelfth century and continued well into the seventeenth and, in some countries, up to the end of the eighteenth century. While we know most about European legislation during this period, there are records of such laws being enacted further afield, such as the eleventh-century Chinese edict that permitted only nobles to wear black sable and ermine, while commoners had to content themselves with ordinary brown sable, sheep and moleskin.[37]

An indicator of the centrality of fur to this long succession of vestimentary legislation is the fact that the very first secular European sumptuary regulation (ecclesiastical edicts directed specifically at the clergy had been in operation for a considerable period before this) 'banned the use of sable furs over the value of 40 *soldi* to trim hems'.[38] As indicated in the *Breve della campagna*, Genoa's legal code, the law was decreed in 1157 and pre-dates the first English laws by some 200 years. This deceptively simple prohibition is an attempt to restrict personal financial expenditure but, more importantly, the visible and excessive display of such expenditure. Medieval European sumptuary legislation emerged from what were originally Christian moral precepts and concerns about the display of wealth and luxury, and its attendant vices. Even before the first European sumptuary legislation, the desire for fur was equated with the deadly sin of pride, which led the eleventh-century German chronicler Adam of Bremen to comment on the craze for marten (the same species as the better known sable and relative of the mink and ferret): 'We strive as hard to come into the possession of a marten skin as if it were everlasting salvation.'[39] The love of fine clothes and adornment was equated to immorality and therefore, in order to curb this growing tide of iniquity, it was felt necessary to legislate against it for the common good. From the outset such laws proved difficult to uphold and applied to certain sections of society only, for what was deemed inappropriate expenditure for some, was upheld for others. So whilst a commoner may have been prohibited from trimming his garment with certain furs, members of the nobility, clergy or judiciary wore those same furs as a mark of their status and office (fig. 2-29).

Sumptuary legislation follows much the same trajectory as shifting attitudes towards luxury itself, which of course it typically concerned itself with. Initially targeting excessive expenditure as immoral and sinful, that same expenditure became understood as wasteful, squandering resources on personal display that could have been more productively spent elsewhere. Finally, this standpoint developed into a form of economic protectionism, legislating against the consumption of imported 'foreign' and therefore nationally deleterious goods, including furs. As these shifts in emphasis imply, the numerous edicts concerning dress issued across Europe for over 500 years, with varying degrees of severity and effectiveness, were not simply about limiting consumption. The first English sumptuary legislation to regulate dress attempted just such a blanket limitation, using fur as its primary target. In 1337 it was decreed that only the royal family, prelates, earls, barons, knights and clerks earning at least £100 per annum could wear fur; for anyone else it was prohibited. Such a ban was obviously impractical at a time when everyone who could do so wore furs to protect themselves against the harsh northern climate. Then in 1363 a further statute was passed, which more clearly defined the types of fur that were permitted for each rank. Nobility, clergy and wealthy citizens were allowed to wear expensive imported furs such

2-28 After Hyacinthe Rigaud (1659–1743), *Louis XV as a Child*, c.1716–24. Oil on canvas, 195.6 x 141 cm. The 5-year-old Louis XV is shown wearing a blue velvet mantle strewn with gold fleur-de-lis and lined with ermine. The use of ermine was an integral part of the coronation robes worn by French monarchs. The Metropolitan Museum of Art, New York. Purchase, Mary Wetmore Shively Bequest, in memory of her husband, Henry L. Shively, M.D., 1960 as ermine, lettice (the snow weasel), Baltic squirrel and budge (imported lamb skin), while the lower orders could wear only lamb, coney, cat or fox, that is, native English furs.[40]

This hierarchising of fur – and the desire to define and differentiate sections of society by the way it could dress, which became the prevailing characteristic of sumptuary legislation – had a number of contradictory effects. Initially, the ability to wear certain furs was a visible marker of rank and social status. This in turn made those furs even more desirable, until finally, by wearing certain furs (or cheaper, but effective imitations) it became possible to assume a superior rank or status. As Alan Hunt eloquently puts it in his history of sumptuary law, 'The result is that far from clarifying social differences, sumptuary law actually provokes increasing competition and imitation since it is "cheaper" (economically and politically) for all parties to compete over the symbols than over what those symbols represent.'[41] Sumptuary legislation concerning fur operated as a two-fold process of permission and prohibition, where certain members of society were allowed to wear furs and others were not. Generally speaking, those of an elevated social standing could wear rarer, imported and softer furs, while those of lowlier status had to wear coarser, native skins. As stated earlier, having clearly defined markers of status makes it much easier to assume, via dress and the display of such markers, an elevated social position, to 'pass' as it might be termed. So it can be argued that rather than maintaining a rigid social hierarchy, sumptuary legislation allowed for a certain degree of social mobility (fig. 2-30). This, of course, did not escape the attention of legislators, who became increasingly concerned that the expanding lower and mercantile classes, and their aspirational imitation of their superiors, threatened the social hierarchy. More and more complex attempts to assign certain furs to particular classes were instituted in England, for example, so that by the reign of Henry VIII and the passing of the Act for Reformation of Excess in Apparel of 1533, we learn that sable furs were reserved exclusively for the royal family; only dukes, earls and barons could wear lynx and black genet (the skins of the civet cat, both black and grey, were highly prized and more valuable than other cat skins); and only those of the rank of gentleman or above could wear an imported variety of fur not produced within the realm.[42] However, records show that even commonly found domestic furs were being imported, which would make it difficult to prove where a fur had originated from, and that even nobles – who were allowed to wear both common and rarer fur – often mixed the two together on the same garment. This practice is evidenced by the inventory of Henry VIII's wardrobe, taken in 1547, which included linings for a jacket consisting of 'squirrelles and sables', and linings and facings for two coats 'of white lambe & face of lizarns' (lynx).[43] Additionally, the fashion for certain colours of fur played a significant role in England, as historian and conservator Maria Hayward notes: 'In the early sixteenth century, dark and light furs were very popular instead of the bright red/brown furs favoured in the fifteenth and fourteenth centuries.'[44]

If sumptuary legislation attempted to simultaneously maintain a rigid social hierarchy and guard against the harmful economic impact of the importation of foreign goods, it also followed a less fiscal, more moral agenda, especially when exercising its power over women's dress. From its beginnings sumptuary law railed against what was considered the excessive displays of expenditure on female dress. Such displays were indicative of the sin of pride and more than likely would lead the wearer down the paths of lust and immorality. Naturally, much legislation concerned itself with the dress of prostitutes, attempting to distinguish members of that profession from virtuous women. This excerpt from a sixteenth-century proclamation concerning the dress of 'Common Women Within the City' [London] is typical: 'No such lewd woman shall be so daring as to be attired either by day or night in any kind of vesture trimmed with miniver [white squirrel], grey work [badger]... or any other manner of noble budge [imported lambs wool]'.[45] The regulations concerning prostitutes followed two broad approaches: one forbade

prostitutes from adopting the forms of dress that distinguished the virtuous woman, such as the 'noble' furs; the other, conversely, permitted prostitutes to wear finery in the hope that good, honourable women would be shamed into not wearing such luxurious fur, which was equated with sinfulness. This somewhat ambiguous attitude to women's dress, their sexuality and aspirational display survives – certainly when considering fur – to the present day.

2-29 Creusa Receiving the Burning Jewellery from Medea, c.1413–15 From *De Casibus Virorum Illustrium* (On the Fates of Famous Men) by Giovanni Boccaccio. Tempera colours, gold leaf, gold paint and ink on parchment. In this illumination Creusa, the daughter of the King of Corinth, wears a rich red gown trimmed with ermine as befits her noble status. Digital image courtesy of the Getty's Open Content Program

2-30 Hans Holbein the Younger (1497–1543), *Hans of Antwerp*, c.1532. Oil on panel, H: 13.1 cm. The sitter, judging from his costly fur-lined garments, was a wealthy merchant, possibly a member of the Hanse or league of German merchants resident in London. © Victoria and Albert Museum, London. Salting Bequest

Sumptuary legislation, at least that which attempted to regulate dress and personal expenditure on conspicuous forms of sartorial display, had disappeared from all countries by the eighteenth century, in some instances much earlier, as in England, where sumptuary laws were repealed in 1604. However, as Hunt argues, this does not mean that we have dispensed with sumptuary legislation and that it is now merely an archaic relic of a pre-modern age. Today's trade restrictions and embargoes are surely modern-day equivalents of the sumptuary legislation that prohibited expenditure on foreign luxury goods and ordered restrictions on dress. Whether self-imposed, decreed by institutions, or a result of the stylistic regulation maintained by the contemporary fashion system, they are still very much with us, in the workplace and amongst our peers. The fear of increased social fluidity and illegitimate elevation that early sumptuary regulation attempted to bar and yet made more possible, via its classification of furs according to status, lingers on in popular culture's understanding of who has the legitimate and, most importantly, moral right to wear fur.

Mainstream cinema has played a pivotal role in shaping our attitudes to dress and while cinematic fiction seems remote from medieval and early modern sumptuary law, it has preserved many of the attitudes to fur regarding social status and morality propagated by such legislation. Cinema's construction of the immoral, the virtuous and the ineligible woman crystallises around the fur coat with surprising frequency, especially in films from the so-called Golden Age of Hollywood. Tropes familiar from sumptuary legislation as to who has the right to wear fur, the assumption of unlawful status via the wearing of fur, and fur as the visible sign of immorality underpin some of the most memorable cinematic moments of the last century. Hollywood's condemnation of women who wear fur other than that given to them by their spouses in recognition of long-serving conjugal duties is remarkably similar to the edicts against 'lewd' women that pepper the history of sumptuary law. The difference between the fur coats gifted by a spouse, as opposed to those offered as a prelude to illicit sexual activity by a lover, the 'matrimonial' and 'extra-marital minks' as I have termed them previously, is regularly reinforced in mainstream films of this period.[46]

By the mid-twentieth century and mink's pre-eminent status as the most desirable of furs, Hollywood dressed many of its memorable female protagonists for their most dramatic scenes in fashionable mink. Amongst a wardrobe full of memorably immoral minks, we can pause to consider Gloria Grahame as the revenging gangster's moll, Debby Marsh, in *The Big Heat* (fig. 2-31; see also fig. 3-69), wearing her mink as a weapon accessorised with smoking gun and bandaged, disfigured face; or Virginia Mayo, playing Verna Jarrett in *White Heat*, auto-erotically admiring herself perched on a chair in underwear and long-coveted mink moments before her psychotic gangster husband kicks her off her pedestal.[47] In a later film, *BUtterfield 8*, we see Elizabeth Taylor as conflicted prostitute Gloria Wandrous, scrawling 'no sale' on her latest client's mirror before absconding with his wife's mink (again wearing only a silk slip beneath) as more suitable recompense for her services than the $250 dollars he has left her (fig. 2-32).[48] All three receive punishment in the finale to all three films, presumably for the assumption of aspirational mink as well as their immoral lifestyles: Marsh is shot, Jarrett imprisoned and Wandrous dies behind the wheel of her scarlet Sunbeam Alpine. As hyperbolic as the cinematic retribution for coveting fur may be, these socially undefined, morally dubious women have ultimately little or no rights and continue to be as regulated by the strictures of celluloid sumptuary legislation as their medieval counterparts had been.

2-31 *The Big Heat*, dir. Fritz Lang, 1953. Film still. Moviestore Collection/ Shutterstock

2-32 *BUtterfield 8*, dir. Daniel Mann, 1960. Film still. MGM/Kobal/Shutterstock

In opposition to these irredeemable fur lovers, Hollywood has also offered up a succession of virtuous women whose honour stays intact despite the allure of fur, women who act as moral correctives for the weak-willed. In *That Touch of Mink*, Doris Day as the innocent Cathy Timberlake fights to retain her honour despite the fur-bearing enticements of her suitor (fig. 2-33).[49] Later in the film the viewer is offered a vestimentary reminder of the original incorporation of fur as lining, common in the era of the original sumptuary legislation, when Cathy succumbs to just a 'touch of mink' lining a Norman Norell-designed coat that she admires at a private fashion show, one of a succession of such seductively fur-lined garments. Swiftly realising that by accepting this extra-marital mink she must also relinquish her virtue, and is now covered in disgrace as well as fine wool and mink, it is only when she finally rejects the furs that have been bought for her that Cathy regains her honour and can shed the shame until those furs are lawfully bestowed upon her within the sanctity of marriage.

If immorality and fur are inextricably linked and ultimately punished in mainstream cinema, then the ability to transcend one's social station by the acquisition of fur is also regularly interrogated. When a $58,000 sable coat is thrown from the penthouse of America's third richest banker and falls into the lap of Jean Arthur, playing poor working girl Mary Smith in the 1937 Depression comedy *Easy Living*, this 'heaven-sent' sable leads to a series of assumptions that cast Smith as the banker's mistress and confer on her an astute business acumen and inside knowledge of the stock market.[50] These mistaken attributes lead to her living rent free in the lap of five-star luxury and being showered with gifts from car dealers, jewellers and couturiers, all eager for the patronage of the banker. *Easy Living* is a perfect cinematic condensation of the fears of unlawful social standing conferred by the wearing of fur, a direct descendant of the same unlawful social elevation that sumptuary laws attempted to prevent.

Even those women who attempt to procure their own minks are condemned, presumably for usurping the rights of men to buy fur for women. Woe betide any cinematic heroine who earns her own furs through honest toil. The only 'lawful' way for a woman to wear mink is if it is bestowed upon her by a grateful or guilty husband. Joan Crawford, resplendent in mink as the principal character in *Mildred Pierce*, finds little recompense in its furry caress for a life of self-sacrifice, enduring a monstrously spoilt daughter and an unfaithful lover (fig. 2-34).[51] Similarly the desire for mink, if not forthcoming as a marital reward, is condemned as unfittingly aspirational and disloyal, a lesson learnt by Nora Connors (Ruth Hussey) in *The Lady Wants Mink* (fig. 2-35). She goes so far as to start her own mink farm, and through honest toil and familial responsibilities is made to see the error of her ways, realising that matrimonial contentment and the gift of children far surpasses fashion and a mink coat.[52]

In the same year that Joan Crawford's portrayal of Mildred Pierce, in all her lustrous, mink-clad angst, illuminated cinema screens, Britain was enduring its most severe period of clothes rationing, a twentieth-century wartime equivalent to sumptuary legislation (fig. 2-36). Instituted in 1941 to reduce the civilian production and consumption of clothing, and divert valuable raw materials and labour towards the war effort, especially the production of military uniforms, every type of clothing was allocated a points value, which was used, alongside cash, to purchase a strictly limited number of items per year. At the start of clothes rationing 66 coupons were issued to each adult, but by the eight-month period between September 1945 and April 1946 this had dropped to just 24. Interestingly, fur as a material was not specifically listed in the original Board of Trade notice of June 1941, which detailed how many coupons were needed for each type of garment. A fur coat would therefore require 14 or 11 coupons, according to length, the same as for coats made from cloth, but with the addition of a prohibitive cash sum as fur attracted a 100 per cent purchase tax during the period. A subsequent list issued in July of the same year does mention fur as one of the materials specified for a 'jacket, blazer, bolero, [or] blouse-type jacket' requiring 13 coupons. However, as the war continued and coupon allocations were revised, there seems to have been a degree of discrepancy as to how many coupons were needed to purchase fur – according to a Fenwick's advertisement, a 'Dyed Grey Indian Lamb' coat required 18 coupons and a starting price of 82 guineas (figs 2-37).[53] The use of fur was encouraged by the Board of Trade during wartime as it saved on the consumption of wool. Embellishing existing garments with fur pieces was encouraged in publications such as British *Vogue*, as, for example, in the article 'Refashion with Fur' from December 1942, which suggests that 'tails and pieces saved from old furs will add definite chic, apparent warmth, to wilting winter clothes' (fig. 2-38). In order to make the 'Mink jabot and bow hat', however, it recommends somewhat unrealistically that one should 'use fourteen tails, of mink or what-you-have...'.[54] Furriers were directed to use up their stocks of pelts, although replenishing them with imported furs would have been impossible due to trade restrictions. In 1940, before rationing was introduced, supplies of fur were down by 75 per cent, the government regarding them as non-essential items.[55] The hardwearing, thermal properties of fur meant that if you owned a fur, or could find a pre-owned one as secondhand clothing was exempt from rationing, or could afford to purchase one, it was an obvious choice as wool and other materials became ever scarcer. Fur used as a trimming, however, suffered the same fate as all embellishments on clothing in Britain during wartime, as once the Utility Clothing Scheme

2-33 *That Touch of Mink*, dir. Delbert Mann, 1962. Film still. Courtesy of the author

2-34 *Mildred Pierce*, dir. Michael Curtiz, 1945. Film still.
Courtesy of the author

2-35 *The Lady Wants Mink*, dir. William A. Seiter, 1953. Film still.
Courtesy of the author

was introduced in 1942, fur, as with other trimmings such as lace, was strictly prohibited, and the number of panels used to make a complete fur coat were similarly restricted.[56] A *Vogue* article from December 1944, entitled 'The Separate Fur Piece', which suggested the use of fur stoles in place of coats, reflects the continued restrictions and a degree of ingenuity in interpreting those same restrictions, declaring, 'Stoles are new favourites in fur (especially since reduced to one coupon only).'[57] What is interesting to consider is that while British wartime clothes rationing and the Utility Scheme imposed restrictions on clothing consumption with a degree of severity and detail that far surpasses earlier sumptuary legislation, it did so with the express intention of safeguarding the national interest and out of egalitarianism, rather than the maintenance of status and hierarchy. The draft notes from the Board of Trade concerning the implementation of an 'austerity campaign' and the introduction of clothes rationing makes this clear: 'The purpose would be (1) to break down the tradition of "respectable" dressing, and (2) to make people wear their clothes to the last gasp and be impervious to the lure of fashion.'[58]

Throughout a track featured on the 1978 album *Giant* by funk supremo Johnny Guitar Watson, over his joyous guitar riffs the phrase 'Wrapped in black mink' is seductively whispered some 24 times. This is abbreviated to 'Wrapped … mink' a further four times, and the song ends with a final triumphal declaration, 'Black mink!'[59] Apart from the song's opening expectant panting, Watson's characteristic scatting, and the one instance of his trademark utterance 'Come here guitar', the line 'Wrapped in black mink' makes up the entire lyric of the song. The phrase is necessarily ambiguous. Does it refer to the possible addressee of the song, being wrapped in black mink? Or Watson's own desire to be wrapped in black mink? When heard rather than read, can it also be understood as 'rapt' or indeed 'rapped', and might it even be a knowing reference to the Blackglama advertising campaign, which fused celebrity, success and black mink so successfully at the time the album was released (see 'Soft Gold', p. 43)? Whatever the enigmatic phrase may mean, its insistent furry repetition creates a powerful soundscape of tactile seduction, desire and assertion. Fur, the more extravagant the better, has long been the characteristic livery for the flamboyant entertainer, and Watson was no exception with his 1970s incarnation as the 'Gangster of Love', a distillation of 'pimp' styling popularised in Blaxploitation films of the period,

2-36 Ankle boots, 1943. Repurposed ocelot coat, with red leather platform soles and tasselled side zips. © Victoria and Albert Museum, London

replete with wide brimmed hats, gold teeth, dark glasses, abundant jewellery and, of course, furs.[60] What this familiar and often denigrated persona both exaggerates and disguises is the persistent deployment of fur by African-Americans throughout the twentieth and twenty-first centuries as a vestimentary mechanism of affirmation. Fur as a sign of arrival, of achievement and, crucially, as presence, has meant that for black Americans, from the devout churchgoer in her Sunday best to today's rap superstars, fur has maintained an ability to signify status by its visual display and consumption (fig. 2-39). The fear of social, sexual and economic fluidity that underpinned historic sumptuary legislation remained in the fictional strictures against unlawful fur espoused by Hollywood, and were augmented both on screen and in reality by the fear of racial mobility signified by the fur coat. The figure of the fur-wearing drug dealer and pimp, and his equally be-furred women, who populated Blaxploitation cinema of the 1970s, simultaneously dismantled some, and upheld other, stereotypes of 'blackness' including that of fur and the African-American consumer. These swaggering hustlers function as a critique of an aspiring underclass, whose love of fur and jewellery is represented as a crude attempt to seize symbolic power and agency, acting as a form of subliminal cinematic sumptuary legislation regulating against the threat of racial ascendancy. Interestingly, this stereotype was revisited, and indeed to some extent dismantled, in the 2007 film *American Gangster* starring Denzel Washington as the real life Harlem drug dealer Frank Lucas, the same Lucas who famously wore a $100,000 full-length chinchilla coat and matching $25,000 hat to the Muhammad Ali v. Joe Frazier fight in 1971.[61] This event is recalled in the film, his extravagant furs attracting the attention of the police, a sartorial misdemeanour that Lucas (Washington) later regrets as we see him destroy the offending fur in a fire.

These cinematic caricatures of fur-clad hustlers and pimps were a necessary contrast to another figure of the African-American in fur, one that spoke of success, of economic and social elevation, of the struggle for equal rights and often-Christian values (fig. 2-40). Prominent black figures were recorded by pioneering African-American photographers, such as James van der Zee, documenter of the Harlem Renaissance whose portraits did much to establish New York's new black American cultural identity in the 1920s and 1930s, or the Washington-based Addison N. Scurlock, who established a successful studio photographing many

2-37 FAR LEFT
Advertisement in British *Vogue*, December 1945. Fenwick of Bond Street, London, announces new fur coats that can be purchased with coupons and cash. Courtesy of the author

2-38 LEFT 'Refashion with Fur', British *Vogue*, December 1942. Courtesy of the author

2-39 OPPOSITE Eve Arnold (1912–2012), *Lady at a Garden Party at Count Basie's in St. Albans*, 1968. From the 'Black is Beautiful' series. © Eve Arnold/Magnum Photos

affluent and socially prominent black Americans living in the Washington area in the early twentieth century, imbuing his portraits with a sense of identity and self worth often signified by the inclusion of fur. Scurlock later famously photographed renowned classical singer Marian Anderson singing at the Lincoln Memorial, resplendent and defiant in mink in 1939 after she was refused admittance to Washington's Constitution Hall by the Daughters of the American Revolution (fig. 2-41).

In the racially segregated America of the first half of the twentieth century, for many black women a fur coat was the only means to signal a sense of achievement and self worth. Other markers of success, such as home ownership, were often impossible with many potential black homeowners ineligible for housing loans or having to face discriminatory housing regulations. But the purchase of a fur coat was something that signified personal prosperity and was a commodity that retained its value and could be passed down from

2-41 Addison N. Scurlock (1883–1964), Marian Anderson at her open-air concert at the Lincoln Memorial, Washington D.C., April 1939. Granger/Shutterstock

2-40 African-American woman, Georgia, United States, c.1899. Granger/Shutterstock

one generation to the next. Fur, for the disenfranchised African-American, offered a tactile reaffirmation of worth, acting as tangible protection from the routine condescension, ignorance and assumptions faced by many throughout the twentieth century. Fur was understood as reward and power, a sign of security and stability in an all too often insecure and insubstantial existence and therefore was worn to give thanks at church, to mourn at funerals, to honour the beloved, to defy authority and to rejoice at celebrations.

The 2019 New York City Council announcement that it was going to consider banning the sale of fur within city limits has mobilised protest from both the Jewish and black communities (see figs 1-34, 1-35). An article, published following the announcement, reported that:

> *A prohibition would fly in the face of centuries of religious and cultural tradition. Black ministers have staged protests, saying that for many African-Americans, wearing furs is a treasured hallmark of achievement. Hasidic rabbis point to the many men who wear fur hats on the Sabbath. And fur shop owners and garment manufacturers have raised alarms over the potential loss of jobs and an attack on an industry with a deep history in New York.*

The article concludes with an interview with Harlem minister the Reverend Johnnie Green Jr., who declares, 'I'm more concerned about saving black lives ... When the activists are more concerned about saving black lives than black minks, let me know.'[62]

New York Times journalist Jasmine Sanders, in an article entitled 'Nothing Faux About It', charts the African-American woman's relationship with fur and how the anti-fur movement can be understood as an attack on a significant form of black female agency. She quotes an observation made by the mother of Paula Marie Seniors, Professor of Africana Studies at Virginia Tech, who suggested that 'As soon as black women could afford to buy mink coats, white society and white women said fur was all wrong, verboten, passé.'[63] Although one could argue that black women were buying fur long before the advent of the anti-fur movement in the 1980s, it is nevertheless possible to understand the primarily white, Eurocentric condemnation of fur-wearing women as a contemporary form of ethically motivated, increasingly racially defined sumptuary legislation, mobilised particularly forcefully against black female celebrities who wear fur.

'Queen of Soul' Aretha Franklin was famous for her furs, as Robin Gihvan, fashion critic for *The Washington Post*, has noted: 'So, so many furs. Worn against the cold and worn in the face of adversity. Worn with hauteur. Worn because she was a star, and furs are what stars wear' (fig. 2-42).[64] A long-standing target of PETA, Franklin remained a loyal fur fan, incorporating furs into her performances and letting them fall from her body as she rose to a crescendo. As Gihvan again notes, 'The coat drop was a signal that Franklin ... was ready to loose her full vocal power in a transformative sermon of gospel, soul and rhythm and blues.'[65]

An arguable successor to Franklin's title, American R&B singer and actress Mary J. Blige has similarly made fur a symbol of her rise from rags and considerable adversity to mink (fig. 2-43). Champion of designers such as Fendi and Dennis Basso, who are renowned for their expertise in working with fur, Blige continues the traditional alliance of black celebrity and

2-42 Aretha Franklin, 1993. Amy Sancetta/AOP/Shutterstock

fur. This was strikingly condensed in the remarkable celebration of fashion, fur and fame that appeared in American *Elle* magazine of November 2011, entitled 'Hail Mary', in which Blige wore that season's furs including designs by Dior, Gucci and Fendi.

Just as the 1970s caricatures of the fur-loving hustler have undergone a process of lyrical and visual *détournement*, so the same process of etymological reclamation has seen offensive terminology formerly used to describe black Americans become part of the linguistic arsenal of contemporary rap. Fur has taken centre stage in rap music's confrontational affirmation of success, the essential clothing in which to drink Cristal or ride in a Lexus and reconstitute the image of black affluence.

However, within the climate of popular sociocultural consciousness, a large part of which concerns itself with animal welfare including a wide-scale

2-43 LEFT 'Hail Mary', featuring Mary J. Blige, *Elle* magazine, November 2011. Courtesy of the author

2-44 BELOW Cardi B leaves Queens County Criminal Court, New York City, January 2019. Media Punch/Shutterstock

advocacy of vegetarianism, even rap's defiant status-affirming attire has not been immune to contemporary ethical sumptuary legislation. As with Aretha Franklin, an increasing number of rap stars are letting the fur fall from their shoulders. Whether or not Beyoncé and Jay-Z's recent exhortation to their fans to embrace veganism negates the earlier celebration of fur by rap/R&B's 'royal couple' remains to be seen. This manifested itself in the 2003 worldwide hit 'Crazy in Love', the video for which included Beyoncé dancing with a fur stole whilst her husband-to-be looks on admiringly, declaring that he is 'cut from a different cloth' and his 'texture is the best fur – chinchilla'.[66] Today's emotive sumptuary legislation against fur is possibly too powerful for the rap establishment to resist. However, it may still be possible to find vestiges of the sixteenth-century 'lewd woman' and her socially disruptive assumption of fur in some of rap's rising stars. Cardi B, famed for her extravagant dress sense and explicit gender realignment of rap's misogynistic visual and linguistic lexicon, chose head-to-toe fur for her court appearance in January 2019 in connection with charges of public affray, brought against her after an altercation in a New York strip club (fig. 2-44). In addition to the customary reading of fur as a visible sign of economic success, this choice also signals a resistance to judicial regulation and, significantly, in a climate of growing intolerance of fur, sumptuary regulation. An act of fur-wearing defiance, it has revived historical concerns as to who has the right to wear fur. Is fur now only worn by the 'wrong' sort of person? This recalls Seniors's statement and continues to affirm historian Alan Hunt's observation that 'Furs have provided a persistent expressive mechanism for the visible display of social hierarchy and thus have been a persistent target of regulation.'[67]

PART THREE

COAT

3 COAT

MODERN PRIMITIVES

The history of fur's utilisation in clothing can be understood as a series of journeys. Unlike the major journeys of exploration and trade, or the mythical sagas and emotional voyages explored elsewhere in this work, the vestimentary journeys that are the subject of this chapter – what might be understood as a history of how fur has been shaped, conceived and displayed, in short, fashioned – are often brief, proximate and transitory. Lining to outerwear, attached or loose, shaggy or sheared, plain or embellished, are all possible units of sartorial distance, at times almost imperceptible, which when identified and assembled construct the seams of fashionable fur.

Fur's centrality to what might be understood as traditional or indigenous dress will be referenced primarily for its impact on the history of European, and latterly North American, fashion with which this chapter is concerned. That the dress of other cultures and societies, both historic and extant, has inevitably informed, inspired and been appropriated by western fashion, is hardly surprising when one considers fur's ancient and universal adoption as clothing. Indigenous dress, however, whilst modified and stylistically developed according to its own temporalities, is exempt from the repetitive, accelerating and inexorable cycles of sartorial change that characterise the developments under discussion here.

For fur's fundamental importance to the history of clothing there is ample material evidence. Tools used in its production have been excavated at sites such as Neumark in Germany, a middle Palaeolithic site where, amongst other artefacts, a stone tool some 100,000 years old was found. Experts have speculated that it was used in the processing of animal skins, attested to by the deposit of oak bark matter found adhered to the blade, which could have been used for tanning.[1] Although no actual physical evidence survives, it is apparent from visual representations of ancient Sumerian culture that fur was extensively worn, particularly in the form of a sheepskin skirt or kilt that was worn with the fleece on the outside and rolled over at the waist to secure the garment. Known as a *kaunakes*, this would have been worn by elite males, such as Ur-Nanshe, King of Lagash, who is depicted in a limestone relief dating from around 2550–2500 BCE. In later periods sheepskin was replaced by woven woollen material but with additional loops or tufts sewn onto the garment to simulate fleece, an early form of 'fake' fur.

Elsewhere, at a number of sites excavated in Scandinavia, remarkably preserved prehistoric fur garments have been discovered, such as the sheepskin cloak found in East Jutland dating from around 350–341 BCE. Made from perfectly matched dark and light sheepskins, it is stitched together with animal

PREVIOUS PAGE The *beurre salé* fur technique (detail). Courtesy of Kopenhagen Fur

3-1 Nicole Wermers (b. 1971), *Infrastruktur*, 2015. Installation view, mixed media. Photograph by Andy Keate. Courtesy of the artist and Herald Street Gallery sinews, a prehistoric reversible garment that could be worn with the fleece inside or out. Another ancient forerunner of the modern sheepskin coat, or 'sheepie', is the wonderfully evocative child's coat preserved in the frozen tombs of the Tashtyk culture in present-day southern Siberia. Now believed to date from the third or fourth centuries BCE, it displays a remarkable degree of skill (fig. 3-2). The body of the coat, made from sheepskin, flares outwards towards the hem, its reinforced leather seams and front edging trimmed with wolf or dog fur (it is known from other prehistoric excavations that dogs were not only used for hunting but also for food, and their fur for clothing).

Even in this nascent form, prehistoric fur clothing, in addition to its practical thermal properties, would have signified status and power, it would have been imbued with the aura of conquest and violence born of the capture and killing of the animal, making fur a supremely transformative material, which reconfigured as clothing accounts for fashioned fur's complex and controversial history. As historian Alan Hunt suggests, 'Starting from the very beginning the first clothes were the trophies of the hunt or war – skins or other relics of animals and human conquests;

these trophies gradually gave way to badges and heraldic symbols. From the beginning dress is never simply functional; it marks distinctions in prowess and rank'.[2] An understanding of the symbolic resonance of clothing made from animal skins permeates the humble prehistoric sheepskin and the ceremonial lion and leopard skin alike.

Pre-dating even these archaeological finds, scientific evidence of our ancient fur-wearing past has been provided by using the DNA of body lice, which are distinct from human head lice and uniquely adapted to living on clothing. Recent research suggests that humans started to wear clothing as early as 170,000 BCE, and by the period of migration from Africa to the colder climes of Europe and Asia that occurred around 100,000–70,000 BCE, such clothing would almost certainly have been made from animal skins.[3]

The world of classical antiquity, however, had less regard for fur, partly due to the fact that the warmer Mediterranean climate meant there was less need for its thermal properties, and partly due to its perceived lowly status. Greeks and Romans dressed primarily in linen and wool, the sophistication of fine woven textiles signifying a level of taste and economic status that animal skins could not. Sheepskins and other coarse, longer haired furs such as goat or wolf were generally the preserve of the rural population, labourers, the poor and 'strangers', and was also the sign of the barbarian 'other'.

The pioneering work carried out by Dorothy K. Burnham in the 1970s, utilising the collections at the Royal Ontario Museum, led her to propose in her seminal work *Cut My Cote* (1973) that while factors such as climate, occupation, status and modesty all determine the look of clothes, it is the fabric from which a garment is made that plays the greatest role in determining its cut and fit.[4] Burnham introduces the idea of a 'skin concept', which survives especially in the construction of traditional garments of colder countries, where cloth is cut horizontally rather than in the more typical vertical direction. She suggests this is determined not by its development from rectilinear loom-woven cloth, but by the fact that 'in ages past

3-2 Child's sheepskin coat, Siberia, 200–400 BCE. Alfredo Dagli/Shutterstock

3-3 Aquascutum coat, 1970s. England; sheepskin. Courtesy of the Westminster Menswear Archive, University of Westminster, London

3-4 Skinheads, one wearing a sheepskin coat or 'sheepie', 1970s. England. Keystone Pictures USA/Keystone/Shutterstock

they were made of skins'.[5] Burnham argues for the persistence of a skin memory in the production of traditional garments in regions where animal skins were the primary material and which evoke the earliest of clothing production techniques, 'a large skin will fold around with no side seams, and inserting sleeves into vertical side slashes and joining the shoulders completes the garment'.[6]

This prototypical fur fashion survives in many examples of traditional global dress where, after being consumed for food, an animal's complete fur or skin is formed into a rudimentary garment. It also survives in the form of the *pilche*, a simple cloak constructed from animal skins that was worn throughout Europe in the medieval and early Renaissance periods, and survived in more remote regions until the early twentieth century. The *pilche*, as Elspeth Veale and other historians have noted, is an exceptional garment in the history of European fur, being, until the nineteenth century, the only garment worn with its fur on the outside. In England, as in much of western Europe during the Middle Ages, the *pilche* was made from indigenous species such as sheep, goat or beaver and was worn by commoners and the wealthy alike, the latter lining theirs with finer furs. Veale records a late fourteenth-century example belonging to the Earl of Derby, later to become Henry IV, who possessed a *pilche* made of goat skins lined with squirrel, while the commoner would more than likely have had to be content with a 'sheepskin hood made long enough to form a shoulder cape', which as she observes is often seen in contemporary depictions of peasant dress.[7] Variants of the *pilche* consisting of a sheepskin or similar coarse, longer haired fur, made into long or short cloaks, simple jerkins or rudimentary sleeved garments, appear in the traditional dress of many cultures, the term itself derived from the Latin *pellis* meaning a skin or hide.

The legacy of the *pilche* survives today in the form of the sheepskin coat (fig. 3-3), often referred to as shearling (a more comfortable term for today's fur-sensitive consumer, which emphasises the shearing rather than the skinning of sheep), and its distant cousin the fur gilet. The precise origin of the classic modern sheepskin coat, of characteristic tan or brown suede and cream fleece (the variant of dark brown suede with chocolate fleece became popular in the late 1970s) and leather 'football' buttons, is difficult to ascertain. The British company Morlands, synonymous with sheepskin products until the company's closure in 1981, can claim to be one of the first producers of this ubiquitous garment. Originating in 1825 under Cyrus Clark – one of the celebrated shoe-manufacturing Clark brothers – the company started

3-5 John Galliano for Dior, jacket, *Hardcore Romance*, Autumn/Winter 2003. Sheepskin. Michael Euler/AP/Shutterstock

to make sheepskin slippers from off-cuts, which became so successful that this aspect of the business expanded. Under the direction of John Morland, a tannery was acquired in Glastonbury in 1870 and the company started producing sheepskin products under the Morlands name. Spurred on by the advent of the automobile, which necessitated the production of warm clothing and accessories for motoring such as sheepskin rugs, coats, boots and foot muffs, the business grew. The thermal properties of sheepskin also proved invaluable for early aeroplane travel and Morlands was an important British manufacturer of that other staple of the twentieth-century fur wardrobe, the fleece-lined, leather flying jacket, which was produced in 1941 along with boots for RAF pilots flying in the Second World War (see p. 150).[8] A testament to the effectiveness of Morlands sheepskin boots was the fact that a number of pairs were included in the kit taken by Sir Edmund Hillary's team on his successful ascent of Everest in 1952, and it is tempting to consider today's ubiquitous UGG boot as perhaps a casualwear descendant of these pioneering boots (see fig. 3-6).

The irresistible combination of comfort, warmth, a certain proletarian ruggedness and 'truth to materials' has led to the sheepskin coat being favoured by all social strata. The patrician Tony chooses a sheepskin for visits

3-6 LEFT Jennifer Lopez in fur gilet and UGG boots, Beverly Hills, California, 2010. BDG/Shutterstock

3-7 RIGHT *His Prehistoric Past*, dir. Charles Chaplin, 1914. Film still. Snap/Shutterstock

to the pub and a weekend in the country in the 1963 film *The Servant*, while 'Del Boy' in the hugely popular British TV series *Only Fools and Horses* crystallised the sheepskin's association with the market trader and used car dealer.[9] The sheepskin has also been regularly conscripted into the uniform of various subcultures, most notably the skinhead's 'sheepie', worn best with Sta-Prests, Dr Martens and a Ben Sherman shirt (fig. 3-4). While critics would declare that classics are best left untouched, some of the most creative fashion designers have transformed and indeed highlighted the sheepskin coat's rich tradition, one of the most startling examples being John Galliano's' geometric reimagining of it for his Autumn/Winter 2003 ready-to-wear collection for Dior (fig. 3-5).

There is a shared skin memory between the sheepskin coat, the *pilche* and the fur gilet, whose popularity, especially for women, is a testament to the attraction of fur in its most basically fashioned form (fig. 3-6). The simple waistcoat beloved of those from all walks of life was the acceptable and democratic face of fur-wearing in the early twenty-first century, adding a dash of primitivism and tactile surprise to jeans and what subsequently became known as 'athleisure' – sweat shirts and pants, worn when shopping, at the school gates or even going to the gym. For more formal social occasions the fur gilet added a sensuous and primeval edginess to evening wear, becoming a staple of both red carpet appearances by celebrities and those aspiring to that status. Made from synthetic fur, shearling or more costly furs such as mink, the gilet was ubiquitous enough to escape comment from the anti-fur lobby and provided entry-level consumption of fur without the formality and commitment required of other fur garments.

The fur gilet provides a route back from the relative sophistication of the sheepskin coat to our primeval fur-wearing past, a past that has fascinated the producers of popular culture and the furrier alike. The 'memory (or rather imagination) of skin garments' and the 'primeval' fashioning of fur captivated early film makers. The figure of the bearskin-wearing caveman was deployed for both 'serious' dramas, such as D.W. Griffith's *Man's Genesis*, and for comedies, transforming both Charlie Chaplin (in *His Prehistoric Past*) and Buster Keaton (in *Three Ages*) into modern primitives (fig. 3-7).[10] Such a wealth of cinematic primitive fur would not be seen again until the 1960s, when leading prehistoric costume designer Carl Toms devised not only the iconic antediluvian 'bikini', worn by Raquel Welch in *One Million Years B.C.* (see fig. 1-18) but also a complete collection of furry fashions for the cast of *When Dinosaurs Ruled the Earth*.[11] Another production from the 'prehistoric' 1960s, a decade that gave us perhaps the most directional of primitive styling in Fred Flintstone's fur tunic with contrasting

3-8 Bonnie Cashin, coat, 1960s. Suede and fur. © The Metropolitan Museum of Art, New York/Art Resource/Scala. Gift of Seena Dundes

These cinematic fantasies of the 1960s are a reflection of the same 'native', skin-wearing, primeval aesthetic that influenced that decade's fur fashions, the complete skin worn almost unaltered, or evoking fundamental skin memories in basic garment shapes such as the tabard, poncho and cape. Ironically, this journey back to primeval fashions informed and inspired some of the most forward-thinking designers of the period. Minimalists such as Bonnie Cashin, synonymous with making casual sportswear both chic and wearable, created in the 1960s a simple tie-fastened, poncho-inspired suede and mink swing coat for Philip Sills & Co., with whom Cashin had a long and productive association and where she first introduced her trademark leather trimmed hem. The coat is expressive of Cashin's belief in wearability and simplicity, coupled with a sense of rugged luxury evocative of indigenous American clothing in its use of animal skins (fig. 3-8).

Fashion's use of 'raw' fur, or at least a raw aesthetic, invokes the wildness and ferocity of the animal kingdom and sits in opposition to the furrier's art, where fur is fashioned and embellished into the most sophisticated of garments. It is this tension between the unfashioned and the fashioned, the 'raw and the cooked', which characterises the history of fur fashion.

tie, sheds more light on the possible construction of these skin concepts. In the 1961 film version of Jules Verne's *Mysterious Island*, now remembered primarily for its special effects in Superdynamation, Lady Mary Fairchild, one of the survivors stranded on the desert island that has been caught in a sort of prehistoric time continuum, demonstrates that not only is she a crack shot but also that she is in possession of remarkable needleworking skills.[12] In the film we see her, with the aid of bone needles, quickly running up a sort of Edwardian fur capelet for herself and a skin minidress for her niece. As the narrator informs us: 'Lady Mary turned out to be quite handy with a needle and thread. She was able to make goatskins into clothing for the men and fashioned a trim garment for Elena'.[13]

3-9 Brian Jones in sheepskin *pilche*, Afghan coat and suit for his court appearance, London, 1967. Worth/AP/Shutterstock

3-10 Jun Takahashi, coat, Autumn/Winter 2006. Shutterstock

3-11 Sarah Burton for Alexander McQueen, coat, Autumn/Winter 2012. Fairchild Archive/Penske Media/Shutterstock

Fur in this way can be understood to join the ranks of Roland Barthes's famous vestemes, units that make up the language or system of fashion, in this case fur, which, when animated by furrier, the wearer and its mediated representation can be understood as a series of oppositions between the rudimentary and the refined.[14] For his 1967 court appearance to appeal his jail sentence for drugs offences, Brian Jones, lead guitarist of the Rolling Stones and passionate fur-wearer, chose a modern-day shaggy sheepskin *pilche* worn over an Afghan jacket, signifying counter-cultural hippie cachet, contrasted with the ultimate symbols of conformity – a white shirt and a tie (fig. 3-9). The result was what must surely rank as one of the decade's most easily 'read' demonstrations of fur as primeval anarchy versus civilised convention.

Much of the history of fashionable fur is characterised by an increasing level of artisanal skill, rendering this primary material into ever more subtle and technically sophisticated garments. This often results in forms and treatments of fur far removed from its natural state (see 'The Force of Fur', p. 141), a process accelerated by contemporary anti-fur sensibilities. However, a desire to return to fur's most primitive, however artfully contrived, appearance has resurfaced in the work of some of the most innovative of contemporary designers. Mongolian lamb, with its characteristically long crimped fleece, is immediately suggestive of primitivism and regularly summons what has been described as a 'yeti' aesthetic onto the most fashionable of runways. Jean Paul Gaultier fashioned his 'big foot' or 'yeti' in camouflage-coloured fur for his Autumn/Winter 1997 haute couture collection, Jun Takahashi for *Undercover* (Autumn/Winter 2006) rendered his shaggy apparitions even more enigmatic by bandaging their heads with studded and pierced lace (fig. 3-10), and Alexander McQueen evoked Himalayan folk costume in the enveloping shaggy blanket cape designed for his Autumn/Winter 2008 menswear collection. Equally transformative, the longer haired goat designs in McQueen's celebrated Autumn/Winter 2009 collection *Horn of Plenty* electrified the audience. Guests witnessed the arrival of a yeti/BDSM 'black-fur-clad becoming', a vision more recently resurrected by Sarah Burton for the McQueen Autumn/Winter 2012 collection (fig. 3-11), and made animal-friendly by Gareth Pugh's grey, synthetic, monk-hooded mountain dweller in that same season.[15]

Autumn/Winter 2012 can be considered one of the most 'primeval' of recent fur seasons, with a number of designers using fur and skins that collapse the temporality between archetypal fur garments and the finesse of the contemporary furrier. When not using shaggy pelts such as those of lamb and goat, the

3-12 Karl Lagerfeld for Fendi, suit, Autumn/Winter 2012. Olycom Spa/Shutterstock

3-13 Miguel Adrover, coat, Autumn/Winter 2012. Fairchild Archive/Penske Media/Shutterstock

3-14 Sean John, oversized scarf, Autumn/Winter 2001. Cavan Pawson/Evening Standard/Shutterstock

collections featured herds of dyed cow, pony and deer that flocked to the runways of Europe. The fur house Revillon, building on its revival under the creative direction of Rick Owens from 2003 to 2006, appointed ex-Givenchy designer Andrew Heather, who for his first collection for the house in 2012 included, amongst sheared mink and skunk garments, a remarkably 'primitive' calf-hair dress coat and two-piece suit. In Milan Karl Lagerfeld chose the equally striking hide of the antelope for Fendi, typifying that season's cattle drive backwards towards a primeval agrarian past (fig. 3-12). Elsewhere that same season, controversial and elusive designer Miguel Adrover made a rare reappearance with his largely recycled collection, including an eviscerated secondhand fur coat, which rendered the model a fur trapper's latest kill (fig. 3-13). Unsurprisingly, this hunter-gatherer concept has more often informed and inspired menswear, especially from those designers who like their fur rugged and testosterone-fuelled, most effectively realised by rap star and producer-turned-fashion designer Sean ('Puffy') Combs with his phenomenally successful Sean John label. His groundbreaking Autumn/Winter 2001 collection combined furs fresh from the Stone Age with luxury streetwear (fig. 3-14).[16] The first look on the runway comprised a lambskin sweatsuit and voluminous, floor-length lynx tail scarf, which set the tone for a show that included deer, fox, goat, karakul and mink alongside ostrich and crocodile skins, a vestimentary Noah's Ark of ghetto fabulousness.

The Bible ends this journey through fashionably primitive fur and an encounter with arguably the first recorded instance of the art of the furrier and, more tellingly perhaps, the first coupling of fur with the notion of sin. In Genesis we learn, 'Unto Adam also and to his wife did the Lord God make coats of skins, and clothed them'. Fur clothing marks Adam and Eve's transition from holy innocence to sinful knowledge, an association that in the Christian world would pervade fur's fashionable journeys, acting as the reason for its proscription and as a catalyst of desire.[17]

NOW YOU SEE ME, NOW YOU DON'T

During the medieval and early modern periods in Europe, the wearing of fur was dominated by three significant factors: trade, technology and status. Over time all three of these factors would be modified and developed, which in turn impacted significantly on the actual manner in which fur was worn and incorporated into garments. Whereas the furs discussed in the previous sub-section were by and large those worn out of necessity by all stratas of society, those considered here will primarily be those of the nobility, the wealthy and figures in positions of influence. Any study of worn fur in this period is inevitably restricted by socio-economic evidence, as for the most part – in the absence of actual garments – we are reliant on visual records such as portraits, and written accounts including inventories, bequests and wills, all of which were commissioned by, and pertain to, the wealthy. Fur, of course, was still widely worn by the lower classes, but the types of fur and styles of these garments remained relatively unchanging and consisted typically of the cloaks and *pilches* considered previously. Most information concerning the wearing of fur at this time can be gleaned from the sumptuary legislation that identified which types of fur should be worn by different sectors of society (see 'Wearer's Rights', p. 63). This meant in effect that the lower classes wore available indigenous species, which in England meant the skins of sheep, goat and cattle, alongside beaver, weasel, otter, native squirrel, wolf, bear and cat, some of which became scarcer and disappeared altogether as the Middle Ages progressed.[18] With the exception of squirrel, which will be discussed shortly, the furs favoured by the wealthy tended to be finer, imported, and consequently more costly.

During the historical period under discussion, fur was chiefly used to provide insulation and for the most part remained unseen except for front facings or edgings and at the hem, neck and wrist (fig. 3-15). The principal task of the furrier was to produce fur

3-15 Sofonisba Anguissola (c.1532–1625), *Prince Alessandro Farnese, later Duke of Parma and Piacenza*, c.1560. Oil on canvas, 107 x 79 cm. The 15-year-old prince's ermine-lined cloak fulfils the dual role of thermal insulation and status affirmation, in addition to the magnificent silver thread and pearl decoration. Gianni Dagli Orti/Shutterstock

linings, which typically would be removable, as a fur would often outlast the original garment and so could be reinserted into a new one. Their removability also maintained the economically important trade in secondhand and renovated furs, a trade often open to malpractice with reconditioned furs sold as new and other abuses that legislation regularly attempted to control. So the term a 'furred' garment was generally understood to mean having a lining of fur. The term 'furrier' is derived from the old French *forrer* meaning to line or sheath, which is an indication of the chief production of the original furriery trade, and this dual encasing and lining operation is important both for discussions concerning fashionable fur's journeys from interior to exterior as well as an understanding

3-16 Cristóbal Balenciaga, coat, 1962. Donegal tweed lined with sable. Balenciaga's sable-lined coat continues an earlier tradition of largely unseen furry luxury. Fondación Cristóbal Balenciaga

of its transformative function. Fur in this period was central to a series of complex vestimentary negotiations between the body and the garment that centred on touch, warmth, visibility and defence. Fur was private, much of it unseen, proximate to flesh, sensed through undergarments, only becoming visible and tactile at the front opening, hem, neck and wrist, demarcating the vulnerable borders of the garment with status-conferring edgings (fig. 3-16).

During the thirteenth and fourteenth centuries squirrel was the most fashionable and widely sought-after fur for those of gentle birth. Garments in this period were typically made from brilliantly coloured fine woollen cloth and the delicate fur of the squirrel – especially the bluish-grey varieties from colder northern countries – was especially suited for lining and offsetting clothing. The grey fur was also trimmed away to leave only the white underbelly and so used to augment ermine furs. The majority of squirrel skins were imported into England from Northern Europe, Russia and Siberia, where the most prized skins were obtained via Constantinople, the largest and most important fur market of the period. Cargo records of the time document the vast quantities of squirrel skins that were traded via the city.

The complex nomenclature and bewildering variety of names for different types of squirrel fur is proof of its centrality to the medieval fur trade. *Greywerk* and *vair* were two of the most common names and tended to indicate the finest skins obtained from the coldest parts of Northern and Central Europe. In addition to these two general terms, squirrel was further classified: according to colour, for example *blackwerk* (dark grey, almost black) or *redwerk* (red/brown skins from Central Europe); according to place of origin, such as *calabre*, which indicated the skin was originally from Calabria; by quality and by the way skins were packed and transported, thus *ledderwerk* (leatherwork) indicated the skins had been packed with skin on the outside and so were 'raw', while *harwerk* indicated that the skins were dressed and had been packed with the hair visible. A further taxonomy was applied to squirrel once it had been made into larger skins and incorporated into garments: *bis* (probably a corruption of 'beasts'), *griy* (grey) or *cristigrey* (early or late winter skins), *miniver* (white, taken from the underbelly) and the confusing term *vair*. The meaning of *vair* changes over the period, but is generally applied to larger assembled skins, the name derived from the varied or variegated effect produced by using both the grey back and white belly of the animal (see 'Translation', p. 211 and fig. 5-29).[19]

By the fifteenth century, and in tandem with economic, mercantile and legislative factors, the concept of fashion, as we might understand it today, began to play a decisive role in the way fur was worn. Any attempt to establish the moment when 'fashion' – meaning successive, stylistic change – as opposed to its etymological origin and historical usage – meaning to make or shape – is first recognised in this way is notoriously complex. The Oxford English Dictionary quotes from Shakespeare's *Hamlet* and gives 1602 as a possible date, but many fashion historians favour the fifteenth century and the Burgundian court as its locus.[20] Famed for its extravagance and splendour, the court, most notably during the reign of Philip the Good, led fashions in Europe during this period. Philip's 16 years of mourning, during which he and the court plunged themselves into black, was to have a pervasive influence on fashion, with more sombre colours for garments, including the fur they were lined and edged with, becoming popular. John Harvey, in his influential study of male black attire, notes: 'It is clear that in the fifteenth century black was beginning to have the value as a fashion colour that it has often had since, and indeed has now – carrying, in its smartness, the suggestions at once of importance and sophistication.'[21]

It is in this same period that the blueish grey of the finest squirrel started to fall from favour and was superseded by the dark hues of sable, pine marten, black genet (the skin of the civet cat), black rabbit (known as 'coney' until the sixteenth century, a name revived in the twentieth century, possibly to lend a certain cachet to the common-sounding rabbit) and black lambskin, which was imported from southwest Europe. By the late fifteenth century in England, squirrel is rarely recorded in fashionable wardrobes and was relegated for use in liveries and ceremonial garments, and worn for mourning. This last usage provides furry, historical support for theories, in particular those of the philosopher Walter Benjamin, who understood fashion as an inexorable succession of mortalities, necessary to give birth to the next new style.[22] Squirrel never recovered from its medieval demotion, and although surfacing periodically in the history of fashionable fur, and according to *The Book of Fur* 'the history of the squirrel, with perhaps that of ermine, beaver and Russian sable, is the history of the fur trade', by the twentieth century its chief use was in the making of children's garments and carriage covers, as an embellishment for other furs or to make paintbrushes (fig. 3-17).[23] J.G. Links, head of the London furriers Calman Links and, in 1956, also director of the Hudson's Bay Company and President of the British Fur Trade Alliance, reveals that although *miniver* (the white belly of the squirrel) was the official trimming for peers' robes for coronations in general, and for that of Queen Elizabeth II in 1953 in particular, the wealthier peers wore ermine, while the less wealthy chose white rabbit, and none wore *miniver*. He goes on to quote from the testimony of a merchant, given to the Hudson's Bay Company in 1749, which states that Canadian furs were worth importing 'except their squirrel skins, which are good for nothing.'[24]

In tandem with the fashion for more sombre colours, as the Middle Ages progressed clothing underwent a distinct change both in the material from which it was constructed and in its overall form. Heavier brocades and velvets replaced finer wool, and styles became more elaborate and padded, all of which required denser, darker and fuller furs to complement

3-17 The 10-year-old heiress Gloria Vanderbilt in a grey squirrel coat, New York, 1935. AP/Shutterstock

this new, more dramatic, structured silhouette. Veale paints a sumptuous picture of late fifteenth-century English court fashions, recording that 'gowns of white or black velvet were furred with ermine, yellow velvet with leopard skin, russet velvet with black rabbit, black damask or crimson tissue with black budge or marten'.[25]

Veale's description, published in 1966, as well as being the result of assiduous scholarship also reflects the popular 'medievalism' that influenced fashions in the 1960s generally, and fur fashions in particular. This is perhaps best seen in the Oscar-winning costume designs by John Truscott for the 1967 production of *Camelot*, for which the film's stars were dressed in an array of 'Arthurian' outfits, including Guinevere's space age/medieval, white fur-trimmed, 'parka'-hooded gown, a look that preoccupied designers of the period resulting in furred, hooded coats and winter wedding dresses (fig. 3-19).[26]

More exotic furs such as lynx, mink and black genet became fashionable, so that by the sixteenth century we find evidence in surviving portraiture and wardrobe accounts of a great variety of furs being used for dramatic effect (fig. 3-18). As Hunt observes, 'Any examination of the history of portraiture will reveal the enormous significance of the fur as the preferred drapery through which to display the social and economic pride of the subject.'[27] The construction and projection of image, using meticulous rendering of clothing and accessories, characterises the work of early sixteenth-century painters such as Holbein, one of the most adept at recording his wealthy sitters' self-assertion through fur and one who would have been able to choose for his clients black furs 'with black gowns to indicate understated wealth' or select pale or spotted furs such as 'lynx and the light coloured belly

3-18 *Portrait of a Man in a Fur-Trimmed Coat*, c.1540. Lombardy, Italy; oil on canvas, 97.5 × 74.9 cm. The Metropolitan Museum of Art, New York. Marquand Collection, Gift of Henry G. Marquand, 1890

3-19 *Camelot*, dir. Joshua Logan, 1967. Film still. Warner Bros/Kobal/Shutterstock

fur of the leopard or libbard ... to striking effect on dark fabrics'.[28] Clothing, furs and jewels in portraiture of the sixteenth century are as important, if not more so, than the face of the sitter, as cultural theorists Ann Jones and Peter Stallybrass put it concerning later Renaissance depictions, 'a subject composed through textiles and jewels, fashioned by clothes.'[29]

It is perhaps with sable above all other furs that the wealthy chose to line and trim their garments during the fifteenth and early sixteenth centuries. Prized for its soft, dense, dark brown, almost black fur, sable is a species of marten, its Latin derivation *Martes zibellina* resulting in the French *zibeline*, a common alternative name for sable, especially in the late nineteenth and early twentieth centuries. Closely related to the pine marten and the beech or stone marten, known during this period as *foynes*, all of which were used extensively for their fur, sable belongs to the family *Mustelidae*, which also includes mink, otter, badger, wolverine and weasel. Sables were imported from Russia and were the most expensive of furs during this period. When the royal houses of France and Brittany were united by the marriage of Charles VIII to Anne of Brittany in 1491, her trousseau included a gown trimmed with some 160 sable skins at a cost of £5,000 (the sterling equivalent of the amount in French francs). Further evidence of the cost of sable fur is to be found in the writings of the sixteenth-century German geographer Jacob Ziegler in his account of the 'North Regions', who noted that the price of sable had 'growne to great excess, next unto

3-20 Karl Lagerfeld for Fendi, coat, Haute Fourrure, Autumn/Winter 2015. 'Silvered' sable. Pixelformula/Sipa/Shutterstock

gold and precious stones'.[30] These fabulous sums have recently been evoked by the sable coat, designed by Karl Lagerfeld for the launch of Fendi's Autumn/Winter haute *fourrure* collection in 2015 (fig. 3-20). Amongst some 36 extravagant mink, chinchilla, fox and feather creations, the 'silvered sable' – with each individual hair coated to achieve a luminescent shimmering blackness – is thought to hold the record for the most expensive contemporary fur coat, and was reputed to retail for €1million.

Sable's rich, very dark brown, approaching blackness made it both eminently fashionable and serviceable, offsetting the most costly of fabrics. It is also unique amongst furs in that it feels as smooth when stroked from head to tail, as it does from tail to head (see 'Under My Skin', p. 163). A testament to sable's desirability is that even in the late sixteenth century, when the wearing of fur was far less prevalent than in the preceding centuries, sable and black fox from Russia were still highly prized and featured prominently in records concerning the exchange of diplomatic gifts between the Russian and English courts. When the Russian ambassador from the court of Ivan the Terrible visited Elizabeth I, in return for the gifts of highly esteemed English silver, he bought eight pairs of sables to be made up into tippets. Sable continued to ease diplomatic relations between the two countries, as John Evelyn recorded in 1662, when the Russian ambassador visited the court of Charles II to congratulate the king on his restoration: 'Then came in the presents, borne by 165 of his retinue, consisting of mantles and other large pieces lined with sable, black fox and ermine'.[31] Furry diplomacy between Russia and Britain, centred on the prestige of sable, has continued until the twentieth century, when Russian leaders Bulganin and Khrushchev on their state visit to Britain in 1956 presented Elizabeth II with a cape made of Russian sable.

The costliness and relatively small size of sable skins has meant that they have been used extensively for accessories such as the tippet, which is discussed in the following subsection, and also for one of the most distinctive elements of traditional dress, the *shtreimel*, worn by married Haredi Jewish men (fig. 3-21). Typically made from the tips of sable, or in some cases beech or pine marten tails, the *shtreimel*, with its

3-21. Haredi Jewish man at the 'Wailing Wall', Jerusalem, wearing a sable *shtreimel*, 2014. Valerio Berdini/Shutterstock

distinctive cylindrical/wheel-like shape, is thought to be derived from similar traditional fur hats worn by Polish or Russian nobility. Worn only on the Sabbath and other special occasions, the number of tails used – typically 13, 18 or 26 – has special significance, with some experts suggesting that these numbers relate to the Thirteen Attributes of Mercy recorded in Exodus. Controversially, Jean Paul Gaultier included variants of traditional sable *shtreimels* in his now notorious Autumn/Winter 1993 *Chic Rabbis* collection.

Although sable, due to its lustre, denseness and colour, has never been subject to the same vagaries of fashion as other furs, it was perhaps in the late nineteenth and early twentieth centuries that sable attained a peak of desirability similar to that in the Renaissance. In 1902 some 28,000 sables were imported into Britain from the Russian winter fur fair held at Irbit. As in earlier periods, sable at the turn of the century was favoured for the contrast it lent to gowns of vibrant hues when used as a trimming, and was also much sought after for accessories of all sorts including stoles, muffs and hats, often adorned with stuffed and mounted sables' heads. The most desirable examples of the newly fashionable sealskin coats and jackets were trimmed and edged with sable and James Laver, in his book *Taste and Fashion*, cites a furrier's catalogue of 1898: it includes 'a dainty sac coatee of Russian sable', a broadtail coat with 'collar, front, and cuffs of either sable or chinchilla', and 'a smart full-length coat of seal, with collar of Russian sable and a double frill down the front of sable and wide edging of the same fur.'[32] But perhaps the quintessential sable item of the period was the fur-lined, fur-collared gentleman's overcoat. As a mark of success, a sable-lined coat had no parallel and was the sign of both the established and aspiring businessman, the man about town, and it swiftly became associated with financiers and impresarios. One of the most telling observations of the centrality of the sable-lined coat to a man's social standing can be found in the short story, *A Cup of Cold Water*, by Edith Wharton, published in 1899. The hero, Woburn, sets great store by his Savile Row

3-22 Advertisement, British *Vogue*, November 1938. Full-length ermine evening coat for Albert Hart furriers of Carlos Place, London. Courtesy of the author

tailored overcoat 'with cuffs and collar of Alaska sable', which 'guarantees his admittance to New York society's balls and allows him to offer his arm encased in its luxurious sleeve to the fair and privileged.'[33]

Rivalling sable in its costliness and the fur most expressive of luxury and nobility is ermine, perhaps the most celebrated fur of the period under discussion and, due to its incorporation into surviving ceremonial dress, immediately evocative of the historical importance of fur (fig. 3-22). Ermine (*Mustela erminea*) is the name given to the stoat or weasel in its winter coat. By the process known as seasonal polyphenism (see 'Manimal', p. 15), the summer coat of the stoat changes from sandy brown on the back and head with a white belly to solid white except for the characteristic black-tipped tail. This occurs in species dwelling in northern colder climates, its southern relatives retaining their brown coats in winter. The brilliant white winter coat of the stoat acts as camouflage against its snowy habitat and it has been suggested that the black tip to its tail functions as a form of decoy. Predatory birds seeing the darting black movement of the tail from the air will swoop in its direction, thus invariably missing the actual body of the stoat.

Due to the whiteness of the ermine's coat, it became symbolic of purity (fig. 3-23). In Henry Peacham's book of emblems, *Minerva Britanna* of 1612, it makes its appearance as number 75 with the heraldic motto *Malo mori quam foedari*, or 'I prefer death to defilement'. This refers to the legend that the ermine would rather be killed than sullied by its coat becoming spotted with dirt, or 'Be torn with dogges' rather than 'defile his daintie skinne'.[34] This belief relates to the practice of encircling an ermine with a ring of mud, positioned by hunters so as to block its path to safety in fear of marking its coat, a scene illustrated in engravings associated with the Order of the Ermine. Although the veracity of this animal behaviour is doubtful, the concept of the ermine maintaining its spotless coat in the face of adversity strengthened its association with purity and thus, by extension, virginity. Hence its appearance in the 'Ermine Portrait' of Elizabeth I,

3-24 Queen Victoria in ermine-trimmed outfit and muff, 1872. Carte de visite, W. & D. Downey; albumen silver print. Digital image courtesy of the Getty's Open Content Program

the 'Virgin Queen' (1585), attributed to Nicholas Hilliard, which depicts an ermine on the queen's left arm with a golden crown around its neck, a symbol of royalty. The ermine's purity also provides a probable explanation for its mysterious presence in Leonardo da Vinci's portrait *Lady with an Ermine* (1489–90), possibly depicting the mistress of Leonardo's employer Ludovico Sforza, Duke of Milan, who was a member of the Order of the Ermine created in 1464 by Ferdinand I of Naples.

As the portrait of Elizabeth I indicates, ermine is associated with royalty, but precisely when this association began is unclear (see fig. 3-24). Suffice it to say, depictions of royalty wearing ermine robes for coronations and other ceremonial occasions in manuscripts, frescoes, effigies and paintings are plentiful by the fourteenth century. However, earlier

3-23 Golanski, cape, late 1950s. London; ermine. Courtesy of the author and Tim Cope

3-25 ABOVE LEFT Valentino, coat, Autumn/Winter, 2013. Dyed and powdered mink. Thibault Camus/AP/Shutterstock
3-26 ABOVE RIGHT Valentino, jacket and overskirt, Autumn/Winter, 2013. Powdered mink. Fairchild Archive/Penske Media/Shutterstock

examples of the association of ermine with royalty are not uncommon, and, if we include biblical as well as secular royalty, the sixth-century mosaics from Ravenna (see 'Translation', p. 211, fig. 5-31) include an ermine-wearing Balthassar. Of the fourteenth-century examples one of the most splendid representations of divine royalty as signified by ermine are the figures of the saintly kings Edward the Confessor and Edmund, presenting Richard II to the Virgin and Child, in the Wilton Diptych (1395–9), both of whom wear sumptuous ermine-lined robes that contrast with the shimmering, celestial background.

The Victorian antiquarian and expert on historical costume James Planché notes that for his coronation Richard III had two sets of robes made, including one of purple velvet furred with ermine, while Henry VIII wore 'Coronacion Robes of purpull Veleute furred with miniver and ermine'.[35] Planché adds that Henry's robe featured a collar and cape of ermine that reached halfway to the elbow, which, as Elizabeth Ewing comments, has 'continued to be worn at coronations to our own day, with little change'.[36] Ede & Ravenscroft, robe-makers to British sovereigns since 1689, states on its website that the robes for the most recent coronation, that of Elizabeth II in 1953, followed strict guidelines laid down for previous coronations and consisted of 'a six yard train in best quality handmade purple silk velvet, trimmed with best quality Canadian ermine 5" on top and underside and fully lined with pure silk English satin, complete with ermine cape and all being tailed ermine in their traditional manner'.[37]

When ermine skins are sewn together, the tails are either left in place or removed and 'powdered' on the skins at regular intervals. Powdering is the process of cutting a slit in the skin, inserting the tail through it, and sewing it in place, a laborious process that added

greatly to the cost of garments furred with ermine (see 'The F Word', p. 151).

Ermine has become so closely associated with nobility, and indeed the traditional robes of many clerical, academic and legal institutions, that the somewhat tongue-in-cheek statement written by the furrier J.G. Links in 1956 still retains an air of truth: 'Kings, Doges, mayors, lawyers, anyone who needs to impress his inferiors with the eminence of his position, puts on a piece of ermine, and takes the trick'.[38] Self-proclaimed emperors from Napoleon I to Jean-Bédel Bokassa, President for Life of the Central African Republic, have utilised ermine as a sign of sovereignty, Bokassa emulating Napoleon with a crimson velvet, ermine-bordered coronation robe some nine metres (29 feet) in length. Cinematically, ermine is also a convenient sign for royalty however ersatz, reaching a pinnacle in the 1948 musical production *That Lady in Ermine*, Ernst Lubitsch's last film as director, which bears all the hallmarks of Lubitsch's characteristic historical kitsch aesthetic. This included a bare-foot Betty Grable playing the dual roles of nineteenth-century Countess Angelina, ruler of Bergamo, and sixteenth-century Countess Francesca. Both appear throughout the film wrapped in a decidedly 1940s style dressing gown made of exaggeratedly powdered ermine, which gave maximum exposure to Grable's celebrated legs.[39]

Today, fully spotted ermine is rarely worn, and most often seen at ceremonial occasions where it acts as a furry relic of an outmoded feudal system. Recent references to members of the British House of Lords as 'Ermine vermin' and 'Bloated, ermine-coated and never been voted' are a testament to the vestimentary symbolism of fur, and ermine in particular, in this case as representative of privilege and entitlement.[40] Peers of the realm typically wear ermine whilst seated in Parliament and only wear powdered ermine at coronations, spotted according to their rank, although, as mentioned previously, according to official regulations the fur should in fact be *miniver* (squirrel).[41] When powdered ermine is used in contemporary fashion, it is usually done so ironically. Vivienne Westwood's *Harris Tweed* collection (Autumn/Winter 1997), featuring red velvet 'mini-crinis' and fake 'ermine' capes topped off by tweed and ermine crowns, is a case in point, a lampooning of British royalty using traditional British cloths. More recently Valentino, under the creative direction of Pier Paolo Piccioli and Maria Grazia Chiuri, produced its own version of the ermine-trimmed robes of peers of the realm, again in imitation with 'red velvet' rendered in dyed mink and 'ermine' in powdered white mink, a direct reference to the medieval origin of this ceremonial collection (figs 3-25, 3-26).

If ermine is only sporadically, and then ironically, used by today's designers, that was not the case in the nineteenth and twentieth centuries, when its regal associations, its exotic appearance and its dazzling whiteness made it one of the most enduringly fashionable furs of the period. Owing to its costliness and, when spotted, its striking appearance, it was often made into smaller accessories or continued its historical usage as trimming and edging. With the advent of photography, and latterly film, its brilliant whiteness, along with other pale furs such as white and silver fox, made it especially fashionable. In the hands of creative designers working at the turn of the century, and on into the 1920s and 1930s, ermine exuded an air of aristocratic elegance and sophistication, its softness and pliability allowing the fur to be draped and hung like cloth. These qualities are acknowledged in *Fur Facts* from 1922, in which ermine is noted as being 'very popular with Her Royal Highness, The American Woman, who uses it principally for evening wraps and opera capes'; it goes on to provide the following fashion tip: 'Ermine rather calls for diamonds and low-cut gowns.'[42]

The stunning ermine coat worn by the Hollywood star Anna May Wong (fig. 3-27), made by the prominent New York furriers H. Jaeckel & Sons and designed

3-27 Madeleine Vionnet, coat made for Anna May Wong, 1935. Ermine, silk. © The Metropolitan Museum of Art/Art Resource/Scala, Florence. Gift of Anna May Wong by Madeleine Vionnet, is the perfect example of the cinematic glamour that would have radiated from both the coat and its wearer. With its high stand-up collar, off-centre opening and dolman sleeves lending it the Hollywood/ Russian/folk costume opulence typical of films of the period, which often featured exotic and glamorous 'White Russian' émigrés, the coat has been 'personalised' for Wong with embroidered Chinese characters on its silk lining.

Interestingly, alongside the fact that ermine was largely favoured by the more mature, sophisticated woman, due to its delicacy it was often used as a lining for infant clothing and blankets. Its potential unsuitability for the younger, innocent wearer is explored in the 1948 film *Enchantment*, a love story set during the Second World War but one that spans generations. It features Teresa Wright as a nineteenth-century ingénue, wracked with guilt and indecision after accepting the gift of an ermine hat and muff from her urbane Italian suitor.[43] The gift, frowned upon by her step-sister, is understood as somewhat improper and too worldly for such a young, innocent girl, who struggles with her conscience each time she wears it and cannot decide whether to keep or reject the glamorous and potentially corrupting gift of ermine.

Alongside sable and ermine, many other varieties of fur, both expensive and less so, were worn and became fashionable in the fur-wearing fifteenth and sixteenth centuries. These included leopard (*libarde* or *leberde*) and lynx (*lucerne*), one of the most expensive furs used in the sixteenth century and seen lining the garments of noblemen and royalty in a number of paintings from the period, such as the portrait of Edward VI attributed to William Scrots (circa 1547). Both genet and civet – cat-like animals with distinctive markings – were highly prized especially the black-spotted, darker grey varieties. Of longer-haired furs, wolf was widely used to line men's garments in the period and fox became especially fashionable in the early sixteenth century with red/brown varieties being the most favoured. Although rabbit was fashionable in the earlier centuries when the skins still had to be imported, once the species had become established in England and was more easily obtainable its popularity as a fashionable fur diminished.[44] Black-coated rabbits remained desirable, however, and, as Elspeth Veale notes, black rabbit skins in the sixteenth century 'were about twelve times as expensive as the grey ones'. There are many accounts of rich garments lined with black rabbit fur during the period, including nightwear: the Earl of Pembroke's black cloth nightgown was trimmed with black silk lace and lined throughout with black coney (rabbit), while Henry VII's '*night boteux*', as Veale refers to them – part leg warmer, part slipper – were lined with black coney and white lambskin.[45]

By the end of the sixteenth century the great period of fashionable fur was drawing to a close and while it was still worn as a status symbol and as part of traditional dress, in Europe it would not be until the nineteenth century that fur became so prominent again. This was due to a number of concurring factors, the most influential being changes in fashion and technological development, especially advances in building techniques and living conditions, for the wealthy at least. Window glass was used more widely, the development of chimney architecture made fires more effective, and walls were panelled in wood and lined with tapestries, all of which made the necessity for wearing fur indoors less imperative. Changes in fashion also had a marked impact on the way fur was worn and 'the period's "culture of appearances" hankered after "fashionable," often imported goods, such as silks, velvets, and fine woollens, which were made into layered, padded, and ever more voluminous styles, thus increasing the inherent thermal qualities of fashion at the time.'[46] Additionally, jewellery began to replace fur as a more convenient and portable status symbol, with the increased importation of exotic gems as a result of growing international trade fuelling the imagination and ingenuity of goldsmiths. At the same time European stocks of indigenous fur-bearing animals began to dwindle as a result of the previous centuries' escalating demand. The development of agriculture and increased population growth resulted

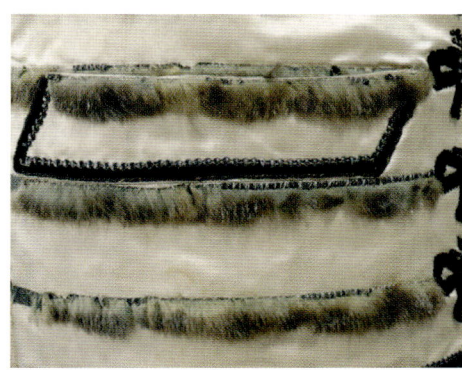

3-28 Man's waistcoat, trimmed with dyed rabbit fur (detail), 1780s. Probably Britain; silk, linen, fur, silver. The fur decoration, originally a bright acidic green, imitates fringing and appears to burst through the body of this elaborate waistcoat. © Victoria and Albert Museum, London. Gift of Theophania Fairfax

in the decline of fur-bearing animals from the most northerly regions too and imported furs became even more costly.

Before proceeding further, it must be stated that just as written accounts of the fur trade show a marked decline, so too do the visual records of dress, which are relied upon when actual examples of early clothing are few. Yet they present an incomplete picture. Such portraits are set in interiors which, due to the advances already mentioned, increasingly obviated the need to wear fur. But they do not reflect the continued wearing of fur outdoors or its use by the lower classes. However, the sixteenth century's decrease in the consumption of fur also marks a shift in moral and psychological attitudes to fur that characterised the medieval and early Renaissance and, it could be argued, the form in which it was displayed and applied to garments. There is an underlying paradox between the status affirming, socially stratifying and institutional display of fur in the period and its accompanying immoral and bestial associations. Such associations are made all the more palpable by its incorporation as unseen linings, proximate to the actual body and skin of the wearer, and as 'border eruptions', which mark the transition from private sensation to public display (fig. 3-28). Hairiness was seen as next to beastliness in an age that depicted the devil, satyrs and wild men with hair-covered bodies. The 'making hairy' that wearing fur signified was a dangerously demoralising process that demanded strict regulation by church and state, hence the preponderance of sumptuary legislation concerning the wearing of fur. It is worth considering that while the largely unseen use of fur in this period is due to its thermal benefit as a lining, the visible wearing of fur as a complete covering, rather than restricted to edgings and facings, would, as Patricia Lurati suggests, have 'raised a series of moral issues related to the animal origins of fur and its wearer's relationship to the bestial and uncivilized world.'[47]

Shorn of its bestial association, the fur lining has survived until the present day, remaining unseen not for fear of the taint of barbarity, but more in celebration of a very personal proximity to luxury, a form of stealth luxury perhaps, that provides the wearer with all the sensory satisfaction of fur without the outward signification of status so important to the medieval wearer. Doris Day, in the 1962 film *That Touch of Mink* (see 'Wearer's Rights', p. 63), succumbs to a mink-lined Norman Norell coat, rather than opting for the 'bestiality', or rather immortality, of a full mink.[48] In that same year Cristóbal Balenciaga, the master of imperceptible luxury, created surely one of the most refined realisations of the 'bestial' within: a deceptively simple coat in Donegal tweed, the sombre colours of the fabric conveying a demure, one might even say dowdy appearance, giving little or no indication, until the wearer chooses to expose it, of its full-length, pure sable lining (see fig. 3-16).

The paradoxical understanding of fur as both a source of shame and prestige that characterised its use in the medieval and Renaissance periods finds its equivalent in the more recent couture tradition, particularly British couture, which prided itself on an evangelical promotion of refined good taste over exhibitionism, a mantra that also characterised its attitude to fur. In an article on the London couture house of Lachasse, published at the beginning of the 1960s, a decade that would also see younger designers celebrating fur in all of its hairy glory, we read that the house was noted for 'a controlled generosity in the handling of beautiful fabrics and furs' and that 'a costume's lining may be one of its chief attractions'. This expression of furry ambivalence links mid-twentieth-century Mayfair to the regulated opulence of the fifteenth-century European courts.[49]

HEADS OR TAILS

The verb to moult – that is, when an animal routinely casts off or sheds a part of its body such as hair, fur or feathers – is derived from the Middle English word *moute*, which in turn is based on the Latin term *mutare*, meaning to change. The process signals new growth, or in some cases transformation. Following furred clothing's decline in Europe from the late sixteenth century, it is possible to understand aspects of its subsequent fashionable journey as undergoing a similar process of moulting. Although fur continued to be used as a lining and edging for garments, and in many cultures was a fundamental component of traditional, ritual or indigenous forms of dress, in the West worn fur's most distinctive and far reaching developments in the early Modern period are in the form of what we today might term accessories (figs 3-29, 3-30). The muff and the tippet, or what later developed into the stole, can be traced to this period of change in the wearing of fur. Similarly, the hat, and in particular the beaver hat, although established long before as a fashionable accessory, reached a peak of popularity in the seventeenth century that would have direct consequences for the subsequent development of the fur trade and its expansion into what was then regarded by Europeans as the New World.

Both the tippet and the muff can be understood as extensions of fur collars and cuffs respectively. Undergoing a process of migration away from the main body of the fur garment, they became detached,

3-29 ABOVE *Zibeline* with jewelled head, c.1550–9. Umbria, Italy; gold and enamel set with seed pearls, rubies and garnets. Walters Art Museum, Baltimore. Museum acquisition by exchange, 1967

3-30 OPPOSITE Model wearing ermine tail hat (maker unknown) with a stuffed ermine on her shoulder, 1950. Mildew Design Ltd/Shutterstock

as with an animal's fur when moulting. As suggested previously, it is possible to understand the use of fur in dress as marked by a series of journeys, some literal and lengthy as in trading journeys in search of new stocks of fur, some metaphorical and minimal as in the journey of fur away from the main body of a garment to the periphery. Whether geographical and mercantile or vestimentary and fashionable, these journeys map the world history of fur, journeys that even in today's increasingly 'fur free' territory remain as emotional, linguistic and topographical signposts.

As with much of the fashionable history of fur, precise origins are impossible to claim with any certainty, and considerable scholarly discussion continues around when the tippet first appeared. Nevertheless, by the late sixteenth century the tippet had become a fashionable accessory recorded in written accounts as well as paintings of the period. During this time the most fashionable tippets took the form of a complete animal skin, typically those of the weasel family; sable, marten, stoat and mink, with the animal's head, paws and claws retained and

3-31 Paolo Veronese (1528–1588), *Countess Livia da Porto Thiene with her Daughter Deidama*, c.1552. Venice, Italy; oil on canvas, 208.4 x 121 cm. The Countess wears a lynx-lined coat and carries a *zibeline* with jewelled head over her arm. Walters Art Museum, Baltimore. Acquired by Henry Walters, 1921

embellished with gold and precious stones. Known also as *zibeline*, from the Italian word for sable or marten, the weasel was also associated with gestation, and bestiaries of the time suggested that weasels conceived and gave birth through either the ear or the mouth, a form of Immaculate Conception akin to that of Christ. Hence *zibellini* became popular during the late fifteenth and early sixteenth centuries as gifts to newly-weds, a symbol of purity and fecundity that, as some historians have suggested, would help the woman fall pregnant swiftly and have an easy childbirth.[50] *Zibellini* also became known in the nineteenth century as 'flea-furs', from the German word *Flohpelz*, due to a belief held by some costume historians of the day that fleas were attracted away from the human body onto the fur of the *zibeline*. This was an interesting if erroneous concept, which seems to confuse the naturally pest-repelling qualities of fur when on the living animal and also foreshadows, inaccurately, contemporary research concerning the development of human head and body lice (see 'Modern Primitives', p. 81).

The Walters Art Museum in Baltimore has a particularly fine example of a *zibeline* mount, dating from the 1550s, in the form of a jewelled marten's head, made from gold and enamel and set with seed pearls, rubies and garnets (see fig. 3-29). Fortuitously the museum also has in its collection a portrait by Veronese of the Countess Livia da Porto Thiene from almost exactly the same date, in which she is wearing just such a *zibeline* and, incidentally, a magnificent lynx-lined robe (fig. 3-31). The fashion for jewelled *zibellini* lasted well into the seventeenth century, Elizabeth Ewing noting the correspondence of Lady Sussex concerning her portrait commissioned from Van Dyck, in which she writes: 'I have seen sables with the clasp of them set with diamonds – if those I am pictured in were done so, I think it would look very well in the picture.'[51]

Tippets, whether jewelled or plain, whether including the heads, tails and paws of the animal or taking the form of simple lengths of fur that may be narrow, as in the contemporary feather boa, or wider as with a stole, have remained a staple fur accessory. For many, the purchase and wearing of a fur tippet or scarf is the affordable, and acceptable, face of fur-wearing today, along with the fur gilet. Following the *zibeline*'s peak of

3-32 Jean-Auguste-Dominique Ingres (1780–1867), *Mademoiselle Caroline Rivière*, 1805. France; oil on canvas, 100 x 70 cm. 15-year-old Caroline is dressed in the height of neoclassical fashion: elbow-length gloves and a remarkably serpentine ermine boa or tippet, typical of the period, accessorise her plain, lightweight gown. Granger/Shutterstock

popularity in the sixteenth and seventeenth centuries, tippets in the eighteenth century became simpler and were very much an extension of the fur trimmings of fashionable gowns of the period, often worn simply twisted around the neck and covering the décolletage. By the early nineteenth century, and necessitated by the fundamental shift towards a neoclassical simplicity in women's fashions influenced by the classical ideals esteemed during the French Revolution, fur's thermal properties became useful once more. Much of the clothing of this period was made from lightweight cloth, and emulated the dress of ancient Greece and Rome, emphasising the body with sheer fabrics that made *déshabillé*, or the appearance of being partly dressed or undressed, fashionable (fig. 3-32). Naturally these fashions, when worn in less temperate climates, demanded the addition of warmer elements and so, along with the Kashmir shawls and short military-inspired Spencer jackets characteristic of the period, fur became desirable again. Many of the fashionably insubstantial dresses were trimmed and edged with deep bands of fur at the hem, long and short cloaks were worn lined with fur and, in addition to the muff, a new variant of the tippet, was developed. Long, narrow and snake-like in form, these fur stoles, or boas as they would subsequently be termed, especially in the twentieth century when made from feathers, were long enough to be worn either looped or draped around the shoulders and down the front of the dress, or more tightly coiled around the body for added warmth.

As the nineteenth century progressed, and with it the rediscovery of fur as a status-affirming fashion fed by an increasingly industrialised and accelerating fur industry, the tippet became a ubiquitous item in the female wardrobe. As part of what might be understood as the later nineteenth century's taxidermied aesthetic, which had the effect of littering interiors with the stuffed bodies of animals, while birds and insects perched, stalked and crawled across fashionable bodies of the period, the tippet regained its teeth and claws. It is as if newly re-formulated as extensions of the furred garment, these taxidermied animal forms act as both a counterpoint to their fashioned 'unrecognisability' as lining and trimming and also serve as a reminder of the violence and mortality incumbent upon that fashioning. Body parts of fur-bearing animals tumble from hats and sweep the ground from hems, while complete animals bite their legs and feet as they lie supine around the shoulders of both the wealthy and aspiring classes. The complete skin of an animal worn as a stole or tie remained fashionable throughout the turn of the century and on into the twentieth, during the earlier part of which the fox fur reigned supreme. Following the successful breeding in captivity of the silver fox, this particular fur, as James Laver has observed, became instantly fashionable in the mid-1920s, adorning both the film star and the office worker alike.[52]

Still favoured as a post-war accessory, a fashionable critique of the fox fur comes from the unlikely voice of the artist Jean Dubuffet, who suggested in characteristically revolutionary tone: 'In the name of what – other than maybe the factor of rarity – do people make necklaces out of shells and not spider webs, the fur of foxes and not their intestines, I would like to know on what grounds?'[53] A characteristic of later twentieth- and twenty-first century fashion has been its regular and accelerating revivals of past styles, and a tried and tested means of instantly evoking previous eras has been to include the ubiquitous fox fur. Whether newly resurrected by contemporary fashion designers or achieved with purchases from vintage stores, the fox fur manages to signify 'style' from the 1890s to the 1940s (fig. 3-33).

Post-war, the complete fur gave way to the stole, typically of mink but fashioned in a bewildering variety of skins to suit every pocket and occasion. The mid-twentieth-century fur stole was the perfect complement to the bare-shouldered, full-skirted eveningwear that became synonymous with the period, providing necessary warmth but without the impediment of voluminous petticoated skirts trapped beneath a full-length fur coat. J.G. Links's *Book of Fur*, written in 1956 for the potential fur purchaser by a celebrated fur producer, acknowledges the importance of this garment to the twentieth-century fur trade and includes a photo essay entitled 'Making up a mink cape'.[54] This shows in detail the various stages from raw skin to 'cape' or stole, the last image showing the finished piece resplendent on a model who looks the quintessence of 1950s glamour – perfectly coiffured, diamond-bedecked and bare-shouldered, emerging from the mink she caresses.

3-33 Edward Molyneux, platinum fox furs, British *Vogue*, May 1932. Courtesy of the author

As a coda to the journey of the tippet, which has never been a masculine fashion, although perhaps the upturned collar of a fur-lined overcoat from the nineteenth century onwards provided an attached version of the tippet for the male, there was a brief moment in the 1950s when the tie, or rather the bow tie, that most masculine of vestimentary symbols, was produced in fur (figs 3-34, 3-35). As has been suggested, historically fur both adorned and demarcated the entry points of clothing, collars, cuffs and hems. More recently the tie, cuff links and belt have proffered closure to the vulnerable points of male attire, the mid-twentieth-century vogue for fur bow ties suggestive of an alliance between protection, adornment and masculine primitivism, adding an accent of tactile danger to the urbane uniform of sports coat and trousers.

As with the tippet, it is difficult to pinpoint the first appearance of the muff. Coming from the Dutch word *mof*, the first muffs appear to have been made of cloth, velvet, satin or wool with fur linings, but this was soon to change as the fur journeyed from the interior to the exterior of the muff. Again, as with the tippet, the muff can be seen as an extension or migration of existing dress, the often interchangeable or renewable deep fur cuffs of dresses journeying out and away from the actual body of the garment and merging to become a separate item of dress. By the latter half of the sixteenth century, muffs had become an established fashion, although at this early stage there was some confusion in England as to their terminology and, while the Dutch-derived word was becoming established, the muff or *muffe* was also known as *snuftkin, snouskin* (snowskin) and *skimskyn*.[55] Although first carried by women, men of fashion swiftly followed suit and started to carry muffs too. Although rarely seen today, the muff remained an established fur fashion for women, men having abandoned it by the first decades of the nineteenth century. And it continued to be so up to and including the first half of the twentieth century, undergoing spectacular increases and diminutions in size, elaboration and in the way in which fur was utilised in its construction.

Some of the most detailed information concerning the muff, and indeed costume in general of the seventeenth century, can be obtained from the remarkable work of Wenceslas Hollar. A bohemian émigré, Hollar came to England in 1637 and amongst a prolific body of etchings and engravings, including religious and secular subjects, landscapes and maritime views, he also produced a series of works recording both fashionable dress and national costume of the period, which has proved invaluable to historians. In addition to plates detailing the complete dress of women, Hollar also produced a unique series of still life compositions, composed of fashionable accessories of the time including muffs, fans, handkerchiefs, gloves and masks. These obsessively observed objects are imbued with an almost surrealist sense of animation, the huddled, writhing masses of fur, lace and leather frozen momentarily before continuing their secret operations. Muffs seem to have fascinated Hollar above all else and, in addition to their inclusion in the accessories groupings, he also

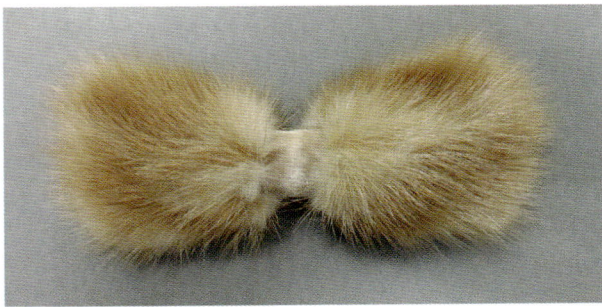

3-34 TOP Actor Robert Wagner wearing a leopardskin bow tie by Aristae Day, New York, 1953. Bob Wands/AP/Shutterstock

3-35 ABOVE Man's bow tie, 1950s. United States; mink or possibly sable. Courtesy of the FIDM Museum at the Fashion Institute of Design & Merchandising, Los Angeles. Gift of Barry Friedman

produced a series of composite views of worn muffs, their ghostly carriers lightly sketched whilst the full virtuosity of his technique is reserved for the muffs themselves; furry prosthetics whose hairy presence dominate the image (fig. 3-36).

Muffs were either carried in the hand or suspended by ribbons about the neck; by the eighteenth century men secured them by means of a side button positioned at the waist of a jacket or from a waistcoat button. A curious atrophied variant of the muff appeared in the

3-36 Wenceslas Hollar (1607–1677), *A Muff in Five Views*, 1645–6. Etching, 83 x 13.1 cm. The Metropolitan Museum of Art, New York. Harris Brisbane Dick Fund, 1917

form of fur wristlets or bracelets, particularly useful during card games to keep the player's wrists and hands warm. Made in pairs from velvet or fur, they became known as *muffetees* in the eighteenth century.[56] Muffs continued to expand and retract in size throughout the eighteenth and early nineteenth centuries, becoming especially popular accessories for the fashion-conscious man, or Macaroni as he was termed in mid-eighteenth-century England (fig. 3-37). It was at this point that muffs grew to enormous proportions and were able to accommodate a number of essential requisites, such as a jewelled snuffbox, a lace handkerchief, and even a 'muff dog', as there was a craze (albeit brief) in the latter part of the seventeenth century for small dogs to be carried inside the capacious muffs of fashionable women. The oversized muff was an essential component of the Macaroni, whose elegant and, to contemporary eyes, effeminate manners and demeanour were lampooned by commentators and considered the product of a debilitating French influence. As with other moments in the history of worn fur, there were gendered and social conventions as to who should, or could, wear which sort of fur, and this certainly applied to muffs in the eighteenth century. Sable and ermine were prized for their softness by women of the upper classes, while men often favoured more rugged furs associated with predatory animals such fox, wolf, lynx, bears and even leopards and tigers.[57] Muffs could also express political allegiance, as in the case of Charles James Fox, the Whig statesman, anti-slavery campaigner, supporter of the French Revolution and, in his youth, a leading Macaroni, whose supporters carried muffs made of fox fur as a vestimentary expression of support. It was reported that style leader, and possible lover of Fox, Georgiana, Duchess of Devonshire, not only carried a fox fur muff but also wore fox tails in her hat.[58]

As with the tippet, the muff became an especially valuable accessory to accompany the insubstantial

3-37 A.B. Duhamel, *Three Views of Muffs*, 1787. Hand-coloured engraving from the *Magasin des Modes Nouvelles Françaises et Anglaises*. This fashion plate illustrates the magnitude of the muff in the 1780s. Courtesy of the Rijksmuseum, Amsterdam. Purchased with the support of the F.G. Waller-Fonds

fashions of the early 1800s and led, understandably, to yet another craze for oversized muffs, which provided extra warmth for scantily clad, fashionable women. And just as the tippet provided the perfect habitat for the bodies of fur-bearing animals in the later nineteenth and early twentieth centuries, so too did the muff. Once again, considerable ingenuity was demonstrated on the part of furriers and mounters as animals' heads, legs and tails dangled from muffs providing warmth for the hands of a style-conscious bourgeoisie, while turning the streets of *fin de siècle* cities into mobile zoos of the dead.

The concept of moulting, or detachment, can not only be understood as a catalyst for the development of important fur items of dress such as the tippet and muff, but also prompts questions concerning the relationship between fur and the history of dress, as well as its migrations through, away from and back into fashion. Similarly, fur's position as integral and discrete, internal and external to clothing, alongside its peripatetic and possibly dysfunctional status, has inspired designers as diverse as Elsa Schiaparelli, Giorgio di Sant'Angelo and Rick Owens. For her collection of 1938, *A Modern Comedy*, Schiaparelli created a coat of blue/black wool trimmed with silver fox fur. The fur, instead of being an integral part of the coat, takes the form of three enlarged pompoms, two at the neckline and one settling at the hip, which becomes a furry pocket attached to the upper two by a velvet ribbon. A reference to balloons and the impossible weightlessness of fur, these incomprehensible furry growths question fur's decorative usefulness and historical signification. Giorgio di Sant'Angelo began his career as a jewellery designer but by the 1970s had started to design clothes initially inspired by Native American and Romany garments. His rejection of traditional tailored forms, as seen in the startling

3-38 Giorgio di Sant'Angelo, cape, Autumn/Winter 1970. Cotton, fur, synthetic. The Metropolitan Museum of Art, New York. Gift of Martin F. Price. © Photo Scala, Florence

embroidered cape from his Autumn/Winter 1970 collection, dripping with dislocated raccoon and fox tails, reflected the prevailing multicultural and indeed counter-cultural hippie aesthetic of the late 1960s and early 1970s (fig. 3-38).

More recently, in 2017 Rick Owens reversed this trend towards detachment and 'grew' onto his characteristically sculptural designs of draped buckram and tulle, semi-detached fur cuffs and atrophied 'muff-like' projections, commenting on the possible nomadic, stateless position of fur in an age of protest (fig. 3-39).

The tail of an animal by its very structure is an extension that is simultaneously independent of the body and yet an intrinsic part of it. The wagging tail of a dog, for example, moves independently and yet anthropomorphically is understood as expressive of its most fundamental emotions. As humans we, of course, retain the coccyx bone as a vestigial reminder of our evolutionary ancestry, yet routinely dock the tails of certain breeds of dogs, and despite the Hunting Act of 2004, which prohibits the hunting of foxes and wild mammals with dogs in the United Kingdom, the tail, or brush, of a fox remains the trophy of a successful kill. An ermine's black-tipped tail, as previously noted, acts as a life-preserving decoy and its fortuitous function is echoed in the animal myths of many cultures. Similarly, myths concerning how animals either gained or lost their tails abound, from the Oneida myth that relates how the bear lost his tail, to the Aboriginal account of how the kangaroo gained its tail, to the Ojibwe legend as to why the beaver's tail is flat.

It is hardly surprising, therefore, that with such a wealth of signification the tail features prominently in fashionable fur as an extension of the constructed garment, as embellishment and as mascot. In addition to their application to tippets and muffs, fur tails have 'grown' from a surprising variety of garments. While many of these incorporate animal parts as a form of fashionable 'primitivism', or as examples of the eternal appropriation of indigenous peoples' use of fur by western fashion designers, others seem to offer a critique of the fashion system itself and its use of animal parts. This can be seen in the remarkable coat named 'Bambury Cross' [sic], designed by the maverick American designer Elizabeth Hawes in 1936 (fig. 3-40).[59] The coat of green broadcloth with integral cape is suggestive of a coachman's, or is possibly a reference to similarly styled nineteenth-century military coats. Sitting on top and covering the upper part of the cape

110 FUR: A SENSITIVE HISTORY

3-39 Rick Owens, dress, Spring/Summer 2017. Thibault Camus/AP/Shutterstock

3-40 Elizabeth Hawes, 'Bambury Cross' coat, Autumn/Winter 1936 United States; wool, fur, silk. Brooklyn Museum Costume Collection at The Metropolitan Museum of Art, New York. Gift of Diane S. Field © Photo Scala, Florence

are a series of glossy brown mink tails, a startling addition to an otherwise sombre coat, which creates the effect of a single, oversized fringed epaulette, reinforcing the military air of the garment. Hawes was a notorious opponent of the concept of fashion, which in the most famous of her treatises, *Fashion is Spinach*, she dismisses as mere 'cellophane' adding a meaningless gloss to its whimsical and transitory products. As such, it has been suggested that the coat is a comment on the then-current fashion for wearing animal tails as embellishment. Interestingly, in *Fashion is Spinach*, as part of a succession of scenarios that Hawes recounts as proof of the unreasonable dictates of seasonal fashion, she includes two concerning fur: 'So, a King gets crowned in England and everything must have an ermine trimming. But you can't find any ermine trimmings in America that spring', and 'I want a coat with no fur trimming in the winter of 1930. All winter coats have fur trimming, the salesgirl says.'[60] As a vestimentary critique of 1930s fur trends, the coat is an example of the more prevalent practice today of a designer critiquing in garment form the very system that it is part of, almost Margiela-like in its stylish reflexivity, but when contrasted with the earlier example of fashion's fascination for the tails of animals it seems especially cogent.

In the collection of the Victoria and Albert Museum is a rare example of a mink jacket dating from the mid-1880s. At a period when it was exceptional to make up a garment with fur on the outside instead of using it for the more customary trimming, the jacket, or more accurately dolman, features a hem entirely trimmed with mink tails (fig. 3-41). The dolman, half-jacket/half-cape with typically loose wide sleeves, was a popular garment in the latter half of the nineteenth century and the cut of this mink example is typical: hip-length with long dipping ends at the front and a shaped back to accommodate a bustle. This exceptional garment was retailed by the Hudson's Bay Furriers in London. As noted by Marion Kite, former Head of the V&A's Furniture, Textiles and Fashion Conservation Department: 'The first experiments in mink farming and captive breeding were not conducted until the late 1870s and selective breeding to obtain a strain which would breed true to type and colour was not undertaken until 1887. It is therefore reasonable to assume that all the pelts came from wild mink.'[61] This jacket, along with Hawes's coat and the previously discussed Sant'Angelo cape, form just three of the many staging posts that punctuate the complex journey of fashionable fur, back and forth through time and across geographical and cultural distances.

An alternative subversion of fashion's 'eternal return' to fur as a status-affirming embellishment, with additional references to its more fundamental transformative properties, is played out in the design of a dress created by Balenciaga around 1964 (fig. 3-42). The black velvet, ermine tail-bustled evening dress recalls the animal's legendary efforts to keep its white coat 'spotless', here contradicted by reversing the ceremonial register of black tips on white to black tips 'lost' against black velvet. This reversal highlights the tail rather than the tip, turning 'dots' to 'dashes', a furry Morse code typical of the designer's insouciance and creating a monochrome peacock's tail that transforms its wearer into an immaculately cut ermine/bird hybrid.

Animal tails worn on the head inevitably evoke images of hunting and trapping, in western popular culture epitomised by the 'coonskin' cap. Derived from Native American headdresses made of the complete skin and fur of an animal, such as the raccoon, which were worn in strict accordance with traditional hunting rituals, such headwear was adopted and modified by white trappers and frontiersmen in the nineteenth century. Most celebrated and mythologised of these figures was Davy Crockett; hunter, politician and opponent of Andrew Jackson and his Indian Removal Act of 1830.[62] Crockett's exploits were fictionalised in his lifetime via stage plays and a series of almanacs recounting his exploits and dealings with Native Americans. A controversial figure in life and in death, it is to Walt Disney that he owes his lasting fame as a popular American folk hero and icon, and the craze for raccoon caps in the 1950s. Disney adapted Crockett's stories into a hugely successful series of TV programmes starring Fess Parker as Crockett, for which he wore the iconic 'coonskin' cap (fig. 3-43).[63] Cheap versions of the caps were marketed for young boys, typically simplified into a fake fur or rabbit skin skullcap with attached raccoon tail, turning suburban American youth into toyshop trappers. At the height of

3-41 Dolman (detail), Hudson's Bay Furriers, c.1885. England; mink lined with quilted satin. © Victoria and Albert Museum, London. Given by Mrs A. C. Bryant

3-43 'Davy Crockett' hat, 1950s. United States; possibly rabbit fur, with black fur tail. Texas Fashion Collection, University of North Texas Libraries

the craze it is estimated that some 5,000 were sold each day, and as an added gendered spin-off, an all-white version made from rabbit fur called the Polly Crockett was marketed for young girls. Indelibly associated with the wild frontiersman and pioneering American spirit, versions of the caps have resurfaced regularly since the 1950s on fashion runways, ski slopes, concert stages and others spaces of public display, crowning the heads of its wearers with a kitsch commodification of fur's ritual transformative function. The belief in the ritualistic transference of the prowess of the hunted animal that is fundamental to traditional cultures worldwide, especially First Nations and Inuit peoples (see 'Shape Shifters', p. 193), is also an underlying motive for another fur tail craze that has resurfaced at least twice in western fashion history.

A 'must' for any well-dressed Ivy-leaguer or 'frat boy' in 1920s America, alongside his full-length raccoon coat (see 'The Force of Fur', p. 141), ukulele and straw boater, would be a raccoon, or sometimes fox, tail to hang from the petrol cap, fender or bumper of his roadster. Simultaneously combining ideas of speed, the 'chase', the trophy and the 'hound dog', this residue of a once fleet animal appended to the essence of early twentieth-century mechanised speed was the equivalent of the 'go faster' stripes of more recent automobilia. The essence of speed represented by an animal tail (an animal so fast all one can see is the tail disappearing from view) was also the basis for one of the most successful advertising campaigns

3-42 Cristóbal Balenciaga, evening dress (and detail of bustle), 1964. Black velvet with bustle trimmed with ermine tails. Texas Fashion Collection, University of North Texas Libraries

COAT 113

3-44 'Steeple' crowned hat, 1590–1670. England; felted beaver fur. © Victoria and Albert Museum, London. Given by Lady Spickernell

of the 1960s. Esso's 'Put a tiger in *your* tank' slogan was created in 1959 and went on to feature a cartoon tiger in a series of advertisements, notably one depicting the tiger filling up the tank of a car with its tail. A masterful exercise in the established tradition of animal/automotive association that started with the notion of horse power and continued to identify some of the fastest cars of their era including the Jaguar, Mustang and Panther. So successful was the campaign that *Time* magazine declared 1964 to be the year of the tiger on Madison Avenue and part of the campaign's success was due to the give-away fake tiger tails obtained when filling up with Esso Extra, feline ferocity reduced to synthetic brand message.

Synchronous with Esso's success was a British relocation of the animal tail as mascot of speed and, in this case, non-conformism, from automobile to scooter. At the height of the mod (moderne) subculture in Britain during the 1960s, as with the earlier Ivy-leaguer, a desirable accoutrement to the uniform of M-1951 fishtail parka, Italian-cut suit and hairstyle was a 'fox' tail, ideally suspended from the top of a six-foot 'whippy' radio aerial projecting from the ubiquitous Vespa or Lambretta scooter. Although termed a 'foxtail', these accessories could be real or fake, resemble either a fox or a raccoon tail, and over time migrated from the scooter to the hoods or backs of the parka. The mod's foxtail expressed the traditional notion of animal velocity with a specifically British foxhunting association, the subversive mod taking on the role of the fox hunted by the establishment.

The various journeys of fur explored so far – from essential element of the garment to accessory – are comparatively brief when compared to the distance, longevity and intensity of the journeys of exploration and exploitation undertaken in pursuit of the beaver. Satisfying the demand for the beaver hat was the impetus for what can be understood as the most significant of fur's many journeys, a journey that would prove to have lasting ecological, economic and political ramifications.

The earliest references to the beaver hat can be found in the fourteenth century when Chaucer (an invaluable reporter of fur fashions) refers to a merchant's 'Flaundryssh bever hat' in the General Prologue to *The Canterbury Tales*. By the thirteenth and fourteenth centuries numbers of both marten and beaver in Britain were severely reduced, primarily as a result of the growth of human settlement, and Veale describes English merchants in the period trading sheep, coney and fox skins for beaver and otter in Flanders.[64] The beaver hat, as an example of economically detrimental foreign fashion, was much lampooned in English literature of the period, most

3-45 Man's top hat, c.1832. Peck & Company, Boston; beaver fur. Courtesy LACMA Collections. Costume Council Curatorial Discretionary Fund. www.lacma.org

notably by critic and pamphleteer Philip Stubbes in his *Anatomie of Abuses* of 1583, who included this about the beaver hat: 'Some of a certaine kind of fine Haire; these they call Bever hattes of xx. xxx. or xl. shillings a peece, fetched from beyond the seas, from whence a greate sorte of other vanities doe come besides.'[65] As had happened with the native British beaver, by the early 1600s numbers of the European beaver (*Castor fiber*) were also in serious decline, resulting in the British and French exploitation of the North American beaver (*Castor Canadensis*) (see 'Soft Gold', p. 43), which in turn made Britain and France the chief European manufacturers of beaver hats, although some historians suggest the trade was first introduced to Britain during the reign of Henry VIII by Spanish and Dutch manufacturers.

The fur of the beaver, the only extant member of the family *Castoridae*, conforms to a typical structure of coarse, outer guard hairs and softer underfur (known as beaver wool), its uniquely scaly keratin component causing the underfur to mesh tightly during the felting process that is central to the production of beaver hat-making (see 'Manimal', p. 15). Beaver hair is supple, waterproof and hardwearing. Due to its felting properties, it is capable of being moulded and able to support a wide variety of crown and brim shapes, from the tall 'steeple' crowns of the seventeenth century, to eighteenth-century tricorns and the ubiquitous top hat of the nineteenth century (figs 3-44, 3-45). Two distinct manufacturing processes were fundamental to the production of beaver hats: felting and hatting. Felting, the intricate process whereby the hair of the beaver is meshed or entangled to form a pliable fabric, is complex and involves a number of processes. Initially the pelt is prepared by removing the outer guard hairs and separating the underfur by tearing or shaving it from the pelt. The process of removing guard hairs was time consuming and difficult, so beaver skins that had over time lost most of their guard hairs, having been obtained in the previous winter and then worn by First Nations trappers throughout the trapping season, were particularly prized. In addition, through contact with human perspiration, the soft underfur would have started to break down, making the felting process of the wool much easier. These pelts, known as *castor gras* ('coat' or 'greasy' pelts), were mixed with *castor sec* ('parchment' beaver), pelts that had been skinned and scarped clean, but were unworn prior to exportation, in a ratio of roughly one *castor gras* to five *castor sec* in the felting process.

The concept of transformation and its multivalent significance, central to this study, is effectively materialised in the historical production of the beaver hat. The desire for beaver hats revolutionised the ecosystem of sixteenth-century Europe, all but making the Eurasian beaver extinct. This localised transformation provided the catalyst for the European mercantile penetration into, and accompanying colonisation of, the beaver-rich territories of present-day Canada, transforming the international fur trade irrevocably. At a material level, and of even more

3-46 'The Art of Hat Making', *The Universal Magazine of Knowledge and Pleasure*, London, 1750. Engraving illustrating the making of beaver hats. Universal History Archive/UIG/Shutterstock

relevance to the journeys of fashioned fur that this section deals with, we see the transformation of beaver fur from 'raw' state, via the mediation and physical proximity of the indigenous body converting the pelt, to 'cooked' fabric, ready for its final transformation into a western fashion item.

Once the guard hairs had been separated from the underfur and removed from the pelt, they were then mixed with *castor gras*, so that beaver oils were redistributed throughout the underfur, and then carded (fig. 3-46). Following carding, the felting process proper commenced and what follows is a brief outline of the production of the beaver hat as it was typically carried out in the early eighteenth century, but which differs little from its production both before and after this period.[66] In a draught-free room the beaver wool was laid on tables perforated by a series of holes or slots. A hatter's bow or bow carder, similar to a large violin bow, was then passed above the surface of the wool while the string was plucked using a wooden pin, striking and agitating the wool beneath, dislodging any loose dirt or vegetable matter, and forming a matted mass of wool known as a *batt*. The *batts* were then covered with a damp cloth or piece of leather, stacked on top of each other over a heat source, and left to bond further and shrink. Following this the *batts* were placed in a container filled with a mixture of wine lees, urine and hot water, and agitated in this solution by hand or using wooden batons, which encouraged further meshing and shrinkage. Once this process was finished the transformed beaver was ready to be stretched over the hat block, heated and moulded over a fire, rubbed smooth with a pumice stone, trimmed and dyed. Finally the hat would be steamed, its interior stiffened with glue, typically made from rabbit, wine lees, or isinglass obtained from fish bladders, to help create and set the final shape, and any loose hairs were then singed off and the nap raised, if desired, with a metal comb or teasels.

The top hat first appeared at the close of the eighteenth century and continued for the next 100 years as the customary formal headwear for men. It

3-47 Women's carriage boots, *c.*1885. Probably United States; leather, fur with grosgrain ribbon. Courtesy LACMA Collections. Mrs. Alice F. Schott Bequest. www.lacma.org

also ushered in the demise of the beaver hat, which had already come under periodic threat due to fluctuating supplies of beaver pelts. This was a result of the ongoing struggle between European and American interests as to which would gain control of the trade, as well as over-trapping, which led to dwindling supplies of North American beaver. The beaver hat's decline was also hastened due to the development of top hats made from silk, or hatter's plush as it was known. There is considerable debate as to where hatter's plush was first developed and also who was the first hatter to fashion a top hat from it as a substitute for the traditional beaver. While London haberdasher John Heatherington famously caused mayhem and frightened children when he first wore his dazzlingly shiny silk hat in 1797, recent evidence suggests that a hatter from Middlesex, one George Dunnage, produced a hat in 1793 from silk plush, a technique he had learned from his father who was in the ribbon trade. Practically and economically, France can lay equal claim to the origin of the silk top hat, given the native expertise in silk production centred around Lyons, the last silk plush manufacturer only closing its doors in 1968. It seems reasonable to suggest that France had the most incentive to switch from beaver to plush, as Frances Backhouse suggests: 'Britain's North American victory over France in 1760 had left London largely in control of the world supply of beaver pelts, and these became inaccessible to French hatters after Napoleon embargoed trade with Britain in 1806.'[67]

Journeying from top to toe, fur-lined footwear signals both historic and contemporary luxury, practical comfort and, in possible etymological disguise, the fairy tale. *Vair*, or squirrel, as well as more costly furs, was used to line the most fashionable of shoes in the medieval period. Various accounts exist of fur-lined footwear: Henry IV's daughter, Philippa, on her marriage to the King of Denmark in 1406, included in her trousseau shoes of polished leather lined with *gris* (the grey back of the squirrel) and white slippers lined with *miniver*. Fur continued to add accents of both comfort and status to the most elegant of footwear. The thermal advantage of fur was understandably most prized when travelling, and fur-lined carriage boots became a necessary accessory for riding in open or draughty horse-drawn vehicles, typically taking the form of overshoes to protect delicate evening shoes and slippers, and often featuring a slashed front opening to allow them to be put on and removed easily (fig. 3-47). With the advent of the automobile and then the airplane, fur, especially sheepskin, provided the necessary insulation for intrepid early twentieth-century travellers. The most recent revival of the fashionable furry foot occurred in Gucci's Autumn/Winter 2015 collection, which featured its now ubiquitous fur-lined, backless 'Princetown' loafer complete with characteristic horse-bit detailing (fig. 3-48). Newly appointed creative director, Alessandro Michele, had been charged with re-energising the brand. Featured amongst a series of fur garments and details in his debut womenswear collection, the furry loafer became the lasting success story of Gucci's eclectic bohemian reinvention, belying perhaps its much publicised decision to go fur-free.[68]

It is fitting, given the transformative goal at the end of the journeys of fur followed in this book, that this subsection should end with Cinderella, and the transformation of the most celebrated of fur shoes into glass (see fig. 3-49). Debate still continues amongst linguists and literary scholars as to whether Charles Perrault's description of Cinderella's glass slippers was simply a mistranslation or an intentional replacement of *vair* (squirrel) for *verre* (glass). The fairy tale itself is based on much earlier traditional stories including the ninth-century Chinese tale, *Ye Xian*. Basile's *Pentamerone* of 1634–6, the first national collection

3-48 Gucci 'Princetown' loafer, worn by attendee at Tokyo Fashion Week, March 2017. Onnie A Koski/WWD/Shutterstock

3-49 Marc Jacobs, shoes for Louis Vuitton, Autumn/Winter 2014. Tooled gilt leather, mink and satin. Courtesy of the Museum at the Fashion Institute of Technology, New York

of fairy tales, included 'La Cenerentola' as an Italian version of the Cinderella narrative. It was, some 60 years later that Perrault included his version of the tale in *Contes de ma mère l'Oye* (or the Tales of Mother Goose), which first appeared in 1697 at a time when fairy tales were fashionable amongst aristocrats in Parisian literary salons. Slippers made of glass, if intentional, were Perrault's invention as all earlier variants describe either golden slippers, or slippers of fur, or omit any detailed description altogether other than fine and invariably dainty. Veale suggests that the substitution of *verre* for *vair* occurred due to the demise of the trade in squirrel fur and along with it the terminology that described much of the early fur trade. She also intimates that Perrault, basing his tale on an earlier thirteenth- or fourteenth-century French version, possibly misunderstood a description of shoes lined with *vair*, which by the end of the seventeenth century were no longer in fashion; indeed, the economic significance of *vair* had fallen into oblivion.[69] Alternatively, one can argue that glass slippers are merely one of a number of impossible, magical objects populating fairy tales to be understood as set apart from the everyday. More recently glass is argued to be the intended material, as it would not stretch or give, unlike fur, and so only Cinderella's impossible dainty foot would fit.[70] While Michel Serres's order to 'give no credence to the glass slipper' is possibly too dogmatic, his understanding of the *vair* slipper as being the only constant in a changing world and the only object not to revert to its dis-enchanted state is convincing, and his description of the fur-lined slipper poetically transformative: 'Touch the vair slipper, caress its warm, soft, gentle fur. A higher, sparse layer of long, thick hair protects another lower layer of fine, short hair. All fur reveals and conceals a similar double property. The skin of the foot is protected by a skin that is protected by another layer, protected in turn by yet another. Quadruple, quintuple variety.'[71]

FURLAND

The title of this section is derived from a 6-minute 42-second film sequence that offers a conceptual framework, or rather, topography, in which we encounter the synthesis of place, culture and transformation that is the persistent attribute of western fashionable fur. Introducing the celebrated, Technicolor, Adrian-designed fashion show scene that punctuates George Cukor's brittle 1939 comedy of sexual manners, *The Women*, the vendeuse welcomes us with the following speech: 'Bonjour mesdames, mademoiselles. It gives me great pleasure to be your cicerone on our adventurous little voyage into Fashionland.'[72] Arriving in 'Fashionland' the viewer is treated to a succession of temporal and spatial shocks as boundaries are collapsed and the department store setting turns from black and white to a series of colourful, increasingly dislocating, fashionable *mises en scène*, including a cardboard cut-out zoo where fur-trimmed models throw peanuts to real monkeys, dressed in identical outfits to their human visitors. Enfolding this Hollywood scripting of Fashionland is a construction of space that demonstrates a wilful abandonment of borders be they geographical, temporal or philosophical; a reflexive and self-referential space that teeters on the edge of collapse. This is a space that reflects and reproduces itself, and bears a relationship to Henri Lefebvre's interrogation of space as a social construct, a space of multiples that focuses on the contradictory, conflictual and, ultimately, political operation and production of space itself.[73] A space similar to that demarcated and cordoned off by the fur coats in artist Nicole Wermer's installation *Infrastruktur* (fig. 3-1, 3-50). The fur coats, acquired secondhand on the Internet, are sewn onto the backs of replica Marcel Breuer *Cesca* chairs. Not only signifying glamour and wealth, the coats are made also complicit in the production and claiming of space, made tangible by the everyday action of reserving a seat by putting one's coat over its back, a space now characterised by the acts of consumption and social regulation represented by the fur coat. Lefebvre's interrogation of space also provides a valuable set of conceptual coordinates with which to map fashionable space, and in particular the space of fashionable fur, which we might term 'Furland'.

The synthesis of real and imagined spaces is effectively demonstrated on the fashionable body. The naming of garments after cities, countries, fabled lands or specific architectural spaces has been a feature of western fashion history from the late eighteenth century, coinciding with the rise of fashion print, fashion journalism and subsequent promotional and marketing strategies. Topographical reality is dispensed with and reimagined on the space of the body itself, utilising vestimentary co-ordinates with which to propel us to Fashionland, or in this case Furland. So powerful is fur's ability to transcend borders, to transport its wearers to undreamt of cultural, erotic and animistic territories, that it has often been able to dispense with Fashionland's fanciful taxonomies altogether. In its very structure, fur, composed of innumerable single hairs, evokes sensations of limitlessness, producing tactile landscapes of lustrous beauty, with no distinct boundaries, its furry edges promising further vistas. These qualities of remoteness and the unfathomable have made it the perfect material for western fashion

3-50 Nicole Wermers, *Infrastruktur,* 2015. Installation view; mixed media. Photograph by Andy Keate. Courtesy of the artist and Herald Street Gallery

to signify the remoteness and unfathomability of other cultures. Throughout history fur has been utilised to transport its fashionable wearers to imagined spaces, spaces of impossible luxury, violence and power, from the tundra to the jungle. Haunted by the misunderstood remnants of ritual and seduction, Furland provides for the fashionable being the ideal space in which to effect the constant re-imagining and re-creating of identities necessary in an increasingly artificial world. Fur in its very realness provides authenticity in a climate of escalating simulation. Occasionally Furland takes on specific national identities, and not always the imagined identities of western fashion's continuing project of cultural appropriation.

During the seventeenth century, the fashionable Dutch garment known as the jack assumed the status of national costume, expressive of a collective identity and allegiance, a furry celebration of luxury and signifier of the Dutch republic's ascendancy during this period. The flowering of domestic genre painting that occurred in the Netherlands at the time has left a unique visual record of how garments assume cultural significance. The jack was a relatively simple garment, a woman's short, loose jacket, with wide sleeves made from velvet or brocade and typically trimmed with ermine or other white fur (fig. 3-51). The jack became the fashionable 'undress' of the period, and for those who could not afford finer furs, rabbit skins or swansdown were also used for the lining. Eminently practical, the fur lining could be removed in warmer seasons and, as depicted by artists of the time, provided their wearers with a garment that was uniquely expressive of the increasing prosperity of Dutch society, at once luxurious and practical, domestic yet indicative of the nation's global mercantile expansion. As an object of self-fashioning the fur-lined jack performed its duties admirably, re-creating its wearers as the beneficiaries of Holland's colonial ventures. And yet these images of fashionable fur by painters such as Vermeer, ter Borch and Maes have none of the self-aggrandisement of portraits from previous centuries. These figures are largely anonymous, captured whilst going about their domestic duties, or at leisure, placing the viewer in the position of a voyeur observing this new species of furred mercantile success.

In the comparatively 'fur-free' eighteenth century the European imagining of Turkey, characterised by a fascination with Ottoman-inflected design, used fur as part of an orientalist 'liberating cultural vocabulary'.[74] Turquerie, as it has become known, was fostered due to improved diplomatic and trading relations between Ottoman and European nations. In addition an increasing number of gentlemen embarking on the Grand Tour extended their travels to Constantinople, dressed in the manner of the people they encountered there, and were memorialised by European painters ready to capture their wealthy patrons in fashionable 'exotic' attire. Most influential of all, in terms of fashion, were the accounts of local dress recorded in the letters of Lady Mary Wortley Montague, wife of the British ambassador to Turkey, who was immediately struck by the contrast between tightly laced western European women's clothing and the relaxed, sumptuous and elegant clothing worn by Turkish women. She described her own adaptation of Turkish clothing in great detail including 'a loose robe they throw off and put on according to the weather, being of a rich brocade (mine is green and gold) either lined with ermine or sables; the sleeves reach very little below the shoulders'.[75] This short-sleeved, fur-lined tunic became an essential component of dressing *à la turque*, alongside trousers or 'drawers' as she termed them, kaftans held in at the waist by a jewelled girdle, turbans, feathered head ornaments, and low-cut, sleeved waistcoat-like garments that Montague described as 'entrary' (*entari*). Her accounts, at first privately circulated amongst her peers and subsequently published in 1763, together with an increasing number of artefacts and customs, increased the craze for all things Ottoman.

Customs included coffee-drinking and the use of such items of interior decoration as the sofa, which the

3-51 Johannes Vermeer (1632–1675), *A Lady Writing*, c.1665. Oil on canvas, 45 x 39.9 cm. The young woman wears a velvet, or silk, ermine-lined 'jack', a short coat. Courtesy National Gallery of Art, Washington D.C. Gift of Harry Waldron Havemeyer and Horace Havemeyer, Jr., in memory of their father, Horace Havemeyer

newly fashionable Turkish costumes made it possible to lounge upon, something prohibited by restrictive western dress. The century's interest in masquerade also meant that along with other imagined cultural disguises, such as 'Chinese' and 'Indian', Turkish dress afforded an opportunity to become, however momentarily, someone else, someone excitingly proximate to the imagined eroticism of the 'foreigner'. Fur was an essential component of this proximity, a tactile encounter with the remote and mysterious 'other', at once liberating and animalistic. The romance of the Ottoman Empire is condensed into the ermine lining nestling against the porcelain skin of the Right Honourable Lady Mary Radcliffe, dressed *à la turque* and daringly décolleté for her marriage portrait by Francis Cotes in 1755, a conjugal vista of the erotic potential of Furland (fig. 3-52).

If, for the fashionable eighteenth-century European explorer, the map of Furland echoed the contours of the Ottoman Empire, at the close of the nineteenth and intermittently throughout the twentieth century its topology increasingly came to resemble Russia. The condensation of constructed ideas about place, in this case an imagined Russia, found its vestimentary expression in Western Europe's re-awakened interest in fur. This functioned in a similar way to the 'rediscovery' and invention of nationalism that historian Benedict Anderson suggests occurred in the eighteenth and nineteenth centuries, when 'a complex "crossing" of discrete historical forces' became articulated and transferred 'to a great variety of social terrains, to merge and be merged with a correspondingly wide variety of political and ideological constellations.'[76] As had happened with the fashionable reconstruction of the Ottoman Empire, the concentration of interest in Russia that was expressed via clothing was the result of political and economic as well as fictional and aesthetic factors.

Fur, of course, always signifies protection against extreme temperatures and by extension the landscape where that protection is most needed. Siberia had long exercised the imagination of Europeans as a place of

unimaginable cold, as well as being the habitat of the most highly prized and fashionable of Russian furs – sable. The splendour of the Russian court with its cast of autocratic rulers, most notably Catherine the Great, similarly exercised the European imagination and fed subsequent furry fantasies centred on unlicensed sexuality, cruelty and extravagance, condensed into innumerable literary and cinematic constructions of the figure of the Russian empress. This finds its most notorious expression in *Venus in Furs*, a novella by Austrian author Leopold von Sacher-Masoch, in which 'fantasies of Catherine, of Russia, and more generally of Eastern Europe thus appear as the crucial fur lining to the fundamental fantasies of slavery, flagellation, and abasement' (see 'Under My Skin', pp. 177–80).[77]

The political and social upheavals that occurred in Russia towards the end of the nineteenth century, part of which resulted in the pogroms and the mass migration of Russian Jews, coincided with an escalating European desire for fur and furred garments. The sudden influx of Jewish fur dealers, furriers and tailors into the capital cities of Europe, most notably London and also New York, resulted in a boom in the fur industry with an accompanying increase in skills, technical ability and creativity.

As the new century dawned a Russian cultural epidemic swept Europe and America, initiated by the fur-collared impresario Serge Diaghilev. Commencing with his ground-breaking *Exhibition of Russian Art* held in Paris in 1906, then performances of Mussorgsky's opera *Boris Godunov*, featuring a fur-crowned Feodor Chaliapin in the title role, followed by successive seasons of his revolutionary Ballets Russes, audiences were introduced to music, art and design based on traditional Russian folklore and motifs. Most notably, the ballet and opera costumes

3-53 Revillon coat, *Gazette du Bon Ton*, 1922. This fashion plate shows a military-style cape, lined and trimmed with astrakhan in the typical 'Russian' style, popular in the 1920s and 1930s. Courtesy of the Rijksmuseum, Amsterdam. On loan from the M.A. Ghering-van Ierlant Collection

3-52 Francis Cotes (1726–1770), *The Right Hon. Lady Mary Radcliffe, Wife of Francis Eyre, Esq.*, 1755. Pastel on paper lined with canvas, 60.7 × 45.7 cm. The sitter wears a 'Turquerie' outfit including a peacock-blue mantle, decorated with gold and trimmed with ermine. The Cleveland Museum of Art. Gift of Edward B. Greene (1946.463)

designed by artists such as Roerich, Goncharova, Benois and Bakst were to have a spectacular effect on western fashion. While fur was sparingly used for the stage costumes, the overall aesthetic of pagan primitivism was translated into western fashionable language by the pervasive use of fur, supplying an instant Slavic chic that transformed the most mundane garments *à la Russe* (fig. 3-53). James Laver quotes a contemporary commentator on the craze, who noted: 'The dark rich touch of fur is seen on practically every description of coat, and, indeed, on all garments – even to nightgowns and pyjamas ... Everything is fur trimmed from our hats and handbags to our lingerie.'[78] Joining the established Russian furs, such as sable and ermine, more unusual skins including astrakhan and wolf became increasingly fashionable and were often advertised with the epithet 'Russian', as Laver again notes: 'One result of the Russian enthusiasm

3-54 *Roberta*, dir. William A. Seiter, 1935. Film still. Irene Dunne (left) plays Princess Stephanie, the émigré Russian designer of the Parisian fashion house, Roberta. Moviestore Collection/Shutterstock was to introduce several new materials for coats, such as Russian pony, a favourite trimming for which was grey opossum'.[79]

Swiftly following Diaghilev's cultural invasion, a further wave of Russian immigration was to have a marked effect on early twentieth-century fashion and its 'Russianisation'. So-called 'White Russians', a loose group of typically patrician, anti-Communist sympathisers, as a result of their defeat by the Red Army in the Russian Civil War, fled to Europe, most notably Paris and Berlin but also further afield to Shanghai and Istanbul. They established tightly knit communities in those cities, often around members of aristocratic families, who waited in exile until the old order was restored. This influx of a cultured Russian elite, which was perceived by a largely anti-Communist Europe and America as tragically disinherited, simultaneously chic, exotic and reassuringly conservative, increased the fascination for all things Russian. Many of these émigrés contributed to the period's cultural milieu becoming artists and designers, as noted by the magazine *Illustrated Russia*, published in Paris from 1924 to 1939:

> *A Russian émigré lady has shyly entered this city. There was a time when her mother and grandmother ordered their dresses from Worth and Poiret, but this young Russian woman has just escaped from the hell of the revolution and civil war! She has arrived in the capital of female elegance and knocked on the doors of a luxury maison de haute couture. And the massive doors opened to let her in and she has captured everyone's heart'.*[80]

This glamorous exile in turn fuelled the celluloid imaginings of Hollywood, resulting in a number of films of the 1930s featuring doomed, fur-clad White Russians, elegantly 'making do' in Paris and America.

The film *Roberta* from 1935 is a classic example, replete with Hollywood stars adopting thick accents, Parisian fashion houses, anti-Communist propaganda and swathes of Russian fur (fig. 3-54).[81] Ostensibly set in the French fashion house, Roberta, the film is a resolutely studio-bound realisation of 1930s Russian Furland, showcasing the talents of Fred Astaire, Ginger Rogers and Irene Dunne. The improbable plot relates the story of exiled White Russian Princess Stephanie (Dunne), the creative genius behind Roberta, her faithful retainer Prince Ladislaw (posing as a footman) and her encounter with 'America' in the guise of Fred Astaire and Ginger Rogers, who plays the phony 'Comtesse Scharwenka'. The true 'stars' of the show, however, are the furs and costumes, designed by Bernard Newman. At the Café Russe Stephanie, in ermine and pearl *kokoshnik* (the traditional Russian headdress), sings 'Smoke Gets in Your Eyes' accompanied by a balalaika orchestra, and later introduces the 'musical fashion show' wearing a 1930s version of eighteenth-century Russian court dress in satin and white Arctic fox. The fashion show includes an astrakhan coat, muff and Cossack-style hat, and for the evening two floor-length ermine and sable capes that require security in the form of liveried footmen to disrobe the models and guard the furs.

Some 30 years later another cinematic journey to Furland reflected a similar preoccupation with an imagined furry Russia. *Doctor Zhivago*, released in 1965, tapped into the West's cold war fascination with a vanished Russian Empire and an anti-establishment support for Communist ideology, which was in turn part of a larger, fashionably counter-cultural identification.[82] Zhivago's fur fantasies satisfied both sartorial directions, Communist and Imperial. The pre-Revolutionary option consisted of extravagant furs accessorised with the obligatory 'Cossack' or *papakha* hat. Traditionally made from shaggy skins such as bear, wolf or sheep in order to resist sabre blows, but following the Revolution made from a variety of materials, the *papakha*, when translated into a western fashion item, became a generic, round, brimless style made from any fur and in any colour. The 'Red Army' option of sartorial rebellion was most typically signified by the fashion for greatcoats and Russian army caps, preferably a furred *ushanka*, winter-style with earflaps,

3-55 *Doctor Zhivago*, dir. David Lean, 1965. Film still. Sharok Harami/Shutterstock

either newly fashioned or the genuine article obtained from the growing number of army surplus outlets and markets servicing the developing trend for military wear of all periods and countries. *Doctor Zhivago*, which won an Oscar for Best Costume for its designer Phyllis Dalton, offered a wardrobe of fantasy fur as authentically 'Russian' as the film's snowy wastes and ice-covered dacha, which was constructed from marble dust and coated beeswax and filmed primarily in Spain. The film fulfils all furry desires, from the dyed mink belonging to Zhivago's wife, to a gun-wielding Lara in black sable, and the fur-swaddled passion of Omar Sharif and Julie Christie as the perfect combination of foreign exoticism and 1960s 'swinging London', intermittently interrupted by Red Army urban chic as worn by Tom Courtenay and his comrades (fig. 3-55).

The pervasive influence of *Doctor Zhivago* can be gauged by the promotion of Jaeger coats that same year as 'the Zhivago look', 'quilted with Hussar-type fastening' and accessorised with white fox and black sable. More upmarket, the winter wedding maxi coatdress designed by Belinda Bellville for the couture label Bellville Sassoon in 1968 resonates with the influence of Zhivago, combined with that decade's other imagined Furland, *Camelot,* and its 1967 Arthurian imaginings (fig. 3-56). Made from ecru damask cloque, the floor-length coat features deep hems and cuffs of white Arctic fox and a detachable fur-trimmed hood. The coat's zip fastening is concealed beneath elaborate silver frogging and galloons, reminiscent of Russian hussars' uniforms and the border decorations of illuminated manuscripts.

As is well known, it was customary for designers to name individual garments in their collections after significant locations, characters and pastimes, and films again provide us with an example of this practice, paying homage to the period's frequent journeys to Russian Furland. The remarkable London couturier sisters, the Rahvis, were especially fond of this vestimentary territorialisation and in a documentary promoting their Russian-themed collection for Autumn/Winter 1966, the narrator suggests it was 'mostly inspired by recent films' and included outfits with names such as *To Russia with Love, Grand Duchess, Tsarina, Russian Lullaby, Commissar, Trotsky, Red Star* and *Samovar*, describing chinchilla-trimmed suits, coats edged with Arctic fox and a reversible silver cloque coat lined in natural wild mink, accessorised with Russian boots and Cossack hats in fur.[83]

Russia as a locale for furry fantasy has continued to fire the imaginations of fashion designers to the present day, most notably that of Yves Saint Laurent and his 'ethnically' inspired collections of the 1970s and 1980s. Here he regularly used fur as a multicultural signifier, especially in his celebrated 'Russian' haute couture collection for Autumn/Winter 1976, which was replete with fur-clad matryoshka (nesting) dolls and tsarinas topped off with turbans, headscarves, fezzes, 'Cossack' hats and Tartary helmets. Ulyana Sergeenko is the most recent reincarnation of the Russian fashion designer in Paris (fig. 3-57). As a guest member of the Fédération de la Haute Couture, she creates garments of oligarchic excess for the partners of Russia's modern-day boyars, rising on sable clouds from the ashes of the Soviet Republic. Her brand of international Russian luxe – part pre-Revolutionary Romanov spectacle, part Dietrich in *The Scarlet Empress*, and part hyper-sexualised Muscovite – comprises the new national costume of an imagined land, where Mother Russia wears a mink headscarf, hand-carved wooden high heels and a sable-lined greatcoat.

As fanciful and atemporal as the Furlands of Turkey and Russia may be, a sense of discrete geographical location is maintained, albeit across epochs and expressed by the reimagining of the clothing of vastly differing inhabitants of these lands, from pashas to peasants and from tsarinas to Bolsheviks. At the same time as Zhivago mania was gripping the 1960s, a more pervasive form of vestimentary cultural appropriation was becoming the norm, and began to dominate the maps of Furland assuming the magnitude of continents and recognised by the name 'ethnic'. Philosopher Michel Foucault suggested in a lecture given in 1967 that 'we are in an epoch of simultaneity,

3-56 Bellville Sassoon, ensemble, 1968. Britain; silk with silver and cream frogging, Arctic fox fur trim and fur-lined detachable hood. Victoria and Albert Museum, London

3-57 Ulyana Sergeenko, ensemble, Haute Couture, Autumn/Winter 2012. Wool and sable. Fairchild Archive/Penske Media/Shutterstock

COAT 127

we are in the epoch of juxtaposition, the epoch of the near and far, of the side by side, of the dispersed'.[84] It is this juxtaposition that characterised the 'pick 'n' mix' approach to distinct forms of cultural dress, which influenced both high street and high fashion at the time, especially in its use of fur.

The remarkable fashion editorial entitled 'The Great Fur Caravan', which appeared in American Vogue in October 1966 (one year before Foucault gave his lecture), is an early example of this cultural bricolage (fig. 3-58). Running to some 26 pages and featuring the talents of Richard Avedon, Veruschka, fashion editor Polly Mellen (although the spread has often been credited to editor-in-chief Diana Vreeland) and hairdresser Ara Gallant, the 'fashion adventure' starts with Veruschka travelling in a 'pale mink windbreaker' on the bullet train from Kyoto to Tokyo,

3-58 'The Great Fur Caravan', American Vogue, October 1966. Courtesy of the author

bound for the 'strange secret snow country of Japan'.[85] The shoot was purported to have cost $1 million and showcased furs from the most inventive furriers of the day, including Emeric Partos, Georges Kaplan and Revillon, and fur accessories by the likes of Halston, Adolfo and Roger Vivier.

The eclectic range of garments that travelled north from Tokyo in a fleet of limousines 'downy inside with a treasure of furs', and which inspired the copy writer Mary Evans to suggest 'there's not been a caravan like this in Asia since Marco Polo', included a multicultural, ahistorical collision of smocks, redingotes, a burnoose, a windbreaker, toques, hoods, ponchos and a coif.[86] The furs, equally global in origin, comprised sealskin, ermine, mink, sheepskin, Russian lynx, chinchilla, snow leopard, fox and goatskin. Partnering Veruschka in the shoot was 'a giant of mythological proportions', an amateur sumo champion some two meters (seven feet) tall, suitably exoticised and indeed eroticised throughout, likened to a horse in its training stable and possessing a body that 'was straight and hard'.[87] On their journeys to places such as 'The Valley of Hell' and a landscape of 'sleek black deviltry where the air smells of sulphur and pine and melting snow', Veruschka in 'savage furs' becomes various characters in turn: a Mongol warrior; a Noh performer with blonde Dynel wig and a mask with eyes delineated as 'long expressionless slits'; a disco diva on a Japanese dance floor; a fox woman; a 'Tartar chief's baby girl'; a dutiful shrine worshipper, and companion to an ermine-hooded child styled for the shoot as an evocation of a *jizo*, or wayside guardian.[88] Foucault's model of the heterotopia provides a key to understanding this period's iteration of Furland as 'capable of juxtaposing in a single real place several spaces, several sites that are in themselves incompatible.'[89]

This incompatibility would continue to be the hallmark of designers, not only those working in fur but also those who regularly explored, or as it was increasingly considered, exploited, the dress of cultures other than their own. The fashionable, furry heterotopia has found successive cartographers including John Galliano at Dior, where both temporal and spatial incompatibility triumphed. But perhaps the most consistent visitor to Furland has been Jean Paul Gaultier, whose numerous expeditions to Mongolia, China, Mexico, Russia, India and the Arctic regions merged with a gender-defying Parisian legacy of the nightclub and revue bar to provide some of the most sustained and spectacular visions of multivalent, globalised fur. Of his many explorations his haute couture collection of Autumn/Winter 1997, titled *Le Grande Voyage*, has accrued equal measures of praise and subsequent criticism. To the sounds of Tuvan (southern Siberian) nomadic throat-singing, a Chinese children's chorus and accordion music, Gaultier's Trans-Siberian expeditionary party included Mongolian guides, Tibetan monks and Chinese empresses, teetering on modern-day chopines and wearing fur, embroidered skins, pinstripe suiting, silk brocade and 'Peruvian' knit. The direct references to the clothing of Inuit peoples, including the parka, was perhaps the most memorable aspect of the collection compounded by the Icelandic singer Björk. In her only runway appearance she appeared as a diminutive Arctic spirit, dressed in a fur and animal skin jacket with the designer's initials branded onto the front in the form of a Chinese logogram. Extravagantly fur-lined and hooded parkas would re-emerge in another of Gaultier's most intense and visceral visits to Furland: his Autumn/Winter 2008 collection, a controversial clash of Inuit and First Nations references that transformed models into part-trapper, part-animal incarnations swathed in animal skins, some left raw, some exquisitely sheared, wearing stuffed animal heads and accessories sprouting tails and claws (see fig. 5-7). The soundtrack, which mixed Michael Jackson's *Thriller*, the howls, bleats and growls of animals, and excerpts from Prokofiev's *Peter and the Wolf*, provided an additional aural soundscape to this most animistic of collections.

Inuit-inspired fashion had a remarkably early, albeit brief, flowering at the beginning of the twentieth century, coinciding with the great era of polar exploration. As discussed by curator Patricia Mears, a radical initiative to foster a specifically American, as opposed to European-influenced, design aesthetic brought together prominent ethnographers and emerging fashion and textile designers in the 1910s, to produce collections inspired by museum objects.[90] Actively promoted by 'M.D.C.' Crawford, an amateur textile enthusiast and editor at *Women's Wear Daily*, amongst the garments produced were Kamchatkan and Siberian style coats made of animal skins and sinews, and a somewhat less authentic range of designs by Max Meyer that utilised decorative elements drawn from traditional Koryak motifs to embellish fur-trimmed garments typical of the fashionable silhouettes of the First World War period.

It is appropriate that western fashion's journeys to Furland end with the most widely recognisable, inspiring and appropriated-Inuit garment, the parka, as its most treasured souvenir. Since the first contact with Inuit people, whether for the purposes of trade, colonisation or latterly exploration, the West has acknowledged the remarkable understanding of fur and skin represented by this garment in terms of its construction, practicality, thermal regulation and economy aside from its aesthetic power. The parka, as traditionally made and worn by Inuit peoples, describes a hip-length coat, cut straight across the bottom, and typically made from seal or caribou skin. The *amauti* is the female version of the male parka but with the addition of front and back apron flaps, the back flap long enough to sit on, and with a larger hood and baby pouch. Many variations on these traditional patterns exist, including the types of animal skin used and the applied decoration, and as with all Inuit clothing they can indicate where the wearer comes from, their age, sex and marital status.

All Inuit clothing is symmetrical with the middle of the animal skin being the middle of the front or back of the garment, echoing Dorothy Burnham's 'skin memory' discussed in 'Modern Primitives' (p. 81). Women and girls are solely responsible for the manufacture of Inuit clothing and traditionally each garment is 'tailor made' to fit the individual. In summer the parka is worn single-layered with fur to the inside; in winter a second garment is added over the top with the fur turned to the outside, trapping warm air between the two layers of clothing and the body, providing excellent insulation against the cold (see fig. 4-16).

In addition to inspiring high fashion, the parka was adapted for use in the 1950s by the American military for soldiers stationed in cold climates, and later for Scandinavian mountain rescue teams (see fig. 3-74). Both the 'snorkel' parka – with its tunnel-like opening for the face, left after the fur-lined hood is fully zipped up against the cold weather – and the 'fishtail' parka, with its characteristic longer pointed back, were made from industrial grade fabrics instead of animal skin and fur. Both retained the fur-lined hood, originally wolverine for its frost resisting properties, although this also gave way eventually to synthetic fur. As with so many items of military dress, the appearance of the parka in army surplus clothing outlets led to it being adopted by successive subcultural groups, most notably in the 1960s by the mods, who found them especially suitable as protection when riding scooters. It could be argued that the fishtail parka, along with the MA-1 flight jacket and Fred Perry tennis shirt, remains the archetypal subcultural garment as seen on mods, punks, skinheads and numerous less defined groups. Today the parka has trickled up from the street, along with so many subcultural styles, to high-end fashion, which increasingly looks to the street for its 'downwards' direction (fig. 3-59).

3-59 Parka-style pullover jacket, late 20th century. Cotton with fur (rabbit?) trim. Courtesy of the Westminster Menswear Archive, University of Westminster, London

3-60 KTZ, sweatshirt and pants, Autumn/Winter collection, 2015. Fairchild Archive/Penske Media/Shutterstock

A parka was at the centre of one of the more recent cases of contested cultural appropriation. For its Autumn/Winter 2015 menswear collection, the London-based label KTZ duplicated an Inuit parka design on a fur sweatshirt (fig. 3-60). The distinctive pattern had been created by the Inuit shaman Aua in 1922, after receiving a vision that he would be drowned. The design of hands and human figures, originally executed in caribou skin, was meant to provide him with protection against his fate. The parka had been illustrated in books and in the 2006 film *The Journals of Knud Rasmussen*, which recreates the encounter between Danish explorer Rasmussen and the Inuit people including Aua (his great-granddaughter assumes this is where KTZ's designer Marjan Pejoski must have seen it). The runway version of the parka was subsequently reproduced in towelling and sold for £500, until KTZ was forced to apologise to Aua's relative and withdraw the design from production. Other designs included one resembling a woman's *amauti*, which had been decorated with a circular KTZ logo mimicking Gaultier's similar 'branding' of traditional dress 18 years earlier. Perhaps more disconcerting than these uncredited cultural duplications and references was the context in which the parka was positioned. The collection was described as 'Inuit meets *A Clockwork Orange*', Stanley Kubrick's film of 1971 providing the inspiration for 'Inuit' parkas accessorised with bowler hats and 'bovver boots', while on the KTZ website the collection is accompanied by key phrases such as 'English Villain', 'To Meet the Inuit People' and 'Taking Innocence From Others'.[91]

Furland knows no boundaries and is multi-directional, as is its clothing. Although this subsection has concentrated on the influence of indigenous dress on western fashion, conversely, indigenous dress is influenced by western culture. In the collection of the McCord Museum in Montreal is a widow's *amauti* from the late nineteenth century, made from sealskin and fur. What is remarkable about this parka is that it is embellished with trade items as evidence of the contact between Inuit people and non-aboriginal whalers and traders. Decorating the back of the garment are American one cent pieces dating from 1848 to 1855, while on the front glass beads, lead drops and a row of spoons run vertically down its centre, making this a definitive example of the clothing of Furland. Such clothing has the 'property of being in relation with all the other sites, but in such a way as to suspect, neutralize, or invert the set of relations that they happen to designate, mirror, or reflect'.[92]

IN BLACK AND WHITE AND COLOUR

In *The Public is Never Wrong*, the 1953 autobiography of the movie mogul Adolph Zukor, he relates how – as a Hungarian Jewish immigrant to America in the 1890s – he learned the fur trade and describes his first success making fox fur neckpieces from a single skin, complete with head: 'Each fur scarf had a hook and eye or some other clasp to hold the ends together around the shoulders. I invented a spring that allowed the mouth to open and close, making the mouth itself a clasp'.[93] This invention led to the formation of Zukor's Novelty Fur Company. With the aid of various partners and by navigating the caprices of fashionable fur at the time, Zukor eventually made a 'killing' when in 1902 he correctly predicted that red fox was going to be the fashionable fur of the season. At the age of 30, his fortune was estimated to be somewhere between $100,000 and $200,000. It was at this time that Zukor began to divert his attention to the burgeoning entertainment industry and invested in a penny arcade on East 14th Street at Broadway, where amongst the automatic fortune-tellers, punch bags and a shooting gallery was a row of peep machines showing 30-second dramas. So successful was this enterprise that by 1903 Zukor expanded the business to Newark, Philadelphia and Boston, and 'decided to close out the fur business to devote full energies to the arcades'.[94] His ability to predict what the public wanted, as demonstrated in the fur business, he now applied to what would become the motion picture industry. However, as has been suggested, profit may not have been Zukor's sole motivation: 'He felt his social mobility was blocked by the fur business; no matter how much wealth he accumulated, he would still be associated with something unmistakably Jewish, as the fur trade was, and slightly déclassé, as all the garment trades were.'[95]

Zukor, who went on to found Paramount Pictures in 1912, is but one of the seminal Hollywood figures – directors, actors and photographers – who can trace their lineage back to the fur industry. Jerry Schatzberg, born to Jewish furriers in the Bronx in 1927, went on to create some of the most memorable fashion images of the late 1950s and his directorial debut in 1970, *Puzzle of a Downfall Child* starring Faye Dunaway, remains one of the great underrated films made about the fashion industry. Richard Jaeckel, one of Hollywood's best-known character actors who had a career spanning some 50 years, came from fur royalty as the son of one half of the New York furriers H. Jaeckel & Sons (see p. 99). His father (also called Richard) moved to Los Angeles in 1934 to expand the business, which would eventually number Hollywood stars such as Marilyn Monroe amongst its illustrious clientele.

In light of the recent decision by Los Angeles and West Hollywood to go fur-free (see 'I'd Rather Go Hairless', p. 30), possibly soon to be joined by New York City, it is ironic to reflect on the key role the fur industry has played in the establishment of Hollywood, and in particular the role cinema has played in the promotion and popular perception of fur, from its infancy until the present day (fig. 3-61). As cultural theorist and author Elizabeth Wilson has observed, cinema was 'influential in creating new ways for men and women to move, dance, dress, make love, *be*', and, one might add, it increased the allure of fur via the construction of aspirational images of fur-wearing screen idols.[96] Film both reflected and initiated fashions in fur, especially those that contributed to a specific black-and-white form of glamour. Longer-haired, pale or white furs, which framed famous screen faces and photographed well, became fashionable. Skunk was favoured for its startling black-and-white

contrast, as were patterned furs such as leopard and ocelot, which created bold graphic statements when filmed in black and white. Furs such as silver and Arctic fox, white mink and ermine, became especially popular during the 1920s and 1930s, the great period of Hollywood dressing as Wilson describes it. A classic example is the glamorous ermine coat created for Anna May Wong (see fig. 3-27).

Historian Anne Hollander describes these black-and-white fantasies, suggesting they 'were built on the newly powerful sensuality of colorless texture in motion in which American dreams were now being acted out. For women's clothes, sequins, marabou, white net, and black lace developed a fresh intensity of sexual meaning in the world of colorless fantasy.'[97] Fur provided another level of primitive sexual intensity, especially when juxtaposed with the shimmering and diaphanous fabrics that she lists.

During the late 1930s another pale fur hit the headlines when, in 1937, two platinum fox pelts, as they became known, fetched a record auction price of

3-61 Joan Crawford, 1930. Publicity photograph. This image represents perfectly the alliance between fur and the glamorous cinematic image-making associated with the Golden Age of Hollywood. George Hurrell/MGM/Kobal/Shutterstock

$1,000 each, as opposed to the average $25 for standard silver fox pelts. The mutant strain of the silver fox was first recorded on a Norwegian fur farm in 1933 when, amongst a litter of six silver foxes, a remarkably light grey cub named 'Mons' was born, with extensive white markings. Platinum fox, characterised by its striking pale fur, was given an immediate fashion boost when the Duchess of Windsor wore a pair at a public appearance in Paris in 1939. A press photograph captured the occasion, showing the Duchess draped in the distinctive furs, anxiously observed by the ex-king, the Duke of Windsor, standing at her side.

Such was the vogue for fox fur that, ironically, even in an age characterised by a monochrome elegance constructed on black and white film, it became fashionable to dye fox a variety of surprising colours, including 'cinnamon' and 'poppy', a trend meta-cinematically referred to in the film *Singin' in the Rain* (1952).[98] The film charts Hollywood's transition from silent to 'talkies' in the 1920s, and includes in its 'Beautiful Girl' musical number, featuring 'living fashion plates', models wearing green fur-trimmed pyjamas and an evening cape trimmed with shocking pink fox. As commented on in the lyrics: 'If you must wear fox to the opera, dame fashion says dye it.'[99] From the 1920s onwards and assisted by the advances made in synthetic dyes, fur has periodically changed its colour, initially as a celebration of artificiality and the technical ability that allowed a leopard to change its spots or mink to turn pink (see 'The F Word', p. 151). Even in films of the 1960s, such as *What a Way to Go!*, this earlier period of fashionably dyed fur was still affectionately evoked (fig. 3-62). But increasingly, as

3-62 *What a Way to Go!*, dir. J. Lee Thompson, 1964. Film still. Shirley MacLaine, as Louisa May Foster, appears in a pink-saturated wedding sequence for her marriage to Hollywood star Pinky Benson. Although the film was made in the 1960s, her costume designed by Edith Head evoked an earlier period of fashionably dyed fur. Don Brinn/AP/Shutterstock

3-63 Tom Ford, coat for Yves Saint Laurent, 2002. Dyed fox fur. A recreation of a coat from the Yves Saint Laurent Spring/Summer 1971 Haute Couture collection. Cavan Pawson/Evening Standard/Shutterstock

3-64 FAR LEFT Swakara fur (karakul). The fur is dyed and embroidered using an intarsia technique to resemble an African landscape seen from the air. Courtesy of Kopenhagen Fur and Mikkel Østergaard Schou

3-65 LEFT Mink 'petals'. Dyed and embellished, fur can even resemble an Impressionist garden. Courtesy of Kopenhagen Fur and Mikkel Østergaard Schou

the anti-fur lobby grew in numbers and became more vociferous, colour became a means of disguising the real as fake. Yves Saint Laurent's celebrated Spring/Summer haute couture collection of 1971, titled *Libération* (or *Happy Hooker* as it was dubbed by a horrified fashion press), anticipated this now common trend (fig. 3-63). In his influential collection, which crystallised the 1970s love affair with the 1930s and 1940s, and that same decade's music-inspired glam rock/camp style, were crêpe dresses hung with fox furs and a short 1940s-style boxy fox jacket dyed a vivid emerald green, a garment that has continued to inspire subsequent creative directors of the house and a roster of contemporary designers.

An article entitled 'Fur For All' appeared in American *Vogue* in September 1990. Reporting on that season's designs, it describes fur as being worked like fabric, made into unconventionally casual styles and dyed every colour of the rainbow: 'From Arnold Scassi's peach mink jackets and boleros that could have walked off a Hollywood set to Claude Montana's neon brights borrowed from Warhol paintings, color explodes in fur.'[100] Today, fur is dyed, stencilled and painted in every conceivable colour and can mimic a bewildering array of textures. Mikkel Østergaard Schou, Kopenhagen Fur's creative lead furrier, is sought after by leading fashion houses around the world for his skill in using fur as a palette on which to produce everything from camouflage to an Impressionist painting, including the sample of dyed mink used for the cover of this book (figs 3-64, 3-65).

Since the advent of cinema, the fashion and film industries have enjoyed a mutually beneficial relationship, becoming increasingly co-dependant. Contemporary commercial cinema's reliance on product placement is only the most recent iteration of a partnership where, fundamentally, films sell clothes and clothes sell films. Nowhere has this relationship been more effective than in film's promotion of the fur industry, and until the 1970s and the rise of the anti-fur movement, mainstream cinema has made visible the aspirational, erotic and at times dangerous potential of fur. Hollywood furriers and fur retailers feature prominently in a number of seminal films from the 1950s and 1960s, the key period of American fur consumption. The promotion of New York department store Bergdorf Goodman and its famous fur salon in the film *That Touch of Mink* is a prime example of plot lines centred around fur. The symbiotic relationship between fur, fashion and film is made explicit in the film's closing credits, which include: 'Our special thanks to Norman Norell for special fashions, Leo Ritter for Miss Day's furs, Cardinal Clothes for Cary Grant's suits, and Bergdorf Goodman for being Bergdorf Goodman.'[101]

Mirroring developments in fashionable fur, by the 1940s it was mink, more than any other fur, that took centre stage in mainstream cinema's furry fictions, a shift in taste in fur that has remained more or less unassailable to the present day, positioning the mink coat at the pinnacle of esteem and desire. As J.G. Links, the furrier and later art historian, declared in 1956, 'The very word has acquired a connotation far beyond that of a fur; there can hardly be a newspaper or magazine issued in which the word mink does not appear in some context. It is used in derision and in admiration, to suggest elegance and to suggest vulgarity, to arouse envy and to arouse scorn.'[102] Amongst many memorable and possibly vulgar movie minks, the jewel-lined mink evening dress worn by Ginger Rogers in the film *Lady in the Dark* (1944) was reported at the time to be the most expensive film costume ever made, estimated at $35,000. Both the costume and the film itself was widely criticised at the time for its extravagance, being produced at the height of the Second World War (fig. 3-66).[103]

The mink is a medium-sized, aquatic, carnivorous member of the weasel family, with two distinct species: the larger American mink (recently re-classified with its own genus of *Neovison*) and the European mink (genus *Mustela*). So pervasive is the reputation of mink in popular consciousness, due in no small part to its representation on film, that it is hard to imagine a time when mink was not in favour. However, its comparatively recent domination of the fur industry can be gauged by the fact that seminal texts such as J.C. Sachs's *Furs and the Fur Trade* of 1930 make no mention of mink at all, and Richard Davey's classic *Furs and Fur Garments* of 1895 apologetically adds this about mink: 'I must not omit to mention ... another fur which, if not so highly esteemed, is nevertheless, very useful'.[104] Davey continues to note historical attempts

3-66 *Lady in the Dark*, dir. Mitchell Leisen, 1944. Film still. C. J. Tavin/Everett/Shutterstock

to establish '*minkeries*' but 'the fur of the tame mink had so deteriorated as to be comparatively useless', while Frank Ashbrook's *Fur-Farming for Profit* of 1928 devotes some 85 pages to fox farming, but only ten to mink, stating that 'no large number of persons are engaged in raising minks' and that 'wild minks are not only difficult to obtain but they do not respond readily to good treatment in captivity', all of which highlights the enormous impact the development of successful mink farming has had on the fur industry.[105]

Although minks have been bred in captivity for some considerable time, the first attempts in North America were recorded during the Civil War, and in

Canada, in Ontario, in the 1870s; it was during the 1930s that mink farming escalated both in America and Europe. The publication of the first edition of *The Mink Book* by the Fur Trade Journal of Canada appeared in 1937. Its opening paragraph reads: 'Today mink ranching belongs to the world' and is being 'carried on in every province in Canada, in many of the United States, in Great Britain and Europe'.[106] The 1930s also saw the formation of the Danish and Finnish fur breeders associations, which would lead to Scandinavia and, in particular, Kopenhagen Fur, today being the leading global marketplace for buying and selling mink with an annual turnover exceeding $1 billion, while farmed mink continues to be the most important fur type produced in North America.

The potential profit to be made from the increasing demand for mink finds one of its most singular expositions in the 1953 film *The Lady Wants Mink* (see fig. 2-35).[107] In the film a suburban housewife, Nora, has everything she desires – a loving husband and adorable children – but her state of 1950s American, consumer-driven wedded bliss is disrupted by her wealthier neighbour Gladys and her new sapphire mink coat. The coat triggers an obsessive desire for mink in Nora, an obsession her husband with his modest income cannot satisfy. So after much deliberation, Nora decides to move to the country and obtain her own coat – by rearing live minks. Naturally, once she is living a rural existence the aspirational significance of fur becomes meaningless, and facing the challenges of mink farming she rediscovers that she already possesses the greatest gift, a loving, supportive spouse. As a representation of both mid-twentieth-century America's obsession with mink and the growing economic importance of fur farming, the film retains a unique position in the cinema of fur.[108]

Nora's comedic attempts to establish her mink farm give no indication of the billion-dollar enterprise that mink farming would represent to both American and European economies. Kopenhagen Fur, owned by a co-operative of some 1,500 Danish fur farmers, has become the leading global marketplace for buying and selling skins, and Denmark is the largest producer of high quality mink with an output of 17 million skins a year (fig. 3-67). Their recent Welfur initiative and certification scheme is an attempt to ensure that animal welfare is prioritised and since 2020 only famers who achieve the appropriate Welfur standards are allowed to sell their skins at Kopenhagen Fur's auctions.[109] As a model of sustainability mink farming is impressive, an example of a circular economy where, after skinning, mink carcasses are used for animal feed, the fat produces mink oil which is important in both the medical and cosmetic industries, and any waste material is converted into biofuel. In turn minks are fed on the heads, feet and guts of chicken and fish, left over from the processing of chicken nuggets and fish sticks.

The model of efficiency apparent on Danish mink farms is matched by the scale and precision of the grading and sorting systems devised to prepare the skins for auction (fig. 3-68). Kopenhagen Fur grades the mink pelts it auctions according to nine different classifications, including type (main, rare and very rare), size, colour, clarity and hair length. In addition there are four quality grades – Purple, Platinum, Burgundy and Ivory – with purple being the premium grade. This is designated to skins that are characterised by their lightness and silkiness, with extra fine guard hairs and dense, full underfur. Farmed mink has now been bred to produce a full spectrum of colours from white, beige, grey and brown to black. Pure black is rare in Scandinavian-bred mink due to dietary regulations, whereas in the United States mink are still fed on a protein-rich diet, which, allied with the presence of original genetic stock, results in pure black fur. Included in the 24 colours listed by Kopenhagen Fur are the evocatively named 'Stardust' (black underfur with silver-grey longer hair), 'Dawn' (mid-to-pale pink/brown) and 'Jaguar' (a spotted black and white hybrid). Currently bolstered by the Chinese demand for fur, mink farming is still a viable business model. However, in the face of growing calls for a ban on fur farming, to which many European countries including the United Kingdom have already responded, the steadily rising number of fashion designers who have renounced fur, and competition from unregulated international fur farming, American and European mink farming as it currently operates is unlikely to survive much further into the twenty-first century.

Prior to the late twentieth century's prevailing anti-fur sentiments, narrative constructions, whether literary or cinematic, reflected the economic and libidinal power of the mink coat. As a status symbol, a sign of 'having made it', on film the mink coat was unassailable, and its economic value rarely challenged – the garment is always 'worth' something. But if its monetary value goes unquestioned, it is often acquired by an additional emotional, sexual or moral expenditure. Literature, conversely, often interrogates fur's actual price and its ability to maintain its value, as well as its emotional expenditure.

Two short stories by Truman Capote – *A Mink of One's Own* (1944) and *The Bargain* (1950) – were written at the peak of the mid-twentieth-century American desire for mink.[110] Both tales describe visits to comfortable middle-class women by former acquaintances. Now in straightened circumstances, the reason for the visits of the once-sophisticated, Paris-residing Vini Rondo in the earlier story and the bohemian, liberated Alice Severn in the later one, is to sell their mink coats, which once added to their former allure but now, as the stories reveal, have deteriorated considerably along with their owners. The decline of both the guests and their mink coats causes Mrs Munson and Mrs Chase considerable embarrassment, as they feel coerced into purchasing the furs. At the close of the stories, both coats are revealed as virtually worthless, as indeed their assumed friendships had been. Mrs Munson, realising her coat is rotten, declares 'I've been taken and taken good' while Mrs Chase realises her coat too is worthless after she had 'rubbed her hand against the lusterless, balding fur' that 'was mouldy, sour, as though it had lain in an attic by the seashore.'[111]

3-67 Mink farm, Strøby, Denmark. Courtesy Kopenhagen Fur/the author

3-68 Mink skins awaiting grading, Kopenhagen Fur, Glostrup, Denmark. Courtesy Kopenhagen Fur/the author

F. Scott Fitzgerald's *The Pearl and the Fur*, written in 1936, reflects the fashions of the time as it is chinchilla, rather than mink, that is the story's subject. However, this fur's 'value' is as unstable as the mink's in the later Capote stories.[112] The teenage Gwen discovers a chinchilla cape in the back of taxi cab and on returning it to its wealthy owner is rewarded with the offer of foreign travel, but on condition that she acts as the owner's companion. Feeling that this offer had too many strings attached, she accepts a mere $200. At the conclusion to the story Gwen attempts to give this sum, far below the cape's true value, to the young cab driver who she has witnessed being mistreated by the affluent friends of the cape's owner. Here the fur becomes a commodity, whose exchange value fluctuates and is ultimately worthless in Gwen's opinion, much as the fabled pearl of the story's title had been to her father.

The value of fur preoccupied lesser-known writers as well as celebrated authors such as Fitzgerald and Capote. In the 1943 three-act play *The Fur Coat* by Archibald Macdonell (now remembered chiefly for the satirical novel *England, Their England*) the declining value of a mink coat is clearly indicated.[113] The somewhat old fashioned comedy of manners concerns a philandering playwright, his actress wife and her admirers, and has a plot that revolves around a mink coat, which is bought, unlawfully pawned, given as an extra marital inducement and then restored to its original owner, the actress Theodora. To Theodora her coat, bought for 800 guineas (£36,000 today), is a substitute for her faithless, impecunious husband, who pawns the coat and receives half of its true value. For Theodora the coat has now been sullied and rendered worthless, less even than the devalued pawnbroker's price: 'My lovely, lovely coat! Lying at this moment in the filthy corner of some foul pawnbroker's, being touched by repulsive hands, by disgusting brutes.'[114] In these literary examples, as in many others, it seems that mink is unable to hold its value, or that its value is unstable, a commodity that is only worth what it can be exchanged for at any one time, and so it joins its cinematic counterparts as the 'worthless mink'.

Amongst the many celebrated Hollywood furriers it is perhaps Al Teitelbaum who can provide a fitting and suitably meta-textual conclusion to this brief account of fictional mink. Known as 'the furrier to the stars', Teitelbaum dressed many of Hollywood's most glamorous celebrities during the 1940s and 1950s, with shops in Palm Springs and on Rodeo Drive in Beverly Hills. His numerous film credits range from classics such as *Bell, Book and Candle*, where his furs complemented Jean Louis's costume designs for Kim Novak and other cast members, to obscure, but for this subsection, pertinent, productions such as *Miss Mink of 1949*.[115] Teitelbaum's chequered career also saw him managing Hollywood's star tenor Mario Lanza at the height of his alcoholism and manufacturing a highly successful line in fur novelties, a sideline that often proved more profitable than his regular fur business. This mirrors the early career of Adolph Zukor, the other Jewish furrier turned producer, with whom this subsection began. It was for *Miss Mink of 1949* that Teitelbaum produced a mink-lined bathtub for a scene that never made it to the final cut, one of many other fur-covered items he made for films and private clients (see 'Furnishing', p. 182). His loyal clientele included Marilyn Monroe, Joan Crawford and Paulette Goddard for whom he made a leopard skin-lined raincoat. He also specialised in fur menswear: 'For hubby, Teitelbaum turns out a galyak [fur obtained from premature or stillborn lambs] suit featuring a cardigan jacket and trousers that hold a good crease'.[116] He also made a pair of peach-dyed ermine trunks for celebrity professional wrestler George Raymond Wagner aka 'Gorgeous George'. Teitelbaum was adept at dyeing fur unusual colours to satisfy the individual tastes of his more flamboyant patrons.

Teitelbaum would have faded into complete obscurity if not for a notorious court case and its subsequent incorporation into a short story by James Ellroy, the American crime fiction writer (see fig. 3-69). In 1956 Teitelbaum was accused of staging a fake robbery in order to claim the insurance. He testified that he was held at gunpoint while armed robbers

escaped with $28,000-worth of furs. Despite calling on celebrity character witnesses, including Mario Lanza and Joan Crawford, he was sentenced to a year in jail, commuted to six months. In 1999 Ellroy published a collection of short stories including 'Tijuana Mon Amour', which in characteristic, profane, 'jive-talking', staccato style conflates the true story of Teitelbaum's fraud with an hallucinatory plot involving robbery, murder, prostitution, drug addiction and fur 'fencing', as the dealing in stolen furs was termed.[117] The story is acted out by a cast of characters including Teitelbaum, described as 'a furtive fur merchant', Frank Sinatra and Sammy Davis Jr. The celebrity felons 'manhandled minks and moved them out fast' to the waiting 'minkmobile', and after shooting the 'real' robbers they wrap the bodies in fur declaring the scene a 'massacre in mink'.[118] Teitelbaum, 84 years old

3-69 *The Big Heat*, dir. Fritz Lang, 1953. Film still. The fictional distillation of fur and violence that characterises films, such as *The Big Heat*, and literature, such as James Ellroy's fur-laden crime fantasies, mirrors the activities of real life Hollywood furriers, namely Al Teitelbaum. Courtesy of the author

at the time it was published, attempted to sue Condé Nast for $20,000,000 (the story originally appeared in *GQ* magazine, owned by Condé Nast) as, in addition to the bogus robbery, Ellroy portrays Teitelbaum naked in bed with Barbara Graham, a real-life murderer who was executed in 1955, and actress Linda Lansing, whom Ellroy suggests Teitelbaum used to model and subsequently 'fence' his 'stolen' furs. Needless to say, due to his less than spotless past the libel case was settled out of court for an undisclosed sum and Teitelbaum's other possible criminal activities remain unverified. It is perhaps fitting to leave Teitelbaum at the height of his fame, with the words that close a 1950 article entitled 'He Makes Mink Telephones', which was devoted to the fur novelties he made for his famous fur lovers: 'He's made his mark in mink, all right'.[119]

THE FORCE OF FUR

In November 1977 American *Vogue* published an editorial entitled 'The "Force" of Fur', featuring the season's latest furs modelled by Jerry Hall and Maria Hanson together with characters from that year's blockbuster hit film *Star Wars* (fig. 3-70).[120] The contrast between the voluminous, soft and 'primitive' furs and the futuristic metallic and plastic 'skins' of C-3PO, Darth Vader and the Imperial Stormtroopers is startling, initially registering as a purely visual, playful device. In addition to the feature's superficial glamour, however, are deeper indicators of the modes of production, consumption and development of fashionable fur in the latter half of the nineteenth and twentieth centuries.

The article's clash of the ancient with the new, the natural with the artificial, not only acknowledges the symbiotic relationship between fur and film discussed previously, but also offers an insight into the epistemic nature of fashioned fur, which along with most luxury products is both the product of, and the catalyst for, technological innovation. Key to this correlation is the concept of volume, whether understood in terms of scale, number, or capacity. The article uses volume as a metaphor throughout from the implied degree or prowess indicated by its title (which paraphrases the famous *Star Wars* maxim 'feel the force') to the record-breaking success of the box office hit. In addition, the spread features 'super' models with 'big hair' (achieved without the use of extensions) wearing that season's 'big furs'. The copy makes constant reference to the fur coats' 'new proportion', 'long hairs', 'bigger shapes'; it celebrates 'more ease, more luxe, more fur'.[121] Whether a souvenir of one of Yves Saint Laurent's expeditions to Furland in the form of a mink described as 'Chinoiserie' with 'passementerie closings', a Pierre Cardin fox coat with knitted sleeves, or a 'wrap and tie' mink coat with a big 'pull-up sable collar that puts fur where it's most

3-70 'The "Force" of Fur', American *Vogue*, November 1977. Courtesy of the author

appealing – all around the face!', the article relentlessly emphasises excess, density and volume.[122]

As discussed previously, the development of fur garments has been both practical, in terms of thermal benefit and the availability of suitable fur-bearing animals, and social, as an indicator of status and economic position. As standards of architecture and domestic arrangements improved, the thermal properties of fur became less important, its focus shifting to aesthetic, fashionable and aspirational display. This function too became less significant from the sixteenth century onwards as alternative forms of self-fashioning became available. Fur continued to retain its significance as an official mark or status for royalty, the aristocracy and those in high office, but became increasingly less dominant as a component of everyday dress in the fashionable western world, especially for those living in more temperate climates.

Fur would not regain its popularity, nor would it attract a similar level of technical innovation and ingenuity in its deployment as dress, until the latter half of the nineteenth century. Its revival was due to a number of coinciding factors, centred once more on its thermal properties, and on scale and volume as the characteristics of the period's industrialisation, accompanied by the demands of a growing consumer society fed by the technological developments of manufacturing. Fur production in Europe and North America increased dramatically as a result of the influx of new skilled labour (see 'Furland', p. 118), in tandem with increasingly effective methods for the production of fur garments. The impact of the sewing machine on the garment industry has been well documented, and by the middle of the nineteenth century its presence was already heralding the mass production of clothing. The making of fur garments, while no doubt benefiting from the invention of mechanical shearing and fur sewing machines, most notably Singer's 46K class machines introduced in 1889, remained, however, a labour-intensive, highly skilled process, involving a number of manual processes that cannot be replicated or replaced by mechanical means. As the *Book of Fur* suggested of the industry in the 1950s, and which remains true today, 'The making up of fur… calls for skill of hand, and the cost of equipment is insignificant; the conveyor belt system cannot be applied'.[123] The fabrication of fur garments involves manual skills that have changed little for centuries. The traditional fur workroom would comprise the furrier, who would buy the skins and have them processed, and his staff, which constituted designers, cutters, machinists, nailers, liners and finishers, as well as a sales staff if there was an attached showroom. Alternatively, furriers without a workroom would send out skins, patterns and linings, together with instructions for assembly, to what were called 'chambermasters' or outworkers, furriers who worked solely for the trade. In either case, skilled fur garment production, as opposed to cheaper furs made from poor quality skins and assembled more in the manner of cloth garments, known as the 'skin-to-skin' method, was, even at the height of fur's popularity, and certainly today, a relatively small-scale, labour-intensive process. Due to the level of skill required, the long apprenticeships needed in order to learn the craft, and the necessary trust placed on a worker using such costly material, fur workers were some of the most highly paid of all those in the apparel industry. They were also some of the most politically active and the first workers to become organised, as evidenced by the International Fur and Leather Workers Union that was formed in America in 1913.

If the sheer volume of cloth garments that characterised the mass production of the industry in the nineteenth century was less applicable to garments made of fur, that is not the case when considering the quantity of separate processes required by fur production and the volume of specialised terminology employed to describe those same processes. Before the cutting and sewing of a fur garment, the skins will come to the manufacturer dressed and possibly dyed. This involves many stages, each with its unique furriering term such as 'beaming' or 'fleshing', 'drumming' and 'kicking' (see 'Under My Skin', p. 163). Once the skin enters the fur workroom it undergoes

3-71 Sewing machine for fur. Courtesy of Kopenhagen Fur

a series of transformations that may commence with shearing and plucking to reduce the length of the wool on the skin, and the removal of some, or all, of the longer guard hairs. Traditionally the skins are then passed to a 'fitter', who groups them in batches to provide the most uniform match of shade and density across the number of skins required to make the garment. The cutter then takes over, dampening the skin side of the pelts, leaving them for a period skin-side together, before removing the heads, necks, sides and sometimes the rumps and tails while still moist. The trimmed skins are then matched again and allocated to a specific part of the garment: front, back, sleeves, collar etc. Following these stages a more complex process of cutting and sewing begins, with the purpose of increasing the size of the skin, making the most of the fur's shading and marking, and rendering it pliable.[124] This can include 'letting-in' (cutting or sewing the skin to make it wider), 'dropping' (cutting a pelt into diagonal strips and resetting them in a staggered formation, taking advantage of a skin's particular shade) and 'leathering' or 'taping' (strips of leather, or sometimes tape, are introduced between the pieces of fur to increase the pliability and overall size of the skin).

All of these processes require accurate cutting followed by sewing and the invention of the fur sewing machine at the close of the nineteenth century facilitated ever more complex cutting and reassembly of pelts (fig. 3-71). In a typical fur machine the two edges of the cut skin, fur sides together, are passed between two 'cups' or discs with milled edges that grip and drive the fur through the machine. A needle moves horizontally in a back and forth motion, as opposed to the customary vertical manner, across the tops of these cups carrying the thread through the fur pieces. At the same time a 'looper' travels below the thread, gathering it up and over to the other side where the needle again pushes it through the skins forming a looped, or chain-stitched seam, which is not only very strong and pliable but also allows easy unpicking if necessary.

Improvements on this basic mechanism, along with other cutting and shearing machines, means that today a bewildering array of effects can be achieved by means of variations on these same transformative processes, where the complex cutting and assembly visible on the skin side of the pelt is hidden in the depths of the hair on the fur side, resulting in remarkably furry deceptions. The 'air gallon' technique is perhaps the most widely used and the most revolutionary in fur

3-72 The *beurre salé* fur technique. Courtesy of Kopenhagen Fur.

garment production, a process whereby a series of regular alternating cuts are made in the skin side of the pelt, so producing a honeycomb effect. The fur takes the form of a mesh that can then be expanded and stretched, making it incredibly light and flexible. Other techniques include 'crossing' (where fur is combined with other fabrics) and 'intarsia' (where a pattern is made by cutting and reassembling furs of different shades and textures into an overall pattern, similar to marquetry in wood). Ever increasing modes of striping, slashing, twisting and re-sewing has resulted in fur that can look quilted, woven and three-dimensionally sculptural, or can imitate other fabrics such as moiré. This is achieved by a technique known as *beurre salé*, or salted butter, where two differently coloured, but evenly piled furs, such as mink, are identically cut into a series of contours or whorls and then reassembled. Every cut piece of skin of one colour is alternated with an identical piece of the other colour, so producing the intarsia effect (3-72, see also p. 79).[125]

Once a skin has been cut and sewn, whether using the simple process of letting out or a complicated technique in order to achieve a more complex effect, the reassembled skin is then dampened again, stretched and nailed to a board, a highly skilled operation carried out by the 'nailer'. After drying, the fur may be 'drummed' (tumbled in a revolving cylinder with sawdust), brushed or air blown to revive its suppleness and pliability. The newly assembled skins are then laid on the pattern and cut out as with a conventional cloth garment, the pieces are assembled, the seams sometimes reinforced, and finally the garment is lined, in itself a highly skilled occupation.

In addition to the semi-automation of the fur garment industry and the influx of skilled migrant labour, of far greater importance to the trade's development in the later nineteenth and twentieth centuries was the escalation of fur trapping, the invention of the automobile and the changes in fashion at the turn of the century that radically altered the silhouette of women's clothes.

The first modern fur coat, as we would understand it today, made entirely of fur and not simply trimmed with it, was most probably made from sealskin. There has been considerable discussion as to when the first of these coats, or more accurately jackets, appeared. J.G. Links suggests it was as early as the 1840s, but some of the earliest museum examples date from the 1870s and would have sold at that time for around 30–40 guineas, or $150–200. Whenever they first appeared we can get a sense of the craze for seal fashions if the consumption figures are considered: 'The fashion world of Europe and America made use of 10,000 skins a year in 1860, 20,000 in 1865, but 150,000 in the 1870s and 200,000 (if they could be obtained) in the 1880s'.[126] This sudden increase was not just the result of a growing demand for seal items of all kinds and for both sexes, but also because the methods for dressing, dehairing and dyeing sealskin improved dramatically around the 1870s. In order for it to be used for garments the coarse outer guard hairs had to be removed to reveal the rich dark brown underfur (figs 3-73 a&b). There was also a vogue for leaving some parts of the garment with its guard hairs still in place, such as on collars and cuffs, in order to contrast with the velvety smooth fur used for the main body of the garment; or to trim seal fur garments with otter and beaver. By the 1890s sealskin was at a premium: 'Sealskin – as coats, wraps, dolmans, sacques, pelisses, muffs, tippets, and gloves – was everywhere to be seen on the streets and in the shop windows. The sealskin jacket in particular was a trophy of middle- to upper-class fashion over a period of some twenty years, coveted by those who could not afford it as well those who could'.[127] The craze for sealskin also mobilised some of the earliest anti-fur sentiment and a number of pamphlets were published decrying the cruelty of seal hunting and the effect the fashion was having on fur seal populations.

A major source of sealskin were the Pribilof Islands in the Bering Sea, which had been densely populated with fur seals. But between 1872 and 1890 the female population had been reduced by 50 per cent and the male by 90 per cent due to indiscriminate pelagic hunting (that is, hunting offshore on sealing vessels), which allows no selectivity and with no regard for breeding seasons. Various attempts were made to regulate seal hunting in the area but ultimately it was economic concern that the population would become extinct, and with it a valuable resource, rather than humanitarian or ecological values that led to the signing of the North Pacific Sealing Convention in 1911.

While the dictates of western fashion brought the fur seal to the brink of extinction in the nineteenth century, to Inuit peoples its hunting and utilisation is fundamental to the maintenance of traditional ways of living. Eating seal is customary in Inuit regions, so they hunt to obtain food. No part of an animal goes to waste as the remaining intestines are fed to the sledge dogs. The skin and sinews are used for clothing or handed in at trading posts. Made into traditional garments such as the parka, sealskin, while not as warm as caribou, the other traditional skin used by the Inuit, is light, incredibly durable, its structure resists wind and

3-73 a&b Jacket (and label above) of James H. Rogers, Toronto, c.1885–9. Quilted seal skin. With permission of the Royal Ontario Museum

3-74 Parka and trousers, c.1897. Eastern Arctic seal fur, canvas and sinew; made by the Nunatsiarmiut, or Baffin Island Inuits. Courtesy McCord Museum, Montreal

its oil content repels water, while its porosity allows it to breathe and be virtually waterproof (fig. 3-74). All of which makes it the perfect cold weather material, a fact discovered by numerous non-indigenous explorers since the great period of polar exploration at the turn of the twentieth century. As observed by Sarah Pickman in her authoritative essay 'Dress, Image, and Cultural Encounter', 'over the course of the nineteenth century an increasing number of Western explorers, whalers and fur traders who ventured into the Arctic acknowledged the superiority of Inuit-style fur clothing over Western textile clothing for survival in that region, in both materials and construction.'[128]

Seal hunting, as in the nineteenth century, has been at the centre of controversy since the 1980s. Those interested in the preservation of Inuit culture regarded the activities of anti-fur organisations, such as Greenpeace, as yet another example of non-indigenous, imperialist interference, their interventions causing sealskin prices to tumble. This in turn had a devastating effect on Inuit, Dene and other First Nations Peoples, who depended on seal fur harvesting.

3-75 Och Sport, ski-wear cardigan (detail), 1930s. Zurich; knitted with dyed seal fur front and suede collar. This unusual example of sealskin used in combination with knit is reflective of the interest in all types of furs and textures in this period, which saw many revivals of previously fashionable furs.
© Victoria and Albert Museum, London

These are peoples for whom, as Julia Emberley suggests, 'fur trapping represents one means of material support, as well as a symbolic tie to traditional ways of life, in an otherwise poverty-inducing system'.[129] Others see seal hunting as an unnecessary practice in the twenty-first century when alternative sources of food and clothing are readily available. The debate continues, resulting in the unsatisfactory situation that exists today whereby the United States banned all imports of seal products from 1972, yet continues to allow a limited period of harvesting of Pribilof fur seals by indigenous islanders, while in the European Union the ban was made official in 2009. However, since 2015 seal products obtained from hunts certified as having been conducted by indigenous peoples in Greenland and Nunavut are exempt from the EU's ban and can be imported.

Returning to the nineteenth century, the capture of fur-bearing animals and advances in the fabrication and marketing of fur garments continued to increase. Items such as the popular sealskin jacket mirrored the tailored silhouette of women's fashions of the period and so furs fine enough to be shaped and fitted remained the most highly prized (see fig. 3-73). That would change at the turn of the century and in the following decade, when the seismic shift in women's dress occurred, ushered in by designers such as Doucet, Paquin and Poiret, and influenced by artistic collaborations such as the Ballets Russes (figs 3-76, 3-77). Women's clothing became looser, relying less on elaborate shaping achieved through cutting, darting and restrictive undergarments. Fashions were characterised by draping and volume, or by simpler straighter lines, which in turn heralded a new era of fur. By 1910 the straighter line, which had become popular for coats, meant that a much greater variety

3-76 Evening coat, 1925. France; silk, black and gold brocade, red fox fur. Texas Fashion Collection, University of North Texas Libraries

3-77 Eduardo Benito, *Dogaresse*, 1925. From the series of fashion prints, 'Dernière lettre persane', for La Maison Fourrures Max, showing an ermine-lined evening cape.
Kharbine-Tapabor/Shutterstock

3-78 '1958 Cars, 1958 Furs', American *Vogue*, November 1957. This article, with photographs by John Rawlings, epitomises American mid-century consumerist aspiration, combining cars, fur and glamour. The mink coat occupied a pre-eminent position in this fantasy. Courtesy of the author

of furs that did not have to be so elaborately worked could be used, including less fine, and therefore more affordable furs. This led to an increase in the popularity and demand for fur, which began to be worn by all generations and nearly all sectors of society. Musquash, skunk, grey squirrel and marten all became fashionable, while the more minimal style of clothing allowed less pliable, but strikingly patterned furs, such as leopard, to be used to great effect. High-street furriers stocking a range of less expensive furs appeared alongside specialist fur salons in the newly established department stores. In short, the first decades of the twentieth century were characterised by volume: more varieties of fur, in more styles, consumed by more people and in more quantity than ever before.

The fur coat took on the characteristic shapes that it would retain throughout the twentieth century. Capacious styles that were wrapped and belted added extra volume, as in the 'fabulous long hairs' featured in American *Vogue*'s 'The "Force" of Fur' editorial of 1977. Earlier styles that flared and draped from the shoulder, as in the classic broad-shouldered minks, were seen as part of a quintessentially mid-twentieth-century consumerist dream that combined fast cars with glamour, as featured in American *Vogue*'s '1958 Cars, 1958 Furs' of 1957, photographed by John Rawlings (fig. 3-78).[130] As with the 1977 *Vogue* piece, the collision between fur and new technology, in this case mink and the latest convertible Cadillacs, emphasises the relationship between fur and progress, fur and fantasy, and importantly for open-topped travel, fur and warmth.

The Rawlings photographs also pay homage to the automobile as an example of how new technology had impacted on the development of fashionable fur in the twentieth century. The first automobiles, developed in the late nineteenth century, were open to the elements and therefore demanded new forms of protective clothing, with thermal insulation a primary requisite. Fur naturally provided the ideal solution for the pioneer motorist, offering a level of warmth and protection afforded by no other material at the time. The new motoring coats and accessories provided a showcase for the new varieties and styles of fur that were shaping the market. Coats for men and women made of skins that had up to this point not been considered suitable for clothing now became fashionable, lined with, or made entirely from, longer, coarser, shaggier furs such as goat, raccoon, bear, wolf and sheepskin. Furs expressive of a primitive power and energy matched the mechanical energy of the automobile. As the twentieth century moved on, and automobiles became more comfortable and sedan cars with closed bodies were developed, bulky fur coats became less practical, although open-topped sports cars, or roadsters, still provided a means of display for extravagant fur coats, nowhere more so than on the backs of American college students in the form of the iconic raccoon coat (fig. 3-79). For the well-dressed Ivy-Leaguer a raccoon coat was essential for driving or attending football matches. When worn over suit and tie or college sweater and accessorised with a straw boater or cap, it became the sartorial cliché of the American Jazz Age. As a sign of elite 'rebellion' the raccoon coat, advertised in 1921 as costing $325–450 (about $6,000 today), was the perfect garment in which to enjoy a period of youthful hedonism before assuming one's position in society. Ideally long-haired, ankle-length and double-breasted, with a wide shawl collar, deep cuffs and large leather buttons, the raccoon craze soon spread beyond the ivy-covered walls of American privilege. It was adopted by entertainers, sportsmen and anybody wishing to cut a dash, and featured in films, literature and music such as bandleader George Olsen's 1928 recording *Doin' the Raccoon*. As with many similar extravagances the Great Depression hastened the demise of the craze, but an ironic transatlantic reminder of this once aspirational garment was to be made famous by Bud Flanagan, the British music hall entertainer. Best known as one half of the double act Flanagan and Allen, and for popular wartime hits such as 'Underneath the Arches', he was recognised by his trademark mangy, oversized fur coat and battered straw hat (fig. 3-80). Often described as a raccoon coat, photographs and films of Flanagan show him wearing a number of different coats, one of which, made from beaver, came up for auction in 2014. Whether raccoon or made from other fur, Flanagan's coat in its dilapidated state remains a sardonic vestimentary critique of furry aspiration, worn by an entertainer adored by the British working classes.

3-79 Man's coat, 1930s. United States; raccoon fur, pockets trimmed with raccoon tails. Texas Fashion Collection, University of North Texas Libraries

3-80 Entertainer Bud Flanagan in his trademark raccoon coat. Moviestore/Shutterstock

3-81 LEFT Karl Heisler, Luftwaffe flight suit, 1939–45. Berlin; leather and sheepskin. Courtesy of the Westminster Menswear Archive, University of Westminster, London

3-82 RIGHT Liam Hodges, flight jacket and trousers, 2013. Sheepskin patchwork. Sheepskin offcuts were patchworked into panels and then painted with two coats of household gloss paint. The legacy of the flight jacket and similar utility garments, employing the thermal properties of fur, continues to exert its influence on contemporary fashion. Courtesy of the Westminster Menswear Archive, University of Westminster, London

3-83 ABOVE Fighter pilot Manfred von Richtofen in his favourite fur coat, c.1914–18. History of Aviation Collection, Special Collections and Archives Division, Eugene McDermott Library, The University of Texas at Dallas

3-84 RIGHT Royal Canadian Mounted Police overcoat, 1965–70. Quebec; buffalo fur, leather and satin lining. This 'Mounties' coat epitomises the use of fur as a model of outdoors, rugged masculinity that repeatedly informs contemporary men's fashion. With permission of the Royal Ontario Museum © ROM

3-85 FAR RIGHT Liam Hodges, coat, 2013. Hand-dyed fox fur. A collaboration with Kopenhagen Fur in which an intarsia technique is used across the garment, swapping undyed and dyed furs to create a patchwork pattern with little waste. Courtesy of the Westminster Menswear Archive, University of Westminster, London

As with the automobile, the advent of the aeroplane had a similar, but perhaps more lasting, effect on fashionable fur (fig. 3-81). Sheepskin came to the fore used for flying suits and jackets and to line aviators' boots (see 'Modern Primitives', p. 81), leaving a legacy that still informs menswear today (fig. 3-82). Before garments specifically designed for flight were produced, fur coats much like those worn by early motorists made the cockpits of pioneer aviators more comfortable. During the First World War, the first conflict to be fought in the air, fur and flying formed a natural partnership, nowhere more effectively than as part of the self-mythologising of Manfred von Richthofen, 'The Red Baron'. A keen hunter and trophy collector of both animals and enemy pilots, von Richthofen's appearance, especially in his beloved fur coat, most probably wolf, was a boon to the German propaganda machine which idolised him as the world's most celebrated flying ace. His coat was a sartorial expression of his hunter's extinct, preying on the enemy and emerging triumphant from his latest kill (fig. 3-83).

The combination of fur, ferocity, speed and technology has proved irresistible to men's fashion ever since and is periodically revisited by designers and stylists alike. Utilitarian fur garments, such as motoring coats, flying suits or those produced for wearing in cold climates – such as the 'Mounties' overcoat of buffalo fur (fig. 3-84) – have been constant sources of inspiration for fashionable reinvented, furry virility (fig. 3-85).

The automotive fantasies of Cadillac or George Lucas's 'droids' are fitting companions for the journeys of technological innovation taken by fashionable fur. These journeys have now come full circle ending with 'primitive' furs, engendered by the latest technology but which imitate the 'Modern Primitives' encountered at the beginning of this chapter. Across the fashioned body, from hand to machine, from imagined past to timeless present, these journeys to Furland have been constantly shaped and sheared, dyed and embellished, hidden or revealed, forbidden or celebrated, but above all they attest to the 'force of fur'.

THE F WORD

In the collections of the National Museum of Denmark can be found what is possibly the earliest extant example of fake fur, a hat belonging to a Bronze Age warrior, the Muldbjerg Man, who died in 1365 BCE and was buried along with this and other precious objects in an artificially built mound in western Jutland, Denmark (fig. 3-86). The hat, which is round and close fitting, recalling the fashionable dome-shaped women's hats designed by Balenciaga in the 1960s, is made from layers of woollen cloth, the outer layer covered in a dense pile of very fine, knotted cords of about one to two centimetres in length, which produces a remarkable fur-like appearance. The Trindhøj Man, buried in his oak coffin in 1347 BCE, wore a similar hat and matching 'furry' cloak.[131] Some 30 years or so later in Thebes, Tutankhamen's tomb was being stocked with provisions for his journey to the afterlife including both real and fake leopard skins (see 'Shape Shifters', p. 193), indicating that fake fur not only has a surprisingly lengthy history but also that the description 'fake', when applied to fur, which has until very recently been understood pejoratively with its associations of cheapness and deception, is in need of reassessment. Neither the Bronze Age warriors' garments, nor Tutankhamen's leopard skin can be considered cheap, as they involved considerable skill, ingenuity and time in their manufacture. The intention was not to imitate fur at all but rather celebrate fur's ability to be translated from its original grown, skinned and sewn materiality into the language of woven textiles, the basis of all subsequent fur 'fabric' (see 'Translation', p. 211).

Having already used the terms 'fake' and fur 'fabric', it is worth considering the specific linguistic irony that determines our perception of synthetic fur, an irony derived in part from the alliterative insistence of the letter F. Joining 'fake' and fur 'fabric' in this lexicon we might consider today's 'faux', 1960's 'fun', 'false' and even 'fish fur' (РЫБИЙ МЕХ), an ironic Russian expression used to describe poor quality fur, both real and fake, and believed to be derived from a Russian proverb that declares 'A poor man's fur coat is of fish fur'. This excess of Fs betrays a shifting of our attitudes towards fake fur, which today are central to the arguments against the use of real fur in the fashion industry. Yet however unnatural the dyeing and shaping of contemporary faux fur has become, it is now irreversibly politicised and can never hope to regain the exuberance and innocence of the fake 'fun' fur of the 1960s. Today's ubiquitous employment of the genteel and more obscure 'faux', in preference to the direct 'fake', is similarly indicative of an avoidance that has characterised imitation fur since affordability was replaced by conscience as the primary reason for wearing it. 'Faux' (for the English-speaking consumer, at least) conveniently bypasses the direct understanding of imitation or replication represented by the word 'fake' and similarly obscures the fundamental paradox of wearing a simulation of the very material that is deemed undesirable and should be prohibited. At the time of writing, due to the growing condemnation of fur, while I use the initial 'F' as a means to discuss the history of fake fur, the 'F' word has now for many people come to stand for the unmentionable, real fur.

3-86 Bronze Age 'fake fur' hat (and detail below), c.1365 BCE. Western Jutland, Denmark; thin threads in imitation of fur. © National Museum of Denmark

Real fur, of course, both in myth and reality, has often had a direct relationship with dissimulation and disguise. Before considering the history of fake fur itself, it is worth considering how real fur has often been used to deceive. As we have already encountered with the example of the fur-clad Adam and Eve and their expulsion from Eden, the Bible imbues fur with

a sense of immorality. Jacob's simulation of his brother Esau's hairy arms, hands and neck by wrapping his own in sheepskin, in order to deceive his blind father Isaac and receive his blessing, is a case in point: 'And he discerned him not, because his hands were hairie, as his brother Esau's hands: So he blessed him' (fig. 3-87).[132] Here the sense of touch, the litmus test of discernment between real and fake fur and its relative quality, fails and Isaac is unable to distinguish between human and animal hair. In a reversal of the Jacob and Isaac story, where fur is used to conceal a hairy deficiency, fairy tales are replete with fur being donned to conceal nobility and smoothness, a marker of distance from bestiality.[133]

Returning to reality, a reliance on assumption and a lack of discernment is equally important to the history of faked or substituted real fur. However, the motivation for this subterfuge is purely economic rather than moral. Throughout western history less costly, more plentiful, furs have been used to imitate or eke out more valuable skins. Elspeth Veale, in her seminal study of the medieval English fur trade, records a number of such practices, giving examples of *purfling*, where a garment would be lined with less expensive fur, the more costly reserved for the visible edging at neck or wrist known as the *purfell* or *purfile*. 'Gowns might be lined with *pured miniver* [the white belly of grey squirrels] but trimmed with

3-87 Jusepe de Ribera (1591–1652), *Isaac and Jacob,* 1637. Oil on canvas, 110 x 291.5 cm. Prado Museum, Madrid. The Art Archive/Shutterstock

ermine, which meant that some four or five ermine skins were used, with perhaps 800 squirrel … Other combinations were *calabre* [squirrel skins from Calabria] and mink, or leopard bellies and lynx.[134] As has been noted elsewhere, from the medieval period until the nineteenth century, with a few exceptions such as the medieval *pilche* or cloak, fur was used primarily as a lining for garments made of other materials. Owing to the durability of fur, this meant that the lining often outlasted the actual garment itself, giving rise to an important aspect of the fur trade which today we would understand as recycling, or even perhaps upcycling. Older fur linings were often used to line new garments, furs were passed down from one generation to the next and bequeathed in wills, and eventually, on becoming too shabby or worn, ended up being sold by dealers in secondhand garments including furs, known as fripperers (another 'F' word). On entering the secondhand market, worn and used fur could be refurbished by a skilful craftsperson, Veale again recording how lamb skins would be cleaned and sheared again while other worn furs would be repaired and new skins inserted to replace the worn out sections.[135] So skilful were these renovations that they were often re-sold as new, giving rise to much consternation within the fur trade during the Middle Ages.

The renovation of skins that flourished during the medieval period has remained an enduring and indeed sustaining service, still offered by the modern furrier today. Fur that is looked after and has been stored under the correct conditions will last the proverbial lifetime, and given its initial cost it has made perfect sense to have furs remodelled to keep pace with changing tastes, something which became increasingly common from the nineteenth century onwards and the birth of what we might understand as the modern fashion system. Along with other luxury goods and services, part of the initial expense of purchasing a garment from a furrier is the assurance that it can also be periodically renovated by skilful craftspeople to maintain the garment in peak condition or transformed to keep it abreast of the dictates of fashion. Indeed, in the face of declining sales and rising overheads, remodelling is an essential element of any modern furrier's trade if they wish to remain in business.

The remodelling of fur garments highlights an important consideration relevant to their unique construction. Unlike other textiles, which when they become worn and are repaired retain the visible scars of that repair such as patching, darning and the contrast between faded and darker areas, fur is able to 'hide' its repairs far more effectively. Insertions and new stitching become 'lost' in its furry surface and only detectable on the reverse, and then only if unlined. This ability to conceal a fur garment's construction is relevant to the present discussion concerning fake fur, for while much remodelling of fur is carried out with no intention to deceive, it has of course also allowed old fur, stolen fur or merely outmoded fur to be sold as new, legal and current. One of the most explicit yet bizarre representations of the remodelling of stolen furs can be found in the British film comedy *Crooks in Cloisters*.[136] Positioned somewhere between an Ealing comedy and a Carry On film, *Crooks in Cloisters* follows the exploits of a group of thieves, including a fur-clad Barbara

3-88 *Crooks in Cloisters*, dir. Jeremy Summers, 1964. Film still. Studio Canal/Shutterstock

Windsor playing the inexplicably named Bikini. The crooks hide out in a Cornish monastery posing as unlikely monks and, whilst living the monastic life, continue their nefarious activities fencing stolen goods. These include a number of fur coats, which Bikini remodels at a sewing machine dressed in a monk's habit, accessorised on one occasion with a mink stole (fig. 3-88).

If the reconditioning and remodelling of fur in order to appear new and *au courant* can be understood as a form of deception, whether the purchaser is aware of it or not, then the direct mimicry of one fur for another has an equally long heritage as part of the furrier's 'art'. Long before modern chemical dyeing processes arrived, the skilled worker of fur was indispensible to a necessary economy of furry substitution. Veale again is invaluable here, detailing the practice of 'powdering', an early example of substitution or perhaps more accurately the embellishment of one fur with another.[137] Especially popular in the late fifteenth and early sixteenth centuries, powdering consisted of making small incisions into a white ermine skin and then sewing into these slits small tufts, or *tavelons* as they were known, of fur from the legs of black lambs (*budge*) to simulate black ermine tails, producing the characteristic spotting or powdering of black tails on a white ground. Presumably this was undertaken to suggest that more ermines had been used in the construction of the garment and to save on the amount of real ermine tails, or possibly to 'fake' white squirrel to resemble ermine. This practice was in great demand during this period of ostentatious display, despite it being costly, laborious and highly skilled. The technique continues today in the maintenance and restoration of ceremonial garments trimmed with ermine or *miniver* (squirrel), such as the British coronation robes worn by peers of the realm.

Dyeing remains the most common method of simulating more expensive or desirable furs. During the medieval period furriers used both European wild and domestic cats. Wild cats were more prized as their fur was denser and more evenly coloured, whereas the coats of domestic cats varied greatly and therefore were hard to match up in a garment. Consequently they were dyed to a uniform shade, furs treated in this way being referred to as 'painted cats'.

The dyeing of fur increased dramatically from the late nineteenth century onwards as fur became subject to the dictates of fashion in a way that it had not been before. Fashions in fur changed almost as quickly as other materials and as demand increased for a specific type of fur, so naturally did its price, leading to a bewildering variety of imitations. This change in how fur was regarded coincided with the invention and application of new aniline dyes, so that furs of less desirable animals were transformed, both chemically and naturally, using vegetable dyes and other manual processes such as shearing and putting different furs together. They were given exotic or composite names to facilitate their marketing. 'Musk sealskin', for example, was in fact sheared and dyed muskrat (also known as 'Hudson Seal') and cost a fraction of the price of a real sealskin coat, while manipulating the fur of the muskrat to simulate otter fur produced 'Otter Fantasy'. Sheared and dyed coney was sold under the name of 'French Seal' or 'Electric Seal', while 'Blended Marmot' (a genus of large squirrel) resembled sable and, according to James Laver, by the 1920s a mink-marmot coat was being advertised that 'worked just like mink'.[138] The craze for silver fox that also occurred in the 1920s made it briefly the most valuable of furs and prompted a process of imitation as complicated as medieval powdering. According to *Fur Facts* of 1922, it was achieved 'by taking the ordinary red fox and dyeing it black, and then, using the white badger hairs, taking a single hair at a time, dipping one end of it in

3-89 Cape (detail), c.1900. Probably United States; plush (possibly silk or cotton) in imitation of seal fur, with braid trim. Texas Fashion Collection, University of North Texas Libraries

glue and then inserting it among the hairs of the dyed fox. Enough of the badger hair is added to the dyed fox to give it the appearance of silver fox, in that it is sprinkled with white hairs.'[139]

It is probably due to the enormous popularity of sealskin towards the end of the nineteenth century that we owe the development of the first 'true' fake furs; that is, imitation fur made from synthetic or natural materials other than actual fur. 'Seal-plush' or 'sealskin cloth' were affordable fabrics that imitated genuine sealskin. These silky, velvet-like fabrics may well have been 'spin offs', originally developed during the transition from the beaver skin to silk top hat that had occurred earlier in the nineteenth century (fig. 3-89). The earliest imitation beaver fabrics were silk shag weaves with a very long defined nap, known as hatter's plush, first woven at the very end of the eighteenth century (see 'Heads or Tails', p. 102). A similar pioneering, natural 'fur fabric' emerged from the alpaca wool industry, established by the British industrialist and philanthropist Titus Salt. Salt's career began as a wool trader and in the 1830s he started to experiment with some unwanted bales of alpaca wool, eventually managing to weave it successfully into a lustrous and immediately fashionable cloth using a cotton warp and alpaca weft. Alpaca wool is similar to hair in its physical structure and is naturally glossy and soft, lending itself, when woven, to the production of deep pile, dense furry fabrics. It was such a fabric that the German company Steiff used to manufacture the first of their famous teddy bear toys in the 1900s, while elsewhere it was being used by British companies such as Motoluxe to fashion travelling rugs and versions of the fur automobile coat popular in America. Most early plush fur fabrics incorporate the same techniques as those used to make fabrics such as velvet, where the yarn is looped and then cut during the weaving process to produce cloth with a dense pile of varying lengths. Astrakhan or Persian lamb was similarly imitated using processed wools during the early twentieth century, when this fur reached the height of its popularity.

The fake fur industry, as we would recognise it today, had to wait until the 1940s and the development of synthetic pile fabrics, such as Orlon in 1948 and Dynel in 1950, which provided the catalyst for the sudden growth in synthetic furs. The revolution that occurred at the end of the nineteenth century due to the discovery of aniline dyes, described by James Laver as the opening of 'a whole new chapter of the fur industry', is equally applicable to the 1940s and the effect that synthetic fibres would have.[140] Establishing which was the first truly synthetic fur is problematic, with a number of manufacturers simultaneously developing – by accident or design – synthetic fabrics that would be used to simulate fur. The history of fake fur is peppered with dimly remembered brand

3-90 Advertisement for Borgana, 1956. Courtesy of the author

3-91 Astraka, coat, 1960s. Imitation Persian lamb (broadtail) coat with coney collar. Courtesy of the author

3-92 Shrimps, coat, Autumn/Winter 2019. FashionPPS/ZUMA Wire/Shutterstock

names, such as Borg, Tissavel and Astraka, while others including Timme-Tation and Glenara remain lost in a furry synthetic haze and are now known only from photographs on vintage clothing websites. One of the first and most enduring of the new synthetic fur manufacturers was Borg, whose trademark fabric was named Borgana (fig. 3-90). Borg produced deep pile fabrics using the new synthetic fibres. According to various sources, George Borg stumbled across their relevance to the fake fur industry whilst developing fabrics to be used for paint rollers in the late 1940s. Realising that the sheepskin-like material he was producing would also be suitable for coats, he took samples to 7th Avenue in New York and began manufacturing garments in the new material. Borgana developed into a highly sought after range of fake fur fabrics that simulated not just sheepskin but also more luxurious mink-like imitations. Borg became synonymous with 'teddy bear fur', especially popular for jackets in the 1970s, and the name lives on today, often used to describe a range of contemporary teddy bear/sheepskin fabrics and garments. Tissavel, a French company founded in 1953 that specialises in upmarket imitation fur, continues to supply imitation fur fabric to some of the world's leading fashion houses and also manufactures fabrics for toys, paint rollers and the high tech cleaning industry, while the versatile, soft and highly flexible fabric called Kanecaron, developed in 1957 by the Japanese company Kaneka, is also still in production today.

Astraka Furs, or Astraka London as the company was sometimes known, started out as Alfred Morris Furs in 1898. By its heyday in the 1960s and 1970s it had changed its name to Astraka and had become a specialist manufacturer of fake fur garments famed for simulated astrakhan, hence their brand name (fig. 3-91). The company employed some 400 workers at their factory in Shildon, County Durham, in the

3-93 Cristóbal Balenciaga, coat, c.1965. Wool. Even Balenciaga, the master of understated luxury, enjoyed the irony of imitation, as in this wool coat that has been textured and finished to simulate the fleece of a sheep before it has been shorn. The Metropolitan Museum of Art, New York. Gift of Countess Edward Bismarck. © Photo Scala, Florence

north-east of England. Licensed by British Nylon Spinners to produce garments from synthetic fur fabrics such as Minkaleen and Bri-Lon Furleen, Astraka supplied coats to leading stores such as Harrods and Selfridges, had a global export business and, with the World Champion ice dancer Courtney Jones as designer, manufactured uniforms for the British Winter Olympics team of 1980. The company eventually went into receivership in 1988.

Real fur has periodically shed its conventional colourways to adopt more fashionable, unnatural shades. Understandably, this has not been the case with fake fur, which, until comparatively recently, has strived with varying degrees of success to replicate real fur as closely as possible. Even the much-vaunted 'fun' furs of the 1960s tended to project their lightheartedness via unconventional cutting and op art effects, achieved with black and white imitation furs rather than vibrant, synthetic shades. For contemporary faux fur designers, however, colour is paramount. It could be argued that today's most directional faux fur designers make a point of using colours more reminiscent of soft toys than the real animals whose fur they imitate. Advances in dyeing techniques and the production of acrylic fibres has led to an explosion of exuberant, vibrant and purposely whimsical fake fur styling, which stands in direct contrast to the perceived serious and sophisticated cachet that contemporary real fur exudes. As a result the new faux fur brands, such as London-based Shrimps, the New York labels House of Fluff and Maison Atia, and Melbourne's Unreal Fur, appeal directly to a younger, ethically aware and animal-friendly consumer.

Interestingly, both House of Fluff and Maison Atia can trace their origins back to fur and furriering. Kym Canter, CEO of House of Fluff, after years working in the luxury industry sold all 26 of the fur coats she had accumulated to help start the company, while its creative director Alex Dymek has transferred his considerable experience in working with fur to the creation of faux fur garments. Maison Atia, whose slogan is 'Unexpected Luxury', was founded by Chloé Mendel, daughter of the creative director of J. Mendel, the established fashion house in Paris and New York that has specialised in fur since its origins in St Petersburg in the 1870s, as furriers to the Russian aristocracy. Maison Atia's intention is 'to disrupt the faux fur market by translating the luxury touch of real fur to this new material'. As to how this touch is 'translated' is unclear, but it is perhaps a linguistic rather than a tactile notion given the faux French names assigned to their fake fur fabrics, including Minque, Mônkée and Léoparde.[141]

Founded in 2011, Melbourne-based Unreal Fur adopts a similar literary approach to its production and promotion of fake fur. The inspiration for the company's accessories collection, Unreal Fur X Sans Beast, is that of 'an imaginary meeting between Tzippy + Moishe from Maurice Sendak's much loved book *Where The Wild Things Are* and intellectual Simone de Beauvoir in Paris in the 1930s. Elegance, eccentricity – and a touch of the wild.'[142] The bestiality of fairy tales is also conscripted into Unreal Fur's agenda 'to end the use of real fur in the fashion industry', as the context of their Furry Tales campaign of 2017 attests: 'Once upon a time, there was a little girl who wanted to save the world. She didn't want to fight the big bad wolf, she wanted to save him. So she went faux.'[143] The label Shrimps has arguably had the greatest impact on the modern faux fur fashion industry. Founded by London designer Hannah Weiland in 2013, its vibrant coats and jackets have been in the vanguard of fur-free fashion since the first of its signature colour-banded and blocked swagger-style coats launched the label. Instantly recognisable, Shrimps designs are regularly seen on a host of red carpet celebrities and fashion industry figures (fig. 3-92).

The majority of fake fur manufactured today is made from modacrylic (modified acrylic), a derivative of oil mixed with synthetics.[144] As with other petroleum-based products, it is made from non-renewable sources, pollutes during production, releases microfibres on washing and is non-biodegradable. Fake fur manufacturers and anti-fur lobbyists attempt to counter these detrimental environmental factors by comparing the levels of pollution caused by the waste produced from fur farms, CO_2 emissions resulting from the refrigeration of fur, and the various toxic chemicals released during the tanning and dyeing of fur, which also considerably lengthens the time a fur coat treated with such chemicals will take to biodegrade. Beyond the ethical arguments against the rearing and killing of animals for their fur – which are frequently confused with environmental issues – modern, responsibly sourced farmed fur is increasingly sustainable as a system (see 'In Black and White and Colour', p. 132). For every assertion that waste material from fur farms runs off into and pollutes local water systems, farmers counter this by highlighting the benefits from using animal-derived, as opposed to synthetic, fertilisers; for example, waste products such as those produced by mink farms are processed into animal feed and biofuels. Harder to determine are the counter arguments put forward by fur producers concerning the chemicals used in its processing, which suggest that natural, plant-based materials and minerals, rather than synthetic chemicals, are used as this results in the best quality fur, which in turn is in the interests of manufacturers and retailers alike.

3-94 Jean Paul Gaultier, puffer coat printed with a photographic image of fox fur, Haute Couture, Autumn/Winter 2019. Shutterstock

With an increasing body of research, much of it commissioned by either pro- or anti-fur organisations, it seems that neither side will emerge as victorious in the sustainability argument. However, the danger to marine systems from microfibres is of increasing concern and is producing some of the most compelling and, crucially, unbiased research.[145]

Microfibres are shed by a variety of synthetic textiles, such as nylon, polyester, rayon, acrylic and spandex. These textiles are made up into everything from underwear to puffer jackets as well as fake fur coats. The majority of tests carried out so far have used synthetic fleece, rather than any other type of synthetic fur, and so further research needs to be carried out on the environmental impact of microfibres shed from longer-haired and plush fake fur. New initiatives that may address the harmful environmental impact of fake fur have recently been announced by the Faux Fur Institute, its online site supported by, and promoting, the Chinese fake fur and leather company ECOPEL.[146] These include a fake fur developed by ECOPEL from recycled plastic bottles, while current research is focusing on a fur made using 40 per cent plant-based materials, so reducing the reliance on petrochemical derivatives.

While real fur is being worked and dyed to look like other fabrics and, when coming from unregulated sources, is often cheaper than synthetic fur, fake fur achieves ever new heights of synthetic imitation and, in the hands of leading designers, is retailed for sums previously only commanded by mink and sable (fig. 3-94). Looks can deceive, but as yet the indication of real fur remains the sensation of touch and for some that will never be faked. For others, perhaps, we have reached a point where the divide between real and fake is collapsing and the reality of fur no longer resides in its materiality but as an idea. Fur can be understood as transformative or controversial, parodic or nostalgic, a concept of 'realness' that is closer to American ball culture and house communities.[147] Here performances are judged on dance skills, costumes, appearance and attitude; 'real' is performed and judged on degrees of conviction, imitation and attitude. As American choreographer Trajal Harrell has suggested, 'realness operates precisely by blurring the line between perceptions and constructions of the fake and the real'.[148]

PART FOUR

SKIN

4 SKIN

UNDER MY SKIN

In his poetic journey through the senses, published originally in 1985 as *Les Cinq Sens*, philosopher Michel Serres begins the work with his contemplation on the sense of touch and skin, entitled 'Veils'. This positioning reflects its importance as an interrogation of the traditional prioritising of sight.[1] He proposes: 'The skin can explore proximities, limits, adhesions, balls and knots, coasts or capes, lakes, promontories and folds. The map on the epidermis most certainly expresses more than just touch, it plunges deeply into the internal sense, but it begins with the sense of touch.'[2] The skin is the primary organ for the sense of touch, containing receptors that respond to different stimuli, such as heat and cold, pain, pressure, vibration and chemical stimuli, and form part of what is termed the somatosensory system. The physiological complexity of this system is matched by an equally complex emotional and political understanding of the sense of touch and its relation to skin. Skin touches and is touched; it is the point of contact with the world and the boundary that separates the self from the world. Skin is the vessel that individuates and contains and yet is porous, leaks, can be pierced and stripped away. Skin is a border that is constantly crossed and joins other borders.

It is unsurprising, therefore, that the skin – as the finest, most sensitive membrane territorialising inside and outside, the self and the world, and the self and others – should have formed such a rich metaphorical layer. We speak of being 'thick' or 'thin skinned'; of 'skin and bone'; of escaping by 'the skin of our teeth'; and feeling our skin 'crawl'. We are constantly reminded that 'beauty is only skin-deep' and the threat of being skinned alive conjures vistas of unimaginable pain. We can 'give people some skin', the 'skin off our backs', be skinny, or be a skinflint. Cole Porter famously wrote 'I've Got You Under My Skin', while on either side of skin's colonial divisions Rudyard Kipling suggested that we 'are sisters under the skin' and Frantz Fanon interrogated that possibility in *Black Skin, White Masks*.[3]

The insistent imagery of skin peeled away, donated, borrowed and covering improbable surfaces, is intensified, most notably in its violence, when animal, rather than human skin is the subject. There are 'more ways to skin a cat' and rabbit is perhaps still the best skin for 'Daddy' to 'wrap the baby Bunting in'.[4] Although the term 'the skin trade' is today most commonly associated with the sex industry, historically it was understood to be an alternative name for the fur trade and the Hudson's Bay Company, the trade's most significant institution, chose as its motto *pro pelle cutem*, or 'a skin for a skin's worth'. *Pellis*, the Latin word for an animal skin, has enriched

PREVIOUS PAGE Zebra skin (detail). Courtesy of the author

4-1 Janine Antoni (b. 1964), *Saddle,* 2000. Full rawhide; 64.8 x 82.6 x 199.4 cm. Museum of Modern Art, New York, Gift of Agnes Gund. © Janine Antoni; Courtesy of the artist and Luhring Augustine, New York

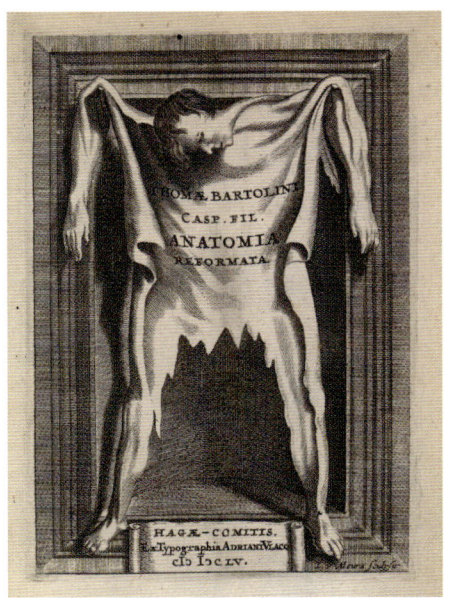

4-2 Frontispiece, *Anatomia Reformata* by Thomas Bartolin. Published by Lugdunum Batavorum, Leiden, 1651, repr. 1655. Wellcome Collection, London

4-3 Damien Hirst (b. 1965), *Saint Bartholomew, Exquisite Pain*, 2006. Installed in the Church of St Bartholomew-the-Great, Smithfield, London. Gilded bronze, 250 x 110 x 95 cm. St Bartholomew is traditionally depicted carrying his own skin, in reference to his martyrdom by being flayed alive. Courtesy of the author

furriering etymology, and has given us the term *pelt*; a now obscure term for a single fur or hide is a *pell*, while *peltry* denotes skins collectively; *pelterie* is the medieval term for the trade of a skinner or *peltmonger*; *pellage* was the duty levied on hides, furs and skins; and in fashion's historical terminology, a *pelisse* was originally a fur-lined robe or gown.

A complex circular network of actions and reactions occurs between the concepts of skin, fur and touch, due especially to their semantic capacity of being both verb and noun. Touching resonates with emotion, sensory stimulation and contact. Skinning evokes acts of removal and violence, while furring, more archaic perhaps, speaks of fashion, status and embellishment. Meanings and possibilities of meaning slide back and forth when confronted, for example, by the fur trade's ironic terminology: the 'dresser' will remove an animal's skin; the 'flesher' will remove the excess fat and flesh from an animal, a process also known as 'beaming'. Similarly, for much of the Renaissance period skin was also understood as clothing, a comparison that is indicative of that era's emphasis on the culture of appearances, where clothing literally made the man. Skin was perceived as mutable, deceptive and detachable, and could be worn and removed like a garment (fig. 4-2). This alarming concept has been made manifest throughout history in a variety of media, amongst which are numerous anatomical drawings, most famously produced by Vesalius depicting flayed human figures carrying their own skin, and *écorchés* (or flayed) wax sculptures that rendered the skinned body in lifelike detail. Classical figures such as Marsyas, the satyr flayed alive as punishment for hubris, occupied artists as did St Bartholomew, the Christian martyr, who met a similar fate and is often depicted with his draped skin and the fleshing knives used to remove it from his body, which led to him becoming the patron saint of skinners, tanners, tailors, glovers and butchers (fig. 4-3).

The concept of the sensate skin, removed from the living being and carried as clothing, is of particular relevance to this study. The belief in the power of skin to retain the essence of the animal it was removed from, which in turn can be transferred to its new wearer, is discussed further in 'Shape Shifters' (p. 193). An understanding of the essential qualities of an animal that reside in its skin, even when fashioned into human garments, has together with the unparalleled tactile responses they elicit, been the instinctual reason for both our attraction to, and abhorrence of, fur. Here, it is perhaps necessary to clarify that 'skin' when referring to that of an animal, for the purposes of this study, can refer to the skin or smooth side of fur, as well as the skin of animals whose hair is comparatively short and dense, such as leopard or tiger, or smooth and flat, such as deer or pony, all of which are referred to as skin rather than fur. What is of importance, however, is that hairless skin, which we might understand as leather or suede, whose history bears marked similarities to, as well as divergences from, the history of fur that this study attempts, will not be included.

Serres's project takes the reader to a space similar to much earlier conceptions of the five senses, which, prior to rationalism's drive to individuate and hierarchise, understood all five as part of a sensorium, facilitated and united by touch. Thomas Aquinas, endorsing Aristotle's view, suggested that touch was the first sense and formed the ground or root of all the others. This belief was maintained until sight became the ascendant sense and was equated to knowledge during the Enlightenment. As late as 1609, professor of anatomy Giulio Cesare Casseri, in his *Pentaestheseion*, maintained that touch was the pre-eminent sense and a template for the others. This historical merging of skin and the sense of touch with all other senses is what Serres reclaims, suggesting:

> *We bear on our skin the complex singularities of which it is composed: germs, pimples, navels and inflorescences, folded, drawn and ocellated, like the bezels of rings. Just as flat or irregular fabric becomes islands, hems, flounces, frills, gatherings, sewn decorations, so does our skin form the continuous backdrop, the base note of the senses, their common denominator. Each sense, originating in the skin, is a strong individual expression of it.*[5]

Fur is most directly experienced through touch; its beauty, while visually apparent, is only fully grasped when touched, stroked, smoothed and ruffled, something that Walter Benjamin found troubling, suggesting the touch of an animal's fur made us too aware of our bestial nature.[6] In the film *Manhunter*, the experience of touched fur is made explicit in the remarkable scene where a blind woman strokes a sedated tiger, feels its soft fur, rigid teeth and its warmth, oblivious to the penetrating gaze of her potential killer, until he closes his eyes in ecstasy and so becomes sightless also (fig. 4-4).[7] The scene is a cinematic synthesis of what can be understood as the

4-4 *Manhunter*, dir. Michael Mann, 1986. Film still. Courtesy of the author

4-5 Roger Vadim and Jane Fonda during a break in filming *La Curée*, 1965. Fonda wears a chinchilla coat designed by Chombert, reputed at the time to be worth 150,000 francs. Godot/AP/Shutterstock

Renaissance culture of touch, which differentiated between the touch of innocence and the touch of the carnal, the soft caress and the forceful blow, the touch of good and the touch of evil.

One fur, however, allegedly defeats our ability to know it through touch. The chinchilla's fur is so soft and fine that furriers would maintain that it was impossible to discern if touched while one's eyes were closed, and so seeing really was believing (fig. 4-5). The fur of the chinchilla, a small member of the rodent family native to the Andes, is the densest of any land mammal, growing on average 60 hairs from each follicle; one square centimetre of fur may bear up to 20,000 hairs. Its fur was introduced into Europe by Spanish explorers in the sixteenth century, but reached a peak of popularity in the late nineteenth and early twentieth centuries. Highly prized for its velvet-like blue-grey fur, and due to its increasing rarity and small size, it was correspondingly costly with a full-length coat requiring up to 150 pelts (fig. 4-6). It became so fashionable that it was driven to the brink of extinction by over-hunting, and wild chinchilla, despite its protected status, continues to be poached and is still in danger today. Nearly all chinchilla used in the fur trade is farmed, and can be traced back to 1923 when a Californian named Mathias Chapman persuaded the Chilean government to allow him to take 11 live animals back to America. These he bred successfully in captivity and it is believed that all farmed chinchilla in Canada, the United States and Europe originate from the original 11.

While skin is the organ of touch, it is the hand that is most readily associated with that sense. We know the world through the hand; to understand something, its texture, temperature, its smoothness and roughness we reach out and touch it with our hands. As the philosopher Jacques Derrida dazzlingly expressed it:

> *Moreover, let us not forget either that the feeling-itself-touching of the finger immediately is a feeling-itself-touched of the finger, even when my finger does not touch another one of my fingers: when it touches anything whatsoever external to my body and my finger, my finger feels itself touched by the thing that it touches.*[8]

The most common emotion we feel when we encounter fur on a living animal is the desire to touch and stroke it, and this same impulse is true of a fur garment, no matter how much we might reject the object on ethical grounds. Encasing the human hand in fur, in the form of gloves fur-lined or with the fur on the outside, in either case seems at once excessive and indicative of a deficiency. If fur-lined, the pleasurable sensation we experience when touching fur is provided perpetually, the hand encased in fur is constantly stimulated to the point of numbness perhaps, ultimately desensitising our hands to the touch of fur.

4-6 John Galliano for Dior Haute Couture, coat, Autumn/Winter 1997. Chinchilla. Michael Euler/AP/Shutterstock

If the fur is external, then the contact we make with the outside world and with others is perpetually mediated by fur, by our own sensitivity. Our reception of stimuli is converted into an act of giving, the transferral of the sensation of fur to the outside world replaces the information we once received, and the new furry skin covering our hands blunts our own tactile sense.

While fur-lined gloves are common today, marketed for their thermal benefits as well as the implied luxury of encasing the hand in fur, in the medieval and Renaissance periods the fashion for gloves made from fur marks a high point in the vestimentary symbolism of the furry hand. In the fourteenth century gloves were made of beaver or hare skins, while more refined pairs made from chamois were elaborately embellished

4-7 Frager, mink boxing gloves made for Sonny Liston, 1963. Liston said he would wear the gloves for the World Heavyweight Championship fight with Cassius Clay, so as not to mark his opponent's face. Heritage Auctions, HA.com

and furred, or trimmed and lined with squirrel.⁹ The giving of gloves in the early Modern period was understood as an act of courtship or diplomacy, when, as authors Peter Stallybrass and Ann Jones note, the glove functioned as an external organ of the body 'that could be transferred from beloved to lover, from monarch to subject, from master to servant'.¹⁰ Gloves made from dog skin were especially fashionable, prized for their softness and flexibility. When given by a man to a woman, the carnal habits associated with the dog, transferred in the form of the flayed skin which, as suggested earlier, retained its essential qualities, becomes a part of the lover, a 'bit of a dog' now united with his intended. Stallybrass, commenting on the correspondence of a Spaniard at the court of Elizabeth I concerning his gift of such a pair of dog skin gloves, observes: 'The lover transformed into gloves, will always be near his beloved. When she wears him he will be able to touch her... Reduced to a malleable layer of skin, the lover can attain his desires, even if it is at the cost of becoming a flayed skin.'¹¹

The subtleties of Elizabethan courtly love, expressed by the fur-gloved suitor, undergo contemporary cinematic translation in the unlikely hands of James Bond. In the 1963 film *Thunderball*, a post-coital Bond attempts to relax his latest conquest by massaging her with a mink glove. The touch of mink, presumably intended to surpass even the tactile expertise of Bond, would appear to fail, as we ascertain from the following exchange:

Bond: 'Mink. Er, it reduces the tensions.'
Patricia Fearing: 'Not mine.'¹²

In 1963 the World Heavyweight Boxing Champion Sonny Liston, as part of the escalating publicity machine surrounding his much anticipated fight against the loquacious newcomer Cassius Clay (as Muhammad Ali was then still called), had a pair of mink boxing gloves made (fig. 4-7). The concept of the iron fist in a velvet glove was brought to new heights, suggesting that the mink punishment Liston would deliver would preserve Clay's 'pretty face'. The mink gloves' symbolic dysfunctionality proved to be ultimately prophetic, as Clay, unmarked, caused a major upset, dominating Liston who conceded defeat at the start of the seventh round. The gloves, which sold at auction in 2016 for just over $13,000 (£10,500), are perhaps a twentieth-century sporting equivalent of Stallybrass's understanding of the incapacitating gloves of the Renaissance, part of the process of 'gentling the gentry'. While Liston was not perhaps gentry, the process of 'gentling' presaged by his mink gloves continued in their rematch, when Clay dispatched him with a first-round knockout.

Our response to the touch of fur is innate and as such affects us deeply from childhood. Lucy, one of the child protagonists in C.S. Lewis's *The Lion, the Witch and the Wardrobe*, is first led to discover Narnia by her attraction to fur. Whilst playing hide and seek, she discovers the wardrobe that unbeknownst to her is the portal to Narnia: 'Looking into the inside, she saw several coats hanging up – mostly long fur coats. There was nothing Lucy liked so much as the smell and feel of fur. She immediately got in among the coats and rubbed her face against them'.[13] This celebrated example of furry transportation is discussed elsewhere (see 'Soft Gold', p. 43), but here reinforces the infantile attraction to fur, which has meant that the softest of furs have traditionally been used to fashion and trim baby clothes and accessories, such as blankets. Another children's book, *Little Fur Family* by Margaret Wise Brown, was originally published, in 1946, as a miniature book with a cover made of real rabbit fur. It was placed in a box with a cut-out hole that allowed children to touch the furry stomach of the character drawn on the front (fig. 4-8). The rather bizarre story opens with the lines: 'There was a little fur family warm as toast, smaller than most in little fur coats.' The story describes an excessive land or 'fur world', where furry creatures don extra fur coats.[14] Later editions replaced the rabbit fur with fake, but the book remains a remarkable example of both literary and fur education for infants.

A training that leads to a particular sensitivity to the feel of fur, above all to its smoothness, is as essential to the fur industry today as it was in 1607, when Edward Topsell in his *History of Four-Footed Beasts* noted that the reason for sable's high esteem resided in the fact that 'if you stroke them from the head to the tail, or on the contrary from the tail to

4-8 Margaret Wise Brown, *Little Fur Family*, 2014. Published by Harper Collins; board book with synthetic fur addition. Courtesy of the author

the head, they do lie every way smooth'.[15] In the grading halls of Kopenhagen Fur, the world's largest fur auction house, after a skin has been mechanically graded using a series of highly sophisticated computer programmes to measure its various characteristics (see 'In Black and White and Colour', p. 132), the final test of its quality is still conferred manually, via the sense of touch, as graders pass the skins between fingers and thumb to determine the degree of softness and tactile quality (fig. 4-9). This is a process that gives practical demonstration to Serres's assertion that 'Pure touch gives access to information, a soft correlate of what was once called the intellect.'[16]

Smoothness has traditionally been considered an attribute of quality, of luxury and of perfection, and the smoothness of fur and fur garments has been similarly prized. Edmund Burke confessed that he did not recollect anything beautiful that was not smooth, adding that 'smooth coats of birds and beasts' were 'animal beauties'.[17] The instinctive action of stroking fur is made in order to receive the pleasurable sensation that smoothness brings, a primal response fundamental to the history of the fur trade and fashion's desire for fur. The apparent smooth seamlessness of a fur garment belies its violent removal from the animal, evidence of the knife now hidden amongst the infinite number of hairs that permit no sight of its scars. Roland Barthes famously likened the smoothness of the Citroën D.S. to a divine object, descending to earth fully formed with no apparent trace of its assembly.[18] A fur garment shares this same magical quality of smoothness; a supernatural object that we know is the product of skinning an animal and yet, once transformed by the furrier's art, appears whole and seamless. Unlike other fabrics, a mistake in cutting fur can be mended and made invisible, its seamed complexity disappearing on the fur side so reinforcing the invisibility of human intervention (fig. 4-10). Serres's use of the metaphor of the reverse side of a tapestry in his exploration of touch is similar to the back of worked fur, revealing the tangled web of connections between the senses and presenting a unified, but infinitely complex, outer surface, while the back remains intricately seamed. This duality, or indeed duplicity, which animal rights advocate Henry Salt suggests reflected a society obsessed by perfect appearances achieved at the expense of others, in this case animals (see 'I'd Rather Go Hairless', p. 30), is central to the concept of the border that skin, and the act of skinning, patrols.

The tension that exists between the inner and outer layers of any structure, the inherent violence associated with the skinning and wearing of animals, and the economic demarcation of society expressed by the ability to own and wear fur, is palpable when we start to journey through fashionable fur's seductive surfaces. The negotiation of this tension between inner and outer is in fact the history of vestimentary fur, and resonates with the same poetic allure that the philosopher Gaston Bachelard found in his masterful exploration of space: 'Outside and inside are both intimate – they are always ready to be reversed, to exchange their hostility. If there exists a borderline surface between such an inside and outside, this surface is painful on both sides.'[19]

The inherent violence associated with the wearing of animal skins is, of course, a highly emotive subject and has meant that there has been little recent reasoned discussion of our ancient and sensorial relationship with fur. It has typically been artists who have most successfully tackled this difficult subject, artists such as Janine Antoni who, in her remarkable work *Saddle* of 2000 (see fig. 4-1), negotiates some of the complex narratives concerning the relationship between skin and presence. *Saddle*, which consists of a full-size cowhide that has been draped over and moulded to the shape of the artist's body, so that when hardened it becomes a transforming carapace, is resonant both of the trace of the artist and the animal,

4-9 ABOVE LEFT Grading mink skins at Kopenhagen Fur, Glostrup, Denmark. Courtesy of Kopenhagen Fur/the author

4-10 ABOVE RIGHT Ileana Zora, coat (detail), 1980s. United States; reverse-seamed mink that intentionally shows its construction on the outside). Courtesy of the author

4-11 Jean Paul Gaultier, coat, Autumn/Winter 2006. Mongolian lamb. The ready-to-wear collection featured models wearing long-haired furs, accompanied down the runway by live furless Manx cats, clipped poodles and greyhounds, and extravagantly hairy breeds such as Afghan hounds and Pulis. This posed questions concerning our tactile responses to both skin and fur. Mark Large/Associated Newspapers/Shutterstock

Betty sings, 'I wanna have a fur coat, have a fur coat. Not until then will I be happy'.[20] So her companions Koko and Bimbo go hunting. Various failed attempts to shoot animals follow, resulting in a fight that becomes a whirlwind, which finally disperses to reveal a pile of fur coats/skins. Betty is at first pleased but then, on seeing the skinned 'naked' (except for their underwear) shivering animals, admonishes Koko and Bimbo and gives the animals back their coats, one by one, which they pull on and 're-fur' themselves with. The cartoon closes with a triumphant parade of restored animals and with Betty at the head, swathed in a huge pneumatic, spotted fur.

A similarly comedic, but overtly racist, account of hunting and the oscillation between the inside and outside of an animal's skin was made in the nineteenth century, creating a tension that continues to inspire fashion collections of the twenty-first century (fig. 4-11). Immediately following the publication of 'The Song of Hiawatha' in 1855, Longfellow's enormously popular epic poem spawned a number of parodies including 'The Song of Milkanwatha: translated from the original Feejee' in 1856, one passage of which became especially popular and was subsequently published separately under the title 'The Modern Hiawatha'. The verse tells

a haunting reminder that asks the viewer to consider the relationship between animal and rider, beasts of burden, the borders of power, ownership and suffering all bound up in our relationship to animals.

The essential antagonism between borders – the borders of skin, the border between containment and dispersal, Bachelard's 'dialectics of the outside and inside' – are nowhere more insistent than in the borders between the furry and the furless. The wearing of fur, the donning of a second, unlawful skin, has provided an insistent reminder of the brutality of borders, no matter how light-hearted those reminders may be. *A Hunting We Will Go* is the title of a 1932 episode of the cartoon series featuring popular character Betty Boop. At the beginning of the episode

4-12 Reverse of intarsia fur sample produced for Louis Vuitton. Courtesy of Kopenhagen Fur/the author

SKIN 171

the story of a pair of mittens made from animal fur, and discernable amongst the poem's insistent trochaic rhythms and alliteration is a surprising understanding of the thermal technology inherent in First Nations Peoples' indigenous use of fur. Meaning and borders begin to collapse with the poem's continuous prefixing of the word 'side' with 'fur', 'skin', 'in' and 'out' in lines such as 'He, to get the warm side inside, Put the inside skin side outside', resulting in an unsettling bricolage of literary game-playing, colonial condescension and furry expertise.[21]

In worked fur, the reverse side bears the scars of its painful creation – the skinning, the cutting, the stitching and even possibly the healing. Human marking of an animal's skin is more commonly associated with the operation of branding, however, which, too, has an equivalency to fashioned fur. The historical understanding of the verb 'to brand' is to indelibly mark the flesh, most typically with a hot iron of some sort, as the property of another. One only has to consult the dictionary to grasp how complete an etymological shift has occurred over time. The primarily sixteenth-century definitions of branding – 'burning', 'the mark made by a hot iron', 'to stamp with infamy', 'to cauterise' – employ a distinctly corporeal, violent discourse, but on reaching the nineteenth century we begin to note the use of definitions such as 'a trademark', or 'a sign of quality', which have a decidedly more commercial, manufacturing implication.[22] Branding and its deployment in the marketing of goods and services is today a global business, and its original bestial and criminal associations are conveniently absent from today's commercial 'brandscape'. However, in the case of products made from the skin of animals, the original concept of branding as a form of identification and ownership merges with the contemporary understanding of 'brand loyalty'. Stamped leather goods, of course, have long been identified with the same operation, that of burning into the skin, that is carried out on livestock. Marking the fur side of a skin, however, is obviously more problematic. Due to the demands of the luxury brand industry, and in tandem with the ever more sophisticated techniques use to process fur, the branded fur has now become a characteristic of twenty-first century luxury design. Using the intarsia method, it is now possible to brand an animal's fur not as a sign of agrarian possession, but as conspicuous luxury brand consumption (fig. 4-12).

One of the earliest and most remarkable examples of branded fur is an haute couture Christian Dior coat, designed by Marc Bohan in 1973 (figs 4-13, 4-14), that

4-13 ABOVE Marc Bohan for Dior Haute Couture, coat, Autumn/Winter 1973. Mink. Gray Reginald/Shutterstock

4-14 OPPOSITE Marc Bohan for Dior Haute Couture, coat (detail), Autumn/Winter 1973. 'Branded' dyed, intarsia mink (see fig. 4-13). Courtesy of the author

stridently proclaims its wearer's loyalty to the house by the repeated Dior logo made from intarsia mink. The seamless transition from living animal to luxury product is only made possible by the hiding of its painful transformation behind linings, which obscure its construction and are only revealed accidentally if the lining is torn. Lost in the luxuriant furry surface and covered by lavish silks and satins lies the 'historiated skin', as Serres refers to it, the true 'history' of the object, which is more real than its imposed skin, the livery of luxury. The hidden skin reveals 'wear and tear, scars from wounds, calluses, wrinkles and furrows of former hopes, blotches, pimples, eczema, psoriasis, birthmarks. Memory is inscribed there, why look elsewhere for it?'[23]

Skin is not only stripped away, cut, shaped and stitched to form other skins, or other clothing. It can also, under exceptional circumstances, offer a form of protection beyond the capabilities of normal garments. Getting inside the skin, rather than just beneath its surface, can provide warmth, protection and disguise. An understanding of the depth of skin, of touch, recalls Aristotle's opinion that the organ of touch was in fact the heart, in tandem with its corresponding medium, flesh. Touch, therefore, resided throughout the body as well as on its surface, and borders exist between the body and the external world as well as within the body itself, so Cole Porter's lyric from 'I've Got You Under My Skin' seems especially perceptive when it continues, 'so deep in my heart, you're really a part of me'.[24]

The evisceration of animals in order to seek protection and warmth inside the body is a motif that reoccurs with surprising regularity (fig. 4-15), but can perhaps be identified as originating, within western culture at least, with Jonah, who resides in the 'belly of the beast', the giant fish that shelters him from the tempestuous seas for three days.[25] Today it is film that has most effectively represented this visceral act of survival, with the emphasis firmly placed on an animal's freshly disembowelled body to provide warmth.

In *The Empire Strikes Back*, the main protagonist Luke Skywalker is discovered freezing to death on

4-15 After Henri de Montaut, *Red Riding Hood Released From the Belly of the Wolf*, c.1865. Wood engraving. In this visceral scene – absent from modern, sanitised versions of the tale – a very small and relaxed Red Riding Hood is revealed safely residing inside the Wolf. Wellcome Collection, London

the ice planet Hoth by Han Solo, one-time smuggler and leader of the Rebel Alliance.[26] To keep him warm while he builds a shelter, Solo eviscerates a recently deceased Tauntaun, a fur-bearing lizard-like creature, which provides protection on the glacial planet. More realistically perhaps, in the Oscar-winning, fur-trading epic *The Revenant* (see fig. 2-27), a horse provides the necessary succour.[27] At the close of his epic journey of survival and salvation that constitutes the majority of screen time, frontiersman and guide Hugh Glass is forced to take shelter and recoup in the belly of his dead horse, emerging to complete his odyssey and seek revenge. Most surprising of

4-16 Gutskin parka or *kamleika*, 1910–15. Western Arctic, made by Yu'pik Inuits from Chukotka. Seal intestines and fur, sinew and feathers and sheath of the crested auklet. © McCord Museum, Montreal

all is the use of an eviscerated cow as the vessel for the three reincarnations of writer Norman Mailer that punctuate Matthew Barney's epic *River of Fundament*.[28] Here the carcass not only provides shelter from the film's eponymous river of fundament or faeces, but also serves as the fleshy casing in which Mailer's son, John Buffalo Mailer (Norman I), is reborn and emerges from the cow as Norman II, the 72-year-old African-American jazz drummer Milford Graves. This final example of being in 'the belly of the beast' is perhaps closest to the transformative skins discussed in 'Translation' (p. 211), but the skin of the animal here serves more as an incubator than as flesh worn to effect a transformation.

Having invoked the image of the thermal benefits derived from the proximity to an animal's internal organs, it seems appropriate to mention a remarkably thermal-efficient garment, which, while not fur exactly, is made from the organs of seals. The *kamleika* is a traditional Inuit outer garment made from seal or walrus intestines, an extremely light, durable and water-resistant material. When sewn with grass or sinews, which expand when soaked, the garment becomes totally waterproof. It is worn as a protective layer over a fur parka or for ceremonial purposes, and traditionally took a month to produce. Many Inuit peoples once believed that gutskin formed a barrier against evil spirits and *kamleika* were often decorated with puffin or auklet beaks as a further preventative measure as their rattle scared away spirits (fig. 4-16).[29]

The dialectic between warmth and coldness that fur clothing attempts to arbitrate takes place within a

4-17 *Eyes of Laura Mars*, dir. Irvin Kershner, 1978. Film still. Columbia/Kobal/Shutterstock

larger emotional conflict between desire and cruelty. Once killed, animals are skinned while still warm as if allowed to go cold they stiffen and the process becomes more difficult. Equally, during summer months fur coats are best stored at temperatures between 50 and 60 degrees Fahrenheit and 45–55 per cent humidity. The desire for, and attraction to, fur is always haunted by the shadow of cruelty implicit in its production, the 'horrible inside outside' to quote Bachelard, which Betty Boop experiences when she sees the skinned animals, her desire for a warm fur coat tempered quite literally by their shivering coldness.[30] The tension between coldness and warmth, between inside and outside, between human and animal flesh accounts for fur's erotic charge.

Sigmund Freud's allusion to fur as a fetishistic replacement for the female genitalia, expressed in his brief but much extrapolated observation that 'no doubt the part played by fur as a fetish owes its origins to an association with the hair of the *mons veneris*', is limited sensorially and, as he himself suggests, is uncertain.[31] His explanation that 'the choice of a fetish is an after-effect of some sexual impression, received as a rule in early childhood', is an unlikely circumstance when it comes to the sight of female genitalia and fur.[32] His later account of fur in the 1927 treatise *Fetishism* emphasises fur's role in the disavowal of a woman/mother's castration. Following the scenario of a little boy peering at female genitals from below, starting from the feet upwards, and, therefore, accounting for the fetishistic preference for shoes, he applies the same logic to the sight of fur. For him, 'fur and velvet – as has long been suspected – are a fixation of the sight of pubic hair, which should have been followed by the longed-for sight of the female member'.[33] Again, this is surely a supposition dependant on the woman/mother wearing fur at that traumatic moment. While the sight of fur against flesh has been the basis for any number of sexual fantasies, it is perhaps the tactile 'impression' of fur and hair, not exclusively pubic, against the skin and the contrast between these two tactile sensations, rather than the gender specific visual impression, that provides the key to its libidinous command.

The ribald directness of the phrase 'all fur coat and no knickers' belies a complexity that collides fur, skin and nakedness with notions of pretence, aspiration and immorality, and a never-to-be resolved tension between warmth and coldness. Helmut Newton's archetypal photograph, *Laura in a Fox Cape* of 1974, which features a model walking along the Avenue Georges V in Paris at night, wearing only high-heeled shoes and a fox fur cape, open to reveal her genitalia, condenses both a mercantile commodification of animal and woman with a primeval understanding of warm fur against flesh. Four years later, Newton's imagery was the inspiration for the 'stylised violence' produced by the fictional fashion photographer in the film *Eyes of Laura Mars*, which contains a collapsing together of Freud's formulation of fur as fetish, the tamed ferocity implicit in the processed skins of animals, warmth, and the misogyny of late 1970s fashion styling.[34] Against a backdrop of burning cars, Laura Mars, a female Newton with an equally objectifying camera lens, shoots an editorial featuring women wearing only fur coats and revealing underwear. They effect a series of choreographed 'flasher' movements, opening and closing their furs while enacting a mock fight (fig. 4-17). This is accompanied by the thermally threatening track 'Burn', which overlays rock keyboards and screams with the lyrics 'Play with fire. You wanna burn?'[35]

The British bedroom farce *Not Now Darling*, set in the West End furriers of Bodley, Bodley and Crouch, makes the relationship between fur, flesh and commodification explicit.[36] Primarily an excuse for the film's leading actresses Julie Ege, Barbara Windsor and Trudi van Doorn to appear in their underwear and then be hastily covered up by fur, the plot entails strippers, mistresses and minks. Both sex and fur is on sale, emphasised in the pivotal scene where Ege strips in the middle of the furriers and refuses to move until she receives her promised mink. The symbolic coldness of commodified sex is here counterpointed by the denial of warmth in an environment full of potential thermal benefit.

The command *Not Now Darling*, and its implication of denial and refusal, brings us inevitably to *Venus in Furs* by Leopold von Sacher-Masoch, a novella published in 1870, which no account of the representation of fur within western popular culture can ignore, and which perhaps more than any other text of the Modern period has confirmed the relationship between fur and erotic desire.[37] *Venus in Furs*'s reputation has grown exponentially, especially since 1886 when psychiatrist Richard von Krafft-Ebbing introduced the term 'masochism' as a clinical category in his *Psychopathia Sexualis*. This was one of the first texts concerning sexual pathology and it discusses a number of what Krafft-Ebbing termed 'cerebral neuroses' including masochism, or, the process of deriving sexual gratification from receiving pain or abuse. Krafft-Ebbing also described fur as a material that can waken or heighten sexual awareness and, unlike Freud, based the attraction of fur purely on its tactile sensation, rather than it being a substitution for pubic hair. So firmly embedded have the concepts of masochism, and indeed sado-masochism, become within contemporary society that, on returning to the source of the term, one is struck by the novella's chasteness and, for the purposes of this work, the relatively simple allegorical status that fur is given. As Gilles Deleuze perceptively noted: 'Indeed, the work of Masoch is on the whole commendable for its unusual decency.'[38]

While *Venus in Furs* makes a concerted effort to establish the visual, art historical ancestry of the novella's protagonist Wanda von Dunajew, the 'Venus in Furs', using Titian's *Venus with a Mirror* and other references to emphasise the contrast between Venus's white skin and dark fur, it is the touch of fur and by extension its warmth that is the focus of the story (fig. 4-18). From the very first page, fur's thermal properties are prioritised: 'The sublime being had wrapped her marble body in a huge fur and, shivering, had curled up like a cat'.[39] Many other allusions to coldness, contrasted with the warmth of fur, follow. A climax

4-18 Titian (active c.1506; d. 1576), *Venus with a Mirror*, c.1555. Oil on canvas, 124.5 x 105.5 cm. Granger/Shutterstock

4-19 *The Scarlet Empress*, dir. Josef von Sternberg, 1933. Film still. Marlene Dietrich as Catherine the Great offers a cinematic evocation of Leopold Sacher-Masoch's novella of 1870, which explores the relationship between fur and erotic desire. Paramount/Kobal/Shutterstock of thermal fantasy is reached a third of the way into the story, where the reader is given a pseudo-scientific account of warmth and electricity that the tropics apparently produce 'more heated peoples' and 'heated atmospheres' and that fur excites all highly-strung people. A rather bizarre analogy between cats and batteries prompts Wanda to declare: 'So a woman in fur is nothing but a big cat, a charged electric battery?'[40] Again, Deleuze provides clarity: 'In the masochistic fantasy, fur retains its utilitarian function; it is worn less for the sake of modesty than from fear of catching cold … Masoch's heroines frequently sneeze. Everything is suggestive of coldness: marble body, women of stone, Venus of ice'.[41]

The other overlooked point about *Venus in Furs* is that it is a novella about fashion, and fur fashion in particular. The vogue for all things Russian, expressed via fashionable fur, is discussed at length in 'Furland' (p. 118), a craze that emerged at exactly the same time as Sacher-Masoch's novel. Wanda, who declares she has 'a talent for despotism – I also own the necessary furs', appears in a variety of Catherine the Great 'looks', while copious descriptions are included of *kazabaikas*, a Slavic vestimentary fantasy imagined by Sacher-Masoch and referred to as a fur-lined coat.[42] These descriptions would grace any contemporary fashion journal in their fetishistic attention to detail: 'A new, fantastic attire: Russian ankle-boots of violet, ermine-trimmed velvet; a gown of the same material, decorated with narrow strips and gathered up with cockades of the identical fur; a short, close-fitting paletot similarly lined and padded with ermine; a high cap à la Catherine the Great' (fig. 4-19).[43]

The power of representation, and in particular the role photography would play in the mediated imagery of fur-clad women, is interestingly signalled in the passage where Severin, Wanda's future slave, obtains a photographic reproduction of the Titian *Venus*: 'What luck! A Jew who dealt in photographs somehow contrived to get me the portrait of my beloved'.[44] How swiftly fur and erotic fixation became established can be gauged by another famous literary example of furry representation. Prior to Gregor's 'metamorphosis' in Franz Kafka's 1916 story of the same name, the only indication of his desires, indeed his humanity, in his otherwise regimented existence as a fabric salesman is the attraction he feels for the photograph of an anonymous fur-clad woman. In his otherwise spartan room, Gregor 'hung the picture which he had recently cut out of an illustrated magazine and put into a pretty gilt frame. It showed a lady, with a fur cap on and a fur stole, sitting upright and holding out to the spectator a huge fur muff into which the whole of her forearm had vanished'.[45] This proffered fur, an invitation to touch and be subsumed in its warmth and softness, remains so potent for Gregor that, even once he has undergone his transformation and his room has been stripped of its furnishings, he guards the image both as memory of his former self and, in his insect guise, as a source of comfort. 'He was struck by the picture of the lady muffled in so much fur and quickly crawled up to it and pressed himself to the glass.'[46] Gregor's desperate attraction to the photograph is a salient example of the libidinal energy that, even as image, fur and in particular fur clothing has generated.

The proffered muff in Gregor's photograph points back through time to another equally compelling image of a muff-carrying woman, emblematic of the erotic association between fur and sexuality. The celebrated series of etchings entitled *The Seasons* (1643–4) by fur-obsessive Wenceslas Hollar (see 'Heads or Tails', p. 102) depicts women's fashions. The personification of Winter shows an anonymous masked woman in a velvet gown and sable tippet carrying a large sable muff. Set against a background of the City of London, she holds up her gown to reveal the embroidered hem of her petticoat and a high-heeled shoe, decorated with a rosette (fig. 4-20). It has been suggested that the woman is a prostitute, as J.L. Nevinson discreetly speculates: 'Winter's success in her profession is obvious to all; her masterful charm has won her a sable tippet and muff'.[47]

Interestingly, the part of the City she foregrounds shows the tower and facade of the original Royal Exchange, where merchants gathered to transact their business. To the extreme right is a building known at the time as the Tun, so-called because of its barrel shape, which was originally erected in 1283 as a prison for 'night-walkers and other suspicious persons'.[48]

The relationship between commercial gain, fashion and sexuality through the medium of fur is made explicit in Winter's accompanying poem:

Winter
The cold, not cruelty makes her weare
In winter, furrs and Wild beasts haire
For a smoother skinn at night
Embraceth her with more delight.[49]

The synthesis between the rough hairy skins of animals and the implied carnality (and indeed cruelty) of wearing fur is equated in the verse to the smoother, less hairy but perhaps no less bestial act of human intercourse. The temporal and chronological distance separating Winter's City of London and Laura's Parisian street in the Newton photograph is condensed by the libidinal force of fur; a force that was recognised long before Freud's fetishistic treatise and which, since the Renaissance, has been understood as a metaphor for sexuality. Historian Patricia Lurati, in her essay examining the Renaissance understanding of fur as an erotic material, discusses how lewd rhymes that equated fur with sexuality were popular especially during carnivals, including the *Song of the Furriers* by Bernardo Giambullari: '[It] listed the many types of pelts – cat, lynx, marten, lamb, sable, vair, fox, ermine, hare and rabbit – used by furriers with the clear intention of referring to the female pubic region'.[50] The substitution of the name of fur, or fur-bearing animals, for the female sexual anatomy is a legacy that has survived with the contemporary usage of 'beaver' and 'pussy', while the first recorded usage of the term 'muff' as a referent for the female genitalia dates from the 1690s, an appellation that Hollar seems to have suggestively pre-empted.

The mid-twentieth-century fashion for mink garters – a pair from this period, owned by the

4-20 Wenceslas Hollar (1607–1677), Winter from *The Seasons*, c.1643–4. Etching, 26 x 18 cm. The Metropolitan Museum of Art, New York. Gift of Barbara E. Fox in Memory of Howard A. Fox, M.D., 2018

Duchess of Windsor, was included in the auction of her personal possessions in 1998 – brought fur into close proximity with the pubic region, garters acting as material realisations of Freud's fetishised substitution of fur for pubic hair (fig. 4-21). Today it is possible to obtain a range of fur 'sex toys' including fur nipple warmers, massage gloves in mink, chinchilla and fox, underwear for men and women in black rabbit, patent leather stockings trimmed with black mink and, for men, white or blue fox 'cock cuffs'.[51] This recent commercialisation of the erotic appeal of fur is merely

4-21 Hal Hunter, garters, c.1945. United States; mink, faux pearls, silk lace. Courtesy of the FIDM Museum at the Fashion Institute of Design & Merchandising, Los Angeles. Gift of Mela Hoyt-Heydon

a contemporary manifestation of our primal response to the touch of fur. Severin, the European nobleman in *Venus in Furs* who desires to be enslaved to a woman, describes himself as a *suprasensual* person. However, as Serres points out, exceptional sensitivity is unnecessary as through our skin we respond to 'fluctuating traces of caresses, memories of silk, wool, velvet, furs, tiny grains of rock, rough bark, scratchy surfaces, ice crystals, flames, the timidity of a subtle touch, the audacity of aggressive contact'.[52]

FURNISHING

Pablo Picasso's possibly apocryphal comment that you can cover almost anything in fur has been credited as the catalyst for the creation of one of Surrealism's most iconic works: Meret Oppenheim's *Object of 1936*, or *Le Déjeuner en Fourrure* as Andre Breton re-titled it (fig. 4-22). The famous cup, saucer and spoon, covered in a thin layer of Chinese gazelle fur, was conceived when Picasso, Oppenheim and Dora Maar met at the Café de Flore in Paris in 1936. Oppenheim, who was freelancing as an accessory designer at the time, was wearing a metal cuff covered in fur, a design she had just sold to the couturier Elsa Schiaparelli, who featured it in her Autumn/Winter 1936 collection. It was the cuff that prompted Picasso's comment, to which Oppenheim is supposed to have responded that even her cup could be covered with fur. Following their meeting, she immediately bought a cup and saucer from Monoprix and on returning to her studio covered the pieces with fur.

Oppenheim's *Object*, 'with its blend of inutility, sexual connotations, and nausea' as art historian Werner Spies has described it, was exhibited by Breton to great acclaim, 'a vortex of art interpretation' leading to its acquisition by the Museum of Modern Art in New York.[53] While much has been made of the work's sexual associations with the spoon being read as phallic, the cup vaginal and the fur pubic, for Oppenheim it was fur's thermal properties that inspired the work as, on finding her coffee growing cold, she is said to have asked the waiter for '*un peu plus de fourrure*' (a little more fur) to keep her cup warm. Thermal pun or sexual allegory, the lasting power of *Object* lies in its essential dysfunctionality. Our recoil from the thought of taking a mouthful of fur is an instinctual revulsion akin to that of psychoanalyst Julia Kristeva's notion of the 'abject', which she compares to food loathing as when 'the lips touch that thin skin on the surface of milk' (fig. 4-23).[54]

Oppenheim made other fur objects including a pair of fur gloves with wooden fingers and red-painted nails, which, together with a number of metamorphic glove drawings, may well have influenced Schiaparelli. Over 30 years later, in 1969, she created *Squirrel*, a glass beer mug with a fur squirrel tail for a handle, a masculine counterpart to the feminine cup and saucer. What distinguishes Oppenheim's fur objects is their uselessness; their impossibility makes them seminal surrealist things. Most other fur-covered objects, while often

4-22 Meret Oppenheim (1913–1985), *Object*, 1936. Cup, saucer and spoon covered in Chinese gazelle fur. John Lindsay/AP/Shutterstock

materially compromised and ridiculously extravagant, still retain the object's original function.

Fur objects often speak of luxury and decadence, such as the fur-covered lipstick case produced by couturier Lucien Lelong, a prototype design for his successful perfumery and cosmetics line. Made sometime between 1935 and 1942, the silver mink-covered lipstick comes perilously close to the oral revulsion of Oppenheim's cup and saucer, the mental proximity between lips and fluffy mink generating a disturbing tactile frisson, possibly erotic, possibly repugnant (fig. 4-24). Fur has also been used to cover books, a less surprising practice when one considers the leather-bound volume, or the gruesome history of books covered in human skin, often the skin of executed criminals, technically known as anthropodermic bibliopegy. Perhaps the most celebrated fur-covered book belonged to the architect Le Corbusier. When his beloved dachshund Pinceau (Brush) died, Le Corbusier had the animal skinned and tanned. The leather was then used to cover a cherished copy of *Don Quixote*, a somewhat macabre gesture but a way, perhaps, of recalling the pleasure he received from stroking the dog each time he opened his favourite volume. Here the tactile benefit is aligned to the concept of the souvenir, or, in the manner of mourning jewellery that incorporates human hair, a reminder of the departed loved one. Denise Hawrysio's artist's books series, entitled *Killing*, uses fur as a salutary reminder of the actual process of obtaining fur. The volumes open to reveal pages made of fur, supremely tactile yet literally unreadable, 'useless' books that are as unintelligible as the killing of animals for their fur (figs 4-25, 4-26).

Al Teitelbaum, the idiosyncratic Hollywood furrier (see 'In Black and White and Colour', p. 132), in addition to providing furs for films and a roster of celebrity clients also had a lucrative side line producing fur-covered objects, including a complete library of books covered in mink. In a populist, surreal idiom, Teitelbaum also produced mink-covered telephones, his best-selling item, which according to an article

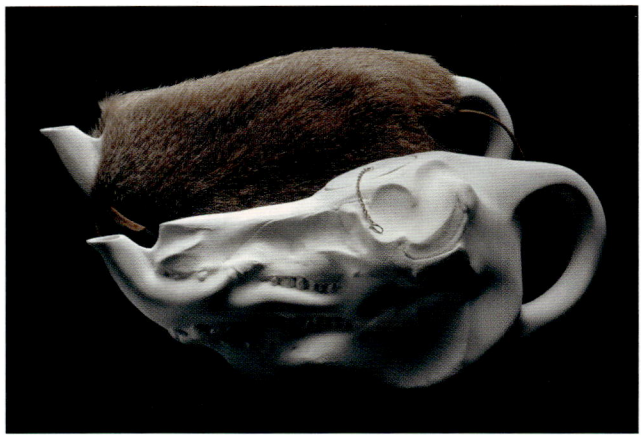

4-23 TOP Wieki Somers (b. 1976), *High Tea Pot*, 2003. Porcelain teapot in the form of a pig's skull, with a fur tea cosy. *High Tea Pot*, a successor perhaps to *Object*, continues the thermal play initiated by Meret Oppenheim, forcing the tea-drinker to consider the repugnant, yet useful, proximity of warming rat fur to an object associated with the bourgeois ritual of tea-drinking. Studio Weiki Somers

4-24 ABOVE Lucien Lelong, mink lipstick case, 1935–42. Courtesy of the FIDM Museum at the Fashion Institute of Design & Merchandising, Los Angeles. Gift of Monique Fink

entitled 'He Makes Mink Telephones' of May 1950, used on average three mink skins each and retailed for $200. Other objects included an ermine-upholstered typewriter for a Hollywood screenwriter, zebra skin upholstery for director Mitchell Leisen's limousine, and lampshades made of white broadtail (Karakul or 'Persian' lamb). The article closes with the copywriter's suitably punning allusion to Oppenheim's *Object*, predicting 'And you can bet an ermine-coated coffee cup, he'll go fur, that phone furrier fella.'[55] The 1950s also saw the production of the 'Johnny Mink', a fur lavatory seat cover, available in natural, silver-blue or white mink, by prominent New York and Detroit furriers Annis Furs, which marked a suitably scatological nadir of the mid-twentieth-century craze for surrealist-inspired fur-covered items.

While novelty fur products may have reached a peak in the 1950s, the use of animal fur and skins in interior decoration has a much longer history. Primeval habitats would no doubt have used skins for their thermal properties, and there are many accounts of the earliest civilisations using furs and skins in their interiors, a practice that continues today in many indigenous societies. Early histories of fur take the Bible as a starting point for the use of skins in decorative schemes, referring to the passage in Exodus that describes the construction of the tabernacle as including 11 curtains of goat hair, a tent of red-dyed ram skins, and an awning of badger skins.[56]

This biblical excess was certainly matched in medieval Europe, where fur was worn extensively and a variety of skins were also used as bed and floor coverings. Elspeth Veale notes that '*counterpoynts*' or bed coverings, either fur-lined or made entirely from skins, were used in wealthy households, including examples made from ermine lined with squirrel, and she also records a London merchant who slept under leopard skins. She goes on to document cradles trimmed with the softest furs and even '*hedesheets*', prototype pillows made from ermine covered with a linen cloth.[57] As improvements were made in domestic architecture, the need for the thermal benefit of furnishings made from skins decreased, and fur in the western interior took on symbolic, rather than practical, functions.

Furs, skins and the body parts of animals used in decorative schemes are emblematic of hunting. The trophy room has long been a mechanism by which to display prowess and rank throughout global culture and history. Such rooms were an indispensable demonstration of privilege and power, the slaughter

4-25 Denise Hawrysio (b. 1957), *Killing III*, 1989. Rabbit fur pages bound in buckram. This series of four books incorporating fur or skin (the other two being *Killing II*, with pages of mink, and *Imaginary Killing*, using imitation deer fur) collectively oscillate between the seductive tactility of fur and repugnance at the senseless slaughter of animals. Photograph by Denise Hawrysio. Courtesy of the artist and Collection of the National Art Library, Victoria and Albert Museum, London

4-26 Denise Hawrysio (b. 1957), *Killing I*, 1988. Leopard skin pages bound in buckram. Photograph by Denise Hawrysio. Courtesy of the artist and Special Collections of Chelsea College of Art & Design Library

and display of animals consolidating the hunter's social status. As Alan Hunt observes:

> *There are deep roots to the ornamental role of trophies: the horns, head or fur of the victim of the chase attest to the prowess of the male hunter and thus become sources of status. Manifestations of the link between trophies and hunting have remained remarkably enduring features of masculinity: taxidermy still flourishes, antlers are still attached to walls and fish that did not get away still achieve a gruesome immortality.*'[58]

Throughout the early Modern period, alongside the obligatory display of antlers and stuffed heads in trophy rooms, animal skins – most commonly leather and often elaborately stamped, moulded and gilded – were used to line the walls of domestic spaces. Spain was the principal centre for this craft and decorative, leather-lined walls became a marker of status and civility. In the Victorian period the trophy room and hunting lodge became newly fashionable, owing to the increasing aristocratic alliance between British and Central and Eastern European dynasties, typified by the marriage of Queen Victoria to Prince Albert of Saxe-Coburg-Gotha, where hunting estates and lodges were a cultural tradition. The Dougarie Estate, built in the 1850s on the Isle of Arran, is typical of the period, its external walls continuing to be adorned with antlers until the 1970s. It still retains many features of the 'baronial slaughter house' style, including deer skins on the passage walls and decorations reflective of the craze for antler furniture, often incongruously included in more modest urban interiors (fig. 4-27).[59]

When not functioning as indicators of their inhabitants' sporting prowess, the use of animals in interior design was intended to be understood as 'exotic', symbolic of decadence and the 'suprasensual' nature described by Sacher-Masoch. The quintessential decadent, the Duc des Esseintes, hero of J-K. Huysmans's 1883 novel *A Rebours* (Against Nature), decorates his new house at Fontenay by binding the walls 'like books in large grained crushed morocco [leather]: skins from the Cape', and, along with his collection of rare books and his cut flowers, he strews 'tiger skins and blue fox furs about the floor'.[60] As the nineteenth century turned into the twentieth, the shift from domestic game animals to rarer breeds as a form of decoration for European and North American interiors was indicative of the increased availability of these skins

4-27 Hall of the Hunting Trophies, Chateau du Haut-Kœnigsbourg, Alsace, France. With its chandeliers made from antlers and wall painting of St Hubert, the patron saint of hunters, this nineteenth-century renovated interior in a medieval castle is typical of the fashion for hunting lodges and other spaces decorated with trophies and objects made from animal parts. Public domain/WikiCommons and the growth of fur production in this period as a whole. *Furs and Fur Garments*, published in 1895 in conjunction with the International Fur Store in London, notes the fashionable shift to 'exotic' animal species in interiors and is worth quoting in full:

> *The introduction of late years of the use of the skins of the larger animals, such as the Polar bear, the buffalo, the bison, the tiger, the leopard, and even the lion, as decorations in the furnishing of large apartments, has led to an increased commerce in these skins, which are unquestionably beautiful, not only as mats and rugs, but also for wall decoration. The skin of the leopard makes exceedingly pretty chair-backs, and so, for a matter of fact, does the undyed seal. Madame Sarah Bernhardt has introduced, with startling effect, a lion's hide in her beautiful study in Paris, and another leading French artiste, Madame Rejane, has a lion (stuffed) rampant as a lamp-bearer. Monkeys can be rendered picturesque objects of furniture as lamp-stands and card-holders.*[61]

This chilling account concludes with a warning against vulgarity and the approbation that skins 'must be prepared to perfection' and can 'be obtained at THE INTERNATIONAL FUR STORE, where a large collection of stuffed animals is exhibited' and 'which well deserves inspection'.[62]

With the use of exotic animal skins in interior schemes came a shift in the perception of these strictly masculine gendered spaces. The testosterone-charged trophy room, or 'man cave', gave way to the space of the predatory female. A space that once celebrated man's mastery over animals now became a space in which man himself was the prey. This popular perception was heralded by figures such as the actress Sarah Bernhardt and crystallised by the publication of Elinor Glyn's scandalous 1907 novel *Three Weeks*. Glyn, sister of the British fashion pioneer Lucile (Lady Duff-Gordon), forged a remarkably modern media career as a novelist, Hollywood screenwriter, stylist and briefly director.[63] *Three Weeks*, with its notorious scene of a Balkan queen seducing a young British aristocrat on a tiger skin rug, led to the popular verse:

> *Would you like to sin*
> *With Elinor Glyn*
> *On a tiger skin?*
> *Or would you prefer*
> *To err with her*
> *On some other fur?*

This fixed forever in the popular imagination the image of her as the 'man-eating' seducer, reclining on a tiger-skin rug. A 1927 image by graphic artist Jean Raoul-Naura for the satirical magazine *Fantasio* depicts a stylish, fur-clad woman, standing on the flayed skin of a man, the naked flesh of her latest conquest replacing the customary tiger skin. It serves to emphasise the role interior decoration played in the construct of the all-devouring female.

More traditional masculine trophy rooms endured, nevertheless, and were part of a larger twentieth-century fascination with African culture, including the colonially commodified phenomena of the big game hunt and the safari, as popularised in numerous Hollywood films and in which many of its stars took part, both on and off the screen. Most notable of these was Gary Cooper, who enjoyed shooting bears and mountain cats in between filming with his friends Ernest Hemingway and Howard Hawks. Following a nervous breakdown in 1931, he went on safari to Kenya and decimated a considerable quantity of wildlife there, bringing back the carcasses to his Beverly Hills retreat (the former residence of Greta Garbo), along with a pet monkey named Toluca. It formed a disquieting decorative melange of popular moderne, Hollywood Spanish revival and hunting lodge luxe (fig. 4-28).

While fur soft furnishings today are almost undetectable from their synthetic imitators, with early twentieth-century animal skin furniture that was not the case. The great era of modernist furniture, the 'apparatus of contemporary life' as the architect and designer Marcel Breuer described it, produced

4-28 Actor Gary Cooper's trophy room in his home at Beverly Hills, California, 1940s. Glasshouse Images/Shutterstock

by figures such as Eileen Gray, Le Corbusier, Pierre Jeanneret and Charlotte Perriand, was noted for its spartan machine aesthetic using industrial materials such as tubular steel and glass. The soft elements of these democratic, affordable pieces were typically made from simple woven fabrics, waxed cotton or plain leather. However, 'de-luxe' versions were produced where pony, leopard or zebra skin replaced the basic textiles, pieces that created a dialogue between western, rational, technological construction and 'primitive', tactile sensuality.

These dichotomous objects were the props for the *mise en scène* of avant-garde design during the 1920s and 1930s, made for interiors that retained a fascination with animal products, but rejected the padded, upholstered spaces of the nineteenth century. Stripped of their heads, claws and paws, animal skins were treated as textures and surface patterns. Similarly *shagreen* (shark or ray skin) was a favoured material for cabinet-making, resulting in pieces of furniture that act as frozen moments in the processing of the organic, in the clash between the mechanical and natural worlds. Typical of these pieces is the startling chair designed by Denham Maclaren around 1930, made of upholstered zebra skin imprisoned behind two massive slabs of industrial grade glass and riveted with metal fittings more commonly seen securing shop windows or display cases (fig. 4-29 a&b). It is as if the animal is in the process of being compressed; its mane, still left intact on the back of the headrest, invests the chair with a surreal cruelty. Completing the typical modernist interior of the period would be animal-skin rugs and African sculpture, symptomatic of a general fascination with African art that expressed itself in jazz, Cubism and indeed leisure pursuits such as the safari.

These modernist trophy rooms, while rejecting the taxidermied displays of the nineteenth century, are indicative of the twentieth century's increasing consumption of natural resources and the annexation of other cultures. Cultural theorist Gunnar Schmidt's observations concerning nineteenth-century interiors – and the final question that he asks in his article 'Trophies: the Aestheticization of Melancholy' – can be just as effectively directed towards these Machine Age slaughter rooms:

> *One constructs for oneself a space, an interior in which objects – as things subject to one's rule – are assigned their final and strictly delineated places. Everything becomes a still life, a nature morte. But it remains to be asked: what kind of home is this, in which objects are at once ornaments and symbols of triumph?*[64]

Fur soft furnishings have continued their uneasy progress into the twenty-first century. Oscar de la Renta, the celebrated fashion and interior designer, used fur for both, most notably for the library of his New York apartment. Photographed by Horst in 1969 for American *Vogue*, the library extended the traditional bibliophile's love of leather-bound volumes onto suede couches, leopard-skin pillows and raccoon-tailed fur throws. A year earlier, the sexual cathexis associated with the fashionable domestic incorporation of fur was given a typically revolutionary reinterpretation in Pasolini's film *Theorem*, in which the enigmatic, Christ-like arrival of a mysterious stranger into the midst of a wealthy bourgeois Italian family is the catalyst for their sexual and political transformation.[65] A central space for these transformations is provided by fur-covered beds, which become the sites for the sexual inadequacy of the father and his subsequent 'healing' by the stranger, played by Terence Stamp, and also for Stamp's seduction of the family's son and heir.

In 1971 it was possible to have the world, or at least the country of your choice, rendered in fur, made by the trail-blazing New York furriers Georges and Jacques Kaplan (see 'Soft Gold', p. 43). Under the title of 'Fur-Niture', they started to produce fur-covered couches in geographical shapes. Their 'four-section all American couch', as it was described, had a foam

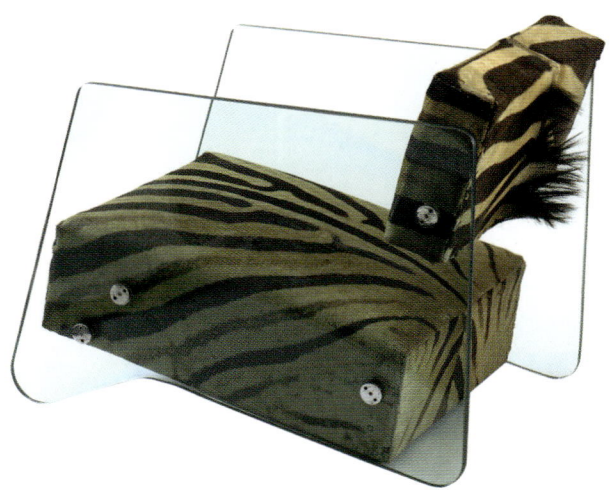

4-29 a&b Denham Maclaren, armchair, c.1930. London; zebra skin, industrial glass and metal fittings. © Victoria and Albert Museum, London

SKIN 189

rubber base and came in four sections which, when arranged together, formed the shape of the United States of America. Covered in Texas bull hide, the dark brown and cream markings of the hide mimicked the outline of individual states – a couch of this kind could be purchased for $5,000. Kaplan could also hand-sculpt Manhattan (for under $1,000), or any state or country that might be desired, 'provided the fur doesn't come from an endangered species', an early ecologically aware example of domestic global domination, achieved in fur.[66]

Today it is possible to buy anything from wild Russian sable blankets, retailing for €57,925 ($65,000), to mink headboards and pillows and bolsters, in furs to suit every budget, while established luxury companies such as Frette produce fur-lined and trimmed bed linen reminiscent of medieval *hedesheets*.

This subsection has concentrated so far on fur interiors and the objects encountered within those spaces, but to conclude we might consider the example of a complete house made from fur. Throughout history and in many cultures, rudimentary structures such as tents have long been made using animal skins, but the Pelzhaus, or fur-house, exhibited at the 1896 Hungarian Millennium Exhibition in Budapest, was a construction entirely rendered in fur (fig. 4-30). The exhibition, which was part of a series of events and public works intended to kickstart the construction of modern Hungary and the establishment of Budapest as a metropolitan capital, attracted a variety of Hungarian exhibitors including Josef Katzer, court furrier and master skinner, who established his business in Budapest in 1876. In the form of a typical farmhouse, the Pelzhaus conforms to dwellings recognisable from fairy tales and children's drawings, complete with gables, a pitched roof, a chimney and a picket fence. Made entirely from skins inside and out, it has foundations of sealskin and squirrel, window shutters of moleskin and main walls of muskrat fur. The fur garden fence posts are topped with hedgehog finials with fur garlands suspended from their mouths. Four full-length fox skins demarcate the corners of the house and the roof is made from overlapping shingles

4-30 Pelzhaus, a house made of fur exhibited at the Hungarian Millennium Exhibition, Budapest, 1896. Published in *The Furrier's Craft*, 1903. Public Domain/WikiCommons

of opossum tails. The chimney, fashioned from bird skin, is topped by taxidermied nesting storks, while a golden eagle perches at the opposite end of the roof. A moose head overlooks the window while the entrance to the interior, which apparently contained an exhibition of the furrier's products, is guarded by a taxidermied adult brown bear.

This hallucinatory Pelzhaus returns us to the world of surrealism, realising André Breton's desire for 'nothing less than the objectification of the activity of dreaming, its transfer into reality'.[67] Known only from a nineteenth-century photograph, its interior remains mysterious as two headless, fur-clad sentinels block further sight of the inside. An interior, one imagines, furnished with mink-covered books, ermine-jacketed telephones, gazelle-fur tea services, and fittingly, for this surreal consumer dream, with 'Johnny Mink' providing the excremental seating.

PART FIVE

FLEECE

5 FLEECE

SHAPE SHIFTERS

Wearing fur is transformative; it initiates 'becoming', becoming-animal, becoming-multiple, becoming-molecular, concepts formulated by Gilles Deleuze and Félix Guattari in *A Thousand Plateaus*, their seminal contribution to late twentieth-century postmodernism.[1] These becomings might be joined by becoming-occelated, the neologism devised by Michel Serres to describe the imagined state of bearing the eye-like markings of a leopard, or becoming-villous and making indefinite our borders with a coating of long fine hair, as with a monkey.[2] What is important is not the assumption of an animal's characteristics or its mythical attributes by the donning of its skin and 'turning' into a tiger, wolf, or bear, but the unsettling of the borders between human and animal. In fact, 'what is real is the becoming itself, the block of becoming, not the supposedly fixed terms through which that which becomes passes'.[3]

Why else is the image of Mae Capone hiding in mink so unnerving (fig. 5-2), or the sight of Marlene Dietrich, caught in the moment of becoming- gorilla/becoming-Dietrich, singing 'Got voodoo, head to toes, Hot voodoo, burn my clothes', so atomising?[4] The countless myths depicting humans transformed into animals, or indeed animals that become human, are at their most potent at the moment of becoming, the growing, pulling on,

5-2 Mae Capone, February 1938. The wife of Chicago gangster Al Capone avoids reporters by obscuring her face in the deep collar of her mink coat following her prison visit to see her husband in Alcatraz. Granger/Shutterstock

PREVIOUS PAGE Naomi Bailey-Cooper, glass 'fur', 2018. Textile sample using spun glass, wild rubber and Tencel. Courtesy of the artist.

5-1 Nayland Blake (b. 1960), *Crossing Object (inside Gnomen)*, 2017–18. Performance exhibit, New Museum, New York. Photograph by Scott Rudd. ©Nayland Blake, Courtesy Matthew Marks Gallery

5-3, 5-4 'Fur Play Redux', French *Vogue*, November 2009. Ideas about savagery, tribalism and transformation are synthesised in an editorial by Inez van Lamsweerde and Vinoodh Matadin, which makes an unusually direct statement about our 'bestial' nature. Courtesy of the author

replacing and disguising of skin, for skin opens up a universe of possibilities (figs 5-3, 5-4). This erosion of the border between flesh and fur, smooth and shaggy, plain and marked, is endlessly re-enacted with the wearing of fur and accounts for its terrifying seductions. The possibility of being multiple, at once animal, human, monstrous, carnal but ultimately dis-human, can 'provoke fear, but also fascination, as their ghostly, same but not quite, threatens to re-position or even to dissolve the boundaries of "normality"'.[5] As discussed throughout this book, the mere touch of fur is enough to make its wearers nomads, restlessly crossing cultural, sexual and economic borders, on their journey towards elsewhere. This sensation is undeniably troubling, today more so than ever, and the disgust at the touch of animals that Walter Benjamin discreetly refers to is due to the awareness 'that in him something lives so akin to the animal that it might be recognized'.[6]

Artist Nayland Blake's performance series, *Crossing Object (inside Gnomen)* (see fig. 5-1), takes the form of a bear-bison creature created as their 'fursona' (Blake is always referred to in the plural). The Gnomen can change sex and gender, and its furry suit is representative of Blake's hybrid identity. While informed by Blake's participation in the furry fandom subculture, which celebrates anthropomorphism principally through the wearing of furry animal costumes, *Crossing Object* can also be understood as part of a larger, primeval alliance between the human and animal worlds, merging via the tactile space of fur: 'The becoming-animal of the human being is real, even if the animal the human being becomes is not.'[7]

The transformative potential of the bear has been celebrated throughout time and across cultures. Claws from a bear were found in the tomb of a prince from southern Zeeland, dated to the 4th century BCE, the claws being all that remained of the bearskin in which the prince's body was wrapped, so honouring his earthly prowess and ensuring his continued ferocity in the afterlife. This ferocity continues to be ceremonially acknowledged today in the military bearskin, most commonly associated with the British Grenadier Guards (fig. 5-5). Made from the fur of the Canadian black bear (although that of the thicker brown bear is sometimes dyed and used), caught by Inuit hunters as part of an annual cull, each headdress takes one whole bearskin to produce and is cut to a traditional pattern, the finished article adding an extra 45 centimetres (18 inches) in height to its wearer. Traditional bearskins have a wicker internal shell over which they are stretched, a procedure that can be seen in a British Pathé newsreel of 1951, the closing scenes of which depict a bizarre multiplicity of headless, decapitated bearskins in formation awaiting their wearers.[8]

The tradition has attracted increasing condemnation from animal rights groups and the British Army is currently investigating suitable synthetic alternatives.

The slaughter of bears, or rather the refusal to do so, was the origin of the infantile sign of becoming or transition that is still re-enacted today. In 1902 President Theodore Roosevelt, a passionate hunter, was touring the Mississippi area and having had no success after a few days' shooting, the embarrassing prospect of a 'kill less' president had to be avoided. So a young bear was captured, tethered to a tree and the President's attention drawn to it. Guessing the subterfuge Roosevelt refused to kill the cub, uttering the famous words: 'If I shoot that bear, I won't be able to look my boys in the face again'.⁹ The story was published, accompanied by a cartoon, in the *Washington Post* and became an immediate media sensation (fig. 5-6). Morris Mitchson, a Russian émigré who owned a toy and sweet shop in Brooklyn, saw

5-5 Princes William and Andrew wearing bearskins at the Trooping the Colour Ceremony, London, June 2018. Guy Bell/Shutterstock

5-6 Clifford Berryman, *Drawing the Line in Mississippi*, 1902. This *Washington Post* cartoon comments on President Theodore Roosevelt's refusal to shoot a chained bear cub while on a hunting trip. Granger/Shutterstock

the cartoon and capitalising on the story's popularity had his wife make a stuffed bear cub. After seeking permission from the White House, he named it the Teddy Bear. This totem of potential becoming is an example of what psychoanalyst Donald Woods Winnicott termed a transitional object, a tactile sentinel guarding the child's negotiation of becoming adult.[10] Blake's *Crossing Object* functions in a similar manner, protecting and facilitating their bi-racial, pan-sexual identities.

Wearing the head and skin of an animal into battle transforms the soldier into a state of terrifying becoming for the opposing forces, becoming-bear, lion, tiger, becoming-brutal, becoming-taller (fig. 5-7). In the later stages of the Roman Empire, exotic non-native species of fur were prized by the wealthy, but primarily worn ceremonially. The Roman army's eagle-standard was carried into battle by a soldier wearing a lion's pelt, his head emerging from the jaws of the animal in a moment of devouring, simultaneously consumed and consuming. The transmission of animal prowess by wearing its skin was, according to legend, a process regularly undergone by the Emperor Nero, whose multiple becomings were acts of liberation, much to the horror of his contemporaries, as Suetonius recorded:

> *He so prostituted his own chastity that after defiling almost every part of his body, he at last devised a kind of game, in which, covered with the skin of some wild animal, he was let loose from a cage and attacked the private parts of men and women, who were bound to stakes, and when he had sated his mad lust, was dispatched by his freedman Doryphorus.*[11]

Classical myth is replete with assorted shape-shifting animal skins. Dionysus was often depicted wearing a panther skin; his followers, the Maenads, also sported the skins of fawns and, most notably, Hercules is depicted on Attic pottery wearing the skin of a slain Nemean lion, his head emerging from

5-7 Jean Paul Gaultier, hat, Autumn/Winter 2008. An example of fashion's response to the military tradition of wearing animal heads, trophies that act as expressions of power.
Sipa/Shutterstock

the lion's jaws. Killing and skinning the lion was Hercules's first labour, a task made especially difficult as its golden fur was impenetrable, and the act was only completed by using the lion's armour-piercing claws to flay its own skin. This preparatory becoming operation has provided many western artists with an opportunity to demonstrate their ability to represent human skin, musculature and fur, realised by Rubens as a visceral lion-human-tiger knot of becoming (fig. 5-8).

While the Greeks and Romans favoured lion skins, other ancient civilisations, including the Egyptians and the Mesoamericans, reserved special regard for the spotted skins of the leopard and jaguar respectively. They associated these animals with specific deities, their skins conferring on their patrician wearers the strength and shape-shifting abilities of these feline

5-8 Copy after Peter Paul Rubens (1577–1640), *Hercules and the Nemean Lion*, late 18th–early 19th century. Oil on canvas, 44.5 x 39 cm. © Victoria and Albert Museum, London. Bequeathed by Mrs Durore

5-9 LEFT Pauline Trigere, coat, 1962. Leopard fur with wooden buttons. Brooklyn Museum Costume Collection at The Metropolitan Museum of Art, New York. Gift of Mr and Mrs Robert Zicklin, 1985. © Photo Scala, Florence

5-10 ABOVE Man's dinner jacket (detail), c.1970. Ontario; leopard fur with leather trim. With permission of the Royal Ontario Museum. © ROM

gods. Evidence of both real and simulated ceremonial pelts has been found, as well as artefacts incorporating their distinctive markings. Lions, tigers, jaguars and leopards, including the snow leopard (also known as *ounce*), all belong to the genus *Panthera*, while the lynx, puma, cougar, ocelot, caracal and cheetah are of the genus *Felinae*. Black panthers are melanistic variants of leopards and jaguars, but do not occur in Felinae, so there are no black variants of cheetahs, for example.

Jaguars and leopards have ring-like markings termed rosettes (becoming- flowers?) (figs 5-9, 5-10). Those of the jaguar are bigger and have one or several spots in the centre, while the leopard has smaller more densely distributed rosettes with no central spot. The cheetah has small round solid spots instead of rosettes, distinctive facial 'tears' and black lips. Each type of coat is tailored to a specific environment, provides camouflage even when the animal is moving, and is individual and unique – as with fingerprints, but in this instance a fur print. Famed for their speed, cheetahs are also highly inbred and due to their greatly reduced gene pool are perpetually at risk of extinction, whether due to human intervention or otherwise.

Perhaps the most delirious of all painted cheetah becomings is Fernand Khnopff's celebrated painting of 1896, *Caresses* (fig. 5-11). The archetypal vision of the 'devouring woman', powerful, dominating and seductive, Khnopff's sphinx- cheetah inbreed is also, possibly incestuously, an image of the artist's beloved sister Marguerite. Her recurring features populate his works, becoming-multiple, becoming-other, even becoming-himself as we also recognise her features in the androgynous figure she purrs against. In the 1982 remake of Jacques Tourneur's film *Cat People*,

a haunting story of unseen feline-becoming, the incestuous bond between Paul and his sister Irena, both cat people in human form, is explained in a dream sequence. Featuring a group of languorous black panthers, Paul explains 'we are an incestuous race, we can only make love with our own'. Mating with ordinary humans transforms cat people back into cats and they must kill in order to become cat people again.[12]

The woman in ocellated fur, as sexual predator, pervades popular culture. Mrs Robinson chooses leopard for her seduction of Benjamin Braddock in the film *The Graduate* (fig. 5-15), while Jeanne Moreau, as the immoral Juliette in Roger Vadim's version of *Les Liaisons Dangereuses*, wears ocelot for her most corrupting tasks but on shedding her protective armour of fur, she is un-becoming and suffers disfiguring burns at the climax to the film.[13]

The promise of erotic transformation has meant that patterned furs remained fashionable throughout most of the twentieth century (figs 5-12, 5-13, 5-14). This has resulted in the near decimation of many species, leading in 1973 to the signing of CITES, a multilateral treaty dedicated to the cessation of the international trade in endangered species.[14] Nevertheless, the illegal poaching of and trade in spotted and other distinctively marked animals continues to supply unregulated areas of today's fur trade. Malayan and Sumatran tigers, snow and Amur leopards, jaguars and lions were all classified in 2019 by the World Wildlife Fund as either 'critically endangered', 'endangered' or 'vulnerable', and

5-11 Fernand Khnopff (1858–1921), *Caresses*, 1896. Oil on canvas, 50.5 x 151 cm. Royal Museums of Fine Art, Belgium. Public Domain/WikiCommons

amongst a wealth of alarming statistics available on the WWF website is the estimate that there are only 3,900 wild tigers and only 90 Amur leopards left in the world.[15] The IUCN Red List of Threatened Species states that more than 28,000 species are threatened with extinction.[16]

Cat-becomings are not restricted to hyper-sexualisation. As with the lion-headed Roman legionaires, prowess, accuracy and speed are also attributes of feline transformation. Animal skins, both actual and in representation, were central to the culture and cosmology of ancient Egypt, its society predicated on notions of becoming, not least becoming immortal (fig. 5-16). High-ranking funerary priests wore leopard skins and heads in the belief that the leopard guaranteed regeneration and rebirth in the afterlife, and 'leopards were associated with the night sky; their spots were the stars'.[17] Amongst Tutankhamen's treasures were two 'leopard skins': one real skin, much degraded but with its decorative golden head still intact; the other, a fake (see 'The F Word', p. 151). Attached to a gilded model of a leopard's head was a mass of woven material, described by the archaeologist Howard Carter in his notes as decorated with the leopard's spots, 'represented by 5-point

5-15 OPPOSITE *The Graduate*, dir. Mike Nichols, 1967. Publicity photograph.Granger/Shutterstock

5-12 Esther Dorothy, coat, c.1964. Zebra hide trimmed with leather. Esther Dorothy was often billed as the world's first female furrier. Texas Fashion Collection, University of North Texas Libraries

5-13 Calman Links, coat, 1970s. Lion fur, collar and revers made from the mane of a lion, with snakeskin buttons. Texas Fashion Collection, University of North Texas Libraries

5-14 Coat, Bergdorf Goodman, New York, 1968. Tiger fur with large sable, or possibly fox, shawl collar. Texas Fashion Collection, University of North Texas Libraries

5-17 Bowl, 8th century. Mayan people, Guatemala or Mexico, Mesoamerica. Ceramic, H: 10.5 cm. The bowl is decorated with a mythological scene featuring a jaguar. The Metropolitan Museum of Art, New York. Gift of Mr and Mrs Morris A. Long, 1987

5-18 *Leopard Man* sculptural group, c.1915. Plaster with metal and cloth additions, awaiting re-display with other works in the Royal Museum for Central Africa, Tervuren, Belgium. Virginia Mayo/AP/Shutterstock

stars of gold. These were hollow, of thin sheet gold'.[18] Carter identified this object as a 'leopard-skin' cloak, presumably intended to be worn by Tutankhamen in the afterlife; at once a ritual becoming garment, luxury item and artefact that translates the vitality and ferocity of the leopard into a precious object, a demonstration of skilled simulation and the belief in the transformative power of fur.

All Mesoamerican cultures feature a jaguar god, an animal revered not only as an aggressive predator but also for its transitional abilities, able to inhabit both trees and water and hunt by night and day. These qualities made it important in ritual, guiding and protecting the shaman on his journey between heaven and earth (fig. 5-17). Jaguar pelts were worn by the ruling classes, who often incorporated the animal's name into their royal titles. A belief in were-jaguars (half-human, half-jaguar) was also common and they were usually depicted in transformative poses, in mid-becoming. Mesoamericans believed, as Frances Backhouse observed of Inuit cultures, in the existence of a 'cross-species bond that is almost unfathomable to those of us not brought up in a world where the boundaries between human and non-human are semi-permeable'.[19]

A more recent and troubling becoming can be found in the Royal Museum for Central Africa in Tervuren, Belgium, in the form of a sculptural group depicting a member of a so-called West African leopard cult, or *anioto*, about to pounce on a sleeping victim beneath his feet (fig. 5-18). The standing plaster figure is dressed in a hood and tunic, decorated with a schematic leopard spot pattern, and is given facsimile metal claws. The sculpture, commissioned by the Ministry of Colonies, was unveiled in 1915. Originally displayed with genuine artefacts including a bark skin tunic, iron claws and sticks with which to make leopard paw prints on the ground, the group is a disturbing hybrid between sculpture and ethnographic display and has become a source of embarrassment to the Museum, a bastion and legacy of the Belgian civilising and colonising project. While secret leopard societies existed in many parts of West Africa in the later nineteenth and early twentieth centuries, primarily as a locus of resistance against colonial

5-16 Wall painting from Tutankhamun's tomb, c.1332–1322 BCE. Pharoah Ay, wearing a leopard skin worn by Egyptian high priests, performing the 'Opening of the Mouth' ceremony for Tutankhamun. Gianni Dagli Orti/Shutterstock rule, they have typically been depicted as violent, cannibalistic criminals preying on white victims. Wearing leopard skins, and using the animal's teeth and claws as weapons, enabled cult members to blame leopards for their crimes. Such was the fear of the supernaturally evil, devouring 'savage' that leopard societies not only gripped visitors to Tervuren, but also inspired examples of overtly racist popular literature, including *Tarzan and the Leopard Men* of 1935 and *Tintin au Congo* of 1946.[20] The sculpture in the context of the Museum is 'tamed', frozen in mid-crime, and remains a uniquely unsettled object, becoming-leopard, becoming-Africa under the European and North American colonial gaze. Here, becoming, and with it the possibility of transformation, has been co-opted by western, white rationality in a process of becoming-endangered, as with the leopard itself.[21]

Wearing the skins of an animal does not always ennoble the wearer, and while the pelts of lions, tigers and jaguars emulate the majesty of the beasts they were stripped from, other furs can defile and cloak the wearer in ignominy. Beauty disguised by baseness, specifically the 'baseness' of animals, is a persistent trope in a number of folk tales, an example being the variants of the European *Peau d'âne (Donkey Skin)*.[22] Also known and translated as *Furry Pelts, All-Kinds-of-Fur, The She-Bear* and *Thousandfurs*, the tale tells the basic story of a beautiful princess/daughter who tries to escape the incestuous attentions of her recently widowed father. In order to do this she puts on animal skins and runs away to live disguised in squalor. As with Cinderella, she is periodically restored to beauty, assisted by fashion in the form of three dresses the colour of the sky, moon and sun, but has always to return to furry undesirability. During these transformations she is observed by, or betrays herself to, her noble admirer by revealing portions of her white, non-bestial skin, or inadequately covering her fine clothes with shameful fur, an interesting reversal of the typical position of interiority that fur occupied for most of western fashion history. Her suitor is rewarded for his patience, or ability to see beyond her furry exterior, and takes her as his bride.

The taboo of sinful union with animals represented in these tales and the danger of proximity to fur is a legacy of Renaissance attitudes to fur, which equated animals with unlawful desire. This sense of disgust is expressed most stridently in the Italian variant, translated as *The She-Bear*, which first appeared in Giambattista Basile's collection of fables, *Il Pentamorone*. Glimpsing her hidden beauty, the prince delivers the following remarkable speech: 'Oh, you beautiful morsel fit for kings, why do you hide your passing beauty in a bear's hide? ... Why are you closed in such an hairy lantern? ... lift the veil from that stinking hide ... who has enclosed in a leather casket such a priceless treasure?'[23] *The She-Bear* offers a reduction of the usual multiplicity of identities made possible by the wearing of fur and instead is beauty and the beast become one.

The variant by the Brothers Grimm, *Bearskin*, recasts the reviled fur wearer as a soldier who makes a pact with the devil to wear a bearskin and not to wash, comb his beard or cut his nails for seven years, in return for good fortune. Although repugnant, Bearskin is charitable and kind and is offered the pick of his three daughters by a grateful innkeeper; one daughter is able to see beyond his hairy surface and is rewarded by wealth and the handsome, newly de-furred soldier.

The previously mentioned and notorious 'Hot Voodoo' sequence, from the film *Blonde Venus*, offers a twentieth-century cinematic translation of this traditional tale (fig. 5-19). An unsettling mixture of early Hollywood camp, racism and jazz, the sequence features Marlene Dietrich led on stage in a gorilla suit by Afro-wigged, shield-carrying 'tribal dancers' to perform her striptease, or more accurately her becoming. First she takes off her fur glove/hands to reveal unblemished white skin, as in *Furry Pelts* where the princess is betrayed by forgetting to re-blacken and make bestial

5-19 *Blonde Venus*, dir. Josef von Sternberg, 1932. Film still. Paramount/Kobal/Shutterstock

again a section of her finger, covered by a ring. Then Dietrich removes the gorilla head in a second disturbing becoming as her prominent forehead surmounts the gorilla's torso of padded and muscled cotton. A platinum-blonde Afro wig, pierced by glittering arrows, is put on her head as the rest of the gorilla skin is stripped away to reveal the next moment of becoming: a bejewelled Dietrich/bird/sex-doll with enlarged sequinned nipples and ostrich tails framing a feathered sporran/pubis. Unlike the furry fairy tales, however, the monstrous skin here reveals further monstrosity. Furry baseness no longer disguises purity and is unable to contain a polluting sexuality, made manifest by the song's lyrics, lasciviously drawled by Dietrich.

Transforming shameful and painful fur is most persistently encountered in the figure of the werewolf (fig. 5-20). The dangerous proximity of these incurably furry becomings to our clean 'hairless' bodies, and their legendary transformative power, is acknowledged by the common name for congenital terminal hypertrichosis (excessive hair growth): 'werewolf syndrome' (see 'Manimal', p. 15). The werewolf's 'monobrow', curved fingernails and, in Russian variants, bristles under the tongue, are all anomalies that betray the fully furred beast lurking within and which must be rejected and made taboo. Werewolves patrol the borders between culture and nature, the crossing of which is marked by the shedding of civilised clothing to reveal the primitive fur beneath. This slippage between the cultivated and the bestial is all too easy, and we can only keep these conditions separate if we suppress the non-things that occupy the hinterland between them, that meander back and forth across the boundaries, so making them taboo. Making something taboo orders and individuates

5-20 *Wolf boy or a creature with two heads, one wolf, one human,* c.1495. Woodcut, 10.4 × 6.5 cm. This print from the Nuremberg Chronicles by Hartmann Schedel possibly shows an instance of conjoined twins. Wellcome Collection, London

5-21 Coat, 1850–90. Britain; woven wool, Russian wolf skin. The skins of 32 wolves were used to make the lining and trimmings of this coat. © Victoria and Albert Museum, London. Given by Mrs A. Pollock

our world, and keeps it from being one unbroken continuum of becoming. It also establishes a sense of self, which is always vulnerable and easily overturned when we wear fur.

The tragedy of the werewolf is that this becoming is uncontrollable, unwanted but inevitable, dressing in fur with the full moon and then reverting to furless form once the dawn breaks. The anticipation and pain of this transformation adds to the despair and mortification of this already supremely troubled creature.

Another aspect of folklore is that in order to detect the werewolf in its hairless, human disguise all one needs to do is cut the flesh to reveal the fur lurking beneath the skin, a supremely painful and disquieting image that nevertheless mirrors our anxieties about our own hair, and the border it patrols between our human and animal forms. Exteriorising the animal within us is at the heart of universal transformation myths and, as with the werewolf's, it is often acutely painful. It also explains our oscillating attraction to, and rejection of, fur, which offers us 'modes of expansion, propagation, occupation, contagion, peopling'.[24]

While not known for wearing fur, Adolf Hitler had none of the werewolf's anxiety accompanying lupine identification. He had referred to himself as a wolf since the early 1930s and those in his inner circle often called him 'the wolf', an identification no doubt compounded by Norse myths that tell of the monstrous wolf Fenrir, who is born to the god Loki and the giantess Agrboda. Additionally the name Adolf is etymologically germane being derived from the Old German Athalwolf, a composite of *athal* meaning 'noble' and wolf, while his headquarters on the Eastern Front was dubbed the 'Wolfschanze' or 'Wolf's Lair'. This megalomaniac fantasy was perhaps ultimately only a more recent, but catastrophic, manifestation of legendary monstrous wolf-becomings. Ancient Nordic warriors, known as Berserkers, went into battle wearing only wolf and bear skins, which acted as symbols and furry facilitators of the state of wild fury that overtook them; the warriors' name survives in the modern phrase 'to go berserk'.

Contemporary popular culture remains haunted but not only by werewolves – the popularity of the *Twilight* series of films, romantic fantasies based on novels by American author Stephenie Meyer, are a testament to this, featuring vampires as well as werewolves. It has also been suggested that the character 'Wolverine', known from the *X Men* comics and movie franchise, is afflicted not only with the werewolf's angst, but also the uncontrollable rage of the Berserker. When considering the resonance of mythic fur in popular culture, it is impossible to deny the influence of *Game of Thrones*, the American fantasy TV series, in which fur is used extensively as a means of vestimentary identification. Keen to emulate their favourite characters, fans of the show were swift to respond to the information that the series' costume designer dyed and distressed sheepskin rugs, obtained from the furniture retailer IKEA, for the principal character Jon Snow and members of the military order Night's Watch. IKEA, swift to capitalise on the newly found popularity of their rugs, issued simple instructions telling fans how to make their own 'wolf' capes.

Fashionable lycanthropes have punctuated fur's history, with wolf-lined overcoats becoming a staple of the elegant 'wolf about town' from the mid-nineteenth century, while along with the raccoon coat (see 'Force of Fur', p. 141) motoring coats of wolf and bearskin were valued for their thermal and appropriately 'wild' aesthetic, suitable for members of the newly motorised wolf packs of the early twentieth century (fig. 5-21).

Edmund Leach's seminal 1964 essay *Anthropological Aspects of Language: Animal Categories and Verbal Abuse* suggests that 'Whatever is taboo is sacred, valuable, important, powerful, dangerous, untouchable, filthy, unmentionable.'[25] While fur clothing in general is fast becoming unmentionable, the final fur to be considered in this subsection on transformative furs is not only unmentionable but also, to contemporary society, incomprehensible. Monkey fur, in particular that of the *colobus* monkey, rose to fashionable prominence at the end of the nineteenth century along with many other exotic furs and continued to be used throughout the first half of the twentieth century. It is possible, however, to find earlier references to its use, as in Edward Topsell's *History of Four-Footed Beasts and Serpents* of 1658, where under the entry for 'Munkey' he notes, 'being tamed and caught, they conceive and work very admirable feats, and their skins pulled of them being dead are dressed for garments.'[26]

Due to its fashionable status the colobus monkey was excessively hunted, leading to its extinction from some parts of Africa, but today its biggest threat is from habitat loss due to human destruction. The colobus is arboreal, rarely coming down from the treetops, and extremely agile. Of the various species, two are black and white and one, extremely rare, is red. The black and white species is characterised by its long, lustrous hair, close in appearance and texture to human hair. The genus as a whole derives its name from the Greek *Kolobós*, meaning 'stunted', 'mutilated' or 'docked', due to the fact that it lacks, or has an extremely atrophied, thumb, unlike all other monkeys.

To the Renaissance imagination the monkey's similarity to man was dangerous, an erosion of borders that allowed the possibility of a defiling becoming (fig. 5-22). As Patricia Lurati points out, the monkey was perceived 'as an ignoble parody of humans to the point that it developed into a symbol of inner chaos, of the propensity for vice and unbridled urges. In the mindset of the day, the hairy monkey was perceived as the icon of the sinner, the personification of the devil's helper or even his incarnation'.²⁷ It is perhaps the infinitesimal distance between ourselves and monkeys, a distance that must be maintained at all costs, which, along with the unthinkable cruelty implicated in their manufacture, makes garments made from monkey fur so abhorrent, so perverse.

The incorporation of monkey fur into high fashion garments, primarily for women, plays with the deep-seated associations of the monkey with unbridled sexuality, which Topsell again observed in the behaviour of what he termed 'another kind of monkey', who 'by his knees, secret parts and face, you would judge him a wilde man' and who 'is so venerous that he will attempt to ravish women.'²⁸ Owing to the fashionable silhouette of the 1930s and 1940s, when

5-22 'A Great Munkey', c.1570. Embroidered canvas with silk, gold and metal thread, 26 x 28 cm. Panel from the Oxburgh Hangings, worked by Mary, Queen of Scots and Elizabeth, Countess of Shrewsbury. The subject is taken from a woodcut in a book of animals (*Icones animalium*) by Conrad Gesner, Zurich, 1550. © Victoria and Albert Museum, London. Presented by the Art Fund

5-23 Jacket, late 1930s. United States; colobus monkey fur, silk. Courtesy of the author

monkey fashions were most popular, its fur was used to emphasise and demarcate the ubiquitous wide, padded shoulders of coats, jackets and dresses (fig. 5-23). The fur's luxuriant length and blackness turned fashionable women into broad-shouldered, 'hairy-chested' expressions of the same period's fascination with the 'other' and the 'savage' (fig. 5-24) . Monkey fur clothing is loaded with the cultural and sexual symbolism of 'primitivism' that pervaded popular culture, initiated by the success of films such as *King Kong* and the *Tarzan* series that dominated cinema screens.

Monkey fur was also highly photogenic and registered well on screen (see 'In Black and White and Colour', p. 132), creating for the mass cinema audience spectacularly stylish primates, as personified in 1937 by Ginger Rogers in *Shall We Dance*, where she makes her head-turning entrance dressed in white monkey fur, or by Irene Dunne in her equally dramatic appearance a year earlier in a full-length black monkey coat and matching hat for *Theodora Goes Wild*.[29] Due no doubt in part to cinema's influence, monkey fur became widely available and relatively affordable. One could purchase a monkey-fur coat for $59.50 in 1927 (roughly $850 today), compared to a raccoon coat that could have cost anything from $300 to $450, ($4,200–$6,300), while in rationed Britain in the 1940s the department store Gorringes was advertising monkey coats as an affordable option.

Arguably the greatest fashionable advocate of monkey fur was Elsa Schiaparelli, who incorporated it in a number of her collections, for accessories as well as garments, such as the much copied monkey fur boots. Made for the heavily surrealist *Circus* collection of 1938, fur sprouts and spills over the top of the boots, covering the feet and reaching the ground. Schiaparelli revisited monkey fur in the 1940s for garments such as 'sweaters', which used fur that had been dyed blonde or tortoiseshell. Monkey fur, like human hair, is relatively easy to dye, proof of which can be gained from the startlingly bright, emerald green and black monkey fur muff and tippet, made in France in 1935, in the collection of the National Gallery of Victoria in Melbourne. Interestingly, monkey fur was at its most fashionable during both world wars, periods when inhumanity was in the ascendant.

The year 1938 is the date of a supremely disconcerting evening dress designed by Paquin (figs 5-25, 5-26). Made of creamy, flesh-coloured silk in the typically simple, almost demure, style of the period, it shatters its youthful femininity by the addition of fringes of monkey fur, emphasising the bust line and graphically demarcating the length of the dress from waist to hem in lines of pubic-like hair. Monkey fur's transformative

5-24 'Le Gout du Jour', Paris, 1920. Fashion plate depicting a taffeta tea dress trimmed with monkey fur; an unsettling combination of the refined and the 'primitive'. Courtesy of the Rijksmuseum, Amsterdam. Purchased with the support of the F.G. Waller-Fonds

5-25, 5-26 Jeanne Paquin, evening dress (and detail opposite), 1938. Silk, cotton, monkey fur. The Metropolitan Museum of Art, New York. Gift of Mrs John Chambers Hughes. © Photo Scala, Florence

properties are here caught in mid-becoming, a relocation of African 'primitivism' to the world of Parisian couture – virginal to bestial, female to male – producing a chic simian-becoming, ready for her first mating ritual.

This dress, I would argue, is an example of the 'deep' fashion that Ann Jones and Peter Stallybrass discuss in their examination of clothing in the Renaissance and Shakespeare's use of the term fashion: '"Fashion" can be "*deeply* put on" or, in other words, clothes [can] permeate the wearer, fashioning him or her within. This notion undoes the opposition of inside and outside, surface and depth. Clothes, like sorrow, inscribe themselves upon a person who comes into being through that inscription.'[30] The Paquin dress has dispensed with borders and is in a state of becoming, with hair sprouting from fabric rather than flesh in unexpected places and tailored silk disrupting the natural/unnatural growth of pubic/monkey hair. There is no need to cut the flesh in order to reveal the werewolf or beast within; this garment has already exposed its primitive possibilities.

TRANSLATION

The visual representation of fur has endured as one of the greatest challenges to the artist. From cave paintings to contemporary digital realisations, fur has acted as a form of litmus test by which to gauge an artist's skill. Technological change and development has been instrumental in our relationship to fur, altering both how fur has been sourced and produced and the ways in which it has been worn. A similar trajectory of technological development has influenced how fur has been represented and its image disseminated. Whether it be via marks made by hand, charcoal, brushes, print culture, photography, film or computer-generated imagery, fur's structural complexity, chromatic variation, lustre and tactile sensuousness has inspired its observers throughout history to bravura displays of furry mimesis.

Fine clothes, including furs, would certainly in the sixteenth and seventeenth centuries have been far more costly than a portrait, and it was not unusual for clothes and jewels to be sent to the artist's studio for their own 'sittings', such was the importance of an accurate rendering of clothing, which, according to the period could be 'read' in a variety of ways with the rich symbolism of fur being an intrinsic part of that process. Portrait painters had plentiful supplies of furs that are known to us today from inventories. Their function was not only to enable the artist to perfect the rendering of fur; they were also used to dress the sitters, acting as an incontrovertible sign of the subject's status and a useful prop that we see reoccurring in the work of certain portrait painters, particularly in the eighteenth century (fig. 5-27). Such artists included Pompeo Batoni, whose many portraits of gentlemen on the Grand Tour often share identical fur-lined garments.[31]

The particular challenge of conveying, via whatever medium, fur's structural complexity, beauty and symbolic resonance has resulted in some of the world's most mesmerising demonstrations of artistic skill, and it would be tempting to write a history of art using fur epistemically, as a way of encompassing the development and dissemination of global pictorial representation. Similarly, the history of which type of animal hair has been used to make artists' brushes could produce a delightfully self-referential 'fur on fur' treatise. Today, camel (in fact usually squirrel), kolinsky sable (actually Siberian weasel), ox, badger and hog are the most commonly used. The linguistic complexity of fur, both its naming and the terms used by the furrier, has been discussed throughout this book and is equally rich and equivocal when considering artists' brushes, as Jo Kirby demonstrates when describing the seventeenth-century painter's studio:

> *The hair used for the soft hair brushes or 'pensills' is not always easy to identify: the English word 'fitch', for example, means polecat, a member of the same family as the weasel and the ermine. Hair from the tails of these species was used for brushmaking. However, 'fitch' also referred to a square-ended brush and this is the more likely interpretation.*[32]

As suitable as these approaches to the study of represented fur may be, it is not within the limits of this book to attempt such histories here. Instead this subsection will concentrate on fur's representation, or rather translation, to spaces other than the painter's studio.

5-27 Pompeo Batoni (1708–1787), *Portrait of Richard Milles*, c.1759. Oil on canvas, 134.6 x 96.3 cm. The sitter is depicted in a red fur-lined cloak that appears in a number of Batoni portraits, suggesting this fashionable garment was a studio 'prop' favoured by the artist. Universal History archive/AIG/Shutterstock

Walter Benjamin, speaking of literary translation, suggests that 'Just as the manifestations of life are intimately connected with the phenomenon of life without being of importance to it, a translation issues from the original – not so much from its life as from its afterlife'; he also suggests that translation marks the 'stage of continued life'.[33] It is this 'afterlife' of fur that this subsection is concerned with; an afterlife, however, not rendered in perfect, naturalistic detail by talented artists using traditional methods, for as Benjamin stresses, exact translation is neither entirely possible, nor of any ultimate use to the original (the reader for

Benjamin is not the object of the translator's efforts). Rather, these translations are closer to the action of displacement, 'to transport', 'to remove from one person, place or condition to another'.[34] While there are examples throughout this book of astonishing feats of traditional representative artistry, it is fur's translation to other forms and by other means that enables fur to attain 'its latest, continually renewed, and most complete unfolding.'[35]

When fur is translated into other materials such as glass, metals or textiles, a necessary simplification, or visual shorthand is devised. This is not to say, of course, that it is not entirely possible to find a glass engraver, for example, as skilled at the faithful reproduction of fur as an oil painter may be, but naturalism is not the subject here. Rather, it is the processes that allow a further 'unfolding' of fur, and which both in the past and today have granted fur an afterlife, free from the tyranny however seductive of the 'life-like', the identical, the 'carbon copy', for as Benjamin insists, 'translation is a form'.[36] The translations in silk, glass or gold that this subsection will briefly consider may be closer to that other process of translation, of increasing urgency today perhaps, that of Freud's concept of 'transference', understood as a direction, or re-direction, of feelings and desires towards a new object.[37] If we take our primary sensory and pleasurable response to fur, discussed at length elsewhere in this book, as our original relationship with fur, then rather than being transferred to an undeserving or unsuitable new object of desire, as Freud might suggest, in a climate of mounting opposition to processed fur, the search for new forms of furry expression, new fur in fact, may provide the most satisfying state in which fur's 'afterlife' can continue.

The translation of fur into a form of graphic shorthand, or perhaps ideogram, where an idea is expressed without recourse to a specific language or naturalistic reproduction, reached an apogee in the medieval period. The conventions of heraldry produced some of the most systematic and abstracted interpretations of fur, remaining its dominant mode of visual translation in the west until the pictorial innovations developed during the Renaissance saw the establishment of naturalism. Collectively, the colours and patterns used in heraldry are known as tinctures and are divided into three main groups: metals, colours and furs. While the first two elements are straightforward and contain a limited colour palette (including sable, which despite its origin as the name used for the dark pelt of the marten, in heraldry always denotes the colour black, rather than the fur) and two metallic shades of gold and silver, the inclusion of 'fur' as the final 'language' of heraldic decoration attests to its importance in medieval society. Its ideogrammatic form as a tincture permits fur's very real tactile presence to be abstracted and understood, not so much as material but as sign.

The two furs used as tinctures in heraldry are ermine and *vair* (fig. 5-28). Ermine is usually depicted as black spots powdering a white ground, although there are a number of variations. Its earliest depictions

5-28 Robert Tyas, *Flowers and Heraldry or Floral Emblems and Heraldic Figures Combined to Express Pure Sentiments, Kind Feelings and Excellent Principles*, 1851. Published by Houlston & Stonemason, London. Page detail showing the heraldic tinctures of both *vair* (nos 12 and 13) and ermine. (no. 6) Public Domain/WikiCommons were the most realistic, taking the form of long tapering points echoing the actual tips of the ermine's tail, but it is also commonly depicted as an arrowhead, which at its base divides into pointed tufts and at its head is surrounded by three spots. This convention is thought to derive again from actual observation of the ermine used to line ceremonial and royal robes, where the hair of the ermine tail, represented by the tufted base, was secured by means of studs to the white fur, hence the three spots, but this has yet to be proved conclusively. The British heraldic tradition recognises three principal variants of the customary white ground with black spots: *ermines* for white spots on a black ground, *erminois* for gold with black spots, and *pean* for a black ground with gold spots.

The second heraldic fur is *vair*, the winter coat of the red squirrel, which is blueish grey on the back and white on the underside of the animal (fig. 5-29). This tincture is always depicted in blue and white (to echo the colour of the actual fur) and consists of alternating rows of small upright ear-shaped shields, a pattern again derived from observation of the actual construction of a *vair* lining, as Arthur Fox-Davies in his *A Complete Guide to Heraldry* suggests: 'It will be readily seen that by sewing a number of these skins together a result is obtained of a series of cup-shaped

5-29 Coat (detail), *c*.1980–90. Bellies of Russian squirrel skins pieced together in the traditional manner. Public Domain/WikiCommons

5-30 a&b Stained glass panels from the Life of St Eustace, Chartres Cathedral, 12th century. Known as 'donor' panels, they depict members of medieval French trades, who may have funded some of the stained glass in the cathedral. Appropriately, given that St Eustace is the patron saint of hunters, two of the donor panels depict the fur trade: one shows a furrier displaying a *vair* cloak and the other a furrier selling a cloak to a customer. The schematic representation of *vair* or squirrel would be immediately understood by a medieval viewer. © Dr Stuart Whatling

figures, alternating bluey-grey and white'.[38] As with ermine, *vair* has a number of alternative depictions, according to the size, number of rows and alignment of the 'shield' or 'bell' shaped units. The three principal variants reflect their origin in the fur trade, with the middle or ordinary size known as *vair*, a smaller size known as *menu-vair* (hence *miniver*) and the largest known as *beffroi* (referring to the pattern's bell-like shape) or *gros vair*.

This heraldic shorthand, established around the twelfth century, becomes convention in other pictorial forms, such as manuscripts, memorial brasses, books of hours and stained glass. The windows of Chartres Cathedral include striking examples of this heraldic system of depicting fur, inserted into secular scenes of the fur trade. These scenes have traditionally been regarded as 'donor windows', paid for by the respective trade guilds, including furriers, whose images are immortalised in glass as recognition of their generosity. This view, however, has been revised, due in no small part to the real cost of financing such windows and the fact that the guilds had not actually been organised in central France (at least in the manner we would recognise today) when these windows were being made in the early thirteenth century.[39] Whatever their origin, their depiction of fur represents a remarkable pictorial collision between the animated scenes of commerce and the formal, non-realistic representation of fur that would, however, be readable as fur to contemporary viewers. The depictions of ermine and *vair* that disrupt the pictorial plane and geometrically overlay the naturalistic furriers and their customer, seen in the windows depicting the Life of St Eustace, are striking even for the conventions of medieval stained glass, producing what might be understood as glass collages (figs 5-30 a&b).

What these early representations of fur communicate is the concept of transformation, of our desire for fur to bring about change, to initiate journeys and to transcend borders. Heraldic

5-31 The Three Magi from Mary and Child Surrounded by Angels, Basilica of Sant'Apollinaire Nuovo, Italy (detail), c.526 CE. Mosaic
This panel shows Balthassar, Melchior and Gaspar bringing gifts for the infant Christ. Public Domain/WikiCommons

representations of fur, such as that seen in the stained glass of Chartres, mark a turning point both art historically and mythically. Another example of glass made fur that depicts a journey and one of the earliest translations of ermine can be seen in the celebrated sixth-century Byzantine mosaics decorating the Basilica of Sant'Apollinaire Nuovo in Ravenna (fig. 5-31). In the section depicting the Three Magi, shown wearing trousers, of spotted fur perhaps, and Phrygian caps that identify them as Anatolian, an important early centre for the fur trade, we see Balthassar wearing what must surely be an ermine mantle, with its distinctive black spots on a white ground, ermine's seductive softness gaining an afterlife as glittering glass. Similar material and metaphorical journeys can be seen in mosaic interpretations of the Expulsion of Eden rendered in mosaic, as in the Palatine Chapel in Palermo and the Cathedral of the Assumption in Monreale, Sicily, but here it is shaggy sheepskin that is vitrified.

Condensing the moral and material space between the sacred and the secular, the temporal space between the sixth and twentieth centuries and between the cult of the divine and the cult of the designer, fur's glassy journeys bring us to the celebrated 'leopard skin' dress featured in Jean Paul Gaultier's Autumn/Winter 1997 couture collection. Over a full-skirted brown silk ball gown, the model let fall the layer she was clutching to her body to reveal a full-sized leopard skin, complete with paws, tail and head (which formed the bodice of the dress), made entirely of glass 'bugle' beads hand-sewn to emulate the fur's distinctive markings (fig. 5-32). One of the most widely admired examples of twentieth- century fashion design, the dress translates ancient beliefs in the transformative power of the leopard into the contemporary worship of haute couture, here the leopard's spots twinkling as they did in ancient Egypt's night sky.

Glass into fur is also the ambition of contemporary designer Naomi Bailey-Cooper, who has been researching alternatives to fur's decorative and tactile qualities without using acrylic fibre and retaining traditionally fashioned fur's level of artisanal skill and exclusivity, a journey towards new sustainable luxury (figs 5-1 and 5-33). Bailey-Cooper uses spun glass filaments hand-threaded onto a lattice of wild rubber, inspired by the furrier's air gallon technique (see 'The Force of Fur', p. 141), so allowing the glass fur to remain light and flexible. Glass cloth, that is, cloth woven from very finely drawn threads of molten glass, which was then spun and after cooling resulted

5-32 Jean Paul Gaultier, 'Leopard skin' dress, Haute Couture, Autumn/Winter 1997. Gaultier recently revisited this celebrated dress in his Autumn/Winter 2019 collection, replacing beads with sequins and hanging the leopard's head and paws at the hem rather than forming the bodice as before. Fairchild Archive/Penske Media/Shutterstock

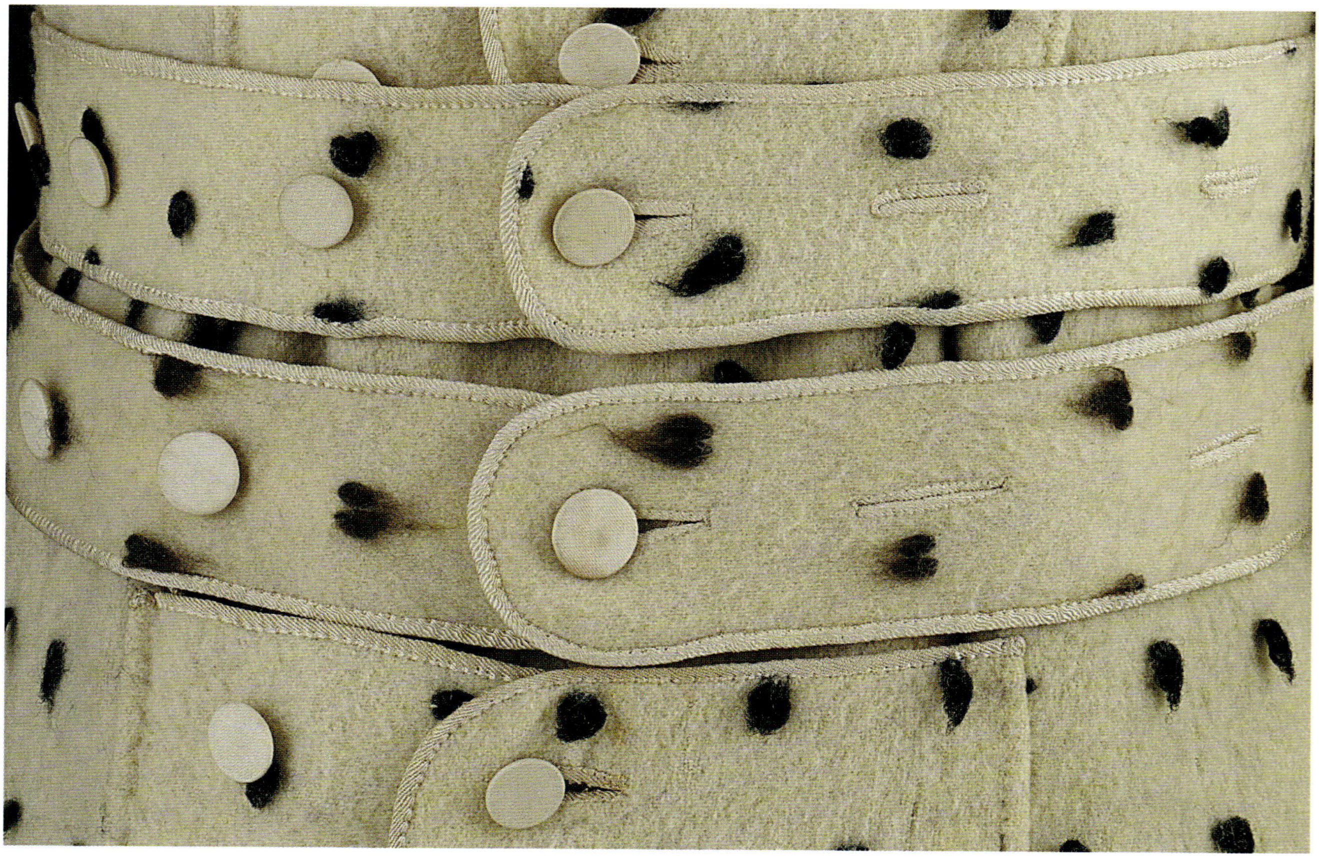

in a light flexible fibre, was first produced in the 1830s and enjoyed considerable success as an alternative to silk, the synthetic manufacture of which eventually halted production of glass cloth.[40] One of glass fibre's uses was to make alternatives to feathers, which Bailey-Cooper's glass fur also references, alongside monkey fur with its silken lustre. As discussed previously, Schiaparelli incorporated monkey fur in her collections, but paradoxically she also produced a monkey fur-like fabric that she named 'angel hair', 'long glistening rayon threads knotted into a loosely scattered fringe that moved as one walked'.[41] This effect is echoed in Bailey-Cooper's glass hair. However, whether Schiaparelli's motivation for this alternative was ethically based is doubtful, perhaps more a product of her endlessly inventive search for alternatives, for translations of one material into another; fur becomes angel hair, the monkey ascends to heaven.

Michel Serres acknowledges in his *The Five Senses* 'that fabrics, textiles and material provide excellent models of knowledge, excellent almost abstract objects, primary varieties: the world is a heap of clothes', to which we might add a heap of fur, abstracted and translated fur providing knowledge not only of the form of the translation but also other bodies of knowledge, surprisingly disparate yet intimately connected to fur.[42]

Ermine, due to its distinctive markings, the high esteem in which it is held and its metaphorical richness centred on the concepts of purity and defilement, has unsurprisingly been translated widely throughout history and across mediums. Its faking and the use of other furs to assume the guise of ermine are discussed in 'The F Word' (p. 151), but here we might consider

5-33 OPPOSITE ABOVE Naomi Bailey-Cooper, glass 'fur', 2018. Textile sample using spun glass, wild rubber and Tencel. Courtesy of the artist.

5-34 OPPOSITE BELOW Man's nightgown (detail), 1815–22. Britain; wool flannel with applied tufts of wool to resemble ermine. © Victoria and Albert Museum, London. Given by Francis Coutts

5-35 Child's jacket, 1855–65. United States; wool. Brooklyn Museum Costume Collection at The Metropolitan Museum of Art, New York. Gift of The Jason and Peggy Westerfield Collection

those examples of ermine rendered in cloth that make no attempt to mimic the fur but rather use it as a furry referent, 'that element in a translation which goes beyond transmittal of subject matter', as Walter Benjamin puts it.[43] The astonishing man's woollen dressing gown of around 1815–22, in the collection of the Victoria and Albert Museum, is a translation of ermine's received noble status and signifier of wealth into humble woollen flannel (fig. 5-34). Black tufts of wool applied to its cream ground echo the furrier's practice of 'powdering', where white furs were tufted with black lamb to emulate ermine. Here, in the gown owned by Thomas Coutts, founding member of the banking dynasty, the impossible is achieved: a debasing of ermine's traditional 'purity', a royal fur rendered domestic and informal, a vestimentary translation that speaks of inversion and irony. In contrast to Coutts's robe is the endearingly minimal woollen child's jacket in the Metropolitan Museum, New York, dated around 1855–65, which pushes the limits of furry translation (fig. 5-35).

The simple red cloth jacket, edged with a highly schematic approximation of ermine constructed from black-stitched cream wool braid, is completely unconvincing, yet insistently still registers as 'ermine'. This is a child's-eye view of ermine that is redolent of dolls' clothes and yet also provides a commentary on the increasing popularity of real ermine for children's clothes towards the end of the nineteenth century, an outfit for American nursery royalty.

The paradox of rendering costly ermine in humble wool is resolved in two examples of French silk brocade from the 1760s: one a length of fabric, the other made up into a sumptuous mantua and petticoat (figs 5-36 a&b). For the mantua the brocaded silver silk is woven into a large, intricate, repeat pattern of flowers and 'ribbons' of ermine, all rendered in the complex and labour-intensive brocade technique. A costly process, it showcases the riches of the natural world in the form of fur and flowers. An added layer of translated 'game playing' is achieved by the addition of real ermine tails, inserted along the neckline and front edge of the bodice. The tails, discreetly caught in metallic silver lace, each with an individual leather sleeve to

attach it to the robe, nestle almost undetected, the usual contrast of dark tails against white fur dispensed with. Instead, the tails offer a private tactile pleasure for the wearer, a 'primary relationship' in the Freudian sense, which is simultaneously transferred onto the substitute and 'public' ermine created on the brocade.[44]

The French silk brocade as a length of fabric displays a similar bravura weaving technique, but this time substitutes leopard for ermine and lace for flowers,

5-36 a & b Court dress mantua (details), 1760s, remodelled 1870–1910. France and England; silk brocade, silver lace and ermine tails. © Victoria and Albert Museum, London

which undulate across the silk forming an animated 'net' in which 'raw' fur and 'refined' lace ensnare one another, a sumptuous translation of the cultural exchange between Europe and the East that characterised the period in which the silk was woven (fig. 5-37).

With the advent of photography it became possible to render textures such as fur with a verisimilitude never before possible. Fur as a subject for photography deserves a study all of its own and would no doubt have to acknowledge Benjamin once more in order to assess how much of the 'aura' of fur is dependant on its tactile encounter.[45] Such a sensation is presumably lost in photography and, unlike the translated examples discussed so far, not reconstituted via the tactile properties of the medium used to achieve the translation. Maison Martin Margiela addressed Benjamin's concerns in his Spring/Summer 1996 collection, which featured clothes made of light, flowing silk, but photographically printed with the image of older pieces of clothing he had acquired from flea markets. The *trompe l'oeil* game playing, where sequins and other textures became flat photographic surfaces and the internal label of the original garments appeared photographically on the backs of these new/old clothes, was enthusiastically received as an interrogation of the 'originality' of fashion. Included in the collection was a simple, fluid wrap dress printed with a fur coat, a somewhat shabby (possibly mink) garment that was transformed into an elegant, lightweight, crucially smooth and hairless garment. This piece, alongside its insistent perceptual illusion, is, I believe, also suggestive of the democratisation of fur, and prophetically offers an ethical alternative to fur – its own image. The interrogation of the aura of fur intensified when, for Margiela's 2013 collaboration with multinational retailer H&M reissued some of the *trompe l'oeil* pieces, including the fur coat/dress, labelling it a 'Re-Edition'. A re-edition of what was in effect already a replica (another of Margiela's favourite forms) of the original fur coat; a translation of a translation.

Whilst photography may offer an exact reproduction of the texture of fur, it is on film that fur has effected its most lasting translations. The symbiotic relationship between fashion, fur and film has been a recurrent theme of this book, but while real fur worn on film needs the expertise of lighting and

5-37 Brocade silk panel, *c.*1760–65. Probably manufactured in Lyons, France. © Victoria and Albert Museum, London. Given by Mrs R. W. Cave-Orme

5-38 ABOVE *King Kong*, dirs Merian C. Cooper and Ernest B. Schoedsack, 1933. Film still. RKO/Kobal/Shutterstock

5-39 OPPOSITE *Monsters, Inc.*, dirs Pete Docter, David Silverman and Lee Unkrich, 2001. Film still. Moviestore Collection/Shutterstock

camera operatives to convey its full lustre and depth, a far greater challenge has been the rendering of imaginary fur, the pelts of new species, so precisely as to make the viewer believe in them. Aldous Huxley's visions of the future have never been so salient than in his apparent anticipation of virtual reality in *Brave New World*, and again it is fur that proves its credibility. 'Going to the Feelies this evening, Henry?' enquired the Assistant Predestinator. 'I hear the new one at the Alhambra is first-rate. There's a love scene on a bearskin rug; they say it's marvellous. Every hair of the bear reproduced. The most amazing tactual effects.'[46]

King Kong, made in 1933, has been hailed as one of the most important films of all time (fig. 5-38).[47] An instant box-office success, the film has become a significant component in the construction of twentieth-century popular culture. Its tale of the 'primitive' undone by civilisation, compassion versus greed and, more disturbingly, as suggested by some critics, the 'threat' of miscegenation, has ensured it remains a seminal work of early Hollywood, when many other similar productions have faded into obscurity. Its chief success is, of course, Kong himself, the realisation of which led to a number of technological innovations that the contemporary film industry is still indebted to. The filming of *King Kong* employed the new technique of stop-motion photography and required four models of the gorilla-like figure covered in rabbit fur and an additional huge torso for close-ups of its face, operated internally by a system of levers and air compressors and covered in bearskin for a more 'life-like' appearance. An additional two arms and hands, also covered in bearskin, were used to achieve sequences featuring Kong's hands. The painstaking stop-motion process, in its infancy in 1931 and taking days to carry out, has led to the deliriously otherworldly air of Kong's fur parting and being ruffled by unseen hands, a translation of fur that is imbued with a curious life at once seductive and disconcerting.

The challenge of transferring 'monstrous' fur from the imagination to the screen remains the quintessential test for fantasy filmmakers today just as much as it was for the crew of *King Kong*, and, as with that film, fur's cinematic realisation has been the driver of technological achievement. While the first film to showcase computer-generated imagery (CGI) of fur was *Babe* in 1995, it is perhaps *Monsters, Inc.* of 2001 that has remained the standard by which fur, monstrous or otherwise, can be realised digitally. Sully, the green and violet spotted furry monster, is the film's main character and here, and in subsequent productions, his luminous fur has been the test of CGI's capabilities (fig. 5-39). Any research into the film and its creators immediately encounters a wealth of superlatives and an excess of statistics concerning how many computer processors were necessary to generate the imagery, the number of new programmes created solely to render fur and hair, and the 2,320,413 separate pieces of hair on Sully. For his appearance in the sequel, Monsters University, Sully's coat consisted of 5.4 million hairs, five times the denseness of his original pelt, an excess that refers, ironically, back to an early medieval understanding of fur as

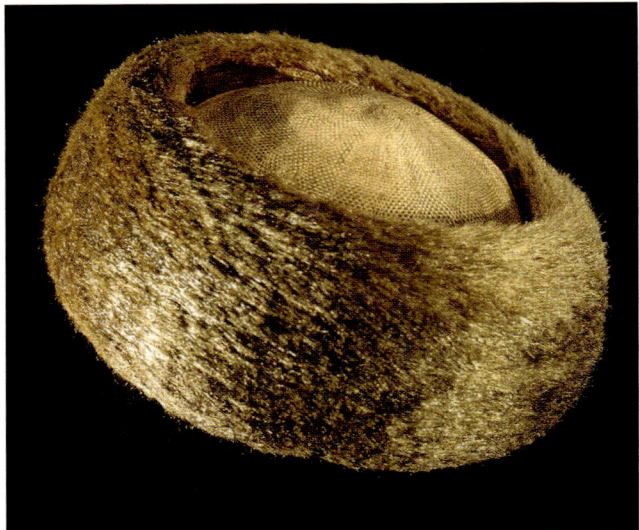 

5-40 a&b Giovanni Corvaja (b. 1971), *Golden Fleece* headpiece (and detail), 2009. 22 carat and 18 carat gold thread. Courtesy of the artist

a potentially corrupting sign of extravagance, even immorality.[48]

How 'monstrous' the monsters of *Monsters, Inc.* may be is questionable, and that is surely one of the film's 'feel good' messages, but to conclude we will remain with the translation of mythical fur, but leave its digital domain and turn to gold, a fitting medium with which to reflect the wealth symbolised by fur and the myth of Jason and the Golden Fleece.

The Golden Fleece is a prize that facilitates the transition to wealth and power, a reaffirmation of fur as material achievement and aspiration. The fleece was originally the skin of a winged ram sired by Poseidon, which was sacrificed by Phrixus and returned to its maker becoming the constellation Aries, a celestial translation that reoccurs in myth, as has already been observed in the Egyptian belief that the leopard's spots were also stars. The fleece is hung on an oak tree in the sacred grove dedicated to the god of war, defended by bulls with breath of fire and hooves of brass, and an ever-watchful dragon. It is from this unassailable location that Jason performs the three tasks necessary to win the fleece and complete its translation.

The Italian goldsmith Giovanni Corvaja has perfected a method that allows him to reduce gold and platinum to the dimension of one-fifth of a human hair. With this impossibly fine and precious thread he creates the semblance of gold fur, from which he makes objects including the remarkable headpiece of 2009 from his *Golden Fleece* collection (figs 5-40 a&b). Entailing thousands of hours of labour and hundreds of kilometres of golden thread, he sees his dedication to his craft as akin to that of an alchemist, always seeking, perfecting but never realising, declaring his work is 'a journey not a destination'.[49] He describes the sensation he receives from touching his pieces as being 'as pleasurable as caressing fur'.[50] Corvaja's *Golden Fleece* headpiece is a fitting final object, inspired by one of the most ancient myths concerning the fortune to be made from fur. His work is a supreme act of translation, a journey inspired by Jason, making fur anew whilst retaining its essential qualities of majesty, beauty and sensory pleasure, constructing a new language for fur but one that fulfills Benjamin's stated 'task of the translator' to produce 'in that language the echo of the original.'[51]

CONCLUSION

FUTUREFUR

The repetitively declared observation that 'fur is old-fashioned', used by newly fur-free designers, is understood as a declaration of ethical and humane principles. But this apparently simple statement can also be understood as an attempt to convince audiences of the 'modernity' of fashion itself. This, as many critics including both Giacomo Leopardi (who declared fashion's sister to be death) and Walter Benjamin (who recognised that 'To the living, fashion defends the rights of the corpse') have assured us, is an impossibility, for fashion must always undergo a process of ageing and dying, a recurring cycle of becoming 'un-modern' and anachronistic in order to become new again.[1]

Fur admittedly belongs to the pre-Modern era in terms of its mythical, magical and cult status. Although traditional forms of myth and magic along with their associated cults have disappeared in the Modern era, the energies and desires bound up in and with them need release – hence our fetishisation of the object, of celebrity, of media and of fashion. Fur is unique in that it acts as a vestimentary reminder of our pre-Modern desires, which, although now forgotten or transferred, are brought back to life, made real once more at the sensuous touch of fur.

As I hope this book has gone some way towards exploring, fur has always been perceived as inextricably constituted by the ancient and the modern, the old and the new, the fundamental and the fashionable. Innovation and exploration have been the essential elements of fur's history of production and consumption. The anti-fur movements are an attempt to establish what is perceived as a rational (although the forms of protest have become increasingly irrational), and by extension 'modern', revision of the fashion industry – hence the emphasis on the consumption of fur as being irrational and 'old fashioned'.

Whether old-fashioned or, rather, outside of the fashion system, nevertheless fashionable fur is dying, and unlike fashion's continuous cycles of death and resurrection, fur's fashionable rebirth, for now, and in its present form, is indefinitely postponed. By fashionable fur I mean fur garments created and promoted by recognisable and esteemed fashion designers and labels, presented as part of seasonal collections, which in turn are disseminated via the fashion media, in short the western fashion system. This system, which aside from its continuing use, or renunciation, of fur is increasingly beleaguered and condemned as unsustainable and irrelevant, does not of course include those traditional, indigenous wearers of fur, for whom its thermal properties, cultural significance and economic benefit far outweighs any ethical or emotional strictures. Neither does it include those from newly ascendant economic regions, who represent the majority of the global fur industry's consumers and who, for now, are keeping that same industry financially buoyant.

As new markets for fur emerge, older ones disappear and while the global fur industry struggles to remain economically viable, it is staggering from the growing impact of widespread opposition. During the course of writing this book, New York City's council speaker, Corey Johnson, announced his intention to join San Francisco and Los Angeles and make the city fur-free, galvanising support from the anti-fur lobby while simultaneously igniting protest from those defending their right to wear fur on religious and cultural grounds, and whose livelihood depends on an industry that was an integral part of New York's early development. This action is also generating cynicism from others who see it merely as a ploy to win Johnson votes in the upcoming mayoral elections. In the United Kingdom, anti-fur and broader political agendas appear to be similarly aligned. In 2018 the Fur-Free Britain Campaign, a coalition of like-minded anti-fur groups, collected more than 425,000 signatures calling on the government to ban all imports of fur to the United Kingdom and co-opted the isolationist agenda of Brexit and the chaos surrounding European trade agreements as a way of realising this goal. A landmark parliamentary debate was held in June 2019 with politicians across the political spectrum calling for the ban, but without securing a commitment from the government to act on the issue. In what may be the sounding of fur's death knell in the United Kingdom, in her recently published memoirs the Queen's dressmaker and confidant, Angela Kelly, revealed that from 2019 any new garments made for the Queen – including ceremonial robes – will use fake rather than real fur.[2]

In the fashion industry itself the number of houses going fur-free continues to grow, most notably the recent addition of Jean Paul Gaultier, whose innovative work with fur appears throughout this book. Gaultier announced at his Autumn/Winter 2019 haute couture collection, which featured printed fur puffer jackets and 'hoodies', and a revisiting of his famous simulation of leopard skin (see 'Translation', p. 211) rendered in sequins, that it was time to tighten regulations and 'stop the massacre'.[3] It is tempting to speculate that Gaultier's announcement that his Spring 2020 haute couture collection, celebrating his 50 years in the fashion business and which will be his last, is reflective of fashion's current prescriptive climate of ethical responsibility, of which the renunciation of fur is characteristic. The death in February 2019 of Karl Lagerfeld, creative director of Chanel and, most significantly for this study, of Fendi, arguably the most innovative of designer furriers and instigator of Fendi's spectacular haute *fourrure* runway shows, has dealt another serious blow to the fashionable status of contemporary fur design. If fashionable fur is dead, then so perhaps is fashion itself. A system that relies on over-production and consumption, is inherently wasteful, disposable and ecologically disastrous, offers little emotional investment to its consumers and makes unacceptable demands on its producers, is ultimately unsustainable.

Reports from the furthest reaches of Furland offer tantalising glimpses of futurefur – fur grown from animal collagen, digitally rendered and printed fur – but these remain currently as mythical as the Golden Fleece. Recycled fur, road-kill fur and remodelled fur offer a possible future for fur, but one that is necessarily limited and indebted to the past. Traditional fur production and consumption, however, can provide us with alternatives to the 'old-fashioned' fashion system as we currently recognise it.

Fur needs to prove it is a relevant and viable material for the twenty-first century, and ironically, this most 'old fashioned' of materials provides a number of alternatives to many of the problems besetting today's fashion industry. Fur is an antidote to fast fashion, with fur garments typically having a much longer life span than other garments. It represents the preservation of traditional manual crafts and skills at a time when these are rapidly

> fur Some animals have soft hair on their skin. It is **fur**. **Fur** keeps them warm. Mother has a **fur** coat.

disappearing and we are becoming increasingly dissociated from the material world. Fur garment construction is sustainable with little or no waste. The fur retailing sector provides an increasingly relevant model of service and aftercare long abandoned in other parts of the clothing industry, with the repurposing and remodelling of fur to ensure its fashionable longevity an established practice within the industry. Fur garments do not attempt to standardise an ideal but adapt to the individual consumer.

They produce a powerful sensory and tactile response in their wearers at a moment when clothing is often disposable, meaningless and un-engaging. Initiatives to make fur more sustainable have included making sure its origins are transparent and can be tracked and labelled to ensure that animal welfare issues are addressed, and that the environmental impact of fur farming is reduced, all of which re-connect the consumer with the garment in an age when we are increasingly disconnected from, or oblivious to, the origin of the products we consume. Open Farm initiatives and schemes such as WelFur (see 'The Force of Fur', p. 141) are an attempt to dispel some of the secrecy and myths surrounding fur production, as are pioneering projects between research institutions and industry partners. One such project is the six-year collaboration between Design School Kolding and Kopenhagen Fur, whose investigation into fur design and sustainability has led to a radical rethinking of not only our relationship to fur and fur garments, but also how that re-thinking might in turn impact on the production and consumption of clothing on a wider scale.[4]

ABOVE Definition of 'fur' from children's picture dictionary, c.1940s. Courtesy of the author

None of this, of course, will overcome the ethical and emotional opposition to fur, and despite Lise Skov's suggestion in her pioneering essay that if 'we consider fashion as some kind of collective unconscious, we can always expect the return of the repressed', fur being the object of contemporary fashion's most enduring repression, wearing the skins of animals for many in developed, non-indigenous cultures is abhorrent, unnecessary and unacceptable, and this is a situation that is unlikely to change and indeed will increase.[5]

Therefore, if the wearing of fur is becoming extinct, then just as historically and biologically extinction is a necessary stage in the development of new species and new forms, perhaps it is time we understood fur's death as the beginning of new life, a life that will utilise aspects of fur's complex and innovative history, its manufacture, its economy, the emotional investment on behalf of producer and consumer, and its sensory connectivity, to help us rethink the way we wear and make clothes in the future. Having invoked a biological metaphor and writing this while the world continues its battle against the Coronavirus pandemic, any system that emerges from the crisis, including the mass production and consumption of clothing, must be radically re-thought. From fur's past, new, or perhaps re-discovered narratives concerning our relationship to clothing, some of which have been encountered in the various journeys to Furland taken in this book, might help us chart our relationship to clothing in the future.

NOTES

INTRODUCTION

1. Elizabeth Ewing, *Fur in Dress* (London: Batsford, 1981), p. 11
2. W.J.T. Mitchell, 'Interdisciplinarity and Visual Culture' in *Art Bulletin*, vol. 77, no. 4 (December 1995), pp. 540–4. See also Jonathan Faiers, 'Dress Thinking: Disciplines and Indisciplinarity' in Charlotte Nicklas and Annebella Pollen (eds), *Dress History: New Directions in Theory and Practice* (London: Bloomsbury, 2015), pp. 15–32
3. Michel Serres, *The Five Senses: A Philosophy of Mingled Bodies* (London: Bloomsbury, 2016)
4. See Laura U. Marks, *The Skin of the Film: Intercultural Cinema, Embodiment, and the Senses* (Durham NC and London: Duke University Press, 2000)
5. Gilles Deleuze and Félix Guattari, *A Thousand Plateaus: Capitalism and Schizophrenia* (London: Athlone Press, 1992)
6. Elspeth M. Veale, *The English Fur Trade in the Later Middle Ages* (New York and Oxford: Oxford University Press, 1966)

PART ONE: HAIR

1. The Bible, King James Version (1611), Matthew 10:30
2. Michel Serres, 'Veils' in *The Five Senses: A Philosophy of Mingled Bodies* (London: Bloomsbury, 2016), p. 59
3. From the introduction to Dan Cameron, Kate Eilertson and Pam McClusky, *Nick Cave: Meet Me at the Center of the Earth* (San Francisco: Yerba Buena Center for the Arts, 2009), p. 18
4. Mary Douglas, *Purity and Danger, An Analysis of Concepts of Pollution and Taboo* (London: Routledge, 2002), pp. 44–5
5. The Bible, King James Version (1611), Judges 16:17
6. Edmund Leach, 'Magical Hair' in *Journal of the Royal Anthropological Institute of Great Britain and Ireland*, vol. 88, no. 2 (July–December 1958), p. 154
7. Jonathan Faiers, 'Nature Boy' in Claire Wilcox (ed.), *Alexander McQueen* (London: V&A Publishing, 2015), p. 127
8. Erich Maria Remarque, *All Quiet on the Western Front* (London: Vintage Classics, 2005), p. 11
9. Patricia Lurati, '"To dust the pelisse": the erotic side of fur in Italian Renaissance art', *Renaissance Studies*, vol. 31, no. 2 (2017), p. 256
10. University of St Andrews Museum and Collections online, https://www.st-andrews.ac.uk/adlib/Details/collect/3426 (accessed 26 March 2019)
11. For more on the activities and histories of both clubs see David Stevenson, *The Beggar's Benison: Sex Clubs of Enlightenment Scotland and their Rituals* (East Lothian: Tuckwell Press, 2001)
12. I am indebted to Marina Hays, who generously shared her research into, and expert knowledge of, the Marisol/Kaplan coat, including her presentation 'Endangered Species: Marisol's Painted Fur Coat', given at the *Cloth and Clothing* colloquium held at the Metropolitan Museum of Art, New York, 1 March 2019
13. From a 1915 advertisement available at http://www.razorarchive.com/p103022929 (accessed 27 March 2019)
14. John Carl Flügel, *The Psychology of Clothes* (London: Hogarth Press, 1940)
15. *One Million Years B.C.*, dir. Don Chaffey, 1966. For more on the fur bikini in *One Million Years B.C.* see Jonathan Faiers, 'Trophies' in Faiers, *Dressing Dangerously: Dysfunctional Fashion in Film* (New Haven CT and London: Yale University Press, 2013) and Sue Walsh, 'Bikini Fur and Fur Bikinis' in Karin Lesnik-Oberstein (ed.), *The Last Taboo: Women and Body Hair* (Manchester: Manchester University Press, 2006)
16. Frank Tashlin, *The Bear That Wasn't* (New York: New York Review Books, Children's Collection, 2010)
17. Dialogue from *Christmas in Connecticut*, 1945, dir. Peter Godfrey
18. Jean-François Lyotard, *Libidinal Economy* (Indiana: Indiana University Press, 1993)
19. For more on the cinematic fur coat see 'Trophies' in Faiers 2013
20. Jeremy Bentham, *An Introduction to the Principles of Morals and Legislation* (Oxford: Clarendon Press, 1907), p. 311
21. For a detailed account of the pioneering female activists and the formation of the RSPB and the Selborne Society see Richard Clarke, *Pioneers of Conservation: The Selborne Society and the Royal SPB*, monograph (London: The Selborne Society and Birkbeck College CEPAR, 2004)
22. 'Dress in Relation to Animal Rights' by Mrs Frank Lemon (Margaretta Louisa Smith Lemon) in Barbara T. Gates, *In Nature's Name: An Anthology of Women's Writing and Illustration 1780–1930* (Chicago: University of Chicago Press, 2002), pp. 170–6
23. Henry Stephens Salt, *Animals' Rights: Considered in Relation to Social Progress* (New York: Centaur Press, 1980), p. viii
24. Salt 1980, p. 84
25. John Galsworthy, *Treatment of Animals*, originally a speech delivered at Kensington Town Hall, London, on 15 December 1913 (London: Animals' Friend Society, 1914) and *For Love of Beasts* (London: Animals' Friend Society, 1912); Jerome K. Jerome, *The Cruel Steel Trap* (London: Animals' Friend Society, 1912). The list of Animals' Friend Society publications makes fascinating reading and provides an insight into the specific historical context in which the British animal rights movement originated, with titles including *Animals in Their Relationship to Empire*, *Horses in Warfare*, *The Sentimental Vegetarian* and *An After-Life For Animals*, alongside specific titles deploring the use of animals in the fur trade such as *The Cost of a Skin* and *The Otter Worry*.
26. For a detailed investigation into the relationship between Nazi ideology and the concept of animal rights see Boria Sax, *Animals in the Third Reich: Pets, Scapegoats, and the Holocaust* (New York and London: Continuum, 2000)
27. *The Animals Film*, dirs Victor Schonfeld and Myriam Alaux, 1981
28. The anti-fur movement's retailing victory has more recently been confounded by the advent of online shopping, which renders the purchase of fur untraceable and beyond public scrutiny. On entering the search term 'fur coat' on Harrods's website, for example, garments of fox, mink, rabbit and kangaroo skin are offered for purchase: https://www.harrods.com/engb/search?searchTerm=fur+coat (accessed 4 February 2019)
29. Stella McCartney interviewed by CNN Style in November 2015; available online at http://edition.cnn.com/style/article/stella-mccartney-sustainable-fashion/index.html (accessed 7 February 2019)
30. Ouida, 'The New Woman' in *North American Review*, vol. 158, no. 450 (May 1894), pp. 610–19
31. Julia Emberley, *The Cultural Politics of Fur* (Ithaca: Cornell University Press, 1997)
32. Emberley 1997, p. xii
33. www.peta.org (accessed 7 February 2019)
34. The other models featured in the original campaign were Naomi Campbell, Claudia Schiffer, Cindy Crawford and Elle Macpherson, all of whom have since chosen to promote or wear fur.
35. From an extract from *Committed: A Rabble-Rouser's Memoir* by Dan Mathews, 2009; published in *The Independent* online: https://www.independent.co.uk/life-style/fashion/features/dan-mathews-petas-fight-against-fur-1678967.html (accessed 5 May 2009). Andrew Cunanan was an American serial killer, who numbered amongst his victims fashion designer Gianni Versace. Mathews himself is gay and the answer was given in response to a question posed by *Genre*, a gay lifestyle magazine, which in 2000 had included Mathews on its list of most influential gay figures.
36. The ban in Los Angeles comes into effect in 2021 and makes it the largest city so far to impose such a ban. There are exemptions, however, including 'used' fur, taxidermy and fur produced from animals taken lawfully under a trapping licence. In addition, the ban is directed specifically towards clothing and accessories retailing and does not appear to include the many interior design and furniture businesses that include fur items in their product ranges.
37. See https://www.peta.org/features/joanna-krupa-gets-almost-naked (accessed 8 February 2019)
38. For a detailed discussion of this campaign and its critical reception see Sue Walsh, 'Bikini Fur and Fur Bikinis' in Lesnik-Oberstein 2006, pp. 166–80
39. See https://www.glamourmagazine.co.uk/article/wear-bare-skin-not-fur (accessed 8 February 2019)
40. Salt 1980, p. xi

PART TWO: PELT

1. Richard Davey, *Furs and Fur Garments* (London: The International Fur Store and Roxburghe Press, 1895), p. 7
2. Elspeth M. Veale, *The English Fur Trade in the Later Middle Ages* (New York and Oxford: Oxford University Press, 1966)

3   Included in the considerable literature on the Hudson's Bay Company (HBC) are these standard works: George Bryce, *The Remarkable History of the Hudson's Bay Company* (London: S. Low, Marston & Co. Ltd, 1900); Sir William Schooling, *The Governor and Company of Adventurers of England Trading into Hudson's Bay During Two Hundred and Fifty Years, 1670–1920* (London: Hudson's Bay Company, 1920); Peter C. Newman, 3 vols, *Company of Adventurers* (Ontario: Viking, 1985), *Caesars of the Wilderness* (Ontario: Viking, 1987), *Merchant Princes* (Ontario: Viking, 1991). Issues of the HBC journal *The Beaver: A Journal of Progress*, since its appearance in October 1920, are available online at: https://canadashistory.partica.online/canadas-history/the-beaver-october-1920/flipbook/1/ (accessed 20 February 2019). Eric Jay Dolin, *Fur, Fortune and Empire: The Epic History of the Fur Trade in America* (New York: Norton, 2010) is both readable and informative.

4   Harold Adams Innis, *The Fur Trade in Canada: An Introduction to Canadian Economic History* (Toronto: University of Toronto Press, 1999)

5   Gilles Deleuze and Félix Guattari, *A Thousand Plateaus: Capitalism and Schizophrenia*, (London: Athlone Press, 1992), p. 314

6   Pierre-François-Xavier de Charlevoix, *Journal of a Voyage to North America* (Chicago: The Caxton Club, 1923), pp. 147–8

7   Frances Backhouse, *Once They Were Hats: In Search of the Mighty Beaver* (Toronto: ECW Press, 2015), pp. 14–15

8   Jules Verne, *The Fur Country* (Toronto: NC Press, 1987), p. 50

9   Deleuze and Guattari 1992, p. 320

10 See the Hudson's Bay Company website: http://www.hbcheritage.ca/history/ fur-trade/standard-of-trade (accessed 17 July 2019)

11 Gustave Flaubert, *Bouvard and Pécuchet: With the Dictionary of Received Ideas* (London: Penguin Books, 1976), p. 306

12 Verne 1987, p. 3. *Pro Pelle Cutem* translates as a 'skin for skin's worth'.

13 Ibid.

14 *A Therapy*, dir. Roman Polanski, 2012; available at: https://www.youtube.com/watch?v=-gl-kaGumng (accessed 24 July 2019)

15 'Representational spaces: space as directly *lived* through its associated images and symbols'; see Henri Lefebvre, *The Production of Space* (Oxford: Wiley Blackwell, 1991), p. 39

16 *New York Times*, 8 September 1940, p. 19

17 Peter Rogers, *What becomes a Legend most? The Blackglama Story* (New York: Simon and Schuster, 1979), p. 8

18 Ibid., p. 7

19 See https://hopeandglitter.wordpress.com/2015/03/10/style-queen/ (accessed 18 July 2019)

20 Alice Beard, '*Nova* Magazine 1965–1975: A History', unpublished PhD thesis, University of London, December 2013, p. 199

21 'Every Hobo Should Have One', *Nova* magazine, November 1971, p. 60

22 Ibid.

23 'Jacques Kaplan's Tour de Furs', *Life* magazine, December 1968, p. 103

24 William Grimes, 'Jacques Kaplan, 83, Bold Furrier, Dies', *New York Times*, 22 July 2008; https://www.nytimes.com/2008/07/22/nyregion/22kaplan.html (accessed 18 April 2019)

25 Tom Wolfe, 'Radical Chic: That Party at Lenny's', *New York* magazine, 8 June 1970; available at http://nymag.com/news/features/46170/ (accessed 18 April 2019)

26 For more on the history of Weil's fragrances see https://weilperfumes.blogspot.com/2013/07/zibeline-by-weil-c1927.html (accessed 6 July 2019). I am grateful to Anthony Salvador for drawing this alliance between fur and fragrance to my attention.

27 Lefebvre 1991, p. 39

28 *Nanook of the North*, dir. Robert H. Flaherty, 1922

29 Fatimah T. Rony, *The Third Eye: Race, Cinema, and Ethnographic Spectacle*, (Durham NC: Duke University Press, 1996), p. 109

30 *Hudson's Bay*, dir. Irving Pichel, 1941

31 Chantal Nadeau, *Fur Nation: From the Beaver to Bardot* (London: Routledge, 2001), p. 40

32 Ibid., p. 30

33 *The Trap*, dir. Sidney Hayers, 1966

34 *The Revenant*, dir. Alexander González Iñárritu, 2015; *Frontier* TV series, premiered in 2016, created by Rob and Peter Blackie

35 Dialogue from *The Revenant*, 2015

36 Lefebvre 1991, p. 229

37 As noted in Alan Hunt, *Governance of the Consuming Passions: A History of Sumptuary Law* (London: Palgrave Macmillan, 1996), p. 23

38 Catherine Kovesi Killerby, *Sumptuary Law in Italy 1200–1500* (Oxford: Oxford University Press, 2002), p. 24

39 Quoted in Dolin 2010, p. 8

40 See Veale 1966, pp. 4–5

41 Hunt 1996, p. 105

42 Ibid., p. 311

43 Maria Hayward, *Rich Apparel: Clothing and the Law in Henry VIII's England* (Farnham: Ashgate Publishing, 2009), p. 102

44 Ibid.

45 Hunt 1996, p. 243

46 Jonathan Faiers, 'Trophies' in *Dressing Dangerously: Dysfunctional Fashion in Film* (New Haven CT and London: Yale University Press, 2013)

47 *The Big Heat*, dir. Fritz Lang, 1953; *White Heat*, dir. Raoul Walsh, 1949

48 *BUtterfield 8*, dir. Daniel Mann, 1960

49 *That Touch of Mink*, dir. Delbert Mann, 1962

50 *Easy Living*, dir. Mitchell Leisen, 1937

51 *Mildred Pierce*, dir. Michael Curtiz, 1945

52 *The Lady Wants Mink*, dir. William A Seiter, 1953

53 http://www.nationalarchives.gov.uk/education/homefront/life/pdf/make.pdf (accessed 13 March 2019); Fenwick advertisement in British *Vogue*, December 1945, p. 17

54 'Refashion with Fur', British *Vogue*, December 1942, p. 64

55 See Julie Summers, *Fashion on the Ration* (London: Profile Books, 2015), p. 65

56 Elizabeth Ewing, *Fur in Dress* (London: Batsford, 1981), p. 131

57 'The Separate Fur Piece', British *Vogue*, December 1944, pp. 50–1

58 http://www.nationalarchives.gov.uk/education/homefront/life/pdf/ make.pdf (accessed 13 March 2019)

59 'Wrapped in Black Mink' from the album *Giant* by Johnny Guitar Watson, DJM Records, 1978

60 'Gangster of Love' also appears on the album *Giant*. By 'Blaxploitation' film, I am referring to those productions specifically aimed at a black audience, made by black filmmakers, such as Mario van Peebles and Gordon Parks (senior and junior), which reached a peak of production between the years 1972 and 1975. They included *Sweet Sweetback's Baad Asssss Song*, dir. Van Peebles, 1971; *Shaft*, dir. Parks Sr., 1971; and *Superfly*, dir. Parks Jr., 1972. For more on Blaxploitation cinema see Lawrence Novotny, *Blaxploitation Films of the 1970s: Blackness and Genre* (London: Routledge, 2007)

61 *American Gangster*, dir. Ridley Scott, 2007

62 William Neuman and Jeffery C. Mays, 'Proposed Fur Ban in New York Pits Animal Rights Advocates Against Black Ministers' in *New York Times* online, 15 May 2019, available at: https://www.nytimes.com/2019/05/15/nyregion /fur-ban-nyc-sales.html (accessed 24 July 2019)

63 Jasmine Sanders, 'Nothing Faux About It', *New York Times*, 31 January 2019

64 https://www.washingtonpost.com/news/arts-and-entertainment/wp/2018/08/17/aretha-franklin-secret-style-icon-with-the-drop-of-a-fur-coat-she-proclaimed-her-self-worth/?utm_term=.8e164d0a072c (accessed 15 March 2019)

65 Ibid.

66 From 'Crazy in Love', written by Beyoncé Knowles, Rich Harrison, Eugene Record and Shawn Carter, 2003

67 Sanders 2019; Hunt 1996, p. 125

PART THREE: COAT

1   See https://www.nespos.org/display/PublicNesposSpace/Neumark-Nord+6.1+-+organic+remains for more on this object (accessed 30 April 2019)

2   Alan Hunt, *Governance of the Consuming Passions* (London: Palgrave Macmillan, 1996), p. 49

3   See Ralf Kittler, Manfred Kayser and Mark Stoneking, 'Molecular Evolution of *Pediculus humanus* and the Origin of Clothing', *Current Biology*, vol. 13, no. 16 (2003)

4   Dorothy K. Burnham, *Cut My Cote* (Toronto: Royal Ontario Museum, 1973), pp. 2–3

5   Ibid., p. 2

6   Ibid., p. 20

7   Elspeth M. Veale, *The English Fur Trade in the Later Middle Ages* (New York and Oxford: Oxford University Press, 1966), p. 14

8   The insulating, fleece-lined flying suit was first developed in 1917 by Australian aviator Sidney Cotton. Variations of the eponymous Sidcot suit were worn in both world wars and it became the prototype for the modern high-altitude flying suit.

9   *The Servant*, dir. Joseph Losey, 1963. The TV sitcom *Only Fools and Horses*, created by John Sullivan, ran to seven series and was broadcast on BBC1 from 1981 to 1991.

10 *Man's Genesis: A Psychological Comedy Founded on Darwin's Theory of the Genesis of Man*, dir. D.W. Griffith, 1912; *His Prehistoric Past*, dir. Charles Chaplin, 1914; *Three Ages*, dir. Edward F. Cline and Buster Keaton, 1923

11 *One Million Years B.C.*, dir. Don Chaffey, 1966; *When Dinosaurs Ruled the Earth*, dir. Val Guest, 1970

12 *Mysterious Island*, dir. Cy Endfield, 1961

13 Dialogue from *Mysterious Island*, as above

14 Roland Barthes, *The Fashion System* (Berkeley CA: University of California Press, 1990)

15 Jonathan Faiers, 'Nature Boy' in *Alexander McQueen*, ed. Claire Wilcox (London: V&A Publishing, 2015), p. 127

16 Combs's celebrity-studded presentation at Bryant Park, New York, was the first fashion collection to be broadcast live on television (live-streaming of fashion shows now being commonplace) and

heralded the arrival of what has been dubbed 'fashion-tainment'. See Suzy Menkes, 'The Collections/New York: Urban Fashion Revolution', *New York Times*, 11 February 2003: https://www.nytimes.com/2003/02/11/style/IHT-the-collections-new-york-urban-fashion-revolution.html (accessed 11 May 2019)
17 The Bible, King James Version (1611), Genesis 3:21
18 Both domestic (*Felis catus*) and wild (*Felis silvestris*) cat fur was widely worn in the period. Wild cats were more prized, however, as their fur was finer and more uniform in colouration compared to domestic cat fur, which varied greatly and was therefore more difficult to match and make up into larger skins. Consequently, once the Scottish population of indigenous wild cat started to diminish, it was increasingly imported from the Continent.
19 This is merely a small selection of the bewildering terminology used by the medieval fur trade to describe the squirrel. For a comprehensive list and explanation of the terms see Veale 1966, especially Section B of the glossary, 'Names Applied to Baltic Squirrel Skins', pp. 223–9
20 'The glasse of Fashion, and the mould of Forme', Hamlet III.i.161
21 John Harvey, *Men in Black* (London: Reaktion Books, 1995), p. 55
22 See 'B [Fashion]' in Walter Benjamin, *The Arcades Project* (Cambridge MA and London: The Belknap Press of Harvard University, 1999), p. 79
23 Joseph G. Links, *The Book of Fur* (London: James Barrie, 1956), p. 106. See Frank G. Ashbrook, *Furs Glamorous and Practical* (New York: D. Van Norstrand Company, Inc., 1954), pp. 35–6 for more on the twentieth-century use of squirrel fur.
24 Links 1956, p. 108
25 Veale 1966, p. 136
26 *Camelot*, dir. Joshua Logan, 1967
27 Hunt 1996, p. 126
28 Maria Hayward, *Rich Apparel* (Farnham: Ashgate Publishing, 2009), p. 102
29 'Composing the subject: making portraits' in Ann Jones and Peter Stallybrass, *Renaissance Clothing and the Materials of Memory* (Cambridge: Cambridge University Press, 2000), p. 35
30 Quoted in Veale 1966, p. 172
31 See Olga Dmitrieva and Tessa Murdoch, *Treasures of the Royal Courts* (London: V&A Publishing, 2013). From the diary of John Evelyn, 29 December 1652, quoted in Murdoch, 'Exhibiting the Renaissance', p. 6; https://edoc.hu-berlin.de/bitstream/handle/18452/8344/murdoch.pdf (accessed 17 May 2019)
32 James Laver, *Taste and Fashion* (London: George G. Harrap & Co. Ltd, 1945), p. 168
33 Edith Wharton [1899], 'A Cup of Cold Water' in Roxana Robinson (ed.), *New York Stories of Edith Wharton* (New York: New York Review of Books, 2007), p. 60; Jonathan Faiers, *Dressing Dangerously* (New Haven CT and London: Yale University Press, 2013), p. 27
34 Henry Peacham, *Minerva Britanna, or a garden of heroical devises. Furnished and adorned with emblems and impresas of sundry natures* (London: 1612). Available at https://archive.org/details/minervabritanna00peac/page/75 (accessed 20 May 2019)
35 James Planché in Elizabeth Ewing, *Fur in Dress* (London: Batsford, 1981), p. 39; Hayward 2009, p. 157
36 Ewing 1981, p. 39
37 Ede & Ravenscroft. See https://www.edeandravenscroft.com/ceremonial-dress/royal-robes/#coronations (accessed 20 May 2019)
38 Links 1956, p. 129
39 *That Lady in Ermine*, dirs Ernst Lubitsch and Otto Preminger, 1948. Lubitsch died eight days into production and Preminger, who refused to be credited as director, completed the film.
40 Scottish National Party spokesperson David Linden was rebuked in 2017 for calling hereditary peers 'ermine vermin' during a debate over the relative size of the houses of Commons and Lords. It was Peter Wishart, the SNP member for Perth and North Perthshire, who, when discussing hereditary peers on social media, used the phrase 'Bloated, ermine-coated …' etc. See https://petewishart.wordpress.com/2015/01/16/reforming-the-lords/ (accessed 10 May 2019)
41 Made of crimson silk velvet, the rows extend around the full width of the cape, with half rows reaching from the right front edge to the centre back. These rows of spots reveal a peer's rank: Duke – 4 rows, Marquess – 3½ rows, Earl – 3 rows, Viscount – 2½ rows and Baron – 2 rows. See https://www.edeandravenscroft.com/ceremonial-dress/peers-robes/#about (accessed 20 May 2019)
42 Albert M. Ahern, *Fur Facts* (St Louis MO: C.P. Curran Printing Company, 1922), p. 179
43 *Enchantment*, dir. Irving Reis, 1948
44 There is considerable debate as to when the rabbit was first introduced into Britain. There is evidence that the Romans brought the species to Britain, but it is thought that these were kept as pets and therefore were unlikely to have escaped into the wild. Other experts, citing records from the thirteenth century that refer to rabbits on mainland England, suggest that they were established as a species during the Norman period.
45 Veale 1966, pp. 176, 15
46 Jonathan Faiers, 'Fur: The Final Frontier' in *Expedition: Fashion From the Extreme*, eds Patricia Mears et al. (London: Thames & Hudson, 2017), p. 112
47 Patricia Lurati, '"To dust the pelisse": the erotic side of fur in Italian Renaissance art', *Renaissance Studies*, vol. 31, no. 2 (2017), p. 241
48 *That Touch of Mink*, dir. Delbert Mann, 1962
49 From 'London Collections, Couture Clothes: Are They Worth Money?', British *Vogue*, September 1960, pp. 98–109
50 For more on *zibellini* and their association with childbirth see Sherrill Tawny, 'Fleas, Fur, and Fashions: *Zibellini* as Luxury Accessories of the Renaissance' in *Medieval Clothing and Textiles*, eds Robin Netherton and Gale R. Owen-Crocker, vol. 2 (Woodbridge: Boydell Press, 2006) and Jacqueline Musacchio, 'Weasels and Pregnancy in Renaissance Italy', *Renaissance Studies*, vol. 15, no. 2 (June 2001)
51 Ewing 1981, p. 50
52 Laver 1945, p. 171. See 'In Black and White and Colour', p. 132 in this volume, for Adolph Zukor's role in the development of the fox fur stole.
53 Jean Dubuffet, 'L'Auteur répond à quelques questions' in *Prospectus et tous écrits suivants*, ed. Hubert Damisch, vol. 2 (Paris: Gallimard, 1967), p. 66. I am grateful to Dr Rachel Perry for bringing this marvellous reference to my attention.
54 Links 1956
55 Ewing 1981, p. 53
56 See Aileen Ribeiro, *Dress in Eighteenth-Century Europe* (New Haven CT and London: Yale University Press, 2002), pp. 161–2
57 See Kimberly Chrisman-Campbell, '"He is not dressed without a muff": muffs, masculinity, and la mode in English satire' in *Seeing Satire in the Eighteenth Century*, eds Elizabeth C. Mansfield and Kelly Malone (Oxford: Voltaire Foundation, University of Oxford, 2013), pp. 131–44
58 See Anna Clark, *Scandal: The Sexual Politics of the British Constitution* (Princeton: Princeton University Press, 2004)
59 Many of Hawes's garments bore somewhat enigmatic titles, and this reference to the more usually titled nursery rhyme 'Ride a cock horse to Banbury Cross' is no exception. The allusion to a 'fine lady with rings on her fingers and bells on her toes' in the rhyme is here a possible critique of the 1930s woman of fashion.
60 Elizabeth Hawes, *Fashion is Spinach* (New York: Dover Publications, 2015), pp. 9–10
61 Marion Kite in Lucy Johnston et al., *Nineteenth-Century Fashion in Detail* (London: V&A Publishing, 2005), p. 218
62 Crockett opposed the Act, which was eventually passed only after bitter debate and in effect gave the government authority to 'resettle' southern Native American tribes in reservations west of the Mississippi, leaving their traditional ancestral territories for white settlers.
63 *Davy Crockett* was a five-part series consisting of hour-long episodes aired on ABC between 1954 and 1955, made by Walt Disney's Disneyland television production company.
64 Ewing 1981, p. 54; Veale 1966, p. 61
65 Philip Stubbes, *The Anatomie of Abuses* (London: Richard Jones, 1583), unnumbered
66 For more on the beaver hat see J.F. Crean, 'Hats and the Fur Trade', *Canadian Journal of Economics and Political Science*, vol. 28, no. 3 (1962); Michael Sonenscher, *The Hatters of Eighteenth-Century France* (Berkeley CA: University of California Press, 1992); and Michael Harrison, *The History of the Hat* (London: Herbert Jenkins Ltd, 1960). The notorious use of mercury in the hat-making trade was primarily reserved for hats made of cheaper or inferior furs, rather than beaver. For a full and fascinating account of the practice of using mercury see 'Toxic Techniques: Mercurial Hats' in Alison Matthews David, *Fashion Victims* (London: Bloomsbury, 2015), pp. 42–67
67 Frances Backhouse, *Once They Were Hats* (Toronto: ECW Press, 2015), p. 119
68 Interestingly, in the light of Gucci CEO Marco Bizzarri's headline grabbing statement in 2017 that using fur is outdated and not modern, Michele placed quotations by Italian philosopher Giorgio Agamben on the audience's seats at his debut collection, stating 'Those who are truly contemporary are those who neither perfectly coincide with their time nor adapt to its demands.' Going fur-free apparently was not considered one of these 'demands'.
69 Veale 1966, p. 138
70 Colleen Hill, *Fairy Tale Fashion* (New Haven CT and London: Yale University Press, 2016), p. 46
71 Michel Serres, *The Five Senses* (London: Bloomsbury, 2016), p. 64
72 Dialogue from *The Women*, dir. George Cukor, 1939
73 Henri Lefebvre, *The Production of Space* (Oxford: Wiley Blackwell, 1991)
74 Alexander Bevilacqua and Helen Pfeifer, 'Turquerie: Culture in Motion, 1650–1750' in *Past & Present*, vol. 221, issue 1 (2013), p. 101
75 Quoted in Ribeiro 2002, p. 266

76 Benedict Anderson, *Imagined Communities* (London: Verso, 1991), p. 4
77 Larry Wolff, Introduction to Leopold von Sacher-Masoch, *Venus in Furs* (London: Penguin Books, 2000), p. x
78 Laver 1945, p. 170
79 Ibid. 'Astrakhan' originally referred to sheep farmed in the synonymous Russian area near the Volga, the skins coming from unborn lambs. Persian lamb is the name used in the West most commonly to describe the fur skins of recently born or unborn lambs, while 'broadtail' is a more contemporary term used to describe such skins. 'Karakul' is a Turkish word for black sheep. 'Swakara' stands for South-West African karakul and is a contemporary brand name rather than a category of fur.
80 As quoted in Inna Fedorova, 'Émigré enterprise: How Russian aristocrats became fashion pioneers', *Lifestyle*, 20 February 2014; see https://www.rbth.com/arts/2014/02/19/emigre_enterprise_how_russian_aristocrats_became_fashion_pioneers_34345.html (accessed 16 June 2019). For more on this subject see Alexandre Vassiliev, *Beauty in Exile* (New York: Harry N. Abrams Inc., 2000).
81 *Roberta*, dir. William A. Seiter, 1935
82 *Dr Zhivago*, dir. David Lean, 1965
83 See Jonathan Faiers, 'Rahvis, Isobel, Helena Geffers, Eva Lutyens, Matilda Etches & Angele Delanghe' in *London Couture 1923–1975: British Luxury*, eds Amy de la Haye and Edwina Ehrman (London: V&A Publishing, 2015), p. 134
84 Michel Foucault, 'Of Other Spaces', *Diacritics*, vol. 16, no. 1 (Spring, 1986), p. 22
85 All commentary and descriptions from 'The Great Fur Caravan', American *Vogue*, October 1966, pp. 88–113
86 Ibid.
87 Ibid.
88 Ibid.
89 Foucault 1986, p. 25
90 See Patricia Mears, 'Fashion from the Extreme: The Poles, Highest Peaks, and Beyond' in Mears et al. 2017, pp. 56–105
91 From the KTZ website: https://k-t-z.co.uk/collections-season/aw15-menswear/ (accessed 21 June 2019)
92 Foucault 1986, p. 25
93 Adolph Zukor, *The Public is Never Wrong* (New York: G.P. Putnam's Sons, 1953), p. 34
94 Ibid., p. 39
95 Neal Gabler, *An Empire of Their Own* (London: W.H. Allen & Co., 1989), p. 17
96 Elizabeth Wilson, *Adorned in Dreams* (London: I.B. Tauris, 2007), p. 169
97 Anne Hollander, *Seeing Through Clothes* (Berkeley CA: University of California Press, 1993), p. 343
98 See Laver 1945, p. 171; *Singin' in the Rain*, dirs Stanley Donen and Gene Kelly, 1952
99 Lyrics from 'Beautiful Girl', sung by Jimmy Thompson in *Singin' in the Rain*, as above
100 'Fur For All', American *Vogue*, September 1990, pp. 224–40
101 Credit line from *That Touch of Mink*, dir. Delbert Mann, 1962
102 Links 1956, p. 148
103 *Lady in the Dark*, dir. Mitchell Leisen, 1944
104 John C. Sachs, *Furs and the Fur Trade* (London: Pitman & Sons, 1930); Richard Davey, *Furs and Fur Garments* (London: The International Fur Store and The Roxburghe Press, 1895), p. 76
105 Davey 1895, p. 76; Frank G. Ashbrook, *Fur-Farming for Profit* (New York: The Macmillan Company, 1928), p. 137
106 Robert G. Hodgson, *The Mink Book*, Fur Trade Journal of Canada (Toronto: 1954), p. 7. Mink farming today, of course, has been banned in the United Kingdom since 2000 and other European countries, such as Austria, have such stringent laws as to make the practice no longer economically viable, while other countries have pledged to discontinue fur farming over the next decade.
107 *The Lady Wants Mink*, dir. William A. Seiter, 1953
108 For more on this film see 'Trophies' in Faiers 2013, pp. 58–83
109 See Kopenhagen Fur's website for more information on the initiative: https://www.kopenhagenfur.com/auction/responsibility/welfur/ (accessed 27 June 2019)
110 Truman Capote, 'A Mink of One's Own' and 'The Bargain' in *Truman Capote: The Complete Stories* (London: Penguin Books, 2005), pp. 9–14, 177–83
111 Ibid., pp. 14, 182
112 F. Scott Fitzgerald, 'The Pearl and the Fur' in *I'd Die For You and Other Lost Stories* (London: Scribner, 2018), pp. 141–57
113 Archibald G. Macdonell, *The Fur Coat* (London: Macmillan & Co. Ltd, 1943)
114 Ibid., p. 33
115 *Bell, Book and Candle*, dir. Richard Quine, 1958; *Miss Mink of 1949*, dir. Glenn Tryon, 1949
116 H.W. Kellick, 'He Makes Mink Telephones', *Mechanix Illustrated*, May 1950, p. 166
117 James Ellroy, 'Tijuana, Mon Amour' in *Crime Wave* (London: Arrow Books, 1999), pp. 126–66
118 Ibid., pp. 147, 148
119 Kellick 1950, p. 166
120 'The "Force" of Fur', American *Vogue*, November 1977, pp. 308–15; *Star Wars*, dir. George Lucas, 1977
121 'The "Force" of Fur' 1977, pp. 308–15
122 Ibid.
123 Links 1956, p. 33
124 Space prohibits a detailed description of the many processes entailed in the making of a fur garment, but Links's *The Book of Fur* and Ashbrook's *Furs Glamorous and Practical*, previously referenced, both contain comprehensive descriptions.
125 A useful series of short videos depicting these and other processes can be found on the Kopenhagen Fur website: https://www.youtube.com/channel/UCqyZqEVUWGxi6XFkrn4uOJg (accessed 30 June 2019)
126 Briton Cooper Busch, *The War Against the Seals* (Kingston, Ontario: McGill-Queen's University Press, 1987), p. 128
127 Nicholas Daly, *The Demographic Imagination and the Nineteenth-Century City* (Cambridge: Cambridge University Press, 2017), p. 181
128 Sarah Pickman, 'Dress, Image, and Cultural Encounter in the Heroic Age of Polar Exploration' in Mears 2017, p. 31
129 Julia Emberley, *The Cultural Politics of Fur* (Ithaca, NY: Cornell University Press, 1997), p. 3
130 '1958 Cars, 1958 Furs', American *Vogue*, November 1957, pp. 136–44
131 For more on these objects see Ulla Mannering, 'Early Scandinavian Textile Design', *ARCHAEOLINGUA*, vol. 33 (2015), pp. 95–102
132 The Bible, King James Version (1611), Genesis 27:23
133 These tales, variants of Charles Perrault's story *Peau d'âne (Donkey Skin)* and the Grimm Brothers' *All-Kinds-of-Fur*, are discussed in some detail in 'Shape Shifters', p. 193–211.
134 Veale 1966, p. 29
135 Ibid., p. 13
136 *Crooks in Cloisters*, dir. Jeremy Summers, 1964
137 Veale 1966, p. 32
138 Laver 1945, p. 171
139 Ahern 1922, p. 39
140 Laver 1945, p. 170
141 See Maison Atia website: https://www.maisonatia.com/pages/faq (accessed 10 February 2019)
142 See Unreal Fur website: https://unrealfur.com.au/collections/unreal-fur-x-sans-beast (accessed 10 February 2019)
143 https://unrealfur.com/pages/furry-tales-campaign (accessed 10 February 2019)
144 Modacrylic refers to fibres with an Acrylonotrile content of 35–85 per cent. Acrylonotrile is a colourless, volatile, highly toxic liquid that decomposes in conjunction with oxygen to form cyanide and formaldehyde.
145 Two of the more recent and useful reports are Niko Hartline et al., 'Microfiber Masses Recovered from Conventional Machine Washing of New or Aged Garments', *Environmental Science & Technology*, vol. 50, no. 21 (2016) and Beverley Henry, Kirsi Laitala and Ingun Klepp, 'Microplastic Pollution from Textiles: A Literature Review', *Consumption Research Norway – SIFO*, Project Report No. 1, 2018
146 See Faux Fur Institute website: https://www.faux-furinstitute.com/ (accessed 23 January 2019)
147 Ball participants are mainly young African-American and Latin American members of the LGBTQ community. Attendees dance, vogue, walk, pose and compete for trophies. Categories both emulate and critique societal norms, attitudes and dress codes, and the accuracy or 'realness' of these performances is awarded accordingly. An underground subculture which can trace its origins to 1920s Harlem, it was first brought to mainstream attention in 1990 by the release of Jennie Livingstone's film *Paris is Burning* and Madonna's hit single 'Vogue'.
148 Trajal Harrell, *Hoochie Koochie*, performance exhibition, Barbican Art Gallery, London, 2017, p. 23

PART FOUR: SKIN

1 Michel Serres, *The Five Senses* (London: Bloomsbury, 2016)
2 Ibid., p. 26
3 'I've Got You Under My Skin', lyrics by Cole Porter, 1936; Rudyard Kipling, 'The Ladies', 1890; Frantz Fanon, *Black Skin, White Masks*, 1952
4 From the children's lullaby 'Bye, Baby Bunting', which was first published in *Gammer Gurton's Garland or The Nursery Parnassus* in 1784.
5 Serres 2016, p. 70
6 I am referring here to the note on 'Gloves' in Walter Benjamin's *One-Way Street* (London: Verso, 1997)
7 *Manhunter*, dir. Michael Mann, 1986. *Manhunter* was the first in a succession of films based on the novels of Thomas Harris featuring the serial killer and cannibal Hannibal Lecter.
8 Jacques Derrida, *On Touching – Jean-Luc Nancy* (Stanford CA: Stanford University Press, 2005), p. 163
9 See Elspeth M. Veale, *The English Fur Trade in the Later Middle Ages* (New York and Oxford; Oxford University Press, 1966), p. 14

10   Peter Stallybrass and Ann Jones, 'Fetishizing the Glove in Renaissance Europe', *Critical Inquiry*, vol. 28, no. 1, Things (Autumn 2001), p. 116
11   Ibid., p. 129
12   Dialogue from *Thunderball*, dir. Terence Young, 1965
13   C.S. Lewis, *The Lion, the Witch and the Wardrobe* (London: Harper Collins, 1999), p. 12
14   Margaret Wise Brown, *Little Fur Family* (New York: Harper Collins, 2014)
15   Edward Topsell, *The History of Four-Footed Beasts and Serpents* (London: G. Sawbridge, 1658), p. 58
16   Serres 2016, p. 82
17   From Edmund Burke [1757], 'A Philosophical Inquiry into the Origin of our Ideas of the Sublime and the Beautiful' in *British Literature: An Anthology 1640–1789*, ed. Robert DeMaria Jr. (Chichester: Wiley Blackwell, 2016), p. 1002
18   Roland Barthes, 'The New Citroën' in *Mythologies* (London: Collins, 1973), pp. 95–7
19   Gaston Bachelard, *The Poetics of Space* (Boston: Beacon Press, 1992), p. 217
20   Lyric from *A Hunting We Will Go*, dir. Dave Fleischer, 1932
21   From 'The Modern Hiawatha' by Rev. George A. Strong (Cincinatti: Jones, Brown and Robinson, 1856), published either anonymously or under a pseudonym and in numerous editions.
22   All definitions from *The Shorter Oxford Dictionary*, vol. 1 (Oxford: Oxford University Press, 1973), p. 230
23   Serres 2016, p. 24
24   From 'I've Got You Under My Skin', Cole Porter, 1936
25   The Bible, King James Version (1611), Jonah 1:17
26   *The Empire Strikes Back*, dir. Irvin Kershner, 1980. I thank Ben Hughes for bringing this scene to my attention.
27   *The Revenant*, dir. Alejandro González Iñárritu, 2015
28   *River of Fundament*, dirs Matthew Barney and Jonathan Bepler, 2014
29   See Betty Kobayashi Issenman, *Sinews of Survival* (Vancouver: UBC Press, 1997) for further information on *kamaleika*
30   Bachelard 1992, p. 217
31   Sigmund Freud, 'Three Essays on the Theory of Sexuality' in *Complete Psychological Works of Sigmund Freud, vol. VII (1901–1905)* (London: Hogarth Press, 2001), p. 155
32   Ibid., p. 154
33   Freud, 'Fetishism' in *Complete Psychological Works, vol. XXI (1927–1931)*, 2001, p. 155
34   *Eyes of Laura Mars*, dir. Irvin Kershner, 1978. I am referring here not only to Newton, but also to fashion photographers with a similar objectifying aesthetic, such as Guy Bourdin.
35   Lyrics from 'Burn', George Michalski and Nikki Oosterveen, 1978
36   *Not Now Darling*, dirs Ray Cooney and David Croft, 1973
37   Leopold von Sacher-Masoch, *Venus in Furs* (London: Penguin Books, 2000)
38   Gilles Deleuze, 'Coldness and Cruelty' in Deleuze and Leopold von Sacher-Masoch, *Masochism* (New York: Zone Books, 1991), p. 25
39   Sacher-Masoch 2000, p. 3
40   Ibid., p. 35
41   Deleuze 1991, p. 53
42   Sacher-Masoch 2000, p. 22
43   Ibid, pp. 95–6
44   Sacher-Masoch 2000, p. 13
45   Franz Kafka, *Metamorphosis & Other Stories* (London: Minerva, 1993), p. 9
46   Ibid., p. 40
47   John Lea Nevinson and Ann Saunders, *The Four Seasons* by Wenceslas Hollar (Norfolk: Daedalus Press, 1979), p. 8
48   See Anon, *The History and Survey of the Cities of London and Westminster* (London: W. Reeve & C. Sympson, 1753), p. 398
49   Nevinson 1979, p. 29
50   Patricia Lurati, '"To dust the pelisse": the erotic side of fur in Italian Renaissance art', *Renaissance Studies*, vol. 31, no. 2 (2017), p. 256
51   Further details can be found on websites such as www.minkglove.com
52   Sacher-Masoch 2000, p. 30; Serres 2016, p. 24
53   Werner Spies, 'Meret Oppenheim's *Objet de Désir*' in Therese Bhattacharya-Stettler and Matthias Frehner (eds), *Meret Oppenheim Retrospective* (Ostfildern: Hatje Cantz Verlag, 2007), pp. 24, 26
54   Julia Kristeva, *Powers of Horror* (New York: Columbia University Press, 1982), p. 3
55   H.W. Kellick, 'He Makes Mink Telephones', *Mechanix Illustrated*, May 1950, p. 166
56   The Bible, King James Version (1611), Exodus 36: 14 and 19
57   Veale 1966, pp. 15–16
58   Alan Hunt, *Governance of the Consuming Passions* (New York: St Martin's Press, 1996), p. 126
59   See Sebastian Hackenschmidt, 'Furniture as Trophies – Design Using Animals' in *Furniture as Trophy*, ed. Peter Noever, exh. cat., Museum of Applied Arts/Contemporary Art, Vienna, 2009, pp. 41–57 for a detailed account of the fashion for antler furniture.
60   J-K. Huysmans, *Against Nature* (London: Penguin Books, 2003), pp. 16, 17
61   Richard Davey, *Furs and Fur Garments* (London: The International Fur Store and Roxburghe Press, 1895), p. 102
62   Ibid., p. 103
63   Credited with transforming actress Gloria Swanson's image from innocent ingénue to vamp, Glyn's 1927 novel *It* defines 'it' as the quality of animal magnetism found in big cats. The novel became a film the same year. Its success inspired her to dub rising star Clara Bow 'the It girl'.
64   Gunnar Schmidt, 'Trophies: the Aestheticization of Melancholy', quoted in Noever 2009, p. 11
65   *Theorem*, dir. Pier Paolo Pasolini, 1968
66   *New York* magazine, 16 August 1971, p. 55
67   André Breton [1936], 'Crise de l'objet', quoted in Bhattacharya-Stettler and Frehner 2007, p. 21

PART FIVE: FLEECE

1   Gilles Deleuze and Félix Guattari, *A Thousand Plateaus* (London: Athlone Press, 1992)
2   Michel Serres, *The Five Senses* (London: Bloomsbury, 2016)
3   Deleuze and Guattari 1992, p. 238
4   From 'Hot Voodoo', lyrics Sam Coslow, music Ralph Rainger, featured in *Blonde Venus*, dir. Josef von Sternberg, 1932
5   Dan Goodley, Katherine Runswick-Cole and Kirsty Liddiard, 'The DisHuman Child' in *Discourse: Studies in the Cultural Politics of Education*, vol. 37, issue 5 (2016), p. 772
6   Walter Benjamin, 'Gloves' in *One-Way Street* (London: Verso, 1997), p. 50
7   Deleuze and Guattari 1992, p. 238
8   *Bear Skins*, 1951, available at https://www.britishpathe.com/video/bear-skins/query/bear+skin (accessed 10 July 2019)
9   See Michel Pastoureau, 'The Revenge of the Bear' in *The Bear: History of a Fallen King* (Cambridge MA: Harvard University Press, 2011), pp. 247–52
10   Donald Woods Winnicott, *Playing and Reality* (London: Routledge, 2005)
11   Suetonius, *The Lives of the Twelve Caesars* (New York: Random House, 1951), p. 259
12   Dialogue from *Cat People*, dir. Paul Schrader, 1982
13   *The Graduate*, dir. Mike Nichols, 1967; *Les Liaisons Dangereuses*, dir. Roger Vadim, 1959
14   The Convention on International Trade in Endangered Species of Wild Fauna and Flora consists of 180 signatory countries including all members of the European Union. Some 5,000 species of animal are protected by its legislation; see https://www.cites.org/ (accessed 21 April 2019)
15   https://www.wwf.org.uk/wildlife (accessed 21 April 2019)
16   https://www.iucnredlist.org/ (accessed 21 April 2019)
17   Christina Riggs, *Unwrapping Ancient Egypt* (London: Bloomsbury, 2014), p. 8
18   The Griffith Institute, *Tutankhamun: Anatomy of an Excavation. The Howard Carter Archives*, no. 021t; http://www.griffith.ox.ac.uk/gri/carter/021t-c021t.html (accessed 18 May 2018)
19   Frances Backhouse, *Once They Were Hats* (Toronto: ECW Press, 2015), p. 43
20   *Tarzan and the Leopard Men* (1935), a novel by Edgar Rice Burroughs, 18th in the *Tarzan* series; *Tintin au Congo* (1946), the second part of the *Adventures of Tintin* comic series, by Belgian cartoonist Hergé.
21   For a detailed discussion of the sculpture and its ramifications see Vicky Van Bockhaven, 'The Leopard Men of the Eastern Congo (ca. 1890–1940): History and Colonial Representation.' Unpublished PhD thesis, 2013.
22   *Peau d'âne* was first published in verse form in 1695. The tale written by the Brothers Grimm, also known as *Thousandfurs* and *Fur Pelts*, was first published in 1812 under the German title *Allerleirauh*. A number of other variants of this story exist, an earlier and notable example being Giambattista Basile's *The She-Bear* from his collection of fables *Il Pentamerone*, first published in instalments between 1634 and 1636.
23   Giambattista Basile, *The She-Bear*, available at https://www.pitt.edu/~dash/type0510b.html#basile (accessed 2 July 2019)
24   Deleuze and Guattari 1992, p. 239
25   Eric Lenneberg (ed.), *New Directions in the Study of Language* (Massachusetts: MIT Press, 1964), pp. 337–8
26   Edward Topsell, *The History of Four-Footed Beasts and Serpents* (London: G. Sawbridge, 1658), p. 6
27   Patricia Lurati, '"To dust the pelisse": the erotic side of fur in Italian Renaissance art', *Renaissance Studies*, vol. 31, no. 2 (2017), p. 246
28   Topsell 1658, p. 8
29   *Shall We Dance*, dir. Mark Sandrich, 1937; *Theodora Goes Wild*, dir. Richard Boleslawski, 1936
30   Ann Jones and Peter Stallybrass, *Renaissance Clothing and the Materials of Memory* (Cambridge: Cambridge University Press, 2000), p. 2
31   I am grateful to Jacqui Ansell for sharing with me her work on the costumes in Batoni's portraits.
32   Jo Kirby, 'The Painter's Trade in the Seventeenth Century: Theory and Practice', *National Gallery Technical Bulletin*, vol. 20 (1999), pp. 15–16

33 Walter Benjamin, 'The Task of the Translator', in Marcus Bullock and Michael Jennings (eds), *Walter Benjamin Selected Writings, vol. 1, 1913–1926* (Cambridge MA: The Belknap Press of Harvard University, 1996), p. 254

34 See 'Translate' in C.T. Onions (ed.), *The Shorter Oxford Dictionary*, 2 vols, (Oxford: Oxford University Press, 1973), p. 2347

35 Benjamin 1996, p. 255

36 Ibid., p. 254

37 See 'The Dynamics of Transference' (1912), in Sigmund Freud, *Complete Psychological Works of Sigmund Freud, vol. XII (1911–1913), Case History of Schreber, Papers on Technique, and Other Works* (London: Hogarth Press, 2001), pp. 97–108

38 Arthur Fox-Davies, *A Complete Guide to Heraldry* (London: T.C. & E.C. Jack, 1909), p. 79

39 For more on the possible origin of these and other such 'donor windows' in Chartres Cathedral see Jane Welch Williams, *Bread, Wine, and Money: The Windows of the Trades at Chartres Cathedral* (Chicago: University of Chicago Press, 1993)

40 See Edwina Ehrman (ed.), *Fashioned from Nature* (London: V&A Publishing, 2018), pp. 72–5 for further information on early glass fibre.

41 Dilys Blum, *Shocking! The Art and Fashion of Elsa Schiaparelli* (Philadelphia: Philadelphia Museum of Art, 2003), p. 285

42 Michel Serres, *The Five Senses* (London: Bloomsbury, 2016), p. 82

43 Benjamin 1996, p. 257

44 See Lesley Miller, 'From Cocoon to Court: An Eighteenth-Century Mantua' in Ehrman 2018, pp. 46–53

45 I am referring here to Benjamin's seminal essay *The Work of Art in the Age of Mechanical Reproduction* of 1935.

46 Aldous Huxley, *Brave New World* (London: Vintage, 2007), p. 29

47 *King Kong*, dirs. Merian C. Cooper and Ernest B. Schoedsack, 1933

48 *Babe*, dir. Chris Noonan, 1995; *Monsters, Inc.*, dirs Pete Docter, David Silverman and Lee Unkrich, 2001; *Monsters University*, dir. Dan Scanlon, 2013

49 Taken from an interview with Corvaja from 2008, available on his website: https://www.giovanni-corvaja.com/the-golden-fleece/ (accessed 30 May 2019)

50 Ibid.

51 Benjamin 1996, p. 258

CONCLUSION

1 Giacomo Leopardi, *Dialogue Between Fashion and Death* (London: Penguin Books 2010); Walter Benjamin, 'B [Fashion]' in *The Arcades Project* (Cambridge MA and London: The Belknap Press of Harvard University, 1999), p. 79.

2 See 'Queen will no longer wear clothes with real fur, Her Majesty's dresser reveals' by Helena Horton and Victoria Ward; https://www.telegraph.co.uk/royal-family/2019/11/05/queen-go-fur-free-first-time-says-official-dresser/ (accessed 6 November 2019)

3 See Vogue.com report on Jean Paul Gaultier, Autumn/Winter 2019 couture collection: https://www.vogue.com/fashion-shows/fall-2019-couture/jean-paul-gaultier (accessed 9 September 2019)

4 See Else Skjold (ed.), *Refurbish* (Kolding: Design School Kolding + Kopenhagen Fur, 2019)

5 Lise Skov, 'The Return of the Fur Coat: A Commodity Chain Perspective', *Current Sociology*, vol. 53, issue 1 (January 2005), p. 9

BIBLIOGRAPHY

BOOKS

Ahern, Albert M., 1922, *Fur Facts: A Book of Knowledge* (St Louis MO: C.P. Curran Printing Company)

Anderson, Benedict, [1983] 1991, *Imagined Communities: Reflections on the Origin and Spread of Nationalism* (London: Verso)

Anon, 1753, *The History and Survey of the Cities of London and Westminster* (London: W. Reeve & C. Sympson)

Ashbrook, Frank G., 1928, *Fur-Farming for Profit* (New York: The Macmillan Company)

----- 1954, *Furs Glamorous and Practical: Fur Buying Mystery Removed* (New York: D. Van Norstrand Company, Inc.)

Bachelard, Gaston, [1958] 1992, *The Poetics of Space* (Boston: Beacon Press)

Backhouse, Frances, 2015, *Once They Were Hats: In Search of the Mighty Beaver* (Toronto: ECW Press)

Barthes, Roland, 1973, *Mythologies* (London: Collins)

----- 1990, *The Fashion System* (Berkeley CA: University of California Press)

Beard, Alice, 2013, 'Nova Magazine 1965–1975: A History', University of London (unpublished PhD thesis)

Benjamin, Walter, 1999, *The Arcades Project*, trans. Howard Eiland and Kevin McLaughlin (Cambridge MA and London: The Belknap Press of Harvard University)

----- [1928] 1997, *One-Way Street and Other Writings* (London: Verso)

Bentham, Jeremy [1789], 1907, *An Introduction to the Principles of Morals and Legislation* (Oxford: Clarendon Press)

Bhattacharya-Stettler, Therese, and Matthias Frehner (eds), 2007, *Meret Oppenheim Retrospective "an enormously tiny bit of a lot"* (Ostfildern: Hatje Cantz Verlag)

Blum, Dilys, 2003, *Shocking! The Art and Fashion of Elsa Schiaparelli* (Philadelphia: Philadelphia Museum of Art)

Brown, Margaret Wise, 2014, *Little Fur Family* (New York: Harper Collins)

Bullock, Marcus and Michael Jennings (eds), 1996, *Walter Benjamin Selected Writings vol. 1, 1913–1926* (Cambridge MA: The Belknap Press of Harvard University)

Burnham, Dorothy K., 1973, *Cut My Cote* (Toronto: Royal Ontario Museum)

----- 1992, *To Please the Caribou* (Toronto: Royal Ontario Museum)

Busch, Briton Cooper, 1987, *The War Against the Seals: A History of the North American Seal Fishery* (Kingston, Ontario: McGill-Queen's University Press)

Cameron, Dan, Kate Eilertson and Pam McClusky, 2009, *Nick Cave: Meet Me at the Center of the Earth* (San Francisco: Yerba Buena Center for the Arts)

Capote, Truman, 2005, *Truman Capote: The Complete Stories* (London: Penguin Books)

Caskey, L.D. and J.D. Beazley, 1963, *Attic Vase Paintings in the Museum of Fine Arts, Boston. Part III* (Boston: Museum of Fine Arts)

Clark, Anna, 2004, *Scandal: The Sexual Politics of the British Constitution* (Princeton: Princeton University Press)

Clarke, Richard, 2004, *Pioneers of Conservation: The Selborne Society and the Royal SPB* (London: Selborne Society)

Collins, Wilkie [1883], 1990, *Heart and Science: A Story of the Present Time* (Gloucester: Alan Sutton)

Daly, Nicholas, 2017, *The Demographic Imagination and the Nineteenth-Century City* (Cambridge: Cambridge University Press)

Damisch, Hubert (ed.), 1967, *Jean Dubuffet. Prospectus et tous écrits suivants*, vol. 2 (Paris: Gallimard)

Davey, Richard, 1895, *Furs and Fur Garments* (London: The International Fur Store and Roxburghe Press)

De Charlevoix, Pierre-François-Xavier, 1923, *Journal of a Voyage to North America* (Chicago: The Caxton Club)

De la Haye, Amy and Edwina Ehrman (eds), 2015, *London Couture 1923–1975: British Luxury* (London: V&A Publishing)

Deleuze, Gilles and Félix Guattari, 1992, *A Thousand Plateaus: Capitalism and Schizophrenia* (London: Athlone Press)

Deleuze, Gilles and Leopold von Sacher-Masoch, 1991, *Masochism: Coldness and Cruelty & Venus in Furs* (New York: Zone Books)

DeMaria, Robert Jr. (ed.), 2016, *British Literature: An Anthology 1640–1789* (Chichester: Wiley Blackwell)

Derrida, Jacques, 2005, *On Touching – Jean-Luc Nancy* (Stanford CA: Stanford University Press)

Dmitrieva, Olga and Tessa Murdoch, 2013, *Treasures of the Royal Courts: Tudors, Stuarts & the Russian Tsars* (London, V&A Publishing)

Dolin, Eric Jay, 2010, *Fur, Fortune and Empire: The Epic History of the Fur Trade in America* (New York: W. W. Norton & Company)

Douglas, Mary, 2002, *Purity and Danger: An Analysis of Concepts of Pollution and Taboo* (London: Routledge)

Ehrman, Edwina (ed.), 2018, *Fashioned from Nature* (London, V&A Publishing)

Ellroy, James, 1999, *Crime Wave* (London: Arrow Books)

Emberley, Julia, 1997, *The Cultural Politics of Fur* (Ithaca NY: Cornell University Press)

Ewing, Elizabeth, 1981, *Fur in Dress* (London: Batsford)

Faiers, Jonathan, 2013, *Dressing Dangerously: Dysfunctional Fashion in Film* (New Haven CT and London: Yale University Press)

Fitzgerald, F. Scott, 2018, *I'd Die For You and Other Lost Stories* (London: Scribner)

Flaubert, Gustave [1911–13], 1976, *Bouvard and Pécuchet: With the Dictionary of Received Ideas* (London: Penguin Books)

Flügel, John Carl, 1940, *The Psychology of Clothes* (London: Hogarth Press)

Fox-Davies, Arthur C., 1909, *Complete Guide to Heraldry* (London: T.C. & E.C. Jack)

Freud, Sigmund, 2001, *Complete Psychological Works of Sigmund Freud, vol. VII (1901–1905): A Case of Hysteria, Three Essays on Sexuality and Other Works* (London: Hogarth Press)

----- 2001, *Complete Psychological Works of Sigmund Freud, vol. XII (1911–1913): Case History of Schreber, Papers on Technique, and Other Works* (London: Hogarth Press)

----- 2001, *Complete Psychological Works of Sigmund Freud, vol. XXI (1927–1931) The Future of an Illusion, Civilization and its Discontents and other Works* (London: Hogarth Press)

Gabler, Neal, 1989, *An Empire of Their Own: How the Jews Invented Hollywood* (London: W.H. Allen & Co.)

Galsworthy, John, 1912, *For Love of Beasts* (London: Animals' Friend Society)

----- 1914, *Treatment of Animals* (London: Animals' Friend Society)

Gates, Barbara T. (ed.), 2002, *In Nature's Name: An Anthology of Women's Writing and Illustration 1780–1930* (Chicago: University of Chicago Press)

Hall, James, 2014, *The Self-Portrait: a Cultural History* (London: Thames & Hudson)

Harrell, Trajal, 2017, *Hoochie Koochie,* performance exhib., Barbican Art Gallery, London

Harrison, Michael, 1960, *The History of the Hat* (London: Herbert Jenkins Ltd)

Harvey, John, 1995, *Men in Black* (London: Reaktion Books)

Hawes, Elizabeth [1938], 2015, *Fashion is Spinach: How to Beat the Fashion Racket* (New York: Dover Publications)

Hayward, Maria, 2009, *Rich Apparel: Clothing and the Law in Henry VIII's England* (Farnham: Ashgate Publishing)

Hill, Colleen, 2016, *Fairy Tale Fashion* (New Haven CT and London: Yale University Press)

Hodgson, Robert G., 1954, *The Mink Book* (Toronto: Fur Trade Journal of Canada)

Hollander, Anne, 1993, *Seeing Through Clothes* (Berkeley CA: University of California Press)

Hunt, Alan, 1996, *Governance of the Consuming Passions: A History of Sumptuary Law* (London: Palgrave Macmillan)

Huxley, A. [1932], 2007, *Brave New World* (London: Vintage)

Huysmans, J-K. [1884], 2003, *Against Nature* (London: Penguin Books)

Innis, Harold Adams, 1999, *The Fur Trade in Canada: An Introduction to Canadian Economic History* (Toronto: University of Toronto Press)

Issenman, Betty Kobayashi, 1997, *Sinews of Survival: The Living Legacy of Inuit Clothing* (Vancouver: UBC Press)

Jerome, Jerome K., 1912, *The Cruel Steel Trap* (London: Animals' Friend Society)

Johnston, Lucy, Marion Kite and Helen Persson, 2005, *Nineteenth-Century Fashion in Detail* (London: V&A Publishing)

Jones, Ann R. and Peter Stallybrass, 2000, *Renaissance Clothing and the Materials of Memory* (Cambridge: Cambridge University Press)

Kafka, Franz, 1993, *Metamorphosis & Other Stories* (London: Minerva)

Kovesi Killerby, Catherine, 2002, *Sumptuary Law in Italy 1200–1500* (Oxford: Oxford University Press)

Kristeva, Julia, 1982, *Powers of Horror: An Essay on Abjection* (New York: Columbia University Press)

Laver, James, 1945, *Taste and Fashion* (London: George G. Harrap & Co. Ltd)

Lefebvre, Henri, [1974] 1991, *The Production of Space* (Oxford: Wiley Blackwell)

Lenneberg, Eric (ed.), 1964, *New Directions in the Study of Language* (Massachusetts: MIT Press)

Leopardi, Giacomo, 2010, *Dialogue Between Fashion and Death* (London: Penguin Books)

Lesnik-Oberstein, Karin (ed.), 2006, *The Last Taboo: Women and Body Hair* (Manchester: Manchester University Press)

Leroi, Armand, 2003, *Mutants: On the Form, Varieties and Errors of the Human Body* (London: Harper Collins)

Lewis, C.S., [1950] 1999, *The Lion, the Witch and the Wardrobe* (London: Harper Collins)

Links, Joseph G., 1956, *The Book of Fur* (London: James Barrie)

Loh, Maria H., 2015, *Still Lives: Death, Desire, and the Portrait of the Old Master* (Princeton: Princeton University Press)

Lyotard, Jean-François, [1974] 1993, *Libidinal Economy* (Bloomington IN: Indiana University Press)

Macdonell, Archibald G., 1943, *The Fur Coat* (London: Macmillan & Co. Ltd)

Mansfield, Elizabeth C., and Kelly Malone (eds), 2013, *Seeing Satire in the Eighteenth Century* (Oxford: Voltaire Foundation, University of Oxford)

Marks, Laura U., 2000, *The Skin of the Film: Intercultural Cinema, Embodiment, and the Senses* (Durham NC: Duke University Press)

Matthews David, A., 2015, *Fashion Victims: The Dangers of Dress Past and Present* (London: Bloomsbury)

McNeil, Peter, 2018, *Pretty Gentlemen: Macaroni Men and the Eighteenth-Century Fashion World* (New Haven CT and London: Yale University Press)

Mears, Patricia et al. (eds), 2017, *Expedition: Fashion From the Extreme* (London: Thames & Hudson)

Nadeau, Chantal, 2001, *Fur Nation: From the Beaver to Bardot* (London: Routledge)

Nevinson, John Lea and Ann Saunders, 1979, *The Four Seasons by Wenceslas Hollar*, Costume Society Extra Series, no. 6 (Norfolk: Daedalus Press)

Noever, Peter (ed.), 2009, *Furniture as Trophy*, exh. cat., Museum of Applied Arts/Contemporary Art, Vienna

Pastoureau, Michel, 2011, *The Bear: History of a Fallen King* (Cambridge MA: Harvard University Press)

Remarque, Erich M., 2005, *All Quiet on the Western Front* (London: Vintage Classics)

Ribeiro, Aileen, 2002, *Dress in Eighteenth-Century Europe* (New Haven CT and London: Yale University Press)

Riggs, Christina, 2014, *Unwrapping Ancient Egypt* (London: Bloomsbury)

Rogers, Peter, 1979, *What becomes a Legend most? The Blackglama Story* (New York: Simon and Schuster)

Rony, Fatimah T., 1996, *The Third Eye: Race, Cinema, and Ethnographic Spectacle* (Durham NC: Duke University Press)

Sacher-Masoch, Leopold von, [1870] 2000, *Venus in Furs* (London: Penguin Books)

Sachs, John C., [1923] 1930, *Furs and the Fur Trade* (London: Pitman & Sons)

Salt, Henry Stephens [1892], 1980, *Animals' Rights: Considered in Relation to Social Progress* (New York: Centaur Press with the Society for Animal Rights Inc., Pennsylvania)

Sax, Boria, 2000, *Animals in the Third Reich: Pets, Scapegoats, and the Holocaust* (New York and London: Continuum)

Serres, Michel [1985], 2016, *The Five Senses: A Philosophy of Mingled Bodies* (London: Bloomsbury)

Singer, Peter [1975], 1995, *Animal Liberation: A New Ethics for Our Treatment of Animals* (London: Random House)

Skjold, Else, 2019, *Refurbish* (Kolding: Design School Kolding + Kopenhagen Fur)

Sonenscher, Michael, 1994, *The Hatters of Eighteenth-Century France* (Berkeley CA: University of California Press)

Stevenson, David, 2001,*The Beggar's Benison: Sex Clubs of Enlightenment Scotland and their Rituals* (East Lothian: Tuckwell Press)

Stubbes, Philip, 1583, *The Anatomie of Abuses* (London: Richard Jones)

Suetonius [AD 121], 1951, *The Lives of the Twelve Caesars* (New York: Random House)

Summers, Julie, 2015, *Fashion on the Ration* (London: Profile Books)

Tashlin, Frank, 2010, *The Bear That Wasn't* (New York: New York Review of Books)

Topsell, Edward, 1658, *The History of Four-Footed Beasts and Serpents* (London: G. Sawbridge)

Turner Wilcox, R. [1951], 2010, *The Mode in Furs* (New York: Dover Publications)

Van Bockhaven, Vicky, 2013, 'The Leopard Men of the Eastern Congo (ca. 1890–1940): History and Colonial Representation', University of East Anglia (unpublished PhD. thesis)

Vassiliev, Alexandre, [1998] 2000, *Beauty in Exile: The Artists, Models and Nobility Who Fled the Russian Revolution and Influenced the World of Fashion* (New York: Harry N. Abrams Inc.)

Veale, Elspeth M., 1966, *The English Fur Trade in the Later Middle Ages* (New York and Oxford: Oxford University Press)

Verne, Jules [1873], 1987, *The Fur Country* (Gloucester: Alan Sutton)

Wilcox, Claire (ed.), 2015, *Alexander McQueen* (London: V&A Publishing)

Williams, Jane Welch, 1993, *Bread, Wine, and Money: The Windows of the Trades at Chartres Cathedral* (Chicago: University of Chicago Press)

Wilson, Elizabeth [1985], 2007, *Adorned in Dreams: Fashion and Modernity* (London: I.B. Tauris)

Winnicott, Donald Woods, 2005, *Playing and Reality* (London: Routledge)

Zukor, Adolph, 1953, *The Public is Never Wrong: My Fifty Years in Motion Pictures* (New York: G.P. Putnam's Sons)

JOURNAL AND NEWSPAPER ARTICLES

Arnold, Dorothea, 1995, 'An Egyptian Bestiary', *Metropolitan Museum of Art Bulletin*, Spring, pp. 7–64

Aubert, M., 2014, 'Pleistocene cave art from Sulawesi, Indonesia', *Nature*, 514, pp. 223–7

Bevilacqua, Alexander and Helen Pfeifer, 2013, 'Turquerie: Culture in Motion 1650–1750', *Past and Present*, vol. 221, issue 1, pp. 75–118

Crean, J.F., 1962, 'Hats and the Fur Trade', *Canadian Journal of Economics and Political Science*, vol. 28, no. 3, pp. 373–86

Foucault, Michel, 1986, 'Of Other Spaces', *Diacritics*, vol. 16, no. 1, Spring, pp. 22–7

Goodley, Dan, Katherine Runswick-Cole and Kirsty Liddiard, 2016, 'The DisHuman Child', *Discourse: Studies in the Cultural Politics of Education*, vol. 37, issue 5, pp. 770–84

Hartline, Niko L., Nicholas J. Bruce, Stephanie N. Karba, Elizabeth O. Ruff, Shreya U. Sonar and Patricia A. Holden, 2016, 'Microfiber Masses Recovered from Conventional Machine Washing of New or Aged Garments', *Environmental Science & Technology*, vol. 50, no. 21, pp. 11532–38

Henry, Beverley, Kirsi Laitala and Ingun G. Klepp, 2018, 'Microplastic Pollution from Textiles: A Literature Review', *Consumption Research Norway – SIFO*, Project Report no. 1

Kirby, Jo, 1999, 'The Painter's Trade in the Seventeenth Century: Theory and Practice', *National Gallery Technical Bulletin*, vol. 20

Kittler, Ralf, Manfred Kayser and Mark Stoneking, 2003, 'Molecular Evolution of *Pediculus humanus* and the Origin of Clothing', *Current Biology*, vol. 13, no. 16, pp. 1414–17

Leach, Edmund R., 1958, 'Magical Hair', *Journal of the Royal Anthropological Institute of Great Britain and Ireland*, vol. 88, no. 2, pp. 147–64

Life Magazine, 1968 'Jacques Kaplan's Tour de Furs', 13 December, pp. 100–3

Lurati, Patricia, 2017, '"To dust the pelisse": the erotic side of fur in Italian Renaissance art', *Renaissance Studies*, vol. 31, no. 2, pp. 240–60

Mannering, Ulla, 2015, 'Early Scandinavian Textile Design', ARCHAEOLINGUA, vol. 33, pp. 95–102

Mitchell, W.J.T., 1995, 'Interdisciplinarity and Visual Culture', *Art Bulletin*, vol. 77, no. 4, December, pp. 540–4

Musacchio, Jacqueline M., 2001, 'Weasels and Pregnancy in Renaissance Italy', *Renaissance Studies*, vol. 15, no. 2, June, pp. 172–87

Nova magazine, 1971, 'Every Hobo Should Have One', November, pp. 60–7

Nova magazine, 1974, 'We're Just Good Fur-Reinds', January, pp. 40–4

Ouida, 1894, 'The New Woman', *The North American Review*, vol. 158, no. 450, May, pp. 610–19

Sanders, Jasmine, 2019, 'Nothing Faux About It', *New York Times*, 31 January

Skov, Lise, 2005, 'The Return of the Fur Coat: A Commodity Chain Perspective', *Current Sociology*, vol. 53, issue 1, January, pp. 9–32

Stallybrass, Peter and Ann R. Jones, 2001, 'Fetishizing the Glove in Renaissance Europe', *Critical Enquiry*, vol. 28, no. 1, Autumn, Things, pp. 114–32

Tawny, Sherrill, 2006, 'Fleas, Furs, and Fashions: *Zibellini* as Luxury Accessories of the Renaissance' in *Medieval Clothing and Textiles*, eds Robin Netherton and Gale R. Owen-Crocker, vol. 2 (Woodbridge, Suffolk: Boydell Press), pp. 121–50

American *Vogue*, 1957, '1958 Cars, 1958 Furs', November, pp. 136–44

American *Vogue*, 1966, 'The Great Fur Caravan', October, pp. 88–113, 175

American *Vogue*, 1977, 'The "Force" of Fur', November, pp. 308–15

WEBSITES

The Griffith Institute, http://www.griffith.ox.ac.uk/griffith.html

https://www.wearefur.com/

https://www.truthaboutfur.com/

Hudson's Bay Company, http://www.hbcheritage.ca/history

ONLINE ARTICLES

Gihvan, Robin, https://www.washingtonpost.com/news/arts-and-entertainment/wp/2018/08/17/aretha-franklin-secret-style-icon-with-the-drop-of-a-fur-coat-she-proclaimed-her-self-worth/?utm_term=.8e164d0a072c (accessed 15 March 2019)

Grimes, William, 2008, 'Jacques Kaplan, 83, Bold Furrier, Dies' *New York Times*, 22 July, https://www.nytimes.com/2008/07/22/nyregion/22kaplan.html (accessed 18 April 2019)

Kellick, H.W., 1950, He Makes Mink Telephones', *Mechanix Illustrated*, May, pp. 74–5, 164, 166, http://blog.modernmechanix.com/he-makes-mink-telephones/ (accessed 27 June 2019)

Menkes, Suzy, 2003, 'The Collections/New York: Urban Fashion Revolution', *New York Times*, 11 February, https://www.nytimes.com/2003/02/11/style/IHT-the-collections-new-york-urban-fashion-revolution.html (accessed 11 May 2019)

Murdoch, Tessa, 2015, 'Exhibiting the Renaissance. *The Golden Age of the English Court from Henry VIII to Charles I* (Moscow Kremlin Museums, 27 October 2012 to 17 January 2013); *Treasures of the Royal Courts. Tudors, Stuarts and the Russian Tsars* (Victoria and Albert Museum, 9 March to 14 July 2013)', 3 August, https://edoc.hu-berlin.de/bitstream/handle/18452/8344/murdoch.pdf (accessed 17 May 2019)

Neuman, William and Jeffery C. Mays, 2019, 'Proposed Fur Ban in New York Pits Animal Rights Advocates Against Black Ministers', *New York Times*, 15 May, https://www.nytimes.com/2019/05/15/nyregion/fur-ban-nyc-sales.html (accessed 24 July 2019)

Sample, Ian, 2014, '35,000 year-old Indonesian cave paintings suggest art came out of Africa', *The Guardian*, 9 October, https://www.theguardian.com/science/2014/oct/08/cave-art-indonesia-sulawesi (accessed 15 May 2018)

Wolfe, Tom, 1970, 'Radical Chic: That Party at Lenny's', *New York* magazine, 8 June, http://nymag.com/news/features/46170/ (accessed 18 April 2019)

Martin, Laura, 2009, 'Dan Mathews: PETA's fight against fur', *The Independent*, Life section, 5 May, https://www.independent.co.uk/life-style/fashion/features/dan-mathews-petas-fight-against-fur-1678967.html (accessed 7 February 2019)

'No, It's Not Fur, but It Looks Like Fur and a Lot of People Like It; Imitation Fur Is Flying High As Fabric for Women's Coats', 1964, *New York Times*, 17 June, https://www.nytimes.com/1964/06/17/archives/no-its-not-fur-but-it-looks-like-fur-and-a-lot-of-people-like-it.html (accessed 16 February 2019)

Stella McCartney, interviewed for CNN Style, 2015, 'Fur's not sexy, not fashionable, and not cool', November, http://edition.cnn.com/style/article/stella-mccartney-sustainable-fashion/index.html (accessed 7 February 2019)

ACKNOWLEDGEMENTS

In the course of researching and writing *Fur: A Sensitive History* I have been especially fortunate to have received the generous support, encouragement and expert advice of many friends and colleagues and I would like to express my thanks and gratitude to the following: To Gillian Malpass without whom this book would not have been written; Anjali Bulley, Clare Davis and Mark Eastment at Yale University Press; Kathrin Jacobsen and Denny Hemming; the Winchester Luxury Research Group, the Library and the Faculty of Arts and Humanities at the University of Southampton and to all at Kopenhagen Fur who provided me with such insight into the subject.

I have been especially fortunate to have benefited from the expertise and generosity of a number of institutions including Patricia Mears and Valerie Steele at the Fashion Institute of Technology, New York; Alex Palmer at the Royal Ontario Museum, Toronto; Karen von Godtsenhoven at the Metropolitan Museum of Art, New York; Danielle Sprecher at the Westminster Menswear Archive, University of Westminster, London; Edwina Ehrman at the Victoria and Albert Museum, London; Kevin Jones at FIDM Los Angeles; Steve Lansdale at Heritage Auctions, Texas and James Butcher and Olivia Twaites at Shutterstock.

I am especially grateful to the following artists and designers who have so generously allowed me to reproduce examples of their work: Janine Antoni; Naomi Bailey-Cooper; Rebecca Belmore; Nayland Blake; Nick Cave; Giovanni Corvaja; Andrew Groves; Denise Hawrysio; Mikkel Østergaard Schou; Wieki Somers and Nicole Wermers. Lastly my sincere thanks to the many individuals who willingly offered their help and advice during the course of this project: Joy Bivins; Marina Hays; Catherine Kovesi; Paul Mathiesen; Morten Pedersen; Else Skjold; Helen Smith; Iain R. Webb and Stuart Whatling.

INDEX

Page numbers in *italic* refer to the illustrations

A
Aboriginal myths 110
accessories 102–18
   boots 73, 84, 85, *116*, *117*, 209
   muffs 102, 106–9, *108–9*, 181
   shoes 117, *117*
   stoles 73, 102, 105, *105*, 106
   tippets 102–5, *102*, *104*
   see also hats
Act for Reformation of Excess in Apparel (1533) 66
Adam and Eve 88, 152
Adam of Bremen 65
Adolfo 128
Adrian 118
Adrover, Miguel 88, *88*
advertising 26, 52–3, *53*, 56–7, 74
aeroplanes 151
Afghan coats 27, *27*, 28, 86, *87*
Africa 24, 82, 187, 189, 203–4, 207, 211
African-Americans 74–7
ageing, hairiness and 28
air gallon technique 143–4, 217
Albany Army Relief Bazaar (1864) 56
Albert, Prince Consort 186
albinos 17
Alexander the Great 43
Alfred Morris Furs 157
Alfus, Albert 29
Allen & Ginter cigarettes *48*
alpaca wool 156
Ambras syndrome 18
American Fur Company 46–7
American Gangster (film) 74
American Society for the Prevention of Cruelty to Animals 31
Anderson, Benedict 121
Anderson, Marian 76, *76*
Andrew, Prince, Duke of York 196
androgenic hair 15
Anguissola, Sofonisba, *Prince Alessandro Farnese 89*
aniline dyes 155
Animal Cruelty 31
Animal Liberation Front 35, *35*
animals: animal rights movement 30–40, 35–7
   camouflage 16–17, 199
   evisceration 174–5
   skinning 176
   transformations 193–211
   see also individual species
The Animals Film 35
Animals' Friend Society 34–5
Anne of Brittany 93
Annis Furs 185
anorexia nervosa 18
anti-fur movement 30, 35–40, 36–7, 58, 76–7, 135, 137–8, 145, 159–60, 225–6

Antoni, Janine, *Saddle 162*, 170–1
Anuszkiewicz, Richard 58
Aquascutum 83
Aquinas, Thomas 165
Arctic fox 17, 125, 127, *127*, 133
Aristae Day 107
Aristotle 165, 174
Armenia 43
Arnold, Eve, *Lady at a Garden Party at Count Basie's in St. Albans 75*
Arthur, Jean 70
artists' brushes 212
Ashbrook, Frank, *Fur-Farming for Profit* 136
Astaire, Fred 125
Astor, John Jacob 46–7, *47*, 48
Astor Place subway station, New York 48, *48*
Astraka Furs 157–8, *157*
astrakhan 123, 156, 157
Aua 131
Avedon, Richard 57, 128
awn hair 15, *16*
axillary hair 15, 21

B
Babe (film) 223
Baccarat 60
Bachelard, Gaston 170, 171, 176
Backhouse, Francis 116–17, 203
badger hairs 155–6
Bailey, David 36
Bailey-Cooper, Naomi *191*, 217–19, *218*
Baker, Caroline 57–8
Bakst, Leon 123
balding 19
Balenciaga, Cristóbal 90, 101, 112, *113*, 151, *158*
Ballets Russes 123, 147
Banton, Travis 62
Bardot, Brigitte 35, 57
Barney, Matthew 175
Barnum, B.T. 18
Barthes, Roland 87, 170
Bartholomew, St 164
Bartolin, Thomas, *Anatomia Reformata 164*
Basile, Giambattista, *Il Pentamorone* 117–18, 204
Basso, Dennis 77
bathtub, mink-lined 139
Batoni, Pompeo 212
   Portrait of Richard Milles 212
Battersea Dogs Home 32
Beard, Alice 58
beards 18, 20, 27
'bears' 28, *29*
bears: bearskins 85, 89, 149, 195–6, *197*
   fairy tales 204
   teddy bears 156, 197
   transformative powers 195–7
Beauvoir, Simone de 159

beaver 44, 89
   castoreum 50, 60–1
   decline of 45, 47
   environment 47
   fake fur 156
   fur trade 45, 48–9
   gloves 167
   hats 45, 102, 114–17, *114–15*
   indigenous peoples and 45, 45, 47–8
   pilches 83
   territorialisation 47–50, *48–9*
   trapping 50
bed coverings 185
Beggar's Benison 22
Belgium 203–4
Bell, Book and Candle (film) 139
Belmore, Rebecca
   Rising to the Occasion 42, 50, *51*
   Twelve Angry Crinolines 50
Belville Sassoon 126, *127*
Benito, Eduardo, *Dogaresse* 147
Benjamin, Walter 91, 165, 195, 212–13, 219, 221, 224, 225
Benois, Alexandre 123
Bentham, Jeremy 40
   Introduction to the Principles of Morals and Legislation 30–1
Bergdorf Goodman, New York 56, 135, 136, *201*
Bergh, Henry *31*
Berlin 125
Bernhardt, Sarah 187
Berryman, Clifford, *Drawing the Line in Mississippi* 196–7, *196*
Berserkers 207
beurre salé technique 79, 144, *144*
Beyoncé 78
Bible 88, 152–3, 185
Bibrowski, Stephan 18
The Big Heat (film) 69, *69*, 140
bikinis 26–7, *26*
Birger Christensen, London 37
Björk 129
black Americans 74–7
black furs 16, 57, 65, 73, 91, 93, 100, 137
Blackglama advertising campaign 56–7, *57*, 73
Blake, Nayland, *Crossing Object (inside Gnomen) 192*, 195, *197*
Blaxploitation films 73–4
Blige, Mary J. 77, *78*
Blonde Venus (film) 204–5, *205*
Board of Trade 71–3
boas 105, *105*
Boccaccio, Giovanni, *De Casibus Virorum Illustrium* 67
Bocour 22
body hair 15, 21, 22–7, 40
body lice 82
Bohan, Marc 172–4, *172–3*
Bokassa, Jean-Bédel 99
Bond, James 168
Bonham Carter, Helena 54

The Book of Fur 91, 142
books, fur-covered 184
boots 73, 84, 85, *116*, *117*, 209
Borg 156, 157
bow ties 106, *107*
boxing gloves, mink 167–9, *168*
branding 172–4
Breton, André 182, 190
Breuer, Marcel 187
   Cesaca chair 118, *119*
Breve della campagna 65
Brexit 226
Bri-Lon Furleen 158
British Animal Defence and Anti-Vivisection Society 32
British Army 195–6
British Empire 56
British Fur Trade Association 58
British Nylon Spinners 158
brocade 220–1, *220–1*
Bronze Age 151, 152
Broome, Rev. Arthur 32
Brown, Margaret Wise, *Little Fur Family* 169, *169*
Bruni, Carla 24
brushes, artists' 212
Budapest 190
buffalo fur 150, 151
Bulganin, Nikolai 94
Burberry 38
Burke, Edmund 170
Burnham, Dorothy 130
Burton, Sarah 87, *87*
BUtterfield 8 (film) 69, 70
Byzantium 43–4, 216, *216*

C
Cadillac 148, 151
Calman Links *201*
Camelot (film) 93, *93*, 126
camouflage 16–17, 199
Canada: farmed furs 137, 167
   fur trade 45–6, 49–52
   see also Inuit peoples
Canter, Kym 159
Capone, Mae 193, *193*
Capote, Truman: *The Bargain* 138–9
   A Mink of One's Own 138–9
Cardi B 78, *78*
Cardin, Pierre 141–2
Cardinal Clothes 136
cars 113–14, 148–9, *148*
Carter, Howard 200–3
Cashin, Bonnie 86, *86*
Casino de Paris, London 27
Casseri, Giulio Cesare, *Pentaestheseion* 165
castoreum 50, 60–1
Cat People (film) 199–200
Catherine the Great, Empress of Russia 123, 180
cats 59, 89, 155

Cave, Nick, *Soundsuit* 14, *17*
celebrity culture 57
Cervantes, Miguel de, *Don Quixote* 184
Chaliapin, Feodor 123
Chanel 226
Chaplin, Charlie 85, *85*
Chapman, Mathias 167
Charles II, King of England 22, 45, 94
Charles VIII, King of France 93
Charlevoix, Pierre François de, *Journal of a Voyage to North America* 47
Chartres Cathedral 215–16, *215*
Château du Haut-Kœnigsbourg, Alsace 186
Chaucer, Geoffrey, *The Canterbury Tales* 114
cheetahs 59, 199, *200*
children 169, 219–20, *219*
China 137
chinchilla 16, 78, 139, 166–7, *166–7*
Chiuri, Maria Grazia 99
Chouart des Groseilliers, Médard 45
Christianity 65, 88
Christie, Julie 35, *35*, 126, *126*
Christmas in Connecticut (film) 30
cinema see films
CITES 200
Citroën D.S. 170
civet cats 66, 91, 100
Clark, Cyrus 83–4
Clay, Cassius (Muhammad Ali) 168–9
cloaks 83
A Clockwork Orange 131
clothing 81–102
   decline in use of fur 100–1, 102
   fur linings 89–90, 101, 120, 153
   making 142–5
   medieval 83
   prehistoric man 81–3, *82*
   rationing 71–3
   remodelling 153–4
   royalty 95
   see also accessories; coats; hats
coats and jackets: flying jackets 84
   jacks 120, *121*
   mink 30, 101, 136, 138
   motoring coats 148–9, 207
   raccoon 149, 209
   sable-lined 95
   sealskin 144–5, *145*, 147
   shapes 148–9
   sheepskin 27, 83–5, *83*
coins 49
Colin, Paul 53
Collins, Wilkie, *Heart and Science* 34
colobus monkey 207, *208*
colonialism 46–7, 48, 54–6
colours: black furs 16, 57, 65, 73, 91, 93, 100, 137

236 FUR: A SENSITIVE HISTORY

dyed furs 134–5, 155, 209
fake fur 158–9
fashions 66
mink 137
Combs, Sean 'Puffy' 88, *88*
computer-generated imagery (CGI) 223
Condé Nast 140
coney 91, 100, 155
Constantinople (Istanbul) 44, 90, 120, 125
consumerism 57
'coonskin' caps 112–13
Cooper, Gary 187, *188*
Corvaja, Giovanni, *Golden Fleece* 224, *224*
Cossack hats 125, 127
Cotes, Francis, *The Right Hon. Lady Mary Radcliffe* 121, *122*
Courtenay, Tom 126
Coutts, Thomas 219
cowhide 22, *23*, 58, 89, 170–1
Cranach, Lucas the Elder, *Samson and Delilah* 19
Crawford, Joan 71, *72*, *133*, 139, 140
Crawford, 'M.D.C.' 129
Cregar, Laird 61
Crockett, Davy 48, 112–13
Crooks in Cloisters (film) 154, *154*
Crystal Palace, London 55
Cukor, George 118
Cunanan, Andrew 38
La Curée (film) 166

D
Dalton, Phyllis 126
Daughters of the American Revolution 76
Davey, Richard 43, 45
Furs and Fur Garments 136
Davis, Sammy Jr 140
'Davy Crockett' hats 112–13, *113*
Day, Doris 70, 101
de la Renta, Oscar 189
deception 152–6
Deleuze, Gilles 10, 12, 47, 50, 52, 177, 180
A Thousand Plateaus 193
Dene peoples 146–7
Denmark 137, 151
depilation 21, 24–7, 39–40
Derrida, Jacques 167
Design School Kolding 227
Devonshire, Georgiana, Duchess of 108
Diaghilev, Serge 123–5
DiCaprio, Leonardo 63
Dietrich, Marlene *179*, 193, 204–5, *205*
Diné people 19
Dionysus 197
Dior 77, *84*, 85, 129, *167*, 172–4, *172–3*
Disney, Walt 112
Doctor Zhivago (film) 125–6, *126*, 127
dogs 82, 110, 168, 184
dolmans *112*, 113
Donovan, Terence 57
Dorothy, Esther *201*
Dors, Diana 27

Doucet, Jacques 147
Dougarie Estate, Isle of Arran 186
Douglas, Mary 19
down hair 15
dress, leopard skin 216–17, *217*
Dubuffet, Jean 106
Duhamel, A.B., *Three Views of Muffs* 109
Dunaway, Faye 132
Dunnage, George 116
Dunne, Irene 124, 125, 209
dyes: fake fur 158–9
furs 134–5, *135*, 155, 209
Dymek, Alex 159
Dynel 156

E
Easy Living (film) 70
ECOPEL 160
Ede & Ravenscroft 97
Edmund, King of England 97
Edward VI, King of England 100
Edward the Confessor, King of England 97
Ege, Julie 177
Egypt, ancient 21, 151, 197–9, 200, 224
Elizabeth I, Queen of England 94, 96
Elizabeth II, Queen of England 91, 94, 97, 226
Elle magazine 77, *78*
Ellis, Havelock 33
Ellroy, James 139
Emberley, Julia 37, 38, 147
The Empire Strikes Back (film) 174
Enchantment (film) 100
endangered species 200
Enlightenment 165
environmental issues 159–60
ermine 17, 43, 90, 95–100, *98*, 133
accessories 100, *103*
in heraldry 213–14, 215
imitations *218–19*, 219–20
in mosaics 216
powdering 97–9, 154–5, 219
and status 55, *64*, 65, 91, 96–9, *96*
as symbol of purity 96
tails 96, 110, 112, *113*, 220, *220*
eroticism 176–82
Esau 153
Esso 113–14
European Union 147
Eustace, St *215*, 215
Evans, Mary 128
Evelyn, John 94
evisceration of animals 174–5
Ewing, Elizabeth 7, 12, 97, 104
Exhibition of Russian Art, Paris (1906) 123
exhibitions 55–6
extinction 200
eyebrows 21, 22
eyelashes 18, 21–2, *21*
Eyes of Laura Mars (film) 176, *177*

F
Fabergé Cosmetics 61
fairy tales 117–18, 153, 159, 190
fake fur 24, 81, 151–2, 156–60
Fanon, Frantz, *Black Skin, White Masks* 163
Fantasio magazine 187
farmed furs 136–8, *138*, 159, 167
Farnese, Alessandro 18, *89*
fashion thinking 8
Fashionland 118–19
faux fur *see* fake fur
Faux Fur Institute 160
fear of fur 15, 28
fear of hair 20, 40
feathers 33, 34, 105
felting, hat-making 45, 115, 116
Fendi 77, 88, *88*, 94, *94*, 226
Fenrir 207
Fenwick's 71, *74*
Ferdinand I of Naples 96
Ferdinand II, Archduke 18
fetishism 176
Feurer, Hans 58
films 132–6
and attitudes to fur 68–71
Blaxploitation films 73–4
on fur trade 61–3, *62–3*
imaginary fur 221–4
mink in 69, 70–1, 139
monkey fur in 209
primitive furs 85–6, *85*
see also individual films
Finland 137
First Nations 112, 129, 172
fur trade 45, 46, 62–3
fur's transformative functions 113
long hair 19
myths 47–8
seal hunting 146–7
see also Inuit peoples
First World War 26, 35, 129, 151, 209
Fitzgerald, Scott, *The Pearl and the Fur* 139
Flaherty, Robert F. 61, *62*
Flanagan, Bud 149, *149*
Flaubert, Gustave, *Dictionary of Received Ideas* 52
flayed skin 164
fleas 104
fleece 15, *158*, 191–224
Golden Fleece 43, *43*, 224, 226
linings 84
prehistoric clothes 81
synthetic 160
see also sheepskin
Fleming, Sir Sandford 49, *49*
Flintstone, Fred 85–6
Florence 44
Flügel, J.C., *The Psychology of Clothes* 26
flying jackets 84
flying suits *150*, 151
foetus, human 17
folklore 204–6
Fonda, Jane *166*
footwear *see* boots; shoes
'The "Force" of Fur' 141–2, *141*, 148
Ford, Tom 134
Fort Albany 50
Foucault, Michel 127–8, 129
Fox, Charles James 108
Fox-Davies, Arthur, *A Complete Guide to Heraldry* 214

fox furs 55, 100, 106, 132
Arctic fox 17, 125, 127, *127*, 133
platinum fox *106*, 133–4
silver fox 99, 106, 133, 134, 155–6
tails 108, 110, 114
France 45–6, 53, 215–16, *215*
Franklin, Aretha 77, *77*, 78
French Revolution 105
Frette 190
Freud, Sigmund 213
Fetishism 176, 177, 181
fripperers 153
Frontier (film) 62, *63*
'fun' fur 59, 152, 158
fur fabric 156
Fur Facts 99, 155–6
Fur-Free Britain Campaign 226
fur trade 43–63
and the anti-fur movement 58, 137–8
and colonialism 46–7, 48–9, 54–6
and films 61–3, *62–3*, 132
history 43–9
retailing 52–4, 53–4, 56–60
tokens 50–2
trapping animals 49–50, *50*
Fur Trade Journal 137
Furland 119–32
furniture 59, 187–90, *189*
furriers 89
perfumes 60–1
regulations 44
shops 52–4, *53–4*, 56–60
workrooms 142
Furs and Fur Garments 186–7
futurefur 226

G
Gallant, Ara 128
Galliano, John *84*, 85, 129, 167
Galsworthy, John: *For Love of Beasts* 34
Treatment of Animals 34
Game of Thrones (TV series) 63, 207
Gandhi, Mahatma 33
garments *see* clothing; coats
garters, mink 181, 182
Gaultier, Jean Paul 87, 131, *160*, 171, 197, 216–17, *217*, 226
Chic Rabbis 95
Le Grande Voyage 129
Gazette du Bon Ton 123
Genesis (film) 85
genet 59, 66, 91, 93, 100
genitalia, female 176–7, 181
Genoa 44, 65
genre paintings 120
George IV, King of England 22
George magazine 140
Germany 81, 151
Giambullari, Bernardo, *Song of the Furriers* 181
Gihvan, Robin 77
gilets, fur 83, 85, *85*
Gillette 24–6, *26*
Glamour magazine 39–40
glass: glass-fibre cloth 217–19, *218*
stained glass 215–16, *215*
Glenara 157
Glover, Mark 35
gloves 167–9, *168*, 182

Glyn, Elinor, *Three Weeks* 187
goat skins 82, 83, 87, 89, 149
Goddard, Paulette 139
Golanski 96
gold 224, *224*
Golden Fleece 43, *43*, 224, 226
Gompertz, Lewis 32, 34
Goncharova, Natalia 123
Gonsalvus family *17–18*, 18
'goose bumps' 17
Gorringes 209
Grable, Betty 99
The Graduate (film) 200, *201*
Graham, Barbara 140
Grahame, Gloria 69
Grand Tour 120, 212
Grant, Cary 136
Gray, Eileen 187
Great Bear Lake 49
Great Depression 149
Great Exhibition, London (1851) 55–6, *55*
'The Great Fur Caravan' (American *Vogue*) 128–9, *128*
Great Lakes Mink Association (GLMA) 57
Greece, ancient 21, 43, 63–5, 82, 105, 197
Green, Rev. Johnnie Jr. 77
Greenland 147
Greenpeace 35, *36*, 37, 146
Grenadier Guards 195–6
Griffiths, D.W. 85
Grimm Brothers, *Bearskin* 204
Groves, Andrew, *Ordinary Madness* 24, *25*
Grueby Faience Company 48
guard hairs 15–16, 115, 143, 145
Guattari, Félix 10, 12, 47, 50, 52
A Thousand Plateaus 193
Gucci 77, 117, *117*
gutskin *175*, 175

H
Haida people 47–8
hair, human 15–16, 17–29
attitudes to 19–21
composition 15
depilation 21, 24–7, 39–40
fear of 20, 40
growth 15
hypertrichosis *17–19*, 18–19, 205
as insulation 18
long, uncut hair 19
phases 19
pigmentation 15
pubic hair 15, 21, 22–4, 27, 39–40, 176, 177, 181
structure 15
hairdressing 21
Hall, Jerry 141
Hall, Minna B. 33
Halston 128
hands, sense of touch 167
Hanseatic League 44
Hanson, Maria 141
Hardy, Tom 63
hare skins 167
Haredi Jews 94–5, *94*
Harlem Renaissance 74
Harrell, Trajal 160

Harrods 36, 158
Hart, Albert 95
Harvey, John 91
hats: beaver 45, 102, 114–17, *114–15*
   'coonskin' caps 112–13
   'Davy Crockett' 112–13, *113*
   feathered 33, 34
   felting 45, 115, 116
   prehistoric man 151, *152*
   Russian 125–6, *127*
   shtreimel 94–5, *94*
   top hats *114*, 116–17
   see also headdresses
hatter's plush 116–17, 156
Hawes, Elizabeth 110–11, *111*, 112
   Fashion is Spinach 111
Hawkins, Benjamin Waterhouse, *Graphic Illustration of Animals* 33
Hawks, Howard 187
Hawrysio, Denise, *Killing 184*, 185
Hayward, Maria 66
Head, Edith 134
headdresses, bearskins 195–6, *197*
Heather, Andrew 88
Heatherington, John 116
Heim, Jacques 26
Heins & LaFarge *48*
Heisler, Karl 150
Hemenway, Harriet 33
Hemingway, Ernest 187
Henri Bendel, New York 56
Henry II, King of France 18
Henry IV, King of England 83
Henry VII, King of England 100
Henry VIII, King of England 66, 97, 115
Henry Heath Hat Factory, London *48*
Heracles (Hercules) 197, *198*
heraldry 213–16, *213*
Hermes 9
hide 164
   antelope 88
   cowhide 22, 23, 58, 89, 170–1
   zebra 201
   see also skin
Hillary, Sir Edmund 84
Hilliard, Nicholas, 'Ermine Portrait' 96
hippies 27, 87, 110
Hirst, Damien, *Saint Bartholomew, Exquisite Pain* 164
His Prehistoric Past (film) 85, *85*
Hitler, Adolf 35, 206–7
Hodges, Liam 150
Hoefnagel, Joris, *Animalia Rationalia et Insecta* 17, 18, *18*
Holbein, Hans the Younger 93
   Hans of Antwerp 68
Hollander, Anne 133
Hollar, Wenceslas 107
   A Muff in Five Views 107, *108*
   The Seasons 180–1, *181*
Hollywood 57, 61, 69–70, 74, 100, 118, 125, 132–6, 139, 187, 222
Holocaust on Your Plate (2003) 38
honey badgers 17
Horst 189
House of Fluff 159
House of Lords 99

Hubert, St *186*
Hudson's Bay Company 9, 10, 44, 46, 47, 53, 56, 63, 91
   Hudson's Bay (film) 61–2
   London headquarters *48–9*
   Made Beavers 50–2
   motto 163
   trading pattern 45–6
Hudson's Bay Furriers 13, 112, *112*
Hungarian Millennium Exhibition, Budapest (1896) 190, *190*
Hunt, Alan 66, 68, 78, 82, 93, 185–6
Hunter, Hal 182
hunting: in films 61–2
   seals 145, 146–7
   trapping animals 49–50, *50*
A Hunting We Will Go (cartoon series) 171
Hurrell, George 133
Hussey, Ruth 71
Hustler magazine 27
Huxley, Aldous, *Brave New World* 222
Huysmans, J-K., *A Rebours* 186
hypertrichosis 17–19, *18–19*, 205

I
IKEA 207
Ill-treatment of Cattle Act (1822) 31–2
Illustrated Russia magazine 125
imitations, ermine 218–19, 219–20
immorality, and fur 66–7, 69–70
indigenous dress, influence of 129–32
Ingres, Jean-Auguste-Dominique, *Mademoiselle Caroline Rivière* 105
Innis, Harold Adams, *The Fur Trade in Canada* 46, 47
insulation, hair as 18
intarsia method 135, 144, 172–4
interior decoration 185–7
International Congress of Women, London (1899) 33
International Fur and Leather Workers Union 142
International Fur Store, London 52, 186–7
Inuit peoples 195, 203
   and anti-fur movement 35, 37
   clothing 130, 145–6, *146*, 175, *175*
   films 61
   influence on fashion 129–32
   seal hunting 49–50, 145–7
   transference of animal powers 113
Isaac 153, *153*
Isham, James, *Indians Hunting Beaver* 45
Isle of Arran 186
IUCN Red List of Threatened Species 200
Ivan the Terrible, Tsar 94

J
jackets *see* coats and jackets
Jackson, Andrew 112
Jackson, Michael, *Thriller* 129
Jacob 153, *153*
Jacobs, Marc *117*
Jaeckel, H. & Sons 99–100
Jaeckel, Gunther 132

Jaeckel, Richard 132
Jaeger 126
Jaguar cars 114
jaguars 16–17, 197–9, 203
Japan 128–9
Jason 43, *43*, 224
Jay-Z 78
Jeanneret, Pierre 187
Jefferson, Thomas 47
Jeftichew, Fedor 18
Jerome, Jerome K. 34
   The Cruel Steel Trap 35
jewellery 22, *22*, 100
Jews 35, 38, 94–5, *94*, 123, 132
'Jo-Jo the Dog-Faced Man' 18
Johnson, Chad 40
Johnson, Corey 226
Jonah 174
Jones, Ann 93, 168, 211
Jones, Brian *86*, 87
Jones, Courtney 158
journalism 57–8
The Journals of Knud Rasmussen (film) 131

K
Kafka, Franz, *Metamorphosis* 180
kamleika (gutskin parka) 175, *175*
Kanecaron 157
Kaplan, Georges 22, 58, 128, 189–90
Kaplan, Jacques 22, 23, 58–60, *59*, *60*, 189–90
Kastoria, Greece 44
Katzer, Josef 190
Keaton, Buster 85
Kelly, Angela 226
Kentish, Lynne 35
keratin 15
Khnopff, Fernand, *Caresses* 199, *200*
Khrushchev, Nikita 94
King, Bill *57*, 57
King Kong (film) 209, 222–3, *222*
Kingsley, Ben 54
Kipling, Rudyard 163
Kirby, Jo 212
Kite, Marion 112
Kopenhagen Fur 135, *135*, 137, 150, 169, *170*, 227
Krafft-Ebbing, Richard von, *Psychopathia Sexualis* 177
Kristeva, Julia 182
Krupa, Joanna 39
KTZ 131, *131*
Kubrick, Stanley 131

L
Lachasse 101–2
Lady in the Dark 136, *136*
The Lady Wants Mink (film) 71, 72, 137
Lagerfeld, Karl 88, *88*, 94, *94*, 226
Laliberte's Fur Parlor, Quebec 53, *54*
Lambretta scooters 114
lambskin 29, 91, 100, 153
Lamsweerde, Inez van 195
Lansing, Linda 140
lanugo hair 17–18
Lanza, Mario 139, 140
Laver, James 106, 123–5, 155, 156
   Taste and Fashion 95
Le Corbusier 184, 187

Leach, Edmund: *Anthropological Aspects of Language* 207
   'Magical Hair' 19–20
Lean, David 126
leather 172, 186
Lefebvre, Henri 56, 61, 63, 118, 119
legislation: for furriers 44
   sumptuary 63–9, 73, 74, 78, 89, 101
Leisen, Mitchell 136, 184
Leiter, Saul 58
Lelong, Lucien 184, *184*
Lemon, Margaretta 33
Leonardo da Vinci, *Lady with an Ermine* 96
leopard skins *41*, 59, 82, 100, 133, 148
   ancient civilisations and 197–9
   bow ties 107
   coats 199
   dress 216–17, *217*
   Egyptian funerary rituals 200–3, *202*
   as endangered species 200
   leopard cults 203–4, *203*
   markings 16, *16*
   in Tutankhamen's tomb 151
Leopardi, Giacomo 225
Lewis, C.S., *The Lion, the Witch and the Wardrobe* 61, 169
LGBTQ community 38
Les Liaisons Dangereuses (film) 200
lice, body 82
Life magazine 58, *59*, *60*
ligers 55
linings, fur 89–90, 101, 120, 153
Links, J.G. 91, 99, 136, 144
   Book of Fur 106
lion skins 82, 197, *201*
'Lionel the Lion-Faced Boy' 18, *18*
Liston, Sonny 168–9, *168*
literature: fairy tales 117–18, 153, 159, 190
   fur in 138–41, 177–80
London 44, 48, 52–3, 123
A London Furrier 54
Longfellow, Henry Wadsworth, 'The Song of Hiawatha' 171–2
Lopez, Jennifer 85
Los Angeles 39, 132, 226
Louis XV, King of France 64
Louis, Jean 139
Lubitsch, Ernst 99
Lucas, George 151
Luftwaffe 150
Lurati, Patricia 21, 101, 181, 208
Lynx 35–6, *36*, 37, 38, 39
lynx fur 66, 93, 100, *104*
Lyotard, Jean-François 30

M
Maar, Dora 182
Macaronis 108
McCartney, Linda 36, *36*
McCartney, Stella 36
McCord Museum, Montreal 131
Macdonell, Archibald, *The Fur Coat* 140
McGahee, Willis 40
MacLaine, Shirley 134
Maclaren, Denham 188–9, *189*
McQueen, Alexander 20, 87, *87*

Eclect Dissect 20
Horn of Plenty 87
Macy's, New York 56
Made Beavers 50–1
Maenads 197
Maes, Nicolaes 120
magazines 57–8
Magritte, René, *Philosophy in the Boudoir* 24
Mailer, Norman 175
Maison Atia 159
Manchester 33
Manhunter (film) 165–6, *165*
Marchant, Edward Dalton, *John Jacob Astor* 47
Margiela, Martin 221
La Mariegola 44
Marisol 22, 23, 24, 58
markings, fur 16–17
Marks, Laura 9
Marsyas 164
marten 65, 93, 114, 148
Martin, Richard 31–2
Mary, Queen of Scots, Oxburgh Hangings 208
masochism 177–80
Massachusetts Audubon Society 33
Matadin, Vinoodh 195
Mathews, Dan 30, 38
Mayan people 203
Mayo, Virginia 69
Mears, Patricia 129
melanin 15
Mellen, Polly 128
Mendel, Chloé 159
Mendel, J. 159
merkins (pubic wigs) 22, 24
Mesoamerica 197–9, 203
Meyer, Max 129
Meyer, Stephenie 207
Michele, Alessandro 117
microfibres, pollution 159, *160*
Middle Ages 21, 65, 89, 90–4, 153–4, 167, 185
Mildred Pierce (film) 71, 72
Milles, Richard 212
Ministry of Colonies (Belgium) 203
Ministry of Waxing 39–40
miniver (squirrel) 66, 90, 91, 99, 117, 153
mink 85, 93, 133
   anti-fur movement 35, 36, 77
   Blackglama advertising campaign 56–7, *57*, 73
   coats 30, 101, 136, 138
   colours 137
   dyed 135, *135*
   eyelashes 21–2, *21*
   farmed fur 36, 136–8, *138*, 159
   in films 69–71, 69–72
   garters 181, *182*
   gloves 168–9, *168*
   grading skins 137, *138*, 169, *170*
   in literature 138–41
   mink-covered telephones 184
   reverse-seamed coat *161*, 170
   stoles 106
   tails 111–12, *112*
The Mink Book 137
Minkaleen 158
Miss Mink of 1949 (film) 139

Mitchell, W.J.T. 8
Mitchson, Morris 196–7
modacrylic 159
'The Modern Hiawatha' 171–2
mods 114, 130
moleskin 65
Molyneux, Edward 106
Momoa, Jason 63
Mongolian lamb 87, 171
monkey fur 28, 37–8, 58, 207–11, 208–11, 219
Monreale Cathedral 216
Monroe, Marilyn 132, 139
Monsters, Inc. 223–4, 223
Montague, Lady Mary Wortley 120
Montana, Claude 135
Montaut, Henri de, *Red Riding Hood Released from the Belly of the Wolf* 174
Montreal 53
Moreau, Jeanne 200
Morlands 83–4
Morris, William 33
mosaics 216, 216
Moscow 53
Motoluxe 156
motoring coats 148–9, 207
moulting 102, 109
mourning clothing 91
mourning jewellery 22
muffs 102, 106–9, 108–9, 181
Muldbjerg Man 151
mummies 20, 20
Muni, Paul 61
Museum of Modern Art, New York 182
museums 55
music 73, 77–8
muskrat 155
musquash 148
Mussorgsky, Modest, *Boris Godunov* 123
Mustang 114
Mysterious Island (film) 86
myths 47–8, 197, 206–7, 224, 225

N

Nadeau, Chantal 61, 62
Nanook of the North (film) 53, 61, 62
Napoleon I, Emperor 99
National Anti-Vivisection Society 32
National Association for the Advancement of Colored People 38
Native Americans *see* First Nations
Navajo people 19
Nazi Party 35, 58
Nero, Emperor 197
Netflix 62
Netherlands 44, 45, 120, 121
Neumark, Germany 81
Nevinson, J.L. 180
New York City 39, 39, 48, 53, 58, 76–7, 123, 132, 226
New York Times 56, 77
Newkirk, Ingrid 37–8
Newman, Bernard 125
Newton, Helmut 57
 Laura in a Fox Cape 177, 181
Nicholay, J.A. & Sons 55–6, 55
Nieman Marcus 29

Norell, Norman 70, 101, 136
Norse myths 206–7
North America: fur trade 44–52, 54
 see also Canada; United States of America
North Pacific Sealing Convention (1911) 145
North West Company 46
Not Now Darling (film) 177
Nova magazine 57–8
Novak, Kim 139
Novelty Fur Company 132
Nunavut 147

O

objects, fur-covered 182–5, 183–4
ocelot 56, 73, 133, 200
Och Sport 147
Ojibwe legends 110
Olsen, George, *Doin' the Raccoon* 149
One Million Years B.C. (film) 26, 27, 85
Oneida myths 110
Only Fools and Horses (TV series) 85
Oppenheim, Meret: *Object* 182, 183, 184–5
 Squirrel 182
Orchard Painter 43
Orlon 156
Orsanmichele, Florence 44
otter 50, 89, 155
Ottoman Empire 120–1
Ouida (Maria Louise Ramé), 'The New Woman' 36–7
Owens, Rick 88, 109, 110, 111

P

Pacheco, Alex 37
paintings, fur in 93, 211–12
Palaeolithic tools 81
Palermo 216
Panther cars 114
panthers 16, 199, 200
papakha (Cossack hat) 125, 127
Paquin 147, 209–11, 210–11
Paramount Pictures 132
Paris 53, 53, 60, 123, 125, 127, 159
parkas 114, 129, 130–2, 130, 145, 146, 175, 175
Parker, Fess 112
Parr, Martin, *Italy, Regio Emilia* 16
Partos, Emeric 128
Pasolini, Pier Paolo 189
Pastrana, Julia 18, 19
Pathé News 195
Peacham, Henry, *Minerva Britanna* 96
Peau d'âne (Donkey Skin) 204
Pejoski, Marjan 131
pelage 15–16
pelt, terminology 164
Pelzhaus 190, 190
Pembroke, Earl of 100
perfumes 60–1
Perrault, Charles 117
 Contes de ma mère l'Oye 118
Perriand, Charlotte 187
Persian lamb 156
PETA (People for the Ethical Treatment of Animals) 30, 37–40, 38, 40, 77

Petersham, Maud and Miska, *The Story Book of Clothes* 6, 11
Philip the Good, Duke of Burgundy 91
Philippa of England, Queen of Denmark 117
Phillips, Eliza 33
phobias, hair 20
photography 74–6, 180, 221
Picasso, Pablo 182
Piccioli, Pier Paolo 99
Pickman, Sarah, 'Dress, Image, and Cultural Encounter' 146
pigmentation 15, 17
pilche (cloak) 83, 85, 86, 87, 153
pilo-motor reflex 16
pine marten 91, 93, 94
Planché, James 97
Plimpton, Freddy 59
Plumage League 33
plush fur fabrics 156
poaching 200
Poiret, Paul 147
Polanski, Roman 53–4
polecat 17
pollution, fake fur 159–60
Pond, Peter 46
porcupines 16
pornography 27
Porter, Cole, 'I've Got You Under My Skin' 163, 174
Porto Thiene, Countess Livia da 104, 104
Portrait of a Man in a Fur-Trimmed Coat 92
portrait paintings 211–12
postage stamps 49, 49
powdering 97–9, 154–5, 219
Prada 53–4
prehistoric man 81–3, 82, 151, 152, 195
Pribilof Islands 145, 147
primitivism 27, 29, 85–6, 110, 123, 151, 152, 209, 211
processing furs 142–3, 164
Prokofyev, Sergei, *Peter and the Wolf* 129
prostitutes 22, 58, 66–7, 180–1
pubic hair 15, 21, 22–4, 27, 39–40, 176, 177, 181
Pugh, Gareth 87
Puzzle of a Downfall Child (film) 132

Q

Quebec 53

R

rabbit 59, 91, 100, 101
raccoon 28, 112, 113, 114, 149, 149, 209
Radcliffe, Lady Mary 121, 122
Radisson, Pierre-Esprit 45
Rahvis sisters 126–7
Rainbow Warrior 36
Raoul-Naura, Jean 187
rap music 77–8
rationing, clothes 71–3
Ravenna 97, 216, 216
Rawlings, John 148, 148
razors 24–6, 26
Réard, Louis 26
Reed, Oliver 62, 62

Rejane, Madame 187
Remarque, Erich Maria 20
remodelling furs 153–4, 226, 227
Renaissance 18, 93, 95, 101, 164, 181, 213
 attitudes to fur 204
 culture of touch 165–6
 gloves 167, 168–9
 monkeys 207–8
 pilche (cloak) 83
Representation of the New Shaving Machine 28
The Revenant (film) 62–3, 63, 174–5
reverse side of fur 172–4
Revillon Frères 53, 53, 56, 60–1, 88, 123, 128
Ribera, Jusepe de, *Isaac and Jacob* 153
Richard II, King of England 97
Richard III, King of England 97
Richtofen, Manfred von 150, 151
Rigaud, Hyacinthe, *Louis XV as a Child* 64
rights to wear fur 63–9
Ritter, Leo 136
rituals 19
River of Fundament (film) 175
Rivière, Caroline 105
Roberta (film) 124, 125
Rodman, Dennis 40, 40
Roerich, Nicholas 123
Rogers, Ginger 125, 136, 136, 209
Rogers, James H. 145
Rogers, Peter 57
Romans 21, 26, 43, 63–5, 82, 105, 197
Rony, Fatimah Tobing 61
Roosevelt, Theodore 196–7, 196
Ross, Diana 57
Ross, Gordon, *The Woman Behind the Gun* 32
Royal Canadian Mounted Police 150, 151
Royal Exchange 180
Royal Museum for Central Africa, Tervuren 203–4, 203
Royal Society for the Prevention of Cruelty to Animals (RSPCA) 32
Royal Society for the Protection of Birds (RSPB) 33
royalty, and ermine 96–9
Rubens, Peter Paul, *Hercules and the Nemean Lion* 197, 198
Rudolf II, Emperor 18
Rupert, Prince 45
Russia: fish fur 151–2
 fur trade 44, 53, 90
 as Furland 121–7, 180
 gifts of fur 94
 influence of 123–5
 royalty and furs 93

S

sable 55, 60, 65, 66, 70, 91, 93–5, 155, 169
Sacher-Masoch, Leopold von 186
 Venus in Furs 123, 177–80, 182
Sachs, J.C., *Furs and the Fur Trade* 136
safaris 187, 189
Saint Laurent, Yves 127, 141

Libération 134, 135
St Petersburg 52–3, 159
Saks, New York 56
Salt, Henry 170
 Animals' Rights Considered in Relation to Human Progress 33–4, 40
Salt, Titus 156
Samson 19, 19
San Francisco 39, 226
Sant'Angelo, Giorgio di 109–10, 110, 112
Sant'Apollinaire Nuovo, Ravenna 216, 216
Saunders, Jasmine 77
Scandinavia 44, 81–2, 130, 137
The Scarlet Empress (film) 127, 179
Scassi, Arnold 135
Schatzberg, Jerry 132
Schedel, Hartmann, *Nuremberg Chronicles* 206
Schiaparelli, Elsa 182, 209, 219
 A Modern Comedy 219
Schmidt, Gunnar, 'Trophies: the Aestheticization of Melancholy' 189
Schou, Mikkel Østergaard 135, 135
scooters 114
Scotland 22
Scrots, William 100
Scurlock, Addison N. 74–6, 76
seals 33
 hunting 33, 37, 49–50, 145, 146–7
 lanugo hair 18
sealskin 55
 fake fur 155, 156
 garments 95, 144–6, 145–7, 147
 Inuit garments 145–6, 146
Sean John 88, 88
Second World War 26, 35, 71–3, 84, 136, 209
Seiter, William A. 72
Selborne Society for the Protection of Birds, Plants and Pleasant Places 33
Selfridges 158
Sendak, Maurice 159
Seniors, Paula Marie 77, 78
sensory hairs 16
sentimental jewellery 22
Sergeenko, Ulyana 127, 127
Serres, Michel 9, 12, 17, 118, 193
 Les Cinq Sens (The Five Senses) 163, 165, 169, 170, 174, 182, 219
The Servant (film) 85
sewing machines 142, 143, 143
sex toys 181–2
sexuality 176–82
Sforza, Ludovico, Duke of Milan 96
shagreen (shark or ray skin) 188
Shakespeare, William 211
 Hamlet 91
Shall We Dance (film) 209
shamans 203
Shanghai 125
shape-shifting 197–9
Sharif, Omar 126, 126
shaving 24–6, 26, 28
Shaw, George Bernard 33
The She-Bear 204
shearling 83, 85
sheepskin 149

INDEX 239

boots 84, 85, 117
coats and jackets 27, 83–5, *83*
flying suits *150*, 151
imitations *158*
and low status 65, 89
patchwork *150*
prehistoric clothing 81–2, *82*
shoes 117–18, *117*
shops, furriers 52–4, *53–4*, 56–60
Shrewsbury, Elizabeth, Countess of, Oxburgh Hangings 208
Shrimps *157*, 159
shtreimel 94–5, *94*
Siberia 44, 82, 90, 121–3
Sikhs 19
silk brocade 220–1, *220–1*
silk plush 47, 116–17, 156
Sills, Philip & Co. 86
Silver Springs Monkey case (1981) 37–8
Sinatra, Frank 140
Singer, Peter 33–4
    Animal Liberation 34, 35
Singer sewing machines 142
Singin' in the Rain 134
skin: and essence of the animal 164–5
    flaying 164
    interior decoration and furniture 186–90, *189*
    sense of touch 163–7, 174
skinheads 85, *85*, 130
Skinners, Worshipful Company of 49
skinning animals 176
Skov, Lise 227
skunks 17, 59, 132–3, 148
slavery 30, 32, 38
Sloane, Julia 30
smoothness, fur 169–70
Society for the Prevention of Cruelty to Animals 32
soft furnishings 187, 189
Somers, Wieki, *High Tea Pot* 184
'The Song of Milkanwatha' 171–2
spaces of fur 56–8
Spain 186
speciesism 34, 35
Spies, Werner 182
spines 16
spotted furs 199–200
squirrel 55–6, 91
    coats *91*, 148, *214*
    dyed furs 59
    linings 83, 117
    medieval clothes 89, 90
    miniver 66, 90, 91, 99, 117, 153
    terminology 90
    vair 90, 117–18, 213, 214–15
stained glass 215–16, *215*
Stallybrass, Peter 93, 168–9, 211
Stamp, Terence 189
Stanwyck, Barbara 30
Star Wars (film) 141
status: fur and 55, 57, 63–71, 74–6, 82, 100
    mink coats 138
Steiff 156
Stella, Frank 22, 58
stoats 17
    see also ermine

stoles 73, 102, 105, *105*, 106
storage, fur coats 176
Stubbes, Philip, *Anatomie of Abuses* 114–15
Suetonius 197
Sumerians 81
sumptuary legislation 63–9, 73, 74, 78, 89, 101
surrealism 182, 190
Sussex, Lady 104
swakara fur 135
synthetic furs *see* fake fur

T
tails 110–14, *110–13*
Takahashi, Jun, *Undercover* 87, *87*
Tanning, Dorothea, *Tales of the American Woods* 56
Tarzan films 209
Tarzan and the Leopard Men 204
Tashtyk culture 82, *82*
Tashlin, Frank, *The Bear That Wasn't* 29
tattoos 22, 27, 29
taxidermy 53, 55, 105
Taylor, Elizabeth 17–18, 69, *70*
teddy bears 156, 197
Teitelbaum, Al 139–41, 184–5
    'Tijuana Mon Amour' 140
telephones, mink-covered 184
ter Borch, Gerard 120
terminal hair 15
That Lady in Ermine (film) 99
That Touch of Mink (film) 70, *71*, 101, 135–6
Thebes 151
Theodora Goes Wild (film) 209
Theorem (film) 189
A Therapy (film) 53–4
thermal properties 15, 71, 82, 105, 142
    boots 117
    flying jackets 84
    gloves 167
    kamleika 175
    motoring coats 148
    Venus in Furs 177–80
Three Ages (film) 85
Thunderball (film) 168
ties, bow 106, *107*
tigers 16, 61, 113–14, *165*, *165*, 187, 200, *201*
Time magazine 114
Timme-Tation 157
Tintin au Congo 204
tippets 94, 102–5, *102*, *104*
Tissavel 157
Titian, *Venus with a Mirror* 177, *178*, 180
Toms, Carl 85
tools, Palaeolithic 81
top hats 114, 116–17
Topsell, Edward, *History of Four-Footed Beasts and Serpents* 169, 207, 208
touch, sense of 163–7, 174
Tourneau, Jacques 199–200
trade *see* fur trade
Trahey, Jane 57
transformations 193–211
The Trap (film) 62, *62*
trapping *see* hunting

trichophobia (fear of hair) 20, 27, 40
Trigere, Pauline 199
Tringhøj Man 151
trompe l'oeil 221
trophy rooms 185–6, *186*, 187, *188*, 189
The Trotula 21
Truscott, John 93
Turkey 120–1
Turlington, Christy 38
Tushingham, Rita 62, *62*
Tutankhamen, Pharaoh 151, 200–3, *202*
Twilight films 207
Tyas, Robert, *Flowers and Heraldry* 213

U
UGG boots 84, 85
underarm hair 15, 26, 27
underfur 15, 115–16
United States of America:
    African-Americans 74–7
    anti-fur movement 37–40, 76–8
    anti-plumage movement 33
    farmed furs 136–7, 167
    fur trade 46–8, 56–7
    raccoon coats 149
    seal product ban 147
The Universal Magazine of Knowledge and Pleasure 115
Unreal Fur 159
Ur-Nanshe, King of Lagash 81
US Army 130
ushanka (Russian army cap) 125–6
Utility Clothing Scheme 71–3

V
Vadim, Roger *166*, 200
vair (squirrel) 90
    and Cinderella 117–18
    in heraldry 213, 214–15
    shoe linings 117, *118*
Valentino 97, 99
van der Zee, James 74
van Doorn, Trudi 177
Van Dyck, Sir Anthony 104
Vanderbilt, Gloria *91*
Veale, Elspeth 12, 44, 83, 93, 100, 114, 118, 153, 154, 185
vegetarianism 34, 35, 78
vellus hair 15, 17
Venice 44
Vermeer, Johannes 120
    A Lady Writing 121
Verne, Jules: *The Fur Country* 49, *49*, 52–3
    Mysterious Island 86
Veronese, Paolo, *Countess Livia da Porto Thiene* 104, *104*
Versace, Gianni 38
Veruschka 128–9
Vesalius, Andreas 164
Vespa scooters 114
vibrissae (sensory hairs) 16
Victoria, Queen of England *96*, 186
Vionnet, Madeleine *98*, 100
Vivier, Roger 128
Vogue (American) 128–9, *128*, 135, 141–2, *141*, 148, *148*, 189
Vogue (British) 71, 73, 74, 95

Vogue (French) 194–5
Vreeland, Diana 128
Vuitton, Louis 117, *171*

W
Wagner, George Raymond ('Gorgeous George') 139
Wagner, Robert 107
Walters Art Museum, Baltimore 104
Warhol, Andy 135
warning markings 17
Washington, Denzel 74
The Washington Post 77, 196–7, *196*
Watson, Johnny Guitar, *Giant* 73–4
weasel 59, 89, 102–4
    see also ermine
Webb, Beatrice 33
Webb, Iain R. 57
Weeks-McLean Migratory Bird Act (1913) 33
Weil 60, *61*
Weiland, Hannah 159
Welch, Raquel 26, 27, 85
WelFur 137, 227
werewolves 205–6, 207
Wermers, Nicole, *Infrastruktur 80*, 118–19, *119*
West Hollywood 39, 132
Westwood, Vivienne: *Harris Tweed* 99
    On Liberty 24, *24*
Weyden, Rogier van der, *Portrait of a Lady* 21, *21*
Wharton, Edith, *A Cup of Cold Water* 95
What a Way to Go! (film) 134, *134*
When Dinosaurs Ruled the Earth (film) 85
whiskers 16
White Heat (film) 69
White Russians 125
Wig Club 22
wigs, pubic (merkins) 22, 24
Wilberforce, William 32
William, Prince, Duke of Cambridge 196
Williamson, Emily 33
Wilson, Elizabeth 132, *133*
Wilton Diptych 97
Windsor, Barbara 154, *154*, 177
Windsor, Duchess of 134, 181
Windsor, Duke of 134
Winnicott, Donald Woods 197
Winter Olympics 158
Wolf boy 206
Wolfe, Tom, 'Radical Chic' 59
wolverine 130
wolves 89, 123, 149
    coat linings 100, *206*, 207
    Hitler's identification with 206–7
    prehistoric garments 82
    werewolves 205–6, 207
women: in films 69–71
    prostitutes 22, 58, 66–7, 180–1
    sumptuary legislation 66–7, 69
    women's liberation movement 27
    women's rights 32
The Women (film) 118
Women's Wear Daily 129
Wong, Anna May *98*, 99–100, 133

World Fairs 55
World Wildlife Fund (WWF) 59, 200
Wright, Teresa 100

X
X Men comics 207

Y
Ye Xian 117
York, Duke and Duchess of 50

Z
zebra skin 188–9, *189*, 201
zibelines (weasel tippets) 93, 102, 104–5, *104*
Ziegler, Jacob 93–4
Zora, Ileana 161, 170
Zukor, Adolph 139
    The Public is Never Wrong 132